GRAMMARS *of* APPROACH

GRAMMARS *of APPROACH*

LANDSCAPE, NARRATIVE, *and the* *LINGUISTIC PICTURESQUE*

Cynthia
WALL

THE UNIVERSITY OF CHICAGO PRESS
Chicago and London

The University of Chicago Press, Chicago 60637
The University of Chicago Press, Ltd., London

Published 2019
Printed in the United States of America

28 27 26 25 24 23 22 21 20 19   1 2 3 4 5

ISBN-13: 978-0-226-46766-5 (cloth)
ISBN-13: 978-0-226-46783-2 (paper)
ISBN-13: 978-0-226-46797-9 (e-book)
DOI: https://doi.org/10.7208/chicago/9780226467979.001.0001

The University of Chicago Press gratefully acknowledges the generous support of the University of Virginia toward the publication of this book.

Library of Congress Cataloging-in-Publication Data

Names: Wall, Cynthia, 1959– author.
Title: Grammars of approach : landscape, narrative, and the linguistic picturesque / Cynthia Wall.
Description: Chicago : The University of Chicago Press, 2019. | Includes bibliographical references and index.
Identifiers: LCCN 2018026869 | ISBN 9780226467665 (cloth : alk. paper) | ISBN 9780226467832 (pbk. : alk. paper) | ISBN 9780226467979 (e-book)
Subjects: LCSH: Picturesque, The, in literature. | Picturesque, The, in architecture. | English prose literature—18th century—History and criticism. | Printing—England—History—18th century. | Visual communication.
Classification: LCC PR769 .W348 2019 | DDC 700/.46—dc23
LC record available at https://lccn.loc.gov/2018026869

♾ This paper meets the requirements of ANSI/NISO Z39.48-1992 (Permanence of Paper).

Contents

Illustrations

Color Plates

(following page 194)

Figures

Table

A Note on My Text

The copyedited manuscript for this book came back to my hands with footnotes rather than endnotes. Given my fondness for the subterranean genre of notes, a goodly number of pages turned out to look like Pope's *Dunciad Variorum* (1729), with two lines of main text bobbing atop an entire underworld of alternate conversations and directions. In a way, that format was its own enactment of the argument; it was its own hand-held landscape of the text (a paraphrase of a line by D. F. McKenzie that will be cited and repeated throughout this book). The impress of the invisible underneath was made visible; the undertext pushed the groundtext up, over, and around. As we all know, a narrative reads very differently if the eye is darting above and below the reference line, or the mind is considering an interruptive leap to the back matter. Footnotes are at best in our peripheral vision; in this case, they sometimes made the main text peripheral. On the one hand, footnotes captured the "form and texture" of my argument (another phrase quoted throughout); on the other, they endangered the *format* of my argument—the long, carefully transcribed passages from sixteenth-, seventeenth-, eighteenth-, and nineteenth-century pages meant to give a near-facsimile sense of spatial elements. In the end, I decided to protect my kerned matter.

I have used first or early editions of primary works throughout, and I have preserved not only their capitals, italics, and punctuation, but also, from chapter 3 on, the *spacing* of the punctuation. As the printer John Smith pointed out in 1755, while the "Full-point" always "join[s] to the matter of the closing period," the "other Points" (semi-colons, colons, question-marks, exclamation points) "not only admit, but require, to be separated from the matter."[1] Part of the argument of this book is to demonstrate how differently things read depending upon how they are typeset. Earlier texts (at least the well-printed ones) had more ventilation within their lines.

I have tried to use the *same* early editions in each chapter, but for various reasons—sometimes to make a different point, or sometimes just because I was in a different library—I can't promise complete consistency.

Acknowledgments

It's been a long and winding road, to say the least. The project has had several working titles as it inched its way along. My first thanks are to all the people whose constructive criticisms helped me strengthen and articulate the argument through its various turnings. I look back to "The Business of Houses," and to presenting "The Paradox of Old London Bridge" to the eighteenth-century workshop at the University of Chicago in Winter 2008, when I was a visiting professor there. The project made two appearances at the Princeton Eighteenth-Century and Romanticism Studies Colloquium, first in February 2009 as "The Business of Houses" and then in February 2014 as "Grammars of Approach: Architecture, Typography, and Narrative Consciousness." In between was "The Impress of the Invisible" (the University of Pennsylvania in 2010 and the University of Washington in 2011). The book finally settled into itself as "Grammars of Approach" through appearances at SUNY-Buffalo (2013), the International John Bunyan Society (2013), the Materialities, Texts and Images Workshop at the Huntington Library and Caltech (2015), the Newberry Library's Colloquium (2016), the University of Chicago's Eighteenth- and Nineteenth-Century Atlantic Cultures Workshop (2016), Harvard University's Roundtable on Description (2016), the International Association of University Professors of English in London (2016), and the University of York (2016). My thanks to all the faculty, graduate students, and staff who made those visits so pleasurable and profitable (intellectually speaking); I know I will miss some names, but here is a special roll call of thanks for those invitations: Dave Alff, David Alworth, John Brewer, Marshall Brown, Jessica Burstein, Timothy Campbell, James K. Chandler, Frances Ferguson, Kevin Gilmartin, Elizabeth Helsinger, Claudia Johnson, Heather Keenleyside, Tom Lockwood, Ruth Mack, John Mee, Julie Park,

Juliet Shields, Eric Slauter, Chloe Wigston Smith, Allison Turner, and David Womble.

We all live happily in libraries. Thank you to the National Endowment for the Humanities for granting me a long-term fellowship at the Newberry Library in 2016. (The Newberry basically raised me from a pup; I started working there when I was a graduate student in philosophy at Northwestern in 1983 and ended up as a reference specialist in Special Collections by the time I finished my PhD in English at the University of Chicago, 1992). I think of it as home. Let me thank James Akerman, John Aubrey, Diane Dillon, Kristen Emery, Jill Gage, Paul Gehl, D. Bradford Hunt, Robert Karrow, Alice Schreyer, and Jessica Walter, as well as my fellow Fellows and Colloquium participants William F. Brooks (who showed up to my talk at his home university, York!), Lisa Freeman, Susan Gaylard, Kate Gustafson, Kara Johnson, Kat Lecky, Lawrence Lipking, Christen Mucher, Raashi Rastogi, Suparna Roychoudry, and Miriam Thaggert. The Lewis Walpole Library is another beloved home; I've spent several visits there, from a week to a month, and have treasured the counsel and collegiality of Nicole Bouché, Kristen McDonald, Margaret Powell, Cynthia Roman, and Susan Walker. I've spent most of my scholarly time—every summer and every winter break since 1998—at the British Library. I thank all the staff of Rare Books and Music (particularly Mr. Anthony). That world, and the world of summer in London on Lamb's Conduit Street, includes Albert Braunmuller, Linda Bree, Alan Cameron, Anne Cameron, Frans DeBruyn, J. Alan Downie, David Fairer, Noelle Gallagher, Linda Gregerson, Elizabeth Horsley, Christine Krueger, Gail McDonald, the late Russ McDonald, Steven Mullaney, Lena Cowen Orlin, John Price, Kate Glover Price, Lynn Strongin Dodds, and Patricia Tatspaugh.

The Department of English at the University of Virginia in Charlottesville has been my warm academic home since 1994. Let me thank particularly Stephen Arata, Alison Booth, Gordon Braden, Elizabeth Fowler, Susan Fraiman, Katharine Maus, Clare Kinney (and Randall Couch), J. Daniel Kinney, Peter Metcalf (unofficial member), John O'Brien, Victoria Olwell, Brad Pasanek, A. C. Spearing, Michael Suarez, and David Vander Meulen. (Those are just the people who have helped me directly or indirectly with this book; many more have helped with Life in General.) Thank you to June Webb, Sarah Arrington, Stacey Trader, Randy Swift, Pamela Marcantel, and Colette Dabney for able and cheerful administration of my practical needs over the years, particularly when I was chair. Outside the English department, Douglas Fordham in art and art history has been specially helpful in, well, matters of art and art history; David Gies in Spanish has been a stalwart coeditor and inspirer; DAVID WHITESELL of Special Collections (and as

Rare Book School instructor) and AMANDA NELSEN in RBS have been so *spectacularly* helpful they deserve small caps. I thank past graduate students, now colleagues around the world, particularly Rivka Swenson, Chloe Wigston Smith, Mike Genovese, and Jennifer Foy Reed, and current graduate students Laura All, James Ascher, Sarah Berkowitz, Evan Cheney, Neal Curtis, Kelly Fleming, and Carol Guarnieri. The Dean's Office awarded the project an Arts, Humanities, and Social Sciences Research Grant to subvent the cost of the illustrations. Thanks most especially to Associate Dean Francesca Fiorani, who has been enthusiastically supportive.

There are people who have read this project in part or whole, or written letters on my behalf, or just talked things through. For years of such support, let me give special thanks to John Bender, Jim Chandler, Frances Ferguson, Tom Keymer, Jayne Lewis, Deidre Lynch, John Richetti, Stuart Sherman, and Patricia Meyer Spacks. I am deeply grateful to the linguistic as well as editorial expertise of Monika Fludernik and Suzanne Keen, who smartened up my grammatical sections for the version that appeared in the special edition of *Style*, "Interior Spaces and Narrative Perspectives before 1850" in 2014. Thank you to my sister Karen Sundberg Meyer, herself a teacher of literature and history, for reading my chapter on prepositions! Parents: Steven and Nancy Johnson, and Richard and Jill Sundberg. To Alan Thomas and Randolph Petilos of the University of Chicago Press, who have been waiting for this since the days of "The Business of Houses," I thank you for your patience and your editorial wizardry. I am very grateful for the constructive criticisms of the readers for the Press, John Richetti and David Spurr. And for the last long lurch, profound thanks to India Cooper and Joel Score, kind as well as meticulous manuscript editors.

I must not—and will never—forget William, our late Betsy, and Elspeth for making sure I was never lonesome or bored at my desk: thank you, everybody, for rearranging papers, padding across laptops, and suggesting a rousing game of String when I needed a break. But most of all, for everything and for always: Paul Hunter.

Introduction

WHAT *is* Grammar?
A. Grammar is the Art of expressing the Relation of Things in Construction, with due Accent in Speaking, and Orthography in Writing, according to the Custom of those whose Language we learn.

Anne Fisher, *A Practical New Grammar* (1759)

THE APPROACH to the mansion is a variety of ROAD peculiar to a house in the country.

J. C. Loudon, *A Treatise on Forming* [. . .] *Country Residences* (1806)

Grammars of Approach is concerned with Things in Construction in eighteenth- and early nineteenth-century Britain that have been individually well studied, but not in Relation to each other: landscape architecture, linguistic and typographical change, and narratological innovation. "Grammar" also refers to the "fundamental principles or rules of an art or science" (*OED* 6a), and that is the other starting premise here. This book begins with the shift in architectural discourse of the term "approach" from verb to noun and explores the ways that the approach as a new perceptual experience visually explains a wider set of changing formal patterns and fundamental principles. The architectural approach was designed to wind from the entrance of the estate "through the most interesting part of the grounds"[1] up to the house itself, and to "form new combinations on every movement of the spectator."[2] It was part of the sweeping picturesque movement that, according to Uvedale Price in 1810, comprised "all that the painter admires— [. . .] all intricacies, [. . .] all the beautiful varieties of form, tint, and light and shade; every deep recess—every bold projection—the fantastic roots of trees—the winding paths of sheep."[3] This book brings together the reshaping of the land with the reshapings of text and language, arguing that the winding paths of the modern approach that shifted the visual and political emphasis had their rootly counterparts in the modern page. The approach changed the perceptual emphasis in two significant ways: first, *away* from the great house (the old-fashioned avenue, wide and straight, kept the house front and center and looming larger with every step) and onto the spectator's own experience; and second, to the *in-between*, the prepositional: the glimpse through the trees, around the bend, across the valley, under the arch. The language used to describe the approach simultaneously enacts it: the rhetorical pattern used by landscape architects and theorists Humphry Repton, Thomas Whately, John Claudius Loudon, William Mason, and Uvedale Price, among others, follows a series of paratactic clauses, variously connected by lively punctuation, "presenting at every bend some new scene to the view,"[4] and then at some key point "bursts upon" the house and ends the sentence. The topography of the page, radically smoothed by sweeping typographical modernizations, opened up the spaces between (the soon to be lower-case) Nouns, allowing the "lesser parts of speech" more play. And play they did. Not only did the grammar books pay more attention to things like prepositions, but narrative patterns in literature developed more prepositional play. The new rhetorical approach encouraged new narrative approaches such as free indirect discourse, its own oblique circling into a mind. The architectural, typographical, and linguistic grammars of approach uncover, in a topography of the page, cultural contexts for narratological change and promote a three-dimensional way of reading that itself forms new combinations in every movement of the page.

I would like to open this book with a description of my approach to this project, which all began with the park gate lodge—that odd little dwelling that introduces the visitor to the estate, that marks the beginning of the approach, and that no one ever sees. Research into the corners of the great estates, by way of Tessa Murdoch's *Noble Households: Eighteenth-Century Inventories of Great English Houses: A Tribute to John Cornforth*,[5] first led me to the architectural phenomenon of the park gate lodge—of which, historians Tim Mowl and Brian Earnshaw assure us, some ten thousand still survive. The lodge reflects "in concentrated form" the "changing architectural fashions of the last two hundred and fifty years."[6] Apart from my first urgent need to live in one myself, I was intrigued by the idea that these "small houses, ambitiously designed, often by famous architects," had received so little historical or critical attention. Mowl and Earnshaw explain that most visitors who "pass through park gates do so in a spirit of near reverential preparation for the unashamedly upper class aesthetic experience which they are about to enjoy," so, since lodges housed persons or families "who had not even the cachet of being intimate house servants," the park gate lodge is "visually ignored as car or coach drives on to the inner class-sanctum of the great house itself" (vii).

Those little prefatory buildings were designed to open the "approach," that "ROAD peculiar to a house in the country." The approach, like the park gate lodge, had great contemporary popularity but little critical attention. I began to look for lodges and approaches in the literature I was reading, and I began to find them. And then, of course, as a literary critic I had to see if they were doing anything literary. They emerged as part of what I began to call the "impress of the invisible": the mark of things culturally prominent but critically invisible, shaping even texts in which they seem to be absent. Lodges, for example, could occupy the page of a novel in much the same way they occupied the topography of the estate: though present, they were often overlooked. It wasn't until I got to page 849 on a rereading of Frances Burney's *Camilla* (1796) that I came across a park gate lodge; I was lucky I hadn't had a little nap just then. The lodge was not glossed; nor were the lodges in *Northanger Abbey* or *Mansfield Park* or *The Mysteries of Udolpho* or *The Pilgrim's Progress* (including the *Pilgrim's Progress* edited by me). And under the formalist microscope, it turned out they *were* up to something literary: performing the usual acts of the liminal, the marginal, the threshold, the *intermédiare*. I called them—at first metaphorically—"prepositional," because they were positioned before the house, because they were on the road to the house, and because they were continually passed by, on the road and in the text.

Pressing the metaphor came next. Investigating the etymology of "preposition" (and the other "lesser" parts of speech) and its entries in encyclopedias, dictionaries, and grammars from the seventeenth through the nineteenth centuries revealed that in fact it led quite an interesting life, almost a fairy tale of upward mobility, a trajectory nearly as remarkable as Tom Jones's from foundling to heir. This research coincided with reading Bertrand Bronson and Richard Wendorf on a long-term interest of mine in eighteenth-century typographical conventions. As an editor of a number of early works, and a teacher of many more, I always relished the *difference* in the reading experience of alien textures—the long *ſ* (and its non-italic form, ſ), the capitalized common Noun, the italicized *Proper Noun*. That was part of the contemporary flavor, and I fully agreed with Benjamin Franklin that while modernization certainly "makes the Line appear more even," ultimately it "renders it less immediately legible; as the paring all Men's Noses might smooth and level their Faces, but would render their Physiognomies less distinguishable."[7] Bronson had magical things to say about printing as an index of taste; John Baskerville's new type, for example, he finds "so suggestive of lapidary depth," his letters "gracious" because they are "treated so openly that air seems to flow through them and around them"; they are spaced on the page "with a judgment so nice as to force the surrounding space to collaborate in completing the outlines of half-suggested [. . .] forms."[8] And Wendorf finely historicizes Bronson's "Great Divide" with a detailed analysis of printing habits across the century, offering a compelling cultural argument for the changes.[9]

The preposition became more prominently visible in the grammar books at more or less the same time that nouns were losing their typographical status. Once those nouns stopped towering over everybody else in the sentence, the spaces *between* the nouns had more room to move. That brought me back to studying landscape architecture and the approach in terms of two contemporary intersections: the great landscape gardener of the mid-eighteenth century, Lancelot "Capability" Brown, called his landscapes "literary compositions," and the nineteenth-century editor of Samuel Richardson, Anna Lætitia Barbauld, contrasted the plot of *Clarissa* as an ancient avenue against the modern approach.

The self-declared differences between the modern approach and the ancient avenue were differences in perspective, in perception, in what Peter de Bolla calls "looking as a cultural form."[10] In the lines of William Mason's *The English Garden* (1786), the design of the approach means that "our sight is led / Gradual to view, the whole"; cedar and larch may for a while "[hide] / The view entire," while here and there a bit of "rose and woodbine" may "burst upon the sight"; we glimpse things "*thro'* a copse," "partially," half excluded and half revealed, so that "each step / Shall wake fresh beauties; each short point present / A different picture, new, and yet the same."[11] This shifting attention to the in-between in landscape architecture, typography, and grammar began to resonate in my rereadings of—in particular—Samuel Richardson, Ann Radcliffe, and Jane Austen. In my previous book, *The Prose of Things: Transformations of Description in the Eighteenth Century*, I read the character Clarissa as perpetually forced to detect and define implied spaces; now she kept appearing prepositionally, between upstairs and down, between family and honor, between a rock and a Lovelace. My new understanding of eighteenth-century commas reoriented *The Mysteries of Udolpho*, and its oddly persistent use of "at length" in the long description of the approach to the castle led to meditations upon changing syntax. The work of M. B. Parkes, Nicholson Baker, and Janine Barchas started fileting formatting onto its own plane, *through* which I was reading the words and meanings below. (Or perhaps above, if I was thinking of punctuation and typography as underground systems of meaning.) The rhetorical patterns of the architectural theorists' descriptions of approaches turned out to enact not only the topography they described but also the syntactical approach of the refurbished periodic sentence: "a *circuit* [. . .] in which the meaning is suspended, till the whole is finished."[12] Each turn in the approach of my research formed new combinations in which the meaning was suspended until at least I *glimpsed* the finished whole—of a historicized narratology and a hermeneutically significant set of shared patterns between topographies of land, page, and narrative.[13]

Thus this is not *exactly* a book about architecture and landscape theory, nor about typography and book history, nor about linguistics and prosody. It is a book about some unexpected formal common denominators between eighteenth-century verbal and visual representations of the domestic landscape, the printed page, and the syntactical turn. It is a book about the enormous power of the little things on a page and in a text. Franco Moretti has said: "The very small, and the very large; these are the forces that shape literary history. Devices and genres; not texts."[14] Dror Wahrman has studied how "the problem of the tiny" was the province of early modern natural science and philosophy.[15] Like Robert Boyle's "little Corpuscles in motion," little words as well as "local motions" "may perform considerable things, either without being much heeded, or without seeming other then [*sic*] faint, at least in relation to the considerableness of the Effects produced by them."[16] Jayne Elizabeth Lewis has called prepositions, unforgettably, "the lynchpins of contingency."[17] And Master Lynchpin of Contingency Himself, the ever-ingenious rake Robert Lovelace in *Clarissa*, declares: "I have often thought, that the little words in the republic of letters, like the little folks in a nation, are the most significant."[18]

My connections between these historical fields of architecture, typography, and grammar share a conceptual family resemblance to Caroline Levine's forms or Bruno Latour's networks. One of the many things I like about Levine's concept is how she "shifts attention away from deep causes to a recognition of the many different shapes and patterns that constitute political, cultural, and social experience."[19] Recent critical traditions, she argues, have treated "aesthetic form as epiphenomenal—as secondary," which "assumes that one kind of form—the political—is always the root or ground of the other—the aesthetic" (14). We might say my "form" is landscape, material and figurative—the common organizing principles and patterns of typography, grammar, narrative, and landscape architecture. The criticism of the last few decades, Levine says, has spent a great deal of attention on "indeterminate spaces and identities, employing such key terms as liminality, borders, migration, hybridity, and passing." She fully acknowledges the importance of this work on "formal failures, incompletions, and indefinability" but urges us to relearn "the major work that [whole] forms do in our world" (9). I cheer this on, but as someone of a more historicist persuasion than Levine, I emphasize the impress that the material, cultural, historical, geographical, and technical worlds have on these forms (or grammars). As a case in point: the in-betweens and borders and minuscules that I investigate here are not exactly failures or incompletions or indefinables (even if they include the "lesser" parts of speech) but lively, performative, connective little stars—the historical predecessors and conceptual *obverses* of the twentieth-century "cultural way of looking": Derridean, deconstructivist, postmodern. The eighteenth-century looker found, in Uvedale Price's words, a "charm [in] expectation" (*Essays* 1:250); she expected a bit of rose or woodbine in the glimpse through the trees, in the spaces in between.[20] As Hugh Kenner says, "New ways of writing, then, for new orders of experience."[21]

My terms will play with the overlapping territory between the literal and the metaphorical. The definition of "grammar" by Richard Johnson (1706) and Anne Fisher (1759) as "the Art of expressing the Relation of Things in Construction" was gently criticized by James Buchanan in 1762: strictly speaking, he said, it should be phrased as "the Art of expressing the Relations of *Words* in Construction."[22] But a number of early linguists argued for a more material connection between words and things (as Swift's satire of Lagado in *Gulliver's Travels* testifies to), and the type and grammar on the page often perform elegantly in this ontological in-between. Commas are their own "forms" with their own "affordances," or latent potential uses (Levine 6); or perhaps we could call them "media" in Clifford Siskin and William Warner's sense of anything that "intervenes, enables, supplements, or is simply in between."[23] The term "picturesque" is used shamelessly loosely throughout the book (except where I am making specific historical or aesthetic claims). As Price himself pointed out, "There are few words, whose meaning has been less accurately determined than that of the word picturesque. In general, I believe, it is applied to every object, and every kind of scenery, which has been, or might be represented with good effect in painting" (*Essays* 1:37). I use it as a prevalent, popular tag for the irregular, the textured, the oblique, the unexpected, the interruptive. And I see a picturesque above ground and below ground (both phrases meant literally *and* metaphorically). The irregular typography of the seventeenth and early eighteenth century gets smoothed into Palladian symmetry somewhere in the middle of the period, but that is what allows (us to see) the play of the fantastic linguistic roots beneath. Grammar is generally regarded as going prescriptivist in the later eighteenth century—more uniform, with prepositions no longer allowed to be stranded—but even if that is true (which I resist to some degree), authors under those prescriptions proved every bit as linguistically ingenious as ever Pope was with a couplet. And what else is free indirect discourse but a narrative picturesque, a winding and sidling into the mind, glimpsing through its self-made trees some opening or enclosure, with or without woodbine and roses?

The key figures in this book are Humphry Repton, Thomas Whately, Samuel Richardson, Frances Burney, Ann Radcliffe, and Jane Austen, and throughout the chapters I will revisit the same scenes from my different approaches. In this way my chapters behave a bit like Repton's famous "slides," the lifting of which reveals a new configuration. Unlike Repton, I am not offering increasingly idealized views but rather a series of palimpsestic readings, watching the passage change through the different lenses of landscape architecture or the semicolon or the summative phrase. What I hope to achieve is a three-dimensional sense of the topographical page, of a practice of reading simultaneously *on* the page as well as *in* or *through* it.[24]

The first two chapters of *Grammars of Approach* explore the physical and etymological landscape of changing perspectives. Chapter 1, "The Architectural Approach," first traces the history of the term, which shifts in grammatical identity as it shifts in spatial purpose and psychological implication. I track "approach" through the dictionaries and encyclopedias of the seventeenth, eighteenth, and nineteenth centuries and through the architectural writings of William Mason, Horace Walpole, Thomas Whately, Humphry Repton, J. C. Loudon, and others. I then show how travelers (Daniel Defoe, Caroline Lybbe Powys, John Byng) and novelists (Samuel Richardson, Charlotte Smith, Ann Radcliffe, Jane Austen) incorporate the concept, vocabulary, and strategies of approach—literal and figurative—into novels.

Chapter 2, "The Prepositional Building," turns to the "prepositional" nature of the approach. An essential part was the architect-designed park gate lodge defining the entrance to the approach and to the estate. But for readers and editors as well as actual visitors, the focus is on the Noun of the House; the lodge tends to disappear from view and page as it is passed *by*, *on* the road and *in* the text. Yet close reading discovers the lodge exerting interpretive pressure as an entrance or threshold or boundary in the works of Burney, Radcliffe, and Austen, and even John Bunyan. The chapter then considers the equally ubiquitous (and equally understudied) "topographical view"—the thousand or so engravings of the great estates collected under titles such as *The Seats of the Nobility and Gentry* (1787) and *Picturesque Views of the Principal Seats of the Nobility and Gentry in England and Wales* (1786–88). I study the position of the house in its frame and the activity of its "staffage." The chapter closes with a coda on Old London Bridge, which had been the only land entrance ("approach") to the city from the south until the mid-eighteenth century. From the twelfth century until 1762 it had been covered with many-storied houses and shops; it was, according to Roger Griffiths in 1758, "more properly called a Village on, or across the River of *Thames.*" But after centuries of almost mythical status, it was completely destroyed, replaced by a modern, symmetrical, utilitarian, houseless, shopless, villageless bridge. The preposition of position, "on," was run over by the preposition of direction, "across." But that leveling and straightening, like the newly uniform line of text, opened up other ways of entering, viewing, and representing London.

The next two chapters turn toward the tiny moving parts of typography and grammar that lever larger textual spaces and meanings and create what I call the linguistic picturesque. In 1782 the landscape gardener Lancelot "Capability" Brown told Hannah More that "he compared his art to literary composition. Now *there,* said he, pointing his finger, I make a comma, and there pointing to another spot where a more decided turn is proper, I make a colon: at another part (where an interruption is desirable to break the view) a parenthesis—now a full stop, and then I begin another subject."[25] Chapter 3 looks at the hand-held landscape of the page (to paraphrase D. F. McKenzie)—at the lexical markers (fonts, capitals and italics, catchwords, and "pointing") that quite literally manage relationships between the abstract and the concrete.[26] "The Topographical Page" surveys seventeenth- through nineteenth-century printers' manuals, correspondence, dictionaries, and encyclopedias not only to expand Jerome McGann's concept of the "radial text" but also to argue for more authorial control than is usually credited beyond the well-known cases of Ben Jonson, Alexander Pope, and Laurence Sterne. (John Smith, in *The Printer's Grammar* of 1755, applauds "Gentlemen who [. . .] point their Copy accordingly, and abide thereby, with strictness." In fact, "were it done by every Writer, Compositors would sing, *Jubile!*")[27]

Samuel Richardson is a pivotal point of this book in so many ways, precisely because of his innovations as printer as well as novelist. In her edition of his correspondence, Anna Lætitia Barbauld describes the plot of *Clarissa* as seen "from afar, as it were through a long avenue, the gradual approach to which, without ever losing sight of the object, has more of simplicity and grandeur" than the "modern" winding approach.[28] But as with the spare smooth lines of roads and texts, new spaces open up underneath this long avenue of plot. As Richardson's rake-hero Lovelace writes to his friend Belford, "the little words in the republic of letters, like the little folks in a nation, are the most significant." And so to chapter 4, "The Grammar in Between," which explores "the little words" galvanized by the linguistic engineering of the late eighteenth century in the explosion of English grammars (before 1700 there were 34 grammars in English about English; between 1700 and 1750 another 34 appeared; between 1750 and 1800 another *205*). Here we document the rise of the "lesser parts of speech." But counter to the traditional view that English grammars became more prescriptivist, we can find in all the new rules and regulations a linguistic playfulness and narrative ingenuity. Clarissa herself lives a pronounced prepositional life, in the end fulfilling her mother's exasperated cry: "Take your own way, and go up!"

The last chapter gathers up the changing architectural and grammatical patterns into more sustained analyses of literary prose within these historical contexts of architecture and print, looking at sentences and paragraphs as spatial angles of narrative approach. It begins with the syntactical architecture of representative writers of the late seventeenth and early eighteenth centuries as context for prosodic change: John Bunyan, Daniel Defoe, and Eliza Haywood. The section considers the arts of pragmatographia, or "the opening and setting abroade those thinges which were included in one word,"[29] the rhythmic power of the summative ("in short," "in a Word," "in fine"), and the paratactic sentence and hypotactic power. Then the chapter considers the narrative move to the interior in these architectural and linguistic contexts. We revisit Radcliffe's passage describing the approach to Udolpho, this time to watch how she obsessively employs the phrase "at length" to mark temporal and spatial shifts from scene to scene and paragraph to paragraph; this both lexically enacts the architectural approach and signals shifting psychological states within its heroine, Emily St. Aubert. Frances Burney's *Camilla*, first discussed in chapter 2 for its park gate lodge, here models not only "Two Ways of looking at the same Thing," but also the many ways to enter the same place.[30] The character Indiana demonstrates an *inability* to enter any other head than her own. The rhetoric of free indirect discourse in Austen, on the other hand, is a perfect model of the architectural description of the approach: a single paragraph can circle from a bird's-eye view overhead, swoop down through a mind, and pop out into direct discourse. Narrative parallax is achieved when one sentence winds into the next for a different perspective.

It is my hope that the combined arguments in this book plausibly make the case that the eighteenth-century architectural approach to the house played into a new narrative approach to the mind, and that attention to the changes in landscape architecture, typography, and grammar can open up new approaches to reading, by seeing simultaneously a typographical landscape, a topographical page, and a narrative picturesque. To read in three dimensions is to see the word, the sentence, the page itself as part of the material world—the "form and texture" of thought.[31]

CHAPTER 1

The Architectural Approach

> Landscape gardening depends greatly on the form of the ground, and therefore to shape that, is the first object.
>
> James Elmes, *Dictionary of the Fine Arts* (1826)

The form of this ground—eighteenth-century landscape gardening—is well trodden, but I would like to do some reshaping of a feature that has not received much attention. My argument begins with the term "approach," which became a noun somewhere in the second half of the eighteenth century—a specifically architectural noun describing that "ROAD peculiar to a house in the country," in the words of landscape gardener John Claudius Loudon (1783–1843).[1] As the tour of the country house became increasingly popular for a wider range of people, the approach was conceptualized as a carefully designed series of changing perspectives from the entrance of the estate, winding "through the most interesting part of the grounds,"[2] to the entrance of the house itself. The approach should "form new combinations on every movement of the spectator" (Loudon, *Treatise* 2:591). Of the *spectator*—not simply the family's visitor but also the estate's tourist. The changes in perspective were not simply of house and grounds but *about* house and grounds, about subject and object, center and periphery, and, most importantly for my purposes, about what lies in between.

"In the ancient style," Loudon explains, "the grand object is, to obtain a straight line," while "in the modern style, a winding line is preferred, as being more easy and natural, and [. . .] displaying a greater variety of scenery."[3] The older approach *to* the great house focused *on* the great house; the approach was a grand avenue, a straight line, dominated by its terminus, the "power house," in Mark Girouard's words.[4] On the avenue, at each step the house (and its implied owner) looms larger, essentially unvarying, perforating even peripheral vision in a sideways glance. The "modern" approach is an architectural means to engineer a different kind of viewing, specifically of the landed estate, the house in the context of its grounds. This idea of landscape gardening as both coming out of and promoting different ways of seeing, viewing, looking, observing, has been a fairly standard and richly varied debate going back a ways, from Richard Payne Knight's contention that the picturesque represented "modes and habits of viewing," to Raymond Williams's observation that the "very idea of landscape implies separation and observation," to John Barrell's argument that a "way of looking" became a "way of *knowing*" the landscape, to Stephen Daniels's "field of vision," to Peter de Bolla's "looking as a cultural form," to David Marshall's question, "What does it mean [. . .] to look at the world through the frame of art?"[5] It is part of what Peter Collins calls the eighteenth-century architectural interest in parallax, or "the apparent displacement of objects caused by an actual change in the point of observation."[6] That is, in architecture, things (objects, buildings, views) are designed to produce the perception of movement in the observer. What is at least temporarily displaced by the new approach is the House (landowner); it is the *observer* (and his or her individual experience) who is focalized here. With carriages and heads turning this way and that, and the Great House remaining hidden (by design) for part of the journey, the weight of the experience thus shifts *from* that House to the route *to* the house and so, necessarily, to the viewer, the visitor, the tourist, *on* the route. The nominalization of "approach" in a sense codifies the importance of the in-between, the on-the-way, the *prepositional*—a concept that has a literal undergirding in the history of grammar, as will be argued in chapter 4. The view, we might say, shifts to the viewer, away from the ultimately viewed. De Bolla argues that the "changing positionalities in the activity of viewing landscape occur at precisely the same moment as changes in the organization of land and property ownership" (de Bolla 106). What this chapter will begin to argue is that this moment of changing positionalities toward landscapes is also reshaping the grounds of text and narrative.

This chapter opens with the oddly spare etymology of "approach" and its evolution from verb to noun. Its life in dictionaries and encyclopedias is skeletal, but the etymology etches the change from the "ancient" style of the straight line of Palladian symmetry to the "modern" style of winding patterns and linguistic picturesque. The second section will look at the word and concept from the point of view of the English landscape designers of the late eighteenth century, as they adapted, rejected, or otherwise responded to the man who relandscaped most of England: Lancelot "Capability" Brown (1716–83). The concept is formally articulated by Thomas Whately (1726–72), Humphry Repton (1752–1818), and Loudon, and their descriptions and definitions share lexical and syntactical patterns that demonstrate what I call the linguistic picturesque—the ways that narrative patterns are designed, syntactically, grammatically, and even to some extent typographically, to replicate the landscaped experience. Then follow a few representative travel writers and novelists to show, first, the more lively lifestyle of the term "approach" in those genres, and then something of the narrative phenomenology of the approach, as their discursions enact the patterns of their excursions. The syntactical architecture of the paragraphs maps onto the stages of the approach, and the language of the descriptions is definitively prepositional: the whole point of the exercise is to go over, under, around, through, and finally up to the house, with the emphasis on the process, on what lies between the entrance and the end.

The etymology of "approach" (*n. s.*)

The term "approach" as a noun in landscape architecture led a double life. It was almost invisible in dictionaries and encyclopedias, the linguistic houses of verbal change. Its nominalization was recorded only as a sort of husk; the older form of "avenue," from which it descended, is given center stage. (Its contemporary cousin, the "circuit-walk" or "belt," does not appear at all.) Its real life was carried out in more popular discourse: the treatises of landscape theorists, the records of travelers, the settings of novels. The first three sections will trace its surface official life; the last two will watch it incarnate itself in other media and ponder the difference.

The first monolingual English dictionary, Robert Cawdrey's *A Table Alphabeticall, conteyning and teaching the true writing, and vnderstanding of hard vsuall English wordes, borrowed from the Hebrew, Greeke, Latine, or French. &c.*, defines "approch" only and quite simply as a verb: "come nigh."[7] Throughout the seventeenth century, the term remains only a verb in the dictionaries, sometimes not even defined (e.g., it is simply divided "ap-proach" in the 1676 *England's Perfect School-Master*), sometimes not appearing at all (Edward Phillips's 1658 *New World of English Words* lists "*Apprentice. / Appretiation. / Approbation. / Approperate. / Appropinquate. / Approver*").[8] The 1706 edition of Phillips's *New World of Words* (continued by lexicographer John Kersey [fl. 1720]) expands the term to include an adjectival version:

To Approach, to draw Nigh, to come Near.

Approachable, that may be Approached.

Kersey's own *Dictionarium Anglo-Britannicum* of 1715 appropriates these definitions, which remain the standard pattern for definitions through most of the eighteenth-century dictionaries as well, as in Nathan Bailey's *Dictionarium Britannicum* (1730), Thomas Dyche's *New General English Dictionary* (1740, 1759), and the *Pocket Dictionary* (1765). Some, like Bailey's in 1730 and John Ash's in 1775, point to the French root "approacher [*sic*] *to come Near*."[9]

"Approach" as a noun appears in the early eighteenth century in a military capacity: "APPROA'CHES [in Fortification] the several Works made by the Besiegers for advancing or getting nearer to a Fortress or besieged Place" (Bailey 1730). (That remains its most constant nounal existence through the century.) Ephraim Chambers, in the 1751 *Cyclopædia*, gives the term more personality (it "cause[s] some sweat among analysts") and a wider appearance in the public sphere (in mathematics and physics), as well as a more detailed description of its life as fortification:

APPROACH. See ACCESS and APPROXIMATION.

The *curve of equable Approach, Accessus æquabilis*, first proposed by M. Leibnitz, has caused some sweat among analysts.—The business is to find a curve, wherein a body descending by the sole power of gravity shall approach the horizon equally in equal times.—This curve has been found by Bernouilli, Varignon, Maupertuis, and others, to be the second cubical parabola, so placed as that its point of regression is uppermost. [. . .]

APPROACHES, in fortification, the several works made by the besiegers for advancing or getting nearer to a fortress, or place besieged. [. . .]

APPROACHES, or *Lines of* APPROACH, are particularly used for trenches cut in the ground, and their earth thrown up on the side next the place besieged; under shelter or defence whereof the besiegers may *approach*, without loss, to the parapet of the covered way; and plant guns, &c. wherewith to cannonade the place.

The lines of *approach* are to be connected by parallels or lines of communication.

The besieged frequently make *counter-approaches*, to interrupt and defeat the enemies *approaches*.[10]

Samuel Johnson's 1755 *Dictionary* gives us:

> *To* APPRO'ACH. *n. s.* [from the verb]
> 1. The act of drawing near. [. . .]
> 2. Access.
>> Honour hath in it the vantage ground to do good; the *ap-proach* to kings and principal persons; and the raising of a man's own fortunes. *Bacon's Essays.*
>
> 3. Hostile advance. [. . .]
> 4. Means of advancing.
>> Against beleagur'd heav'n the giants move,
>> Hills pil'd on hills, on mountains mountains lie,
>> To make their mad *approaches* to the sky. *Dryden's Ovid.*[11]

The definitions remain the same through at least the 1799 edition. In short, in the dictionaries and encyclopedias of the seventeenth and eighteenth centuries, the life of "approach" was lived largely as a verb or as a military substantive. Even James Elmes's 1826 *General and Biographical Dictionary of the Fine Arts* gives no separate definition of "approach," incorporating the term instead into the definition of "avenue." And in the twenty-first century, the *Oxford English Dictionary* defines the term of our interest as: "5.a. A means or way of approach; an access, passage, avenue. Also fig.," with contextual examples from George Herbert ("¶ *Dulness*") and William Cowper:

> 1633 G. Herbert *Temple: Sacred Poems* 108 Where are my lines then? my approaches? views?

> 1791 W. Cowper tr. Homer *Odyssey* in *Iliad & Odyssey* II. vii. 109 Mastiffs in gold and silver lined the approach.

Even here, the examples of "approach" from Herbert and Cowper do not actually match up with the modern domestic meaning of a "variety of ROAD peculiar to a house in the country."[12] Herbert's "approaches," embedded between "lines" and "views," keeps the word tied to the military meanings: the 1720 edition of Phillips's *New World of Words* identifies "Lines of Approach or of Attack" as "the Ways of Trenches dug along in the Earth, toward a Town that is besieged, in order to gain the Moat and the Body of the Place"; and to "View a place, (in the Art of War) is to ride about it before the Siege is laid, observing the strength or weakness of its Situation and Fortification, in order to attack the weakest part."[13] The example from Cowper's translation of the *Odyssey* suggests the Johnsonian "access" (Bacon's "*approach* to kings"), as the dogs of your garden-variety eighteenth-century English country estate were not typically lining the local approach in their gold and silver collars.

"Approach road" is the term used by the *OED*. It cites the first use as: "1833 J. C. Loudon *Encycl. Cottage Archit.* 463 The approach-road to the house." The actual term "approach" for the "ROAD peculiar to a house in the country" was in regular use by the 1770s, as we will see. But throughout the eighteenth century, the more usual term for "approach road" to appear in the dictionaries and encyclopedias is "avenue":

> AVE'NUE [*avenue, F.*] *a Passage, Entrance or Way lying open to a Place.*
> AVENUE [in a *Garden*] a Walk or Row of Trees, *&c.* or a Walk planted on each Side with Trees. (Bailey, 1730)

> A'VENUE (S.) an entrance, passage, path, or way, to, or from a castle, or other building; with the *Gardeners*, it is called a walk. (Dyche, 1740)

> AVENUE, in gardening, is a walk, planted on each side with trees, and leading to some place.
>
> > All *avenues*, Mortimer says, should lead to the front of an house, garden-gate, highway-gate, or wood, and terminate in a prospect.—In an *avenue* to an house, whatever the length of the walk is, it ought to be as wide as the whole breadth of the front; and if wider, it is so much the better. (Chambers, 1750)

> A'VENUE. *n. s.* [*avenue,* Fr. It is sometimes pronounced with the accent on the second syllable, as *Watts* observes; but it is generally placed on the first.]
> 1. A way by which any place may be entered. [. . .]
> 2. An alley, or walk of trees before a house. (Johnson, 1755)

> A'VENUE (S.) 1. A passage to a place,
> 2. A walk or visto of trees. *F.* (*Pocket Dictionary*, 1765)

> AVEN'UE, (*Avenue*, F. *Quo licit venire ad*) a Passage or Way lying open to a Place.
> AVEN'UE, (among *Gardener's*) a walk or Row of Trees, &c. (Buys, 1768–69)

But among landscape gardeners and in fashionable discourse (as we will see in the next sections), "avenue" is most definitely the angle of the past, as Loudon explains: "In the ancient or geometrical style of laying out grounds, the approach road or avenue advances directly in front of the house" (Loudon, *Encyclopædia* 769). Somewhere in the middle of the eighteenth century the grand straight avenue was supplanted by the winding approach. The last sentence of Elmes's definition of "avenue" leaves room for the changing of this cultural form:

> AVENUE. [Fr. From *ad venire,* Lat.] *In architecture.* A way to, access, approach. A long walk of columns, arcades, statues, trees, &c. used for the decoration of an approach to a palace or mansion. The avenue, in the hands of a man of taste, is susceptible of great variety and beauty of design.[14]

The "great variety and beauty" of the way to the palace or mansion received concentrated, dedicated attention by the late eighteenth century.

It may be objected that the etymological absence of "approach" in the dictionaries and encyclopedias as a term defining the designed road to a house—even in those devoted to architecture and the fine arts—makes it a less visible, less influential concept than I want to argue. I confess I was surprised that James Elmes's *Dictionary of the Fine Arts* did *not* include the modern term "approach." Perhaps, as an architect and civil engineer working primarily in London, Elmes (1782–1862) was not as familiar with the landscape gardener's lexicon. Or perhaps, as an antiquarian, he privileged the avenue.[15] In any case, in practice, "approach" replaces "avenue" not only in the grammars of the landscape architects and theorists but also in the vernacular of the traveler and the narrative of the novel. It is through the contemporary articulation of landscape theory that the word and concept of "approach" enter ordinary discourse and popular imagination.

The concept of approach (*n. s.* and *v.*): The "ancient" and the "modern" lines

As Loudon explained it, "In the ancient style, the grand object is, to obtain a straight line," while "in the modern style, a winding line is preferred, as being more easy and natural, and [. . .] displaying a greater variety of scenery" (*Encyclopœdia* 769). But how did the line get where it was going? What happened on the road between the straight and the winding way, the avenue and the approach? There is an enormous body of literature on the subject of the history of landscape gardening; in this section I want to recapitulate the standard story (acknowledging the oversimplifications involved in summaries) to shape the ground, as it were, into a context for seeing similarly shaped ground in nonarchitectural contexts. I will look at the language as well as the images of the basic concepts in landscape theory and design as a backdrop for the syntactical analysis of the next sections of this chapter and the later chapters of this book. The dominant players here are Capability Brown on one side and the champions of the picturesque, such as William Gilpin, Uvedale Price, and Richard Payne Knight, on the other; Humphry Repton lies poised in between, as Brown's self-styled heir but also as innovator, folding aspects of the picturesque into the domesticity of common sense—and an emblem of my interest in the in-between.

The landscape of the English country house that still dominates the cultural imagination is a Brownian one, consisting of "undulating grass that leads somewhere down to an irregularly shaped piece of water over which a bridge arches, of trees grouped casually, with cattle or deer about the slopes, and of houses and other buildings glimpsed in the middle or far distance," such as Richard Wilson's depiction of Croome Court in Worcestershire (plate I).[16] And rightly so. Much of Georgian England was resculpted by Capability Brown. Between 1751 and 1783 he designed or redesigned the gardens of over 170 of England's stately homes from Devon to the Scottish border; his clients included five prime ministers and a dozen dukes. (Born in Northumberland to a chambermaid, he first worked as vegetable gardener to the local squire [who was, whisper had it, his father], Sir William Loraine. He later relegated all vegetable gardens to the margins of the estate.) Brown literally as well as conceptually transformed the English countryside. Horace Walpole called him "the second monarch of landscape."[17] And in 2016, for the 300th anniversary of his birth, the National Trust published a website, "How to Spot a Capability Brown Landscape."

The English landscape was transformed across the eighteenth century by many other factors as well, of course: rapid urban expansion, the improvement of roads, enclosures, agricultural innovations, and so forth.[18] As Stephen Daniels puts it, these transformations "were in a full sense geographical, involving new regional formations, networks of exchange, systems of circulation, spaces of identity and exclusion, concrete, physical places as well as more abstract spheres of influence." Daniels appropriates Humphry Repton's phrase "field of vision"—what we can see with and without moving our head and body—to include the "capacity to comprehend a range of new information and to address the relation between commercial progress and social order."[19] Recognition of these and other conceptual formations, implicit in this chapter, will become more visible in later turns of this argument in the succeeding chapters. Here, my emphasis is on "the form of the ground," in Elmes's words, as it was consciously reshaped by Brown and his successors into a concept of "approach" that was not only an innovation in crossing ground but also an example and emblem of new modes of expression and representation, a way of bringing the unseen into the field of vision, of discerning the impress of the invisible.[20]

Brown acquired his nickname in the 1760s by touring a prospective property on horseback for an hour or so and then pronouncing on its "capabilities."[21] In 1775 he wrote that to "produce [the] effects" of "all the elegance and all the comforts which Mankind wants in the Country and (I will add) if right, be exactly fit for the owner, the Poet and the Painter," one must have "a good plan, good execution, a perfect knowledge of the country and the objects in it, whether natural or artificial [. . .] hideing what is disagreeable and shewing what is beautifull."[22] He set out to "destroy" (Repton's word) the Dutch-style gardens characterized by "sloped terraces of grass, regular shapes of land and water formed by art, [. . .] quaintly adorned with trees in pots [. . .] and clipped, to preserve the most perfect regularity of shape."[23] He fashioned a gentle variety, making slopes out of flat land, shaping large streams into Hogarthian serpentines, damming small streams to create serene lakes, planting and scything vast sweeps of grass, clumping distinctive trees, marking the boundaries with belts of darker trees, removing parterres, and generally creating a vista with a sense of undulating peace, gentle irregularity, pleasant surprise, and satisfying activity.[24] It was all about bringing some things forward and pushing other things down or away, of rearranging the visual field, the pattern of emphasis.

As John Dixon Hunt and Peter Willis remind us, the Brownian shift in spatial sensibility was the product of some hundred and fifty years of experimentation. "What came to be thought of variously as 'the English landscape garden,' '*le jardin anglais*,' '*il giardino inglese*,' or '*der englische Garten*,' was the outcome of a long process whereby the stiff and geometric gardens of Tudor and Stuart England were transformed into an art that the rest of Europe imitated" (Hunt and Willis 1). For the sixteenth and seventeenth centuries, beauty lay in symmetry, in "the geometrical pattern made by circular pools and the intersecting straight lines of avenues, allées, terraces, hedges,"[25] as captured by the Dutch artists and draftsmen Leonard Knyff (1650–1722) and Johannes Kip (1652–1722) in their collection of views of English country houses, *Britannia Illustrata; or, Views of Several of the Queens Palaces, as Also of the Principal seats of the Nobility and Gentry of Great Britain, Curiously Engraven on 80 Copper Plates, London* (1707). As Loudon explains in his *Encyclopædia of Cottage, Farm, and Villa Architecture*: "The beauties aimed at by the ancient style, whether with respect to the house or the grounds, were, to present regular, symmetrical, architectural views" (769). Note that at "Knowle" (Knole), the winding road and tumbling grass are stopped firmly at the gate (figure 1).

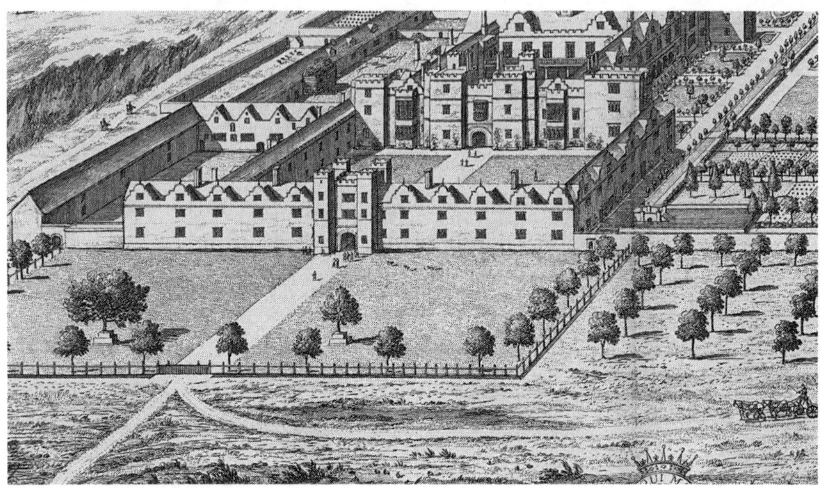

1. Leonard Knyff, "Knowle," Kent. Engraved by Johannes Kip. From *Britannia Illustrata* (1720) (detail). Photograph courtesy of the Virginia Historical Society.

Resistance to the symmetry of Renaissance past and Continental Other was already stirring early in the eighteenth century (think of Pope's *Epistle to Burlington* [1731], where at Timon's villa "Grove nods at grove, each Alley has a brother" [l. 117]—and not in a good way[26]). It only grew. William Shenstone, in "Unconnected Thoughts on Gardening" (1764), puzzles: "It is not easy to account for the fondness of former times for strait-lined avenues to their houses; strait-lined walks through their woods; and, in short, every kind of strait-line; where the foot is to travel over, what the eye has done before."[27] Horace Walpole, a keen fan of his own century, airily dismisses the Dutch-French formalism of the past in *The History of the Modern Taste in Gardening* (1770):

> In Kip's views of the seats of our nobility and gentry, we see the same tiresome and returning uniformity. Every house is approached by two or three gardens, consisting perhaps of a gravel-walk and two grass-plats, or borders of flowers. Each rises above the other by two or three steps, and as many walls and terrasses; and so many iron-gates, that we recollect those ancient romances, in which every entrance was guarded by nymphs or dragons.[28]

It is a chorus: symmetry is at best tiresome, at worst authoritarian, prescripting response.

Naturally, there weren't exactly Team Straightlines and Team Windings (Big Endians and Little Endians); Repton, for example, recognized that "a perfectly straight line, drawn across a valley diagonally, appears to the eye the same as this line of fancied beauty," the Hogarthian serpentine (*Observations* 87). And both Repton and Picturesque Price would at times acknowledge the beauty of the avenue.[29] But the broad strokes are visible. William Kent, according to Walpole's dramatic narrative, "leaped the fence, and saw that all nature was a garden":

> He felt the delicious contrast of hill and valley changing imperceptibly into each other, tasted the beauty of the gentle swell, or concave scoop, and remarked how loose groves crowned an easy eminence with happy ornament, and while they called in the distant view between their graceful stems, removed and extended the perspective by delusive comparison. (*Modern Taste* 43–44)

As the notorious historian J. F. Shade (1898–1959) put it, "we are drawing attention not so much to different aesthetic principles as to different responses to the world."[30] Walpole's language pays attention to the space *between* hill and valley, in the "imperceptibl[e]" interstices of change, and to the experience of the prospect extended by its frame *between* trees. Kent, along with architect (and playwright) Sir John Vanbrugh and designer Charles Bridgeman (inventor of the "ha-ha"), developed the gardens at Stowe in Buckinghamshire, where Brown had moved in 1740. The ha-ha, or sunken fence (designed to keep the deer and sheep from wandering onto the lawn without breaking the prospect with a fence), allowed the parkland beyond the fence "to be harmonized with the lawn within; and the garden in its turn was to be set free from its prim regularity, that it might assort with the wilder country without" (Walpole, *Modern Taste* 43). The inner and outer circles of landscape blend into each other. And the rococo gardens of the 1740s and '50s developed a "magical way in which every feature is gradually revealed and then lost from sight."[31] Although Walpole makes larger claims than garden historians are always happy with, it is true enough that contrast and change edged out symmetry and repetition; the in-between displaced the front-and-center, paving the ground, so to speak, for Brown and Repton on the one hand and the picturesque practitioners on the other.[32]

The "picturesque" movement, springing from William Gilpin's 1768 definition of the term as "expressive of that peculiar kind of beauty, which is agreeable in a picture,"[33] sledge-hammered the smooth Brownian contours in favor of what Uvedale Price (1747–1829) described as "all that the painter admires—[. . .] all intricacies, [. . .] all the beautiful varieties of form, tint, and light and shade; every deep recess—every bold projection—the fantastic roots of trees—the winding paths of sheep."[34] Gilpin had infamously suggested in *Observations on the River Wye* that a "mallet judiciously used (but who durst use it?) might be of service in fracturing some" of the remaining gable-ends of Tintern Abbey.[35] Price and Richard Payne Knight (1750–1824), country-gentlemen-friends-and-neighbors in Herefordshire and avid estate-alterers, were its most prominent and published theoreticians. Knight's poem *The Landscape* (1794), Price's *An Essay on the Picturesque* (1794, 1796, 1810), and his printed reply (1795) to Humphry Repton's *A Letter to Uvedale Price* (1794), which he included in his collected *Essays on the Picturesque* (1810), articulated the code of the picturesque. The essays were translated into German and were extremely influential in Britain and on the Continent.[36]

A quick word on the term itself. As Price himself admits, "There are few words, whose meaning has been less accurately determined than that of the word picturesque" (*Essays* 1:37). Where for Price the term had been applied indiscriminately "to every object, and every kind of scenery," in modern criticism it has been subjected to political, social, religious, and sexual analysis, not to mention further aesthetic extensions. Price worked to position the term as a fairly precise alternative in between the Burkean sublime and the beautiful; I will limit my discussion of the picturesque to its most common denominators as a pattern for narratological analysis. As Ian McLean puts it, "Because the picturesque was structured like a language, it could be everywhere at once."[37] My shorthand will tend to be "the fantastic roots of trees—the winding paths of sheep."

Knight was as scathing about the "fav'rite Brown" as ever Walpole could be about the formalists; in *The Landscape* it is Brown's "innovating hand" that "First dealt thy curses o'er this fertile land":

> Our modern taste, alas! no limit knows:—
> O'er hill, o'er dale, through woods and fields it flows;
> Spreading o'er all its unprolific spawn,
> In never-ending sheets of vapid lawn.[38]

Even the indefatigable traveler John Byng (later Viscount Torrington), generally a champion of the past, dismisses the Brownian present in favor of the rising picturesque sensibility on a visit to "the house and parkish grounds of Mr [James] Evelyn," noting: "Our ancestors were happy to ride from field to field, from wood to wood; but now all is to be lawn'd, to be clump'd: all to be seen at once! Surely modest nature should make but partial discoveries; to eager the eye, to indulge the imagination; and not start all her charms at one display."[39] William Kent had originally rejected views in which all might be "beheld at once" (Walpole, *Modern Taste* 44). As Peter de Bolla argues, the shift to a "linear temporal structure of the view," to a progression of perspectives, a sequence of experiences, was a shift to a form of narrative. "If one views everything 'all at once' the complexities of the sequential look [are] collapsed into a single gestalt" (110). Price particularly criticizes Brown's creation of the "belt" (of trees), comparing it unfavorably to an avenue, which at least has a "simple grandeur" going for it: "in an avenue you see the same objects from beginning to end, and in the belt a new set every twenty yards, yet each successive part of this insipid circle is so like the preceding, that though really different, the difference is scarcely felt" (*Essays* 1:247). It is "perpetual change without variety," from which "there is no escaping," and "the charm of expectation is over" (1:247, 250). There is no narrative.

But although the picturesque practitioners positioned themselves directly against Brown, the line from Brown to the picturesque is itself predicated on Brown's transformative insistence on the winding and the undulating. Brown himself was in fact dramatically incarnating and popularizing an increasing cultural preference for the winding line, the partial vision, the managed surprise—a new kind of narrative, in fact. Ronald Paulson has explored the ways that the 1740s pictorial circuits "(sometimes called 'perimeter belts') had begun to appear in gardens: instead of wandering through the garden, the path made a circuit of it, and the benches revealed a series of perspectives or different points of view on the same scene."[40] The "narrative" could be a swath of different responses to the same object, as Pope had arranged in the 1720s at Twickenham, or as Shenstone later orchestrated at Leasowes: "the grand, the savage, the sprightly, the melancholy, the horrid, or the beautiful" (Shenstone, "Unconnected Thoughts" 2:113). John Dixon Hunt quotes Robert Southey referring in 1807 to the picturesque as "a new science for which a new language has been formed."[41] Brown's famous words to Hannah More will echo more than once in this book: "Now *there*, said he, pointing his finger, I make a comma, and there pointing to another spot where a more decided turn is proper, I make a colon: at another part (where an interruption is desirable to break the view) a parenthesis—now a full stop, and then I begin another subject."[42] Landscape spoke not just as emblem but with plot and character, with a shape of beginning, middle, and end, of expectation, surprise, revelation, resolution.

Although Humphry Repton was a full contemporary of Price and Knight, and all three were of a generation after Brown, Repton comes between Brown and the ideological picturesque in at least three ways. First, he considered himself Brown's heir, and so came in for some of the same ridicule. Second, his own works of landscape, architecture, and publication temporally preceded the full picturesque movement. And third, his work evolved within and against both the Brownian and the picturesque aesthetics, bringing the bold projections, fantastic roots of trees, and windings of sheep into the compass of the humanly comfortable. Repton for me is both a historical and a metaphorical representation of the root system connecting the synchronically changing appearances and emphases of landscape, narrative, and their common topography of the page: his Red Books, those morocco-bound volumes capturing the realities and the possibilities of the estates of his prospective clients, combine graphic vision with textual narration in patterns that work to enact the experience of the designs themselves.

Repton was born into the rural middle class at Bury St. Edmunds. He was educated in England and Holland, and for the first part of his life he set up as a merchant. When his business failed, he pottered happily as a country gentleman in Norfolk, busying himself with botany and gardening, sketching and painting. But his finances wouldn't sustain this life indefinitely, and eventually (at age thirty-six) he decided to become a professional landscape gardener, writing to his well-connected friends and getting himself a number of immediate commissions. "No pursuit seems to have afforded him so much pleasure as that of making drawings of the seats of every nobleman and gentleman within his reach," says Loudon, his first biographer. "Many of these he presented to their respective owners, and others he gave to illustrate the '*History of Norfolk*'; a work then publishing in ten volumes, and for which he also supplied the letter-press describing the Hundreds of North and South Erpingham."[43]

Repton defended Brown consistently (but not entirely uncritically) throughout his career:

> [B]ecause the immortal BROWN was originally a kitchen gardener, it is too common to find every man, who can handle a rake or spade, pretending to give his opinion on the most difficult points of improvement. It may perhaps be asked, from whence Mr. Brown derived his knowledge?—the answer is obvious: that, being at first patronised by a few persons of rank and acknowledged good taste, he acquired, by degrees, the faculty of *prejudging effects;* partly from repeated trials, and partly from the experience of those to whose conversation and intimacy his genius had introduced him: and, although he could not design, himself, there exist many pictures of scenery, made under his instruction, which his imagination alone had painted.[44]

"Prejudging effects" suggests the narrative sensibility of beginning, middle, and end, of reader response. It was not Brown himself but his vast legacy of imitators who were responsible for "all that bad taste" which was attributed to him. According to Repton, after Brown's death "a numerous herd of his foremen and working gardeners" were then "*consulted* as well as *employed*, in the several works which he had entrusted them to superintend," the result of which generated "the immeasurable extent of naked lawn; the tedious length of belts and drives; the useless breadth of meandering roads; [. . .] the naked expanses of waters, unaccompanied by trees" (*Enquiry* 7, 8).

By the time Repton published his first work, *Sketches and Hints* (1795), he was clearly recognized as heir apparent by the Brown family. Repton acknowledges his "obligations to Launcelot Brown, Esq., [. . .] the son of my predecessor, for having presented me with the maps of the greatest works in which his late father had been consulted, both in their original and imprinted states" (30). A letter of 26 August 1788 to his friend the Rev. Norton Nicholls (a close friend of Thomas Gray) outlines his plans for his new career and his influences:

> I have been advised to render my leisure proffitable by a profession which since the loss of Brown and Richmond has been understood by no one so well as yourself. My habit of landscape sketching I have considerably improved by practice and this may be of great use in shewing effects where descriptions are not sufficient. Mason, Gilpin, Whatley [*sic*] and Gerardin have been of late my breviary, and the works of Kent, Brown and Richmond have been the places of my worship. (Qtd. in Stroud, *Repton* 27–28)

By the mid-1790s, Repton was well known and in relatively high demand, although he never achieved success on the grand scale of Brown. "Brown's world was one of large horizons: great estates, high politics, big money and, in the writings of admirers such as Thomas Whately, grand theory. With contracts of up to twenty thousand pounds, and a one thousand pound salary as Royal Gardener, Brown became a rich and favoured man" (Daniels, *Repton* 149). Repton's landscape canvas was smaller, more domestic, more interested in the garden immediately surrounding a house (more Austen than Scott); he was consulted by not only the Prince of Wales, concerning his palace at Brighton, but also "the humble citizen, who, in his villa near town, asked for his assistance to arrange his rows of poplars, or to exclude the dusty road by his fir plantation." All in all, he "was successful, was eminent, was rich, [. . .] was happy" (Loudon, "Biographical Notice" 16, 15).

As evident from his "breviary," Repton was influenced by the picturesque as well as by Brownian contours. He created the term "landscape gardening" as the peculiarly English art of displaying the beauty of scenery by "improving" it, uniting the "powers of the *landscape painter* and the *practical gardener*" (*Sketches* 29). (Brown used the term "Place-making."[45]) Repton loved movement—a plume of smoke from a distant cottage, the sight of travelers on the road, a river rather than a lake. Like Knight and Price, he viewed architecture as an element of landscape, their characters to be reconciled.[46] But he disagreed with the fundamental premise of a picturesque landscape: that it be like a picture. He argues for several crucial differences between a scene in nature and a scene on canvas, most importantly:

> The spot from whence the view is taken, is in a fixed state to the painter; but the gardener surveys his scenery while in motion; and, from different windows in the same front, he sees objects in different situations; therefore, to give an accurate portrait of the gardener's improvement, would require pictures from each separate window, and even a different drawing at the most trifling change of situation, either in the approach, the walks, or the drives, about each place. (*Sketches* 96)

The landscape is alive and moving in ways the painting can never be; its "quantity of view, or field of vision, is much greater than any picture will admit," and some of the most compelling views from the house (such as "from an eminence down a steep hill") do not appear in paintings; its light is more varied, and the practical pleasures of the domestic landscape (a "neat gravel walk" or a "close mown lawn") do not carry the same power in a representation. The "field of vision" in a living landscape shifts moment by moment both in itself, in its light and shade, water and wind, travelers and sheep, and also with each movement of the spectator, the visitor, the inhabitant.[47] Thus Repton admired Brown for his attention to "what related to the comfort, convenience, tastes, and propriety of design in the several mansions and other buildings which he planned" (*Observations* 168n). Human beings in a real landscape move around, change their perspective, and in general have to live in the houses and walk through the gardens designed for them.[48] If, as John Lucas argues, "concern with detail is itself something of a challenge to the picturesque concern with a distanced viewpoint and 'vague emotion, expressed in shadowy mass and luminous base,'"[49] then Repton's clearest distinction from the Picturesquers is his concern with detail—the details of domestic human comfort at all levels (as we shall see in chapter 2) as well as the details of the estate. But in the language of the approach—in the acts of its description—they are all on remarkably common ground.

The language of approach (*v.*): architectural and syntactical design

Repton closes his Red Book to Brandsbury (1789) by transcribing lines from William Mason's poem *The English Garden* (1772–82) that capture the vocabulary and the plot-line—the narrative—used by all the landscape designers and theorists when describing the approach:

> ____________________ *"enrich with all the hues*
> *"That flowers, that shrubs, that trees can yield, the sides*
> *"Of that fair path, from whence our sight is led*
> *"Gradual to view, the whole. Where'er thou wind'st*
> *"That path, take heed between the scene and eye,*
> *"To vary and to mix thy chosen greens.*
> *"Here for a while with cedar or with larch,*
> *"That from the ground spread their close texture, hides*
> *"The view entire. Then o'er some lowly tuft,*
> *"Where rose and woodbine bloom, permit its charms*
> *"To burst upon the sight; now thro' a copse*
> *"Of beech, that rear their smooth and stately trunks,*
> *"Admit it partially, and half exclude,*
> *"And half, reveal its graces: in this path,*
> *"How long soe'er the wanderer roves, each step*
> *"Shall wake fresh beauties; each short point present*
> *"A different picture, new, and yet the same.*
> Mason's Garden Book 1st 50

The entire experience focuses on its prepositional aspects—between, from, o'er, thro'—and on the betweennesses generated by them as one moves from the hidden to the revealed: "Gradual to view, the whole." "Each step," "each short point" marks a different bend in the path (as each clause or line or paragraph tends to mark a different narrative bend); the journey is to end in a bursting-into-view of some sort—of the house, usually, or a prospect, or whatever constitutes "the view entire." The "end" of the approach is, first, to present the house as a perceptual surprise to the viewer, and second, *to never end*. That is, even though the "surprise" of the appearance of the house around the last bend of the approach can only be, strictly speaking, a surprise on one's first visit, yet "How long *soe'er* the wanderer roves, each step / Shall wake fresh beauties; each short point present / A different picture, *new, and yet the same*." Each experience has its own fresh change of light, color, season, temperature, companion, emotional interior. (These differences would of course obtain for the circuit walk and the avenue as well; it seems to be a matter of degree that the theorists preferred to consider a matter of kind.)

Repton's first formally published words on the subject of the approach appear in his 1795 *Sketches and Hints on Landscape Gardening*, in response to Knight's *The Landscape* (addressed to Price). Repton explains in "CHAP. VII CONCERNING APPROACHES; WITH SOME REMARKS ON THE AFFINITY BETWIXT PAINTING AND GARDENING":

> It was not my original intention to have treated of *Approaches* in this volume, as it is a subject that requires to be elucidated by many plates; but the publication of a didactic poem, where much is said on that subject, under the sanction and authority of two gentlemen of acknowledged taste, obliges me to defend not only my own principles, and the reputation of my late predecessor, Mr. Brown, but also the *art* itself, from attacks. (90)

Knight's poem mocks the "grand approach" he says Repton advocated to "announce the owner's state; / His vast possessions, and his wide domains" and concludes by asking, instead of hauling the visitor over "lawn that never ends" (bk. I, ll. 159–73), why not simply hang up a map of the estate at the porter's lodge? But I am less interested in the finer points of the aesthetic quarrels between Repton, Knight, and Price, and more in the ways that each of them was analyzing the concept of approach as a particular visual and psychological experience of connection and combination—of paying attention to what lies *between* the center and the boundary, the entrance and the terminus.

Repton fully joined the criticism of the exaggerated *neo*-Brownian approach:

> There is no part of the Art of Landscape Gardening in which so much absurdity has been displayed by the followers of Brown, as in the line or road, which should lead to the house: and because before his time every road was straight along an avenue to the front, and in the shortest line from the high road, it has been supposed that an approach is now perfect, in proportion to its curvature, and to its length: but good taste, which is only plain common sense, aided by

> observation, directs us to make the road as easy as possible, consistently with the shape of the grounds; and if one line shews more beauty and interest than another, to prefer it; and if it is not actually the nearest possible, to make it more natural and easy.[51]

In fact, OBJECTION No. 3 in his *Observations*, one of the ten explicit dicta on which he wishes his "Fame to be established," states point-blank: "An approach which does not evidently lead to the house, or which does not take the shortest course, cannot be right" (preface 13). The line of approach is not serpentine for serpentine's sake; it is not the anti-avenue; it is a road defined by ease and beauty and that marks the shape of the grounds rather than entirely redefining them. While not direct, like the avenue, it is not wilfully indirect either: as with any good costume or cosmetic, it accentuates the positive, eliminates (or at least mitigates) the negative. The approach to Wingerworth, in Derbyshire, for example, is designed to "shew the most interesting scenery" and to "ascend the hill more gradually" (Repton, *Fragments* 62). The approach from Chesterfield, he decided, was both too steep and too uninteresting; he made it "more easy by a little more curvature to ascend the hill," so it then would "direct the eye to some grass-land beyond the road, which will appear a continuation of the Park" (63).

Repton declares simply: "The road by which a stranger is supposed to pass through the park or lawn to the house, is called an approach; and there seems the same relation betwixt the approach and the house externally, that there is internally betwixt the hall or entrance, and the several apartments to which it leads" (*Sketches* 90). He rebuts Knight by quoting himself in his Red Book for Cobham Hall, where he explicitly condemns the artificial twisting of the approach as absurd as cutting through a hill to make a straight avenue. "Thus do improvers seem to have mistaken the most obvious meaning of an *approach*, which is simply this—A ROAD TO THE HOUSE. If that road be greatly circuitous, no one will use it when a much nearer is discovered: but if there be two roads of nearly the same length, and one be more beautiful than the other, the man of taste will certainly prefer it" (91).[52] The connection between point A and point B has to make sense, and the experience must have continuity: "As soon as the house is visible from the approach, there should be no temptation to quit it; which will ever be the case, if the road be at all circuitous; unless sufficient obstacles, such as water, or inaccessible ground, appear to justify its course" (92). As Repton knows, Knight argues in his poem pretty much the same thing: "The best approach to ev'ry beauteous scene" is one that doesn't bring the landscape "piecemeal to the eyes," because although "beauteous objects, *unconnected* seen" and surrounded by "wide blank spaces" might dazzle the "rude unskilful eye". The mark of true taste "is aptly to conceal; / To lead, with secret guile, the prying sight / To where component parts may best unite, / And form one beauteous, nicely blended whole, / To charm the eye and captivate the soul" (bk. I, ll. 177, 180, 185 [my emphasis], 186, 188, 192–96). The beauty of the estate is a phenomenological whole, created by the connections *between* its objects.

Repton's Red Books, in which he presented his projected improvements to his prospective clients, were exquisitely crafted collections of watercolors, ground plans, and copperplate-hand descriptions bound in red morocco. In each Red Book, Repton aimed to collate the different and sometimes conflicting perspectives of "the painter, the kitchen gardener, the engineer, the land agent, and the architect" by making "a complete digest of each subject proposed to [his] consideration." It is a gestalt approach. Each aspect of every page was meant to capture the experience of motion, surprise, and delight in the approach.

Each Red Book begins with a plan of the grounds. That for Glemham Hall, for example, situates the house at the bottom center, at the upside-down apex of the two approaches, from London and from Yarmouth (plate II): the ground plan itself suggests motion and narrative: at the bottom left, the road "from London" has burst through the double-rule border on its way to the lodge (the little box in the crook where the approaches separate). The two-dimensional is torn.

Repton also "invented [a] peculiar kind of slides to [his] sketches" (*Sketches* 32). The "slides" were flaps of paper bound in over the watercolor, so that the first image is of the property as it is now—a "before" image (plate III). Lift the slide, and *voilà*, Repton's improvements (plate IV). These slides demonstrate the approach to Glemham Hall, first nondescriptly wandering into some trees, and then firmly announced by a park gate lodge (the subject of chapter 2). But slides and plans weren't the end of the matter:

> To make my designs intelligible, I found that a mere *map* was insufficient; as being no more capable of conveying an idea of the *landscape*, than the *ground-plan* of a house does of its *elevation*. To remedy this deficiency, I delivered my opinions in writing, that they might not be misconceived or misrepresented. (Repton, *Sketches* 32)

The narrative is always a kind of grammatical tour, as in the Red Book description of the approach to Tewin Water, "*in Hertfordshire, a Seat of Henry Cowper Esq*" (1799–1800). Here Repton advocates for two different approaches to the seat, from Welwyn and from Hertford, because "approaching the house in two ways each road has its separate advantages and its separate beauties." He easily waves away the current difficulties, offering a visual and aural glimpse of its possibilities:

> The approach from Welwin should enter the meadow to the west, which tho' neglected and overgrown with weeds may easily be drained, and made sound; while the masses of brushwood and trees scattered here and there, sometimes fringing the water which silently glides along in its deep worn channel, and sometimes overhanging and partially concealing it, as it rattles along its pebbled bed, will give this part of the ground the interesting character of natural forest scenery.
>
> The temporary bridge was necessary for the conveyance of materials while the house was building, but may be removed to the place where the road will cross the water when the reason for its remaining ceases; after passing the bridge, the road instead of running parallel to the fence of the kitchen garden in the line of the foot path, should skirt along the outside of a plantation to conceal the pale, leaving a sufficient depth between the plantation and the pale for back road to the offices, while the approach-road sweeps round the skreen with views into a delightful valley beyond the pale, which by a sunk fence might seem to be actually a part of the park, and after passing a corner of the open grove which consists of several rows of large trees, it bursts upon the house, the water, and the opposite bank in an interesting point of view.[53]

Besides the sonic motion of the water, Repton gives us a narrative of motion as well: clause multiplies clause as perspective multiplies perspective, the road passing the bridge, skirting outside the plantation, while the approach sweeps and passes and finally bursts upon the house with the reward of a view.

Thomas Whately (1726–72), English MP and landscape theorist, shared Repton's views on the approach. He wrote his influential *Observations on Modern Gardening* (1770) while living in the Mansion House in Nonsuch Park.[54] Chapter XLV, titled "Of the approach,"[55] defines it in contrast to the avenue, or rather, as something that can now be conceived *beyond* the avenue.[56] He notes that "regularity" has historically been required in the approach because "the idea of a seat is thereby extended to a distance; but that may be done by other means than by an avenue." The problem with the avenue is that it is "confined to one termination" and "exclud[es] every view on the sides"; it therefore "has a tedious sameness throughout; to be great, it must be dull; and the object to which it is appropriated, is after all seldom shewn to advantage" (138–39).

Thomas Jefferson carried Whately's 1770 *Observations* with him on his visits to English gardens because, he wrote, "While his descriptions in point of style are models of perfect elegance and classical correctness, they are as remarkeable for their exactness. I always walked over the gardens with his book in my hand, examined with attention the particular spots he described, found them so justly characterised by him as to be easily recognised, and saw with wonder, that his fine imagination had never been able to seduce him from the truth."[57]

Walking over the gardens with Whately's book in his hand, Jefferson in some real way experienced its "exactness" textually. Repton's verbal as well as architectural patterns of entering, passing, winding, and bursting followed a kind of template for landscape theorists and designers (as well as for travel writers and novelists, as we will see). The major descriptions of approaches are exercises in textual travel, in verbal representation that syntactically, typographically, and grammatically attempts to recreate the visual, physical experience of new combinations on every movement. Syntactically, the descriptions are constructed with clauses clinging to their objects in a series that follows the topography of the landscape; typographically, the clauses are joined (or separated) by a variety of punctuational interventions; and grammatically, the description and the experience (both physical and readerly) are prepositional. They achieve a kind of linguistic version of Peter Collins's sense of eighteenth-century parallax ("the apparent displacement of objects caused by an actual change in the point of observation" [27]).

Whately's description of the approach to Caversham in Oxfordshire, for example, is rhetorically extraordinary. It occupies one paragraph of nine sentences. I have created a quasi-facsimile of the text with the different sentences highlighted to try to capture the sense of its topography (plate V). Each of the internal seven descriptive sentences has an average of six clauses, marked by semicolons or colons—double that if you count the nonlist commas—and together supply a kind of paratactic accumulation. Each long sentence presents a different thematic experience. The first marks the approach from the "elegant lodge" at the entrance as it gently winds through a valley to the mansion, "where the eminence, which seemed inconsiderable, is found to be a very elevated situation, to which the approach, without once qui[t]ting the valley, had been insensibly ascending all the way" (Whately, *Observations* 140). The sentence itself never once quits its line, and the sentences that follow present "some new scene to the view." The next sentence comments generally on the ways the scenes appear to the spectator: unbroken, uninterrupted, "connected" and belonging "purely" to the park (141). The clauses of the third sentence clump the clumps (the "clump" of trees or shrubs being a favorite Brownian introduction to the landscape): the hawthorns, beeches, and oaks at the entrance, "thickened by the perspective as the valley winds"; a clump, a "groupe," a grove, more groupes, a glade, a single tree, some beeches, some clusters, and "openings for the gleams of light to pour in between them" (141). The next sentence tracks the approach to the edge of the estate and rolls with the topography, where "the falls of the ground are more tamed," the bottom is flattened, the banks are gentled, and there's a "knole." The fifth sentence has only two main clauses, but it's the centerpiece of the paragraph: there's an open space, and then the road goes through "a narrow darksome passage" and then "suddenly bursts out upon a rich and extensive prospect" as it reaches the house. The next sentence has the most clauses (twelve), for the best reasons: "Such a view at the end of a long avenue, would have been, at the best, but a compensation for the tediousness of the way; but here the approach is as delightful as the termination" (142). There is "every variety of open plantation," not "confusedly thrown together" but comprising composition: sometimes they do this, sometimes they do that; in one place they do one thing, in another they do another. What the seventh descriptive sentence says about the landscape also describes its syntactical self: "The ground, without being broken into diminutive parts, is cast into an infinite number of elegant shapes" (143). Although the full paragraph is itself rather broken into diminutive parts, especially considering the commas, it does present a great number of elegant bits, and it does create an impressive view at the end of its long avenue.

Uvedale Price offers two descriptions of two different roads: the "winding" and the "dressed." Here, too, the syntax maps onto the topography. In a dressed lane, for example,

> every effort of art seems directed against that disposition of the ground: the sides are so regularly sloped, so regularly planted, and the space, when there is any, between them and the road, so uniformly levelled; the sweeps of the road so plainly artificial, the verges of grass that bound it so nicely edged; the whole, in short, has such an appearance of having been made by a receipt, that curiosity, that most active principle of pleasure, is almost extinguished. (*Essays* 1:24)

The repetition of "regularly" cements regularity; the repetition of "so" is a sibilant series of sighs; the repetition of short, uniform clauses measures the syntactical tread and performs the "receipt" it describes.

But things are different in "hollow lanes and bye roads," untended, left to themselves and therefore to "the natural intricacy of the ground":

> [T]he turns are sudden and unprepared; the banks sometimes broken and abrupt; sometimes smooth, and gently, but not uniformly sloping; now wildly

> over-hung with thickets of trees and bushes; now loosely skirted with wood: no regular verge of grass, no cut edges, no distinct lines of separation; all is mixed and blended together, and the border of the road itself, shaped by the mere tread of passengers and animals, is as unconstrained as the footsteps that formed it. Even the tracks of wheels (for no circumstance is indifferent) contribute to the picturesque effect of the whole: the varied lines they describe just mark the way among trees and bushes; often some obstacle, a cluster of low thorns, a furze-bush, a tussuck, a large stone, forces the wheels into sudden and intricate turns[.] (1:24–25)

Repetition occurs in this passage as well, but there may be more than one furze-bush in the lane, after all. The clauses vary in length and emphasis (sometimes abrupt, sometimes smooth); the punctuation is livelier, mixing and blending in one sentence clauses of varying things that exist with things notably not present; in the center of the passage cluster the agents of this shaping: the passengers, animals, their footsteps, and then the tracks of wheels with their surprise design.

John Claudius Loudon defined the approach (under "*OF THE CONVENIENCES PECULIAR TO A COUNTRY RESIDENCE*" in his 1806 *A Treatise on Forming, Improving, and Managing Country Residences*) as "a variety of ROAD peculiar to a house in the country" (2:590). In its character it should "neither be affectedly graceful or waving" nor "vulgarly rectilineal, direct, or abrupt," and it should "form new combinations on every movement of the spectator." The only thing that will give a proper idea of the effect of the approach is a "model of the *whole* residence" (2:590–91). His approach for North Berwick follows the syntactical patterns of Repton, Whately, and Price in its numerous paratactic clauses defining and describing the windings of the road, emphasizing its fundamentally prepositional experience, and in the end bursting out upon its final destination point:

> The new approach which I designed for North Berwick will pass through a straight level avenue one mile in length, already formed, and containing as its termination North Berwick Law [a hill]. At the end of this avenue the road enters a winding valley, with the lawn or mountain close on the right, shewing a towering cone of wood, rock, and pasture; and on the left the irregular boundary of a plantation in the forest style. It winds in this valley sometimes under perpendicular rocks at the base of the law; at other times through a smooth surface of verdure; sometimes the wood descends to the road, and appears to stretch across the valley; and at other times it retires into dark recesses: every where it is broken by thickets of thorns and hollies, mingled with forest trees;

> which, with the rocks and cattle, form new combinations on every movement of the spectator. This style will continue another mile, until, entering a thick wood, and crossing a brook, it will ascend to the intended mansion. The west and north approaches are shortly and widely different, but equally interesting. One of these passes along high grounds, and exhibits prospects of the sea, Edinburgh, the noble view of Dirleton Castle, and the opposite coast of the Forth: another passes through the marine village of North Berwick, and ascends into the park near the ruins of a fine old abbey. And the last proceeds from the shore, through a hollow wooded dell, which bursts into a level valley at the rocky base of the steepest side of the mountain. Nothing can convey an adequate idea of these approaches but a model of the whole residence. (2:591–92)

The long, single-paragraph approach to describing the elaborate approach is textually mimetic; the reading experience excites the physical, phenomenological one. The old avenue is dissected by the modern approaches, which pass through, wind under, descend and ascend to, stretch across, retire into, pass along, and at last end in exhibiting prospects, ascending to ruins, or bursting into a valley. The grammatical descriptions of the approach *become* a "model of the whole residence."

The traveler's approach

Although "approach" in the architects' sense is oddly missing from the dictionaries, the landscape theorists' term migrated easily into popular discourse. The *sense* of approaching an estate was an early part of the travel writer's self-imposed obligation to supply in the narrative. Here again the language of the accounts reflects the etymology of use—of the landscape theorists' use if not the dictionaries'. In his 1722 *A Journey through England*, for example, John Macky describes the rectilinear avenue at Cannons, seat of the Duke of Chandos:

> You ascend the great Avenue to *Cannons* from the Town of *Edgar*, by a fine Iron Gate, with the Dukes Arms and Supporters on the stone Pillars of the Gate, with Balustrades of Iron on each Side, and two neat Lodges in the Inside; this Avenue is near a Mile long, and Three Coaches may go a-breast; in the middle or half Way of this Avenue, is a large round Bason of Water, not unlike that on the great Road through *Busby-Park* to *Hampton Court*. This Avenue fronts an Angle of the House, and thereby shewing you two Fronts at once, makes the House seem at a Distance the larger.[58]

This avenue does its appointed duty of making the house seem larger; although the narrative focuses on "you," the point is that "you" ascend the great avenue, noticing the arms, the pillars, the gate, the balustrades, the bason, in this mile-long stretch, and it is "you" for whom this temporal and spatial length, this elongated experience, this Palladian symmetry, this approach from an angle, makes "the House seem at a Distance the larger." This description intriguingly notes that the avenue is designed to show "two Fronts at once"—a tactic that Mark Girouard argues does not emerge in visual representations until later in the eighteenth century: "Up to the early eighteenth century the conventional—and for architects almost the invariable—way to show a house was full-frontal, from a central axis. During the eighteenth century it became increasingly common to draw them from an angle" (212). The architectural experience of *seeing* two fronts at an angle—in a wider "field of vision"—preceded its representation. Daniel Defoe also describes the grand avenue of Cannons and its presentation of two fronts in *A Tour Thro' the Whole Island of Great Britain* (1724): "The Avenue is Spacious and Majestick, and as it gives you the view of two Fronts, join'd as it were in one, the Distance not admitting you to see the Angle, which is in the Centre; so you are agreeably drawn in, to think the Front of the House almost twice as large as it really is."[59]

Defoe also emphasizes the pleasurable surprise that a shift in perspective from a winding passage can provide: "And yet when you come nearer you are again surprized, by seeing the Winding Passage opening as it were a new Front to the Eye, of near 120 Foot wide, which you had not seen before, so that you are lost a while in looking" (2.3:9). Defoe, like his literary contemporary (if not kindred spirit) Pope, discovers an interest in the winding, and the "you" experiencing the winding, bubbling up in practice well before its theoretical expression later in the century. As is their wont, philosophers and theorists often simply articulate and codify what is already culturally familiar.

Defoe regularly notes the effects of the avenue on the perception of the building; Burleigh House, for example, looks "more like a Town than a House, at which Avenue soever you come to it" (2.4:160); Kinross in Scotland does not have "any large Avenue or Prospect from the Entrance, but it is a Prospect in itself" (3.3:136). Consistently with the dictionaries, he uses the term "approach" only in its military sense, as when he describes Portsmouth, which has a "good Counterscarp, and double Mote, with Ravelins in the Ditch, and double Palisadoes, and advanc'd Works to cover the Place from any approach, where it may be practicable" (1.2:74).

The fifth edition of the *Tour* (1753), expanded into a fourth volume and printed by Samuel Richardson, incorporates "approach" in an early version of its nounal architectural sense: the entrance to the house. Horseheath-Hall, seat of Lord Montford, has a noble hall: "The Approach to this Hall is by a noble Flight of Stone Steps" (and the roads "through the Park, are made very good, though it is in a very dirty Country; this has been done at the Expence of the present Lord, who is now beautifying the House and Park").[60] Eastbury, in Dorset, seat of the Right Hon. George Dodington, Esq., is "one of the largest and most stately new Fabrics in the Kingdom," and "[y]ou approach this House through a beautiful little lawn; and, passing through the grand Arcade, on each Side of which the Offices are ranged, you land from a Flight of Steps 11 Feet high, under a noble *Doric* Portico" (1:328). "A stately Bridge, or Rialto rather, now leads along the grand Approach to the present Castle"—the royal palace in Woodstock, near Oxford (2:251); for Chatsworth in Derbyshire (see figure 8, p. 73), "the usual Approach to this noble Fabric [. . .] presents itself thus: First, the River, which, in calm Weather, glides gently by; then a venerable Walk of Trees, where the famous *Hobbes* used often to contemplate; a noble Piece of Iron-work Gates and Baluster, expose the Front of the House and Court, terminated at the Corners next the Road" (3:94). "Surprise" had been a feature of Chatworth's situation since it was first built; in Defoe's edition, he declares that "Nothing can be more surprising of its Kind, than for a Stranger coming from the North" from "a waste and houling Wilderness," to look down "from a frightful height, and a comfortless, barren, and, as he thought, endless Moor, into the most delightful Valley, with the most pleasant Garden, and most beautiful Palace in the World" (3:70–71); as the *Tour*'s new narrator puts it, "The Surprize that is occasioned in a Traveller, descending from such a rocky and barren Mountain, and from such a dreary Wilderness, at once upon so glorious a Palace," gave rise to Latin lines (by Hobbes) translated by Colley Cibber as "*from the Mountains, Strangers with Delight / See unexpected* Chatsworth *charm the Sight*" (3:93). (See figure 8.)

Midcentury, in George Bickham's *The Beauties of Stow* (1750), the "ancient" linear perspective still predominates: "From *Buckingham* Town you pass through a little Village called *Chatmore*, and from thence to the *New-Inn* at the South Entrance of the Garden called *Stow*. This is a Prospect, that agreeably surprises you; for, upon quitting an unpleasant Road, you perceive all at once a long Avenue; at the End of which rises a fine View of my Lord's House, though a little confin'd by the inward Row of Arbail-Trees."[61] The indefatigable traveler Richard Pococke, bishop of Meath (1704–65), would note "an avenue to the house" of Mr. Fox in Bramham (4 August 1750), or "a long avenue to the house" of the Earl of Portland (28–29 April 1757).[62] "Approach" was used fairly regularly in travel narratives in relation to cities by the mid-eighteenth century; Gilpin in 1770 pronounces that "the approach to Bristol is grand" (*Observations* 91). Caroline Girle (later known as the travel diarist Caroline Lybbe Powys) exactly reproduces the lexical transition in her diary. She comments in 1756 on the long straight avenue of Holkham Hall in Norfolk (designed by William Kent), and the following year describes "the approach to [Barleborough Hall]" as "fine an avenue of ancient elms as I ever saw."[63] By 1778 she more systematically uses "approach" in its technical sense: she describes the "present approach" to Bletchingdon House, Oxon., as "thro' a fine stone gateway with iron rails" (195). In 1784 she notes: "The approach to Fawley Rectory from the Marlow high-road is a gradual ascent of about two miles, through the typical beech-woods so familiar to all dwellers near the Chilterns" (215). Harleyford, the "elegant brick house" of Mr. Clayton, in Buckinghamshire, has an "approach to the house uncommonly pleasing" ("*July* 28*th*, 1767"; 119). "Avenue" doesn't disappear—a coach-and-six drives up the "avenue" of Fawley Court, one of the family homes, in 1785 (219)—but in her diary she records "Alterations made at Hardwick [House, not Hall] from 1765," and that includes: "1774. — [. . .] Forty-six walnut trees were cut down that year in the approach to the house, and by grubbing up a hedge on the other side laid the two fields together, the road only between them. New fancy gates at each end, a clump planted at the farther one, and a grass walk made round Culmar Field" (385). Nine years later:

> 1783. — Pulled down that part of the pleasure garden wall before mentioned, opposite my dressing-room window, from the bottom of the gravel walk to the canal, continued on the Ha-ha to the clump at bottom, and put up the white pillar which was one of those at the old Ha-ha, formerly belonged to iron gates there, as I've heard my father Powys say, though never was the approach to the house. Could it be made so, and the stucco parlour as the hall, 'twould be much more eligible than at present, as the entrance is the worst part of the house. (386)

In 1792, the picturesque advocate Powys properly despises a straight, pre-Brownian road:

> Soon after you are through the village [of Redbridge] and that of Totton you reach the New Forest, and see your straight road for many miles, which to me is ever a disagreeable view; but the beauty of that forest in some measure makes amends, as the trees are so noble, and many grand clumps, through which, in the most picturesque manner, one sees other woody lanes, uncommon, and therefore very striking to the eye. (271)

By the 1790s it has clearly become disagreeable for the well-read eye to confront a straight line, or rather, to be unconfronted with things in between. Powys records the recoil against the inflexible presentation of the end; here, at least, when she gets to the end, the New Forest allows her views *through* clumps; the swing of the field of vision from side to side is rewarded with *other* woody lanes going elsewhere.

The novelist's approach

The travel writer's discourse incorporating and appreciating different senses of "approach" and "avenue" is employed by the novelistic traveler as well. In Charlotte Smith's *The Old Manor House* (1793), the Old Manor House itself—Rayland Hall—is an "ancient and splendid seat," and so it is not surprising that there is no Reptonian approach; rather, the virtually imprisoned heroine Monimia for "many many hours [. . .] vainly prayed for the sight of a coach or chaise at the end of the long avenue, which was to her the blessed signal of transient liberty."[64] For her, the very length of the avenue is the emblem of captivity, the long line anchoring the seat to the past. In Ann Radcliffe's *The Italian* (1797), "the extensive remains of what seemed to have been a villa" is discovered by the heroine Ellena and her presumed father, the monk Schedoni, on their way back to Naples from her recent imprisonment; the travelers discover an approach that is both old avenue and new picturesque:

> [T]he party alighted before the portal of a deep and broad avenue of arched stone, which seemed to have been the grand approach to the villa. The entrance was obstructed by the fallen fragments of columns, and by the underwood that had taken root amongst them. [. . .] [T]he avenue was of considerable extent, and as its only light proceeded from the portal, except what a few narrow loops in the walls admitted, they often found themselves involved in an obscurity that rendered the way difficult.[65]

Uvedale Price's "light and shade" and "fantastic roots of trees" make this scene a small emblem of the eighteenth-century transition of the approach: the old avenue is literally as well as historically overgrown and overtaken by the picturesque.

Samuel Richardson's midcentury novels enact the changing architectural perspective in different ways. Appropriately, there is no "approach" to Grandison Hall in *Sir Charles Grandison* (1751–53), either in the sense of that peculiar road or in the sense of drawing nigh; Harriet, the new Lady Grandison, and her best-of-men husband simply arrive. We know that Grandison Hall has avenues rather than approaches because the obliging Miss Lucy Selby gives us a textual tour of the grounds, to match Harriet's guide to the house: "This large and convenient house is situated in a spacious park; which has several fine avenues leading to it."[66] But we do not see the avenue in the text until Lucy points it out; we do not see the house from its road; Harriet simply writes to her grandmother: "But by eleven this morning we arrived here. / At our alighting, Sir Charles clasping me in his arms, I congratulate you, my dearest life, said he, on your entrance into *your own* house" (6:19).[67] As I will show in more detail in chapter 5, characters in eighteenth-century novels enter spaces differently across time. Harriet is arrived; she has an entrance (noun) rather than enters (verb). The moment is decisive, possibly inevitable in a long novel that has a Dramatis Personae featuring "Men," "Women," and "Italians." (Harriet's longtime rival was an Italian noblewoman who eventually went insane.)

Perhaps the most striking encapsulation of the architectural change rendered as literary change is Anna Lætitia Barbauld's description of Samuel Richardson's midcentury novel *Clarissa* (1747–48):

> With Clarissa it begins,—with Clarissa it ends. We do not come upon unexpected adventures and wonderful recognition, by quick turns and surprises: we see her fate from afar, as it were through a long avenue, the gradual approach to which, without ever losing sight of the object, has more of simplicity and grandeur than the most cunning labyrinth that can be contrived by art. In the approach to the modern country seat, we are made to catch transiently a side-view of it through an opening of the trees, or to burst upon it from a sudden turning in the road; but the old mansion stood full in the eye of the traveller, as he drew near it, contemplating its turret, which grew larger and more distinct every step that he advanced; and leisurely filling his eye and his imagination with still increasing ideas of its magnificence.[68]

This is the emblematic opposite of the Radcliffe scene above; there, the grand approach is overgrown by the fantastic roots of the picturesque; here, the avenue cuts through the modern underbrush. Richardson's novels are firmly midcentury, and Richardson himself was both innovator and marker of change. It is no coincidence that Barbauld, early nineteenth-century editor, poet, and essaysist, would place *Clarissa* at the end of an avenue. This is the borderline, with the early nineteenth century looking through its own landscaped lenses at the mid-eighteenth, through its own metaphors.

By the time Barbauld was editing Richardson, an anti-picturesque movement was emerging.[69] James Elmes, in his *Dictionary of the Fine Arts* (1826), cites the author of "Walks round London" (which appeared in the *Literary Pocket Book* for 1822), who defended "the stateliness of the old English method, which is an imitation of the Dutch without its clipped conceits." After various aesthetic investigations of the modern with the past style, the author concludes:

> The old gardeners were, therefore, right in selecting flat spots in which to lay out their plantations, and where their avenues might stretch away uninterruptedly; for there are few objects in Nature finer than those old-fashioned long perspectives, and few accidental effects more grateful to the eye than remote figures in them, coming, as they must, so palpably in the line of vision, and yet looking so fairy-like in their size and noiseless footfalls. These are vistas, if we may speak profanely, finer than Nature ever made. (Elmes, EE2)

Even Price and Repton acknowledged the occasional beauty of an avenue.[70] Barbauld is arguing for the fine "old-fashioned long perspectives," the "remote figures" *approaching us* in our line of vision; in the avenue, it appears that the house approaches us; it is the house that gets larger, that increasingly fills the frame of vision, that "commands" the view. (As we will see in the next chapter, the eighteenth-century country house sometimes "afforded" but usually "commanded" prospects and views from its windows, its "scituation." The language of visual dominance shifts; Repton's sense of "appropriation" swings to the viewer and visitor from the house and owner.)

But just as Elmes himself diplomatically concludes that "both manners have their peculiar charms, nor should an attachment to the one necessarily exclude admiration of the other" (EE2v), so *Clarissa* is both/and, poised transitionally both *in* the mid-eighteenth century and *for* the early nineteenth. On the one hand, the "plot" of *Clarissa*—strikingly nonlinear in one sense (Samuel Johnson famously said, "Why, Sir, if you were to read Richardson for the story, your impatience would be so much fretted that you would hang yourself"[71])—is as Barbauld says always in full sight of the traveler, the reader; there is almost no such thing as a "first time" reading of the novel, whether because the contemporary readers were agonizing about its "end" (the rape and death) or because the Penguin paperback spills the beans on its back cover or because that is simply what *Clarissa* is. Tragedy is predetermined. And as an epistolary novel, *Clarissa* is an example of completely direct discourse in the literary technical sense. But on the other hand, both plot and discourse also pivot on the emerging "modern" approach. Each letter reveals some small new thing, a twist in the narrative, a sense of something lurking along the side of the avenue, gliding in the shadows; and of course, textually speaking, the Main Event *does* burst upon us from a sudden turning in the road (figure 2):

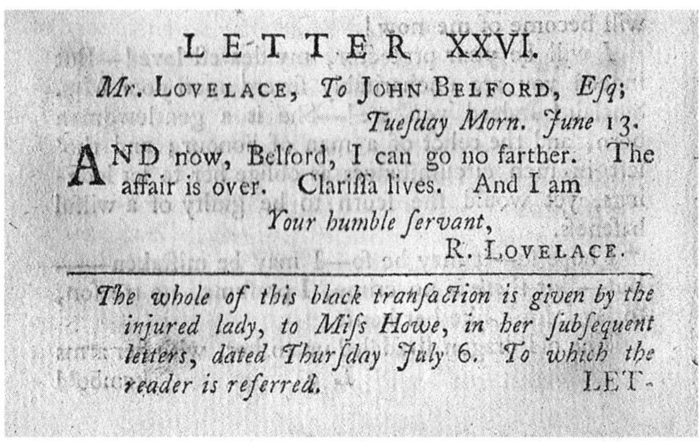
LETTER XXVI.

Mr. LOVELACE, *To* JOHN BELFORD, *Efq;*

Tuefday Morn. June 13.

AND now, Belford, I can go no farther. The affair is over. Clariffa lives. And I am

Your humble fervant,

R. LOVELACE.

The whole of this black tranfaction is given by the injured lady, to Mifs Howe, in her fubfequent letters, dated Thurfday July 6. *To which the reader is referred.*

LET-

2. Samuel Richardson, *Clarissa* (1748), 5:222. ". . . I can go no farther."

Henry Fielding wrote to Richardson about the narrative effects this letter had on him:

> When Clarissa returns to her Lodgings at St. Clairs the Alarm begins, and here my Heart begins its Narrative. I am Shocked; my Terrors are raised, and I have the utmost Apprehensions for the poor betrayed Creature.––But when I see her enter with the Letter in her Hand, and after some natural effects of Despair, clasping her Arms about the Knees of the Villain, call him her Dear Lovelace, desirous and yet unable to implore his Protection or rather his mercy; I then melt into Compassion, and find what is called an Effeminate Relief for my Terror, to continue to the End of the Scene. When I read the next Letter I am Thunderstruck; nor can many Lines explain what I feel from Two.[72]

This is the gothic version of the approach, the bursting upon from the sudden turning in the road. As on the approach we of course know we're headed to the House, no matter how much it winds, so we know, nightmarishly, what we are advancing toward in the novel. It is both avenue and approach, inescapable and recombinant, direct and deviating.

Psychologically, the novel is winding as well: Johnson also said that Richardson's heroines all had "a kind of obliquity in their moral vision"; of Clarissa in particular he noted: "You may observe there is always something which she prefers to truth."[73] The characters close-read each other; they read *between* the lines and listen *beyond* the immediate. Anna Howe rereads Clarissa's words about Lovelace back to her:

> You are pleased to say, and *upon your word too!*—That your *regards* (a mighty quaint word for *affections*) *are not so much engag'd, as some of your friends suppose, to another person*. What need you give one to imagine, my dear, that the last month or two has been a period extremely favourable to that *other* person!— [. . .]
>
> But, to pass that by—*So much* engaged!—*How much*, my dear?—Shall I infer? *Some of your friends* suppose *a great deal*. — You seem to own *a little*.[74]

Clarissa herself senses something *behind* Lovelace's manner: "In short, his very Politeness, notwithstanding the advantages he must have had from his birth and education, appears to me to be constrained; and, with the most remarkably easy and genteel person, something, at times, seems to be behind in his *manner* that is too studiously kept in" (*Clarissa* 1:64; letter XI). The characters frequently extrapolate events *beyond* their immediate visual field, as when Lovelace arrives at the back gate of Harlowe Place to frighten Clarissa off with him: "The moment I heard the door unbolt, I was sure of her" (3:52; letter VI). And, of course, Clarissa herself has been interpreted in multiple and directly contradictory ways *within* and *without* the novel. Lovelace to Belford: "But seest thou not now (as I think I do) the wind-outstripping Fair-one flying *from* her Love *to* her Love?—Is there not such a game?—Nay, flying from friends she was resolved not to abandon, to the man she was determined not to go off with?— [. . .] —Charming contradiction!—Hah, hah, hah, hah!—" (3:55; letter VI). Clarissa's flights are the obverse of the coming approach—a sort of desperate *de*-proach (from the always *en*croaching Lovelace)—her steps, her letters, winding their way through the countryside, through London streets, through inns and aliases, trying to escape the avenue of inevitability, flying from but inexorably heading toward, until she stops—and walks straight up to her Father's House.

One of the most famous novelistic approaches occurs over several duodecimo pages of Ann Radcliffe's *The Mysteries of Udolpho* (1794). Many contemporary reviewers would quote the description in full.[75] It begins:

> At length, the travellers began to ascend among the Apennines. The immense pine-forests, which, at that period, overhung these mountains, and between which the road wound, excluded all view but of the cliffs aspiring above, except, that, now and then, an opening through the dark woods allowed the eye a momentary glimpse of the country below.[76]

And it ends: "At length, the carriages emerged upon a heathy rock, and, soon after, reached the castle gates." In between is the winding road, with "momentary glimpses" through "openings" in the woods, "steep over steep" and "mountains seem[ing] to multiply," mountains "stretched in long perspectives," and a scene that "seemed perpetually changing, and its features to assume new forms, as the winding road brought them to the eye in different attitudes" (2:167–68)—in short, a Central Casting appearance of an Approach. I will treat this passage in detail in chapter 5; here, I want to note that where Loudon had argued that the object of the modern style is "to show two fronts at once, or what is called by Architects an angular view" (*Encyclopædia* 769), the Radcliffean approach is not just the modern "two fronts at once" but a typically gothic extravaganza of them. As Sir Walter Scott put it, "The beautiful description of the Castle of Udolpho, upon Emily's first approach to it, [. . .] affords a noble subject for the pencil; but were six artists to attempt to embody it, upon canvas, they would probably produce six drawings entirely dissimilar to each other, all of them equally authorized by the printed description."[77] Even envisioned as a painting, its turns elude repetition.

Radcliffe also excels at the concept of the "deproach," as we might call the crafted act of moving *away* from the center in winding stages. In *The Italian* (1797), when the hero Vivaldi reluctantly leaves the heroine Ellena, who has been abducted and imprisoned in a distant convent by the henchmen of Vivaldi's scheming mother, the Marchesa, he retreats the way he came, ledge by ledge, cliff by cliff, through the winding thickets, and back into invisibility:

> He lingered on the rock till the last moments of departing light, and then, with a heart fluttering with hopes and fears, bade Ellena farewel, and descended; while she watched his progress through the silent gloom, faintly distinguishing him gliding along ledges of the precipice, and making his adventurous way from cliff to cliff, till the winding thickets concealed him from her. Still anxious, she remained at the lattice, but he appeared no more; no voice announced disaster; and, at length, she returned to her cell, to deliberate on the subject of her departure. (1:328)

Their eventual escape from the convent is an extended deproach, narratively and choreographically, as they wend their breathless way through a series of gates, circuitous routes, long perspectives, remote windings, very short paragraphs (see chapter 5), and very agitated punctuation (see chapter 3), until they are "Released, at length, from immediate apprehension" (2:14–44).

Radcliffe is very much aware of the architectural concept (and term) of approach. At one point the monk Schedoni, "wearied and exhausted" from his cross-country travels, comes across what appears to be a deserted villa, although he had seen someone flitting among its ruins:

> [H]e determined to ascertain whether any refreshment could be procured from the inhabitants within, and the party alighted before the portal of a deep and broad avenue of arched stone, which seemed to have been the grand approach to the villa. The entrance was obstructed by the fallen fragments of columns, and by the underwood that had taken root amongst them. The travellers, however, easily overcame these interruptions: but as the avenue was of considerable extent, and as its only light proceeded from the portal, except what a few narrow loops in the walls admitted, they often found themselves involved in an obscurity that rendered the way difficult. (3:5)

This "grand approach" is in the old, Continental style of a long avenue, modernized by its ruins, its obstructions and obscurities.

The architectural approaches are the overground sign of the psychological approaches. "Approach" as a verb is actively employed throughout the novel, and typically in relation to an architectural feature, a pattern of motion and light, and a psychological implication. In the very first prefatory scene, the "modern style" of a "winding line," in Loudon's terms, sets the spatial and kinetic patterns for the whole. A group of English travelers enters the church of Santa Maria del Pianto in Naples in 1764 (the year of Radcliffe's birth, as it happens), and witnesses the first of many disappearing tricks:

> Within the shade of the portico, a person with folded arms, and eyes directed towards the ground, was pacing behind the pillars the whole extent of the pavement, and was apparently so engaged by his own thoughts, as not to observe that strangers were approaching. He turned, however, suddenly, as if startled by the sound of steps, and then, without further pausing, glided to a door that opened into the church, and disappeared. [. . .]
>
> The travellers, on entering the church, looked round for the stranger, who had passed thither before them, but he was no where to be seen, and, through all the shade of the long aisles, only one other person appeared. (1:iv)

The center of the scene, that-which-is-approached, disappears into its own setting of pillars and pavements and long shady aisles. Upon entering, things change. Approach precipitates a reorganization of the visible, of the perceptual. Later in the first chapter, Bonarmo, Vivaldi's manservant, articulates their physical approach as they hunt for the figure who had mysteriously warned them away from Ellena's villa the night before:

> "Hush!" said Bonarmo, as they turned the foot of a rock that overhung the road, "we are approaching the spot; yonder is the arch!" It appeared duskily in the perspective, suspended between two cliffs, where the road wound from sight, on one of which were the ruins of the Roman fort it belonged to, and on the other, shadowing pines, and thickets of oak that tufted the rock to its base. (1:36)

The narrator takes over the description and extends the verbal approach into the nounal: the arch (the gate) marks where the road winds away; it is a function of perspective, and its combinations include both the buildings and the vegetation of the well-designed approach. The scene continues with the last prescription of the approach: the bursting: "As [Bonarmo] approached the mass of ruins [. . .] a person rushed forth from a doorway of the ruin, carrying a drawn sword. It was Vivaldi himself" (1:45). The whole point of the architectural approach is that its end burst into the visual scene around the last turn; the usefulness of the narrative approach lies in the element of surprise.

As in Real Life, the Approach can in fact be revisited with different perceptions, different experiences. After Schedoni has discovered—in the act of attempted murder—that Ellena is (it seems) his daughter, he retreats in horror from her room. He decides to move her to a safer place, out of reach of the Marchesa's dark designs:

> Having released [the servant] Spalatro from his chamber, and given him directions to procure horses and a guide immediately from the neighbouring hamlet, he repaired to Ellena's room, to prepare her for this hasty removal. On approaching it, a remembrance of the purpose, with which he had last passed through these same passages and stair-case, appealed so powerfully to his feelings, that he was unable to proceed, and he turned back to his own apartment to recover some command over himself. A few moments restored to him his usual address, though not his tranquillity, and he again approached the chamber; it was now, however, by way of the corridor. As he unbarred the door, his hand trembled; but, when he entered the room, his countenance and manner had resumed their usual solemnity, and his voice only would have betrayed, to an attentive observer, the agitation of his mind. (2:327–28)

The attentive observer would also mark that the second approach to her room invests the same passages and staircase with an entirely different phenomenological force; his third approach looks out a different route. As Repton had pointed out, in rebutting Knight, the experience is as much psychological and perceptual as architectural; if the design of the approach centripetally draws us toward the center of the house, "forming new combinations" is the centrifugal consequence of a turn of the head, a different sky, another companion, an altered emotional interior.

One of the most famous novelistic approaches (involving altered emotional interiors) to one of the most famous country houses of all time is the approach of Elizabeth Bennet to Pemberley—often interpreted as being modeled on Chatsworth, described above (and see figure 8, p. 73). This approach opens volume III of Jane Austen's *Pride and Prejudice* (1813) both visually and narratively. A vast deal of attention has been paid to what precisely was going on in Lizzie's head when she acknowledged it "might be something" to be mistress of Pemberley; the extent and detail of the landscape description are often overlooked. Just as in paintings (and, as we will see in chapter 2, topographical views), the central figures of human thought, motive, and action (or the corresponding emblem, such as the House) too often preoccupy critical attention; the peripheral and prepositional, the background and the in-between, much less so. It is worth paying attention to the narrative pace of her party's approach—in a carriage, not on foot, so with images in quicker succession—in the context of designs "to form new combinations on every movement of the spectator" when rereading:

> Elizabeth, as they drove along, watched for the first appearance of Pemberley Woods with some perturbation; and when at length they turned in at the lodge, her spirits were in a high flutter.
>
> The park was very large, and contained great variety of ground. They entered it in one of its lowest points, and drove for some time through a beautiful wood, stretching over a wide extent.
>
> Elizabeth's mind was too full for conversation, but she saw and admired every remarkable spot and point of view. They gradually ascended for half a mile, and then found themselves at the top of a considerable eminence, where the wood ceased, and the eye was instantly caught by Pemberley House, situated on the opposite side of a valley, into which the road with some abruptness wound. It was a large, handsome, stone building, standing well on rising ground, and backed by a ridge of high woody hills;—and in front, a stream of some natural importance was swelled into greater, but without any artificial appearance. Its banks were neither formal, nor falsely adorned. Elizabeth was delighted. She had never seen a place for which nature had done more, or where natural beauty had been so little counteracted by an awkward taste. They were all of them warm in their admiration; and at that moment she felt, that to be mistress of Pemberley might be something!
>
> They descended the hill, crossed the bridge, and drove to the door; and,

> while examining the nearer aspect of the house, all her apprehensions of meeting its owner returned.[78]

The term "approach" does not appear, but the description and narration fit every requirement. They enter at the park gate lodge (see chapter 2); the first sentence is general and takes in the extent and variety of the park landscape; we see simultaneously through Elizabeth's eyes (her "mind was too full for conversation, but she saw and admired" everything), through the third-person collective party of aunt, uncle, niece, and presumably driver; and through "the eye"—the dislocated, generalized spectator. The road ascends to an eminence, and they see the house across the valley and the route of their road (somewhat abrupt) ahead. The grounds of Pemberley are not of the "ancient" geometrical, classical, statuaried style; nor do they seem the rolled, clipped, undulating grounds of Brown; and they certainly are not wildly picturesque. They seem, in fact, to have the easy order and unaffected dignity of a Repton estate. (As we will see in chapter 5, Austen knew the works of Walpole, Whately, Gilpin, Repton, Price, and Knight, she knew the debates over the Brownian emparkments and the picturesque craze, and she relished the absurdities in each.) The critical attention often ends where Elizabeth imagines herself mistress-of-Pemberley-exclamation-point; certainly the beginning of the next paragraph zips them with dispatch across that wide distance, through the valley, and up to the door in three short clauses. But the long preamble to get there is precisely to experience and understand the psychological as well as topographical terrain of approach. After the first meeting with Darcy is past, the Gardiners and Elizabeth tour the grounds in extremely extended detail, first on a "beautiful walk by the side of the water" where every movement of the spectators "was bringing forward a nobler fall or ground, or a finer reach of woods" (and "approach" appears here as experiential verb). Though Elizabeth's mind is fastened only on Darcy's thoughts, she does "at length" return to consciousness of her surroundings and the textual details of woods, river, the openings of the trees, crossing the bridge, longing to explore windings, for quite some narrative time until "they were again surprised [. . .] by the sight of Mr. Darcy approaching them" (*Pride and Prejudice* 253). The description of the approach winds round and bursts upon. Darcy *is* the House, per eighteenth-century architectural theory; Darcy *is* the Noun of the narrative pattern. Elizabeth is the concept of approach.

CHAPTER 2
The Prepositional Building

> A LODGE [*loge,* F.] a Hut or Apartment for a Porter of a Gate, &c.
>
> Nathan Bailey, *An Universal Etymological Dictionary* (1766)

The approach to the estate begins at its gate, and by the second half of the eighteenth century, the "gate" most likely included a lodge, designed as the visual prelude to and architectural complement of the great house (see plate VI). (As we saw in the last chapter, Elizabeth and her aunt and uncle Gardiner "turned in at the lodge" at the beginning of the approach to Pemberley.[1]) Small hunting lodges had existed for centuries, as well as inhabited castle- and city-gates.[2] But the park gate lodge was almost entirely an eighteenth-century phenomenon, very much a part of the *conceptual* approach and in the "modern" style, and well advanced beyond the "Hut or Apartment" as defined by Bailey's *Universal Etymological Dictionary* in 1766. Works such as Johannes Kip and Leonard Knyff's *Britannia Illustrata* (1707) delineate in great detail the great estates with their long formal avenues, sometimes ending in a gate, but rarely in a gate lodge.[3] (See figure 1.)

The park gate lodge became ubiquitously popular among the country house set; Tim Mowl and Brian Earnshaw, foremost historians of the phenomenon, estimate that there are perhaps ten thousand surviving lodges: "small houses, ambitiously designed, often by famous architects, [that] reflect in concentrated form, the changing architecture fashions of the last two hundred and fifty years."[4] And yet, historically, critically, and experientially, the park gate lodge has received little attention. Mowl and Earnshaw speculate that, as most visitors who "pass through park gates do so in a spirit of near reverential preparation for the unashamedly upper class aesthetic experience which they are about to enjoy," and as lodges housed persons or families "who had not even the cachet of being intimate house servants" (no housekeeper to Mr. Darcy there), so the park gate lodge is "visually ignored as car or coach drives on to the inner class-sanctum of the great house itself" (vii). The lodge is driven *by* and *overlooked* not only by the visitor but also by the characters in and editors of novels.

This chapter will begin by looking at the park gate lodge as, metaphorically speaking, a *prepositional* sort of building. A 1740 dictionary defines "preposition" as "a placing or putting before any thing; and particularly spoke of those small particles in a language that are put or set before others."[5] And in 1751 James Harris added that "the original use of Prepositions was to denote *the Relations of Place*."[6] Chapter 4 will deal directly and historically with the grammatical life of the actual preposition and the other "lesser words" that were bypassed and overlooked in favor of the (capitalized) Noun and its agent of change, the verb. Here, the park gate lodge, a sort of small particle in the architectural scheme of things, bypassed and overlooked in favor of the House, is pre-positioned in front of the house and, in combination with the approach (that nominalized verb), initiates the Relations of Place between entrance and end. Just as the preposition was becoming more visible in the later eighteenth century (in an underground sort of way) and exerting more influence over narrative patterns, so the approach with its park gate lodge was reshaping the estate, reemphasizing its boundaries, and redirecting perceptual experience.

The changing line of the architectural approach—winding rather than linear, moving prepositionally around, over, under, alongside, up, down, and toward instead of simply "to" the house, emphasizing things on the way and in between—is matched by the changing representations of the country house in the topographical views of the late eighteenth and early nineteenth centuries, the topic of a later section of this chapter. As Mark Girouard has pointed out, "The way people looked at houses affected the way they drew them. [. . .] [I]t became increasingly common to draw [those houses] from an angle."[7] The enormously popular compendia of engravings of "the seats of the nobility and gentry" rendered the houses not only from various angles but from various perspectives: front and center, in the middle distance, far away behind the trees, dominating the frame to disappearing in a corner, and populated with the "staffage" of gentlemen and ladies, fishermen and frisking dogs, contented laborers and impressive young landscape architects. Both the positioning of the houses and the presence of the figures emphasize the inclusionary practice of the approach; the reader is positioned to enter the scene, the narrative. And the ubiquity of the views—from dinner services to pocket diaries to collected plates for extra-illustrated texts—meant that the view *of* as well as *from* the country estate was packaged for the hand, eye, and pocket of the reader, the tourist, the visitor, the guest, the casual observer. Great Britain was on view, "appropriateable" in Humphry Repton's sense of visual command.

The chapter will close with a coda, a bridge to the next chapter across Old London Bridge, itself described by a contemporary as "a Village on, or across the River of *Thames*"[8] because of its many-storied houses and shops, its community street life, its visual stability. It was also, until 1750, almost the only entrance to London from the south, apart from boats. But in the middle of the eighteenth century the "Village" *on* the river was summarily scraped off, and the bridge *across* was rebuilt, straight, uniform, unencumbered—much the way the topography of the page around the same time was swept clean and sliced uniform, common nouns decapitated, italics uprighted. In both cases, the symmetricization, the straightening, the reordering, paradoxically opened up spaces for the things in between to become visible, enabling a different kind of winding approach.

The park gate lodge

"Lodges are necessary both for approaches and drives," John Claudius Loudon prescribes in the 1806 *Treatise on Forming, Improving, and Managing Country Residences*.[9] "Those for the approach should be designed in a character analogous to that of the mansion" (2:592). Humphry Repton contextualized the "Entrance Lodge or Cottage" as a requirement "to mark the entrance to a place with importance" which is "in compliance with the modern custom of placing the house in the centre of the grounds." He then describes its best situation and character:

> The entrance to a place is generally best marked at any branching off from a public road; and where the boundary of a park is at some distance from the road, and the entrance a kind of private cross-road, a mere Cottage may perhaps be sufficient, of any style of architecture, without reference to the style of the house, and a proper gate will distinguish it as an entrance to a place. But where the gate immediately opens into a park, strongly marked, and bounded by a wall or park-paling, a Lodge seems more appropriate than a Cottage: that it should partake of the style and character of the mansion seems also to be required by the *laws of unity of design*, which good taste adopts in every art. If the architecture of the house be Grecian, the style of the Lodge should be

> the same; as in the design for a Lodge at Wingerworth House [. . .] and for the Entrance to Longnor, where the house is Gothic.[10]

From the architects' point of view, the lodge was definitely not a negligible, bypassable feature. John Papworth, in *Rural Residences* (1818) (plate VI), explains that the lodge was intended to attract the attention of the traveler, for as "the entrance of a property effecting the earliest impression on the mind of a visitant, it is of some importance" that these impressions should be of "a cheerful and inviting character [. . .] being contrived to [. . .] induce the traveller to desire a further investigation."[11] P. F. Robinson declares: "The Gate Lodge is a feature of considerable importance, inasmuch as it should indicate the character of the structure to which it affords an approach."[12] That approach should be marked, says Thomas Dearn, by "neatness and [an] air of comfort."[13] And Humphry Repton, one of the landscape architects who made the park gate lodge a central, not peripheral, part of his whole design, argued firmly that it is "by the attention to the neatness, comfort, and simple ornament of such buildings, that we should then judge of the style of the neighbouring palace."[14] The slides of the approach to Glemham Hall ("in Suffolk A Seat of Dudley Long North Esq[r]:"), for example, feature the lodge as the principal focus of the relandscaped experience (see plates III, IV). In the approach from London, Repton explains,

> there is fortunately a Curvature in the Turnpike-road, a few yards before the present entrance, of which, I wish this advantage to be taken, viz. let a single Lodge be placed to front the road, and let the approach pass nearly over the spot, in which there is a break in the pale, and a gap of sunk fence; which being shut in by a plantation, will produce the effect I have endeavoured to shew in the following sketch, representing the sort of Lodge that I think would be applicable to the House and Situation. (*Red Book for Glemham Hall*, "Approaches," n.p.)

The "Before" sketch of the existing approach shows a carriage full of guests going round the curve on the left, passing tree after same old tree; lift the slide and there is the neat, dignified Lodge, sitting squarely in the middle of the sketch, looking quite like the Noun of the composition in that it controls *our* focus and determines *their* route, closing off the right-hand way with a delicate but firm paling. The carriage-group almost looks *nudged* behind and to the left. The lodge, to reweight my earlier proposition, is prepositional, in that it was built to be driven past, *on* the approach and *toward* the house—but it was also meant to be *seen*. In Repton and the others we see the preposition Nominalized.

As a structure to house the "Porter of the Gate," the lodge was not simply an ornamental prelude but a dwelling, "usually intended, either for an old man, an old woman, or both, or for a mother and daughter" (Dearn 6). But in its earlier incarnations, it was frequently less a *machine à habiter* than a *machine de fantasie* (Mowl and Earnshaw xii). Mid-eighteenth-century designs, such as the gothic lodge introduced by the antiquarian Sanderson Miller in Warwickshire in 1745–47, or Humphry Repton's lodge at Blaise Castle (figure 3), illustrate the possibilities of *fantasie*. Miller's Edgehill Tower loomed dramatically over a steep carriage drive down to his modest Elizabethan home below. He used the lodge as a dining pavilion, treating his guests to an experience of drawbridges and terrifying carriage rides. Miller's near neighbor, the 3rd Earl of Jersey, almost immediately asked him to design one for his Oxfordshire estate, and over the next fifty years the gothic lodge "was well on the way to being absorbed into the standard repertory of suburban architectural practice" (Mowl and Earnshaw 55). Repton's design for the park gate lodge at Blaise Castle achieved "a kind of immortality by being the lodge under whose arch Catherine Morland did not ride" (Mowl and Earnshaw 54).[15] Catherine, of Jane Austen's *Northanger Abbey*, newly indoctrinated into the mysteries of the gothic novel, had longed to visit Blaise Castle, assured by the pompous ignoramus John Thorpe that it was the "oldest in the kingdom" with "dozens" of "towers and long galleries."[16] She expected a Radcliffean gateway "of gigantic size, [. . .] defended by two round towers,

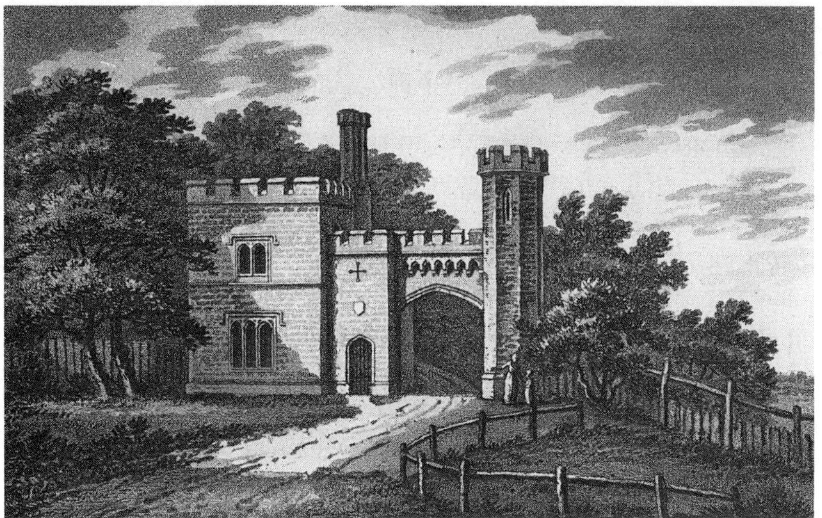

3. Humphry Repton, "Entrance to Blaize Castle," Bristol. From *Observations on the Theory and Practice of Landscape Gardening* (1803). Photograph: Special Collections, University of Virginia, Charlottesville (SB471 .R427 1803).

crowned by overhanging turrets."[17] She did not know—because Thorpe did not know, though presumably Austen *did*—that "Blaise Castle" was the name of the modern mansion built in 1796–98, designed by William Paty; the ancient castle Thorpe promises was a gothic folly built in 1766. And it was probably a good thing that she never did get there, because in fact Repton had been improving the house and grounds to the extent that he prophesied: "The stranger will be agreeably surprised to find that on quitting this wood, he is *not* going to a mouldering castle whose ruined turrets threaten destruction, and revive the horrors of feudal strife; but to a mansion of elegance, cheerfulness, and hospitality where the comfort of neatness is blended with the rude features of nature."[18]

When the lodge was indeed a park gate lodge, housing the gatekeeper, the interior as it presented itself to its occupant was not often a matter of concern for the owner. Indeed, the idea of a "family" living in the park gate lodge was itself aesthetically problematic: "A group of small children, though occasionally picturesque in a situation like this, is not, on the whole, desirable. That neatness and air of comfort, which should mark the approach to a gentleman's residence, would, by such an assemblage, be too frequently destroyed" (Dearn 6). And when the passion for Palladian symmetry met the passion for demonstrative grandeur, the *machine à habiter* virtually ceased to exist.

J. Miller's "Design for a Lodge" divides the space into two single-roomed, double-floored buildings on either side of the gate. A typical park gate lodge, such as that of Boughton House in Northamptonshire, might have "A Bed-Stead matt and Cord A Feather / Bed and Bolster a Blanket a Rugg a Table A Form [a bench or long stool] / A Chair / two Locks and Keys."[19] The lodge at Holkham Hall offered a little more luxury: "A mahogany Tea Table wth. a Cupboard under for Tea / Cups/A Stove Grate, Fireshovel, Tongs, Poker Fender and / Broom" (Murdoch 226). Ruth Perry has looked at the eviction scenes in eighteenth-century novels and observes: "The minimum space required for the comfort of the body is an oblong the size of a grave or a mattress."[20] The doubled octagon is hardly an improvement. Repton objected strongly to the practice, first for its architectural hypocrisy, but then more viscerally for its inhumanity:

> The custom of placing a gate between two square boxes, or, as it is called, "a pair of lodges," has always appeared to me absurd, because it is an attempt to give consequence to that which is mean: the habitation of a single labourer, or perhaps of a solitary old woman, to open the gate, is split into two houses for the sake of childish symmetry, and very often the most squalid misery is found in the person thus banished from society, who inhabits a dirty room a few feet square. (*Observations* 142)

He adds in a footnote: "I cannot help mentioning the witty comment of a celebrated lady, who, because they looked like tea-caddies, wrote on two such lodges in large letters, GREEN and BOHEA" (142d).

Repton was one of the first to consider the larger social issues of landscape gardening, bringing those "banished from society" between the park gates into view. He insisted that his clients not only keep but also repair or renovate the cottages of their laborers. "It was this concern for the housing of the rural poor which led him to attack the fashionable fad for pairs of small symmetrical lodges" and to advocate instead for "a substantial cottage on one side of the gateway only."[21] On the whole, the increasing prosperity of a middle class interested in architecture, in landscape design, in gardens, in furnishings, in traveling, in the interiors of other people's houses, included an increasing interest in improving and even depicting interiors of the poor as well as the rich.[22] Between 1790 and 1835 over sixty illustrated design books for cottages and small villas were published, and their format as well as their content reflects the impress of the landscape movement and the later picturesque: "the crisp contrast and incisive line of the copper engraving" of the earlier eighteenth-century Palladian aesthetic, with the building and plan etched in blank space, transformed into imaginatively lived landscapes and dwellings through various watercolor and aquatint techniques.[23] As Stephen Daniels puts it, "Watercolor in England was becoming more highly esteemed, and inextricably linked to the rising taste for English landscape. Repton's Red Books are part of that picturesque construction of the nation undertaken by a touring army of amateur and professional watercolorist enjoying fast and efficient travel in improved carriages over improved roads."[24]

Later architects improved on this visualization of the overlooked, the centralization of the peripheral. Thomas Dearn's 1811 lodge with sitting room (12' × 14'), bedroom (14' × 10'), wash house (10' × 9'6"), and pantry (10' × 4') is "pleasing" in "outline," and its "arrangements are convenient and economical" (6). The plate shows its occupant walking home in the evening light, with his stout stick and sturdy boots, looking up at his wee castle, presumably with pride in its pleasing outlines and convenient arrangements.[25] Thomas Frederick Hunt creates a similar material idealization of the generally invisible laboring life, bringing the park gate lodge into an imaginative, imaged center. *Half a Dozen Hints on Picturesque Domestic Architecture, in A Series of Designs for Gate Lodges, Gamekeepers' Cottages, and Other Rural Residences* (1825), addressed to those who have "the liberality to make comfortable provision for their dependents," three-dimensionalizes a prospect of contented, comfortable servitude.[26] His first plate, "A Gate Lodge," is "designed for the Entrance, and as a Gardener's Residence to the Grounds of a moderate-sized Gentleman's House. It consists of a Sitting Room, Kitchen, and Out-House, with a Bed Room, and Seed Loft in the Roof." The cottage has a man resting against the rail of his front porch, looking out over his view. The seventh plate of a Gate Lodge has dogs sporting about the lawn. Another has rooms "on a larger scale than the others," and would "not be inapplicable to the Entrance of a Park, leading to a House, in the style of King James the First." These images, says Hunt, picturesque and comfortable as they already appear, are merely indications of even better possibilities: "It will be seen that the Buildings are represented as they would appear when left by the workmen,—the outlines new and unbroken,—no attempt having been made to give them that pictorial effect which they could only acquire by time and the growth of ivy, roses, or other embellishing plants" ("Address," n.p.). There is narrative embedded in these plates, in these prospects, imagined also by Papworth in *Rural Residences* (1818):

> The porch in which [the British labourer] rests after the fatigues of the day, ornamented by some flowering creeper, at once affords him shade and repose; neatness and cleanliness connected with these and other means of external cheerfulness, bespeak the elasticity of mind, and spring of action, which produce industry and cheerfulness, and demonstrate that peace and content at least dwell with its inhabitant. (10)

Repton had inserted a cottage into the background hills of his watercolor of the grounds of Blaise Castle because the image of an inhabited cottage expresses "the ideas of motion, animation, and inhabitancy" that constitute the "chief beauty" of a view. For the landscape designers and architects, the lodge, built as entrance *to* the approach—like every other bit of its winding and turning and in-betweening—had become a central focus, made visible, seen inside.

But as Mowl and Earnshaw pointed out, historically and experientially, the lodge slipped past the traveler's eye and below the historian's notice in the wake of the drive to the center. Like the preposition, which, as Ian Michael explains, "was traditionally 'to be set before' another word," so "the grammarian's eye was fastened not on the preposition itself but on the word it governed"[27]—thus literally over-looked—the park gate lodge was passed by. So it was in Literature as in History.[28]

The pilgrim Christian, in John Bunyan's *The Pilgrim's Progress* (1678), narratively illustrates the problem as he approaches the "very stately Palace before him, the name whereof was *Beautiful*."[29] He sees the palace *first* and *then* "made haste and went forward, that if possible he might get Lodging there; now before he had gone far, he entered into a very narrow passage, which was about a furlong off of the Porters Lodge" (*TPP* 38). The Porter's Lodge, which precedes the house and is actually approached first, sits *behind* the house in the paragraph, in Christian's experience and in his narrative. Catherine Morland's approach to Northanger Abbey has a similar narrative position. That approach is designed, in the narrative and in Catherine's imagination, on the criteria established by Whately, Repton, and Loudon: "Every bend in the road was expected with solemn awe to afford a glimpse of its massy walls of grey stone, rising amidst a grove of ancient oaks, with the last beams of the sun playing in beautiful splendour on its high Gothic windows" (*NA* 161). This is, of course, a neat compression of the elaborate several-page approach to Udolpho by Emily, the Montonis, and their retinue, where the setting sun's "sloping rays, shooting through an opening of the cliffs, touched with a yellow gleam the summits of the forest, that hung upon the opposite steeps, and streamed in full splendour upon the towers and battlements of a castle, that spread its extensive ramparts along the brow of a precipice above" (*Udolpho* 2:169–70). But Catherine's approach does not end with massy walls:

> As they drew near the end of the journey, her impatience for a sight of the abbey—for some time suspended by [Henry Tilney's] conversation on subjects very different—returned in full force. [. . .] But so low did the buildings stand, that she found herself passing through the great gates of the lodge into the very grounds of Northanger, without having discovered an antique chimney. (*NA* 161)

To add insult to injury, those lodges themselves sport "a modern appearance" (*NA* 161). Christian and Catherine—and, for the record, most of their literary editors—have their sights fixed on the great Noun of the House, and pass by the prepositional building.[30]

But when we slow down and look around and between instead of simply straight ahead, things like the park gate lodge swing into view. In Frances Burney's *Camilla* (1796), for example, there are four family estates, each one presumably with its park gate lodge. The estate gates are mentioned frequently, but an actual lodge only appears once. And yet its presence is narratively and psychologically telling: although it does not explicitly mark the beginning of an architectural approach, it opens the gate quite literally to a flurry of narrative and psychological approaches to the house.[31] Camilla has learned that her imprudent hidden debts have landed her father in jail; terrified of her parents' rejection, appalled that she has ruined everyone's lives, she flies frantically from London to her sister Eugenia's home, Belfont; from there to an inn near Etherington (her own home); and from there to Cleves (the estate of her uncle Sir Hugh Tyrold) to seek counsel from her sister Lavinia. As with the landscape theorists' descriptions of approaches (chapter 1), Camilla's approach to the house and then her haunting search within it replicate in prose the rhythms of approach. The drive to Cleves is rendered in a breathless series of sentences looking this way and that:

> When she came upon the cross road leading from Winchester to Cleves, and felt her quick approach to the spot so loved yet dreaded, the horses seemed to her to fly. Twenty times she called out to the driver not to hurry; who as often assured her the bad roads prevented any haste; she wanted to form some appropriate plan and speech for every emergence; but she could suggest none for any. She was now at the feet of her Mother, now kissing the hands of her Father, now embraced again by her fond uncle;—and now rejected by them all. But while her fancy was at work alternately to soothe and to torture her, the park lodge met her eyes, with no resolution taken.[32]

The next paragraph curtails the prose as abruptly as the ride: "Vehemently she stopped the chaise." As she approaches Cleves, the lodge becomes visible as the entrance to what she must face—and it is the noun at the end of its own one-sentence paragraph:

> To drive in through the park would call a general attention, and she wished, ere her arrival were announced, to consult alone with Lavinia. She resolved, therefore, to get out of the carriage, and run by a private path, to a small door at the back of the house, whence she could glide to the chamber commonly appropriated to her sister.
>
> She told the postilion to wait, and alighting, walked quick and fearfully towards the lodge.
>
> She passed through the park-gate for foot passengers without notice from the porter. (5:396)

The scene beyond the entrance lodge becomes gothic: twilight, Camilla invisible to the porter, the shadows of the trees seeming "the precursors of the approach of Mrs. Tyrold"; at the end of the approach (or approaches: multiplied and confounded, imaginary and dramatic), is a full stop in both senses: "but when she came to the little door by which she meant to enter, she found it fastened" (5:396). The next few pages continue the internal "approach" in more breathless sentences and paragraphs turning quick textual corners as she steals from one room to another in the preternaturally empty house:

> She descended the stairs with almost equal apprehension of meeting any one or seeing no one. The stone passage was now nearly dark. It was always the first part of the house that was lighted, as its windows were small and high: but no preparations were now making for that purpose. She went to the housekeeper's room, which was at the foot of the stairs she had descended. The door was shut, and she could not open it. She tried repeatedly, but vainly, to be heard by soft taps and whispering; no one answered.
>
> Amazed, confounded, she turned slowly another away [*sic*]: not a soul was in sight, not a sound within hearing. Every thing looked desolate, all the family seemed to be vanished.
>
> Insensibly, yet irresistibly, she now moved on towards the drawing-room. The door was shut. She hesitated whether or not to attempt it. She listened. She hoped to catch the voice of her uncle: but all was inviolably still. (5:401–2)

Camilla, from a distance and through inaction and avoidance, had managed to fling her family centrifugally from their center, herself creating the gothically empty mansion. No wonder she is reluctant to cross the threshold. The title of the chapter is, after all, "*A new View of an old Mansion*" (5:394). The approach is designed to make the approacher see differently—a new View with each new approach.

That this gate lodge looms with significance here is further supported by the fact that earlier, in an outing to "Knowle" (Knole House, home of the Dukes of Dorset and Barons Sackville [see figure 1]), the house is visited but not entered; the works of Sir Joshua Reynolds are admired, as are the venerable trees, but the party is simply inside and then outside, never crossing (3:209)—like Harriet, Lady Byron, arriving at Grandison Hall but not *approaching* it (chapter 1). When an approach is described, it is *emphasized*—as being more important than the actual arrival. The great gates of Knole are not noticed in the novel, and yet Burney knew them well, having described them to her sister Susanna in October 1779: "The House, which is very old, has the appearance of an Antique Chapel, or rather Cathedral:—2 immense Gates and 2 Court Yards preceded the Entrance into the Dwelling part of the House."[33] The gates of Knole are enormous, unmistakable; they make an Entrance in both senses. One Enters. (And in fact, says Repton's son John, such arched gatehouses "are more appropriate to the courtyards of the mansions, as at Knowle, Penshurst, Hampton-Court, &c. than as Entrances to a park" [*Fragments* 187]). But not on a simple outing, not for Camilla; only when the entrance must be significant, must reveal something hidden or demand something immense, make something visible—even emptiness. The gothic chapter ends with wonderful grammatical ambiguity, as "Camilla, ejaculating, 'Adieu, dear happy Cleves!' was driven out of the park" (*Camilla* 5:855). The passive construction echoes backward over Camilla's destructive passivity.

The idea of approach and entrance, of procedural impressions and the power of passing-through, actively as well as passively, can be textually embedded in more ways than one. Catherine Morland had Emily St. Aubert's language in her head as she passed through the lodges of Northanger Abbey; in Austen's *Mansfield Park* (1814), portals seem to mark a number of Fanny Price's major experiences, and the Radcliffean language of approach seems to rumble textually underground here as well. As Emily entered Udolpho, "the carriage-wheels rolled heavily under the portcullis. Emily's heart sunk, and she seemed, as if she was going into her prison" (*Udolpho* 2:173). When Fanny leaves Mansfield Park and the Bertrams, which and whom she now loves, to return to her family in the naval town of Portsmouth, another massive gate, and another set of carriage sound effects, line the entrance:

> [T]hey regularly advanced, and were in the environs of Portsmouth while there was yet daylight for Fanny to look around her, and wonder at the new buildings.—They passed the Drawbridge, and entered the town: and the light was only beginning to fail, as [. . .] they were rattled into a narrow street, leading from the high street, and drawn up before the door of a small house now inhabited by Mr. Price.[34]

The "Drawbridge" is not glossed in the half-dozen most popular paperback editions, nor is the fact that Portsmouth was a walled town. Landport Gate was the former principal entrance into Portsmouth, built in 1760 to a design possibly by Nicholas Hawksmoor. It originally had a moat in front: the drawbridge led to what was then known as the London Road. What was essentially a repositioning of the gate in 1760 to the center of the northern ramparts meant that "on entering the town visitors were confronted with the relatively minor Warblington Street rather than the main thoroughfare of High Street."[35] Fanny's entrance into Portsmouth is one of distinctly diminishing returns. The light is failing for her as well as for Emily, and in both scenes the carriage wheels rattle or roll as both women enter forms of darkness and confinement. The walls and closed gates of Portsmouth redouble in the spaces of Fanny's experience:

> She was then taken into a parlour, so small that her first conviction was of its being only a passage-room to something better, and she stood for a moment expecting to be invited on; but when she saw there was no other door, and

> that there were signs of habitation before her, she called back her thoughts, reproved herself, and grieved lest they should have been suspected. (377–78)

Fanny is by this point well used to carriage drives and stately approaches, to passing from a small space into a larger, to be invited on rather than foreclosed by an entrance. She makes a psychologically spatial gesture in calling back her thoughts, which had in innocent arrogance moved on through the nonexistent Entrance. "Fanny was almost stunned. The smallness of the house, and thinness of the walls, brought every thing so close to her, that [. . .] she hardly knew how to bear it" (*MP* 382). Rather like the punctuation of the text (chapter 3), the combination of lodge-and-approach is meant simultaneously to connect and to separate, to spin out anticipation in the spaces of between, to presage and project but not, most definitely not, to bring the entrance or the house itself "so close" to its visitor's first perceptions.

The further in she goes, the tighter the pressure:

> There was nothing to raise her spirits in the confined and scantily-furnished chamber that she was to share with Susan. The smallness of the rooms above and below indeed, and the narrowness of the passage and staircase, struck her beyond her imagination. She soon learnt to think with respect of her own little attic at Mansfield Park, in *that* house reckoned too small for anybody's comfort. (387)

Soon not even her imagination can move, can approach, can enter; the narrowness closes her off. Being Fanny, she of course makes the best of things, and hollows out a little space and order in the place, but the descriptive noun used as she leaves confirms the pressure of the psychological through the architectural walls: "How her heart swelled with joy and gratitude, as she passed the barriers of Portsmouth" (445). Where Camilla had passively "been driven," Fanny, deproaching Portsmouth to go back to a Mansfield Park where she will actually Be Someone Who Does Things, actively passes the barriers.

Christian, Emily, Camilla, Catherine, and Fanny all pass under gates and by lodges into palaces, castles, houses, abbeys, and fortified towns in key moments of metamorphic stress; those fictional gates and lodges, however, like their historical landscape counterparts, sink virtually unremarked in the wake of reading, editing, touring. The park gate lodge becomes a prepositional building in that it is passed by, on the road and in the text. But the odd, charming little building that repays attention in an architectural glance—designed as it was by architects to be looked *at* as well as driven *by*—has its barely visible textual counterpart that also impresses itself on the shape of its narrative landscape. Excavating the textual lodge leads our eye along the branching lines of psychological and narrative as well as landscaped approach.

The topographical view

Humphry Repton designed his trade card (figure 4) as a "topographical view"—the popular late-eighteenth- and early nineteenth-century engraving of a country estate—to show himself as surveyor-in-the-landscape, with his assistant, or perhaps a client, attentively to hand. Every Red Book had this image affixed to the inside of its front cover. As his Red Books combined ground plans, watercolor slides, and narrative, so the image here has a text embedded in the trees and rocks, and inserted below (underneath) the engraving. The text carved in the landscape is from Milton's *L'Allegro*:

> Straight mine eye hath caught new pleasure,
> Whilst the landscape around it measures, [. . .]
> Towers and battlements it sees
> Bosom'd high in tufted trees.

The pleasure lies in the measure, the individual "eye" that locates and frames the scene. The text below the image identifies designer and engraver: "H. Repton inv. & delin.r / T. Medland Sculp.r" Both text and engraving are *doing*: surveying, lounging, digging, engraving. The high tower is a focus, and the water reflects the landscape that surrounds it. The arrangement of the scene is actively prepositional, as Stephen Daniels describes it: "*Next* to him is a figure with a ranging rod who looks less like an assistant than one of Gainsborough's lounging young landowners. *Behind* them labourers dig and shovel earth by a lakeside. *Beyond* is a wooded hillside with a tower" (*Repton* 11, my emphasis). Repton's trade card is a snapshot in miniature of the (often overlooked) imaginative appeal and power—the narrative possibilities—of the topographical view. The surging popularity of these views, collected under titles such as William Watts's *The Seats of the Nobility and Gentry, in a Collection of the Most Interesting Picturesque Views* (1779–86) and William Angus's *The Seats of the Nobility and Gentry in Great Britain and Wales* (1787–97), has a variety of political, social, and aesthetic sources; in this section I want to draw attention to the genres of their ubiquity and the nature of their compositional patterns to illustrate their part in the rising conceptual interest in the prepositional spaces of the in-between.

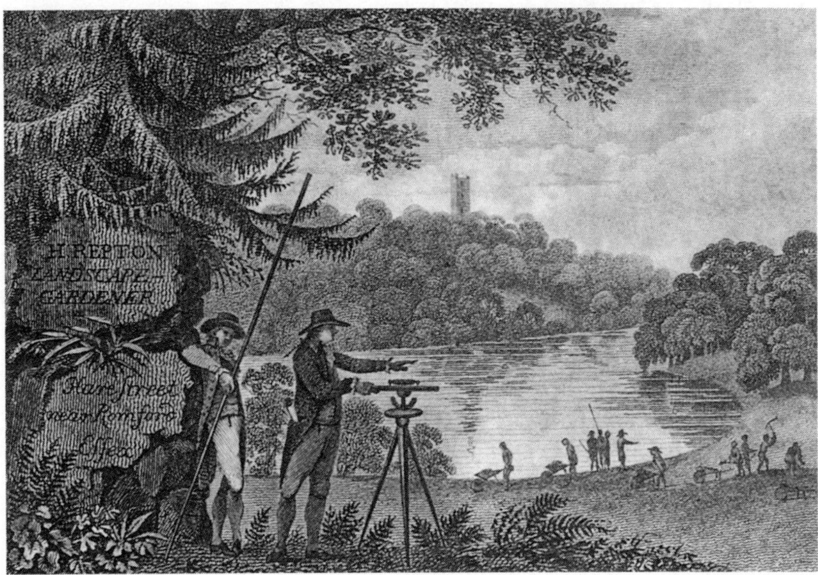

4. Thomas Medland (after Humphry Repton) trade card. From *H. Repton, Landscape Gardener [graphic]*, [Essex?], [ca. 1797?], engraving. Photograph courtesy of the Yale Center for British Arts, Paul Mellon Fund (Folio A 2011 13).

The antiquarian Richard Gough (1735–1809) honored John Leland (1503–52), whose "particular and regular" descriptions of "the state of cities, towns, and villages, [. . .]castles, palaces, churches, with their monuments, and every other building that came his way," first allowed the English "to be acquainted with the face of [their] own country."[36] From Sir Robert Cotton's (d. 1631) Tudor maps, plans, and views of estates, to the "prospect" paintings by immigrant Dutch and Flemish artists such as Wenceslaus Hollar in the seventeenth century and Kip and Knyff's *Britannia Illustrata* in the early eighteenth, to the landscape paintings of the eighteenth century, the English print industry improved in technique and expanded in popularity. By the 1770s "British engravers were a force to be reckoned with,"[37] and by the early nineteenth century upwards of one thousand different engravings of country houses had been published. As touring the great country estates grew in popularity, so the topographical view became one of the most popular forms of art.[38]

Despite its popularity—even ubiquity, as we will see—the topographical view, like the park gate lodge and the preposition, has received relatively little critical attention. "Topography," explains Ronald Russell, "is often regarded as a sort of poor relation of landscape. [And] until comparatively recently, landscape itself was thought of as a poor relation" (11). It was a "humble[r] art" (Payne 9): in the aesthetic hierarchy of painting, "A History is preferable to a Landscape," argued Jonathan Richardson in 1719; in 1759

Horace Walpole declared, "I don't know so contemptible a class of writers as topographers";[39] in 1768 Gough sniffed at topographers such as Johannes Kip, who filled their works "with views of private houses, interesting to none but the owners vanity" (Gough xxviii); and Henry Fuseli rejected "that kind of landscape which is entirely occupied with the tame delineation of a given spot [. . .] what is commonly called Views" (qtd. in Russell 11). Even in more recent art-historical circles, the topographical view is often "excluded as of peripheral reference" in wider studies of architectural prints (Clayton, "Publishing Houses" 43).[40]

The problem with the topographical view was that it was too anchored in the ordinary and everyday—even if the ordinary and everyday meant a house with 101 hearths. Like description itself in the eighteenth century, the topographical view was too *particular*, too individual, too local, to be widely meaningful.[41] "The business of a poet," as Imlac says in Samuel Johnson's *Rasselas* (1759), "is to examine, not the individual, but the species; to remark general properties and large appearance; he does not number the streaks of the tulip, or describe the different shades in the verdure of the forest."[42] John Constable (1776–1837) himself had said modestly, "My limited and abstract art is to be found under every hedge and in every lane, and therefore nobody thinks it worth picking up" (qtd. in Russell 11); but as he was exhibiting his work in the Royal Academy by 1803, so the little things under the hedge and in the lane—the particulars of visual description in print and the particulars of *The Seats of the Nobility and Gentry in Great Britain and Wales* in the world of the print—became first visible and then popular. And as John Lewis Roger noted in his *History of the Old Water-Colour Society* (1891), the "old topographic print[s]" illustrated "in the simple graphic language of their day the outward appearance, not only of the objects, but of the people [. . .] costumed as they really were, and engaged in their ordinary pursuits. [. . .] They indicate, even by their omissions, to what kind of visible objects public interest was then chiefly confined" (qtd. in Russell 25). Topographical views offer another approach to the changing angles of visibility. Indeed, by the early eighteenth century, the publishers of the various collections of topographic views of gentlemen's seats argued that the contents were not so much the stripes of the tulip but comprised the whole British forest. As J. P. Neale asserted in the introduction to his six-volume *Views of the Seats of the Noblemen and Gentlemen in England, Wales, Scotland and Ireland* (1818–23): "Great Britain may justly boast her decided superiority over every other state in Europe, in the grand display of its numerous Country Seats" (qtd. in Clayton, "Publishing Houses" 43).

The topographical view became practically ubiquitous. Proliferating like the country house guide in the wake of the country house tour,[43] the print of the country house (or the picturesque landscape) could tempt you to travel or remind you where you'd been. Alongside the publishing profusion of prints was the equal longing to create one's own personal views: "Drawing masters became available in almost every part of the country. Whole families were given instruction in the principles and techniques of making pictures in pencil or watercolour and went out to practise the craft [. . .] At times, as the 18th century turned to the 19th, it must have seemed as if every artist in England, the trained and the half-trained, was out and about, sketchbook in hand, criss-crossing the land in search of the 'picturesque' view" (Payne 41). (We remember Catherine Morland learning foregrounds and middle distances in the space of an afternoon with Henry and Elinor Tilney.)

The ubiquity had its imperial as well as personal resonances.[44] In 1773–74 Josiah Wedgwood and Thomas Bentley created the "Green Frog Service" for the suburban palace of Catherine the Great, Kekerekeksinen (Finnish for "frog marsh"). All 944 or so pieces of the service (dinner for fifty) were decorated with views of the castles, abbeys, stately homes, gardens, towns, countrysides, and curiosities of Great Britain. Each image is adapted to its particular dish: "The tureen lids have views on either side separated by vignettes, which show details of garden pavilions or castle ruins. The rounded shapes of the sauceboats are matched by landscapes with a low horizon and high cloudy sky."[45] The larger dishes have wide, detailed panoramic views; the "dynamic shapes of the cream bowls" have "especially picturesque views" (Voronikhina 9). Like the narrative descriptions of approaches, porcelain is employed as another medium on which to represent motion and perspective, the choice of subject answering to the shape of the dish. And the dishes were answering to the shape of the country. In Thomas Bentley's introduction to the catalogue he explains:

> We have attempted [. . .] to give a true and picturesque idea of the beauties of this country, both natural and artificial. Though we have purposely omitted to represent the most modern buildings, considering them unpicturesque, there will be found nevertheless specimens of architecture of all ages and styles, from the most ancient to our present day; from rural cottages and farms, to the most superb palaces; and from huts of the Hebrides to the masterpieces of the best known English Architects.[46]

These are the images of Britain, palatial and cottagial, brought to imperial Russia; the *way* of seeing (in) England becomes an export.

The topographical view could ride in your pocket as well as serve you at table. From 1788 through the first decade of the nineteenth century, *Peacock's Polite Repository, or Pocket Companion*, for example, not only contained an "almanack, [. . .] and various other articles of useful information" but was also "ornamented with elegant engravings."[47] The miniature illustrations heading the verso of every monthly double spread of the diary pages featured country seats, as well as gardens and landscapes. (The other "articles of useful information" would include, for example, information on royalty, politicians, lawyers, offices, the banks of England, and eclipses.) By 1789, when Humphry Repton was in his second year as a landscape gardener, he had reached an agreement with William Peacock of Salisbury Court, Fleet Street, London, to publish six monthly headpieces in the *Repository*.[48] The *Repository* for 1800 in the British Library, for example, is a tiny little fellow (about 8 cm × 11.5 cm [3" × 4.5"]), bound in a cherry leather wallet with a cunning card pocket. Each month is illustrated by the houses and gardens where Repton had received commissions. The "Address" to the issues of 1793–95 acknowledges Repton's influence as the means whereby "*The Polite Repository* becomes a pleasing record of the most recent ornaments and improvements to the country" (qtd. in Temple 163). The miniature engraving for January 1800 just so happens to be "*The Cottage of H. Repton Esq. Hare-Street, Essex*" (figure 5).[49] The detail is exquisite. Although the engravings do not generally feature the approach (as they tend to do in the larger topographical prints considered below), the miniature engravings compress the seats—and cottages—of England with what Susan Stewart calls the power of the miniature to "interiorize an outside," to point continually "to the physical world."[50]

For Repton asserted, in fact, that the "most interesting subject" he had ever known was the "View from [his] humble Cottage" (*Fragments* 235). In several places he describes what he calls the concept of "appropriation," which in its particular sense means "the views from a house, and particularly those from the drawing-room," which exhibit the "objects which evidently belong to the place": typically, "such a portion of wood and lawn, as may be supposed to belong to the proprietor of the mansion, occupied by himself, not so much for the purposes of gain as of pleasure and convenience" (*Observations* 110–11). Later, in the *Fragments*, he expands the concept to "describe that sort of command over the Landscape, visible from the windows, which denotes it to be private property belonging to the place" (233). Although he blends into it a bit of *schadenfreude*, in that ownership implies "the power of refusing that others should share our pleasure" (233), he acknowledges that even "the most romantic spot, the most picturesque situations, and the most delightful assemblage of Nature's choicest materials, will not long engage our interest, without some appropriation; something we can call our own; and if

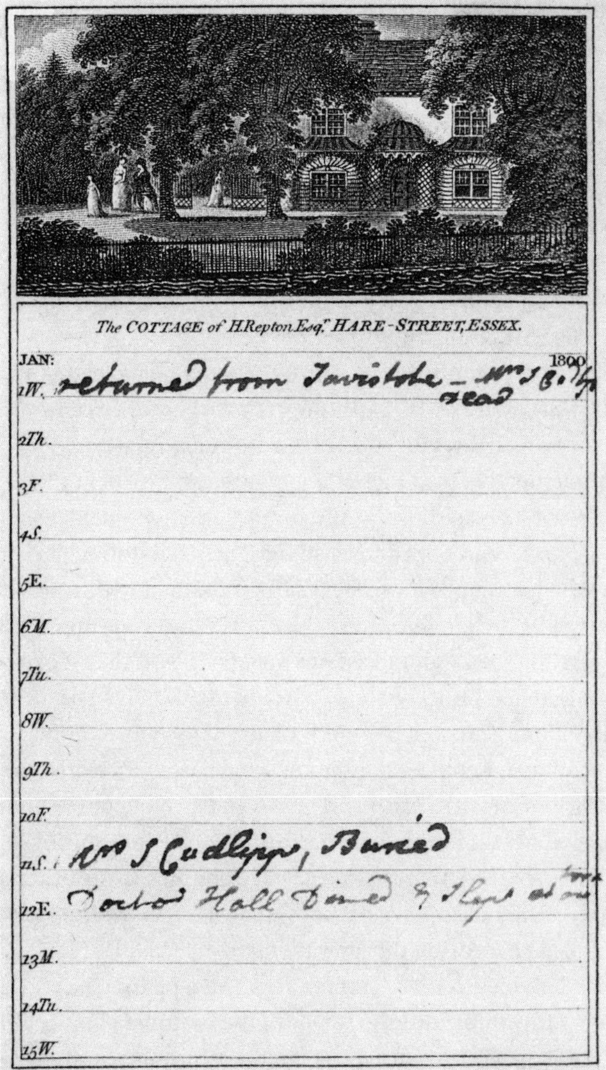

5. Humphry Repton, "The Cottage of H. Repton Esqr. Hare Street, Essex." From *Peacock's Polite Repository* (1800). Photograph © British Library Board (C.59.aa.12).

not our own property, at least it may be endeared to us by calling it *our own Home*" (235). Thus the grand "command over landscape" can just as easily be contracted to "twenty-five yards of Garden" (235). What Repton achieved in Hare Street by relocating a village fence was "a frame to [his] Landscape [. . .] composed of flowering shrubs and evergreens; beyond which are seen the cheerful village, the high road, and that constant moving scene, which I would not exchange for any of the lonely parks" (235).

There is a sort of appropriation of Britain possible in the *Polite Repository*, with halls, lodges, castles, temples, and mausoleums, from the Isle of Wight to Wales, caught and framed on the small page in the small book that is carried in the pocket (and has its own pocket). The nobility's and gentlemen's seats are in the hand and under the command of the eye of the traveler, the diarist, the man in the street (figure 6). As one *Repository* owner made free to point out in his 1791 copy, just under the frontispiece image with "Repository" inscribed on an oval at the base of a large blasted tree: "aristocrates are enemies to the revolution."[51] Here, presumably, is one owner with a revolutionarily inclined take on "appropriation."

Mark Girouard points out that "The way people looked at houses affected the way they drew them" (212). In the 1707 *Britannia Illustrata*, the houses and their formal gardens are portrayed from a bird's-eye view, with little attempt at perspective (see figure 1)—"figures and trees in the distance are shown the same size as those in the foreground" (Russell 28). On-ground views in the late seventeenth and early eighteenth centuries, such as the 1680 engraving of Clarendon House by William Skillman (fl. 1660–85), or the popular image of Alexander Pope's villa in 1735, were primarily full-frontal studies (figure 7). The five hundred or so engravings in the 1720s and 1730s by Samuel and Nathaniel Buck were, according to Susan Owens, primarily topographical records, "austere pen-and-ink drawings aimed at maximum clarity: linear shading is kept to a minimum, small dashes indicated masonry and other details; outlines are crisp and clear; and strong contrasts of light and shade, which imply three-dimensional form, are provided by ink washes. The overall effect is somewhat mechanical."[52] Owens, like many other art historians, remains slightly dismissive of the "somewhat mechanical" topographical view, her language favoring the later picturesque; Ralph Hyde, on the other hand, in his book-length study of the Bucks' town panoramas, squeezed himself through a tiny door into the tower of the Norman church of All Saints, gasped at the same view recorded by the Buck brothers, and throughout the rest of his peregrinatory studies felt "always the excitement, the identification with the artist, an ever-increasing appreciation of what the Bucks had achieved."[53]

During the eighteenth century people began to look at houses differently—from a different angle, so to speak—and so, Girouard points out, "it became increasingly common to draw [those houses] from an angle" (212). The reasons for the different way of looking at houses—for the changing aesthetic—are myriad, of course, and have been thoroughly covered: the rise of domestic tourism coming from greater ease in domestic travel; the French Revolution and the Napoleonic Wars curtailing foreign travel; the consequent (or concomitant) rise of a new nationalism; the interest in picturesque views and landscape paintings (which as Tim Clayton notes predated Gilpin by at least fifteen years[54]). The point here is to look at the new angles, the new perspectives, and the many ways they were represented, and the ways those representations overlapped and interlocked with—as well as, figuratively, illustrating—the shifting patterns of language and narrative. Girouard aligns the increasing number of asymmetrical views with increasingly asymmetrical domestic designs: "Once symmetry of the exterior was no longer the expression of a symmetrical interior, and people were anyway thinking of buildings in terms of views from an angle rather than an axis, there was no very strong reason for even the exterior to remain symmetrical. Nor did it" (212). Girouard's next chapter in the eternally wonderful *Life in the English Country House* is titled "The Arrival of Informality: 1770–1830" and features the 1781 portrait of Sir Brooke Boothby by Joseph Wright of Derby, an image of a young man lounging on a landscape, book closed on the ground, his chin cupped in his hand, looking rather *italicized*. The relaxation of posture, the dispensing of the formal circle of chairs, the increasing informality of the common rooms, and the gradual "sinking" of the country house "into the ground and opening up to the surrounding landscape" (218) is the behavioral parallel to the linguistic picturesque explored in chapters 3 and 4.

Where the picturesque landscapes of Gilpin and others privileged ruins, rocks, cottages, waterfalls, and blasted trees, with the occasional rustic herding cattle,[55] the topographical view of the country seats celebrated in precise graphic detail the house and grounds of the nobility and gentry. But the essential peripheralizing of the genre not only misses its historical popularity and significance, as Clayton demonstrates; it also misses the remarkable range of angles and perspectives explored by the topographical views. The first important late eighteenth-century collections of engravings of country seats (with textual annotations) were William Watts's *The Seats of the Nobility and Gentry, in a Collection of the Most Interesting Picturesque Views* (1779–86), Harrison's *Picturesque Views of the Principal Seats of the Nobility and Gentry* (1786–88), and William Angus's *The Seats of the Nobility and Gentry in Great Britain and Wales* (1787–97). In these collections the houses appear from an astonishing variety of perspectives, from front and center in the foreground to vast yet tiny in a corner distance. André Rogger explains that while the engravings in the various *Seats* compendia "were derived from drawings produced by several artists, [. . .] there is usually just one view per family seat, generally of the house in its landscaped setting as it would be perceived by a visitor approaching from the public highway."[56] But that viewing visitor can enter the frame of the picture from an indefinite number of approaches. In a

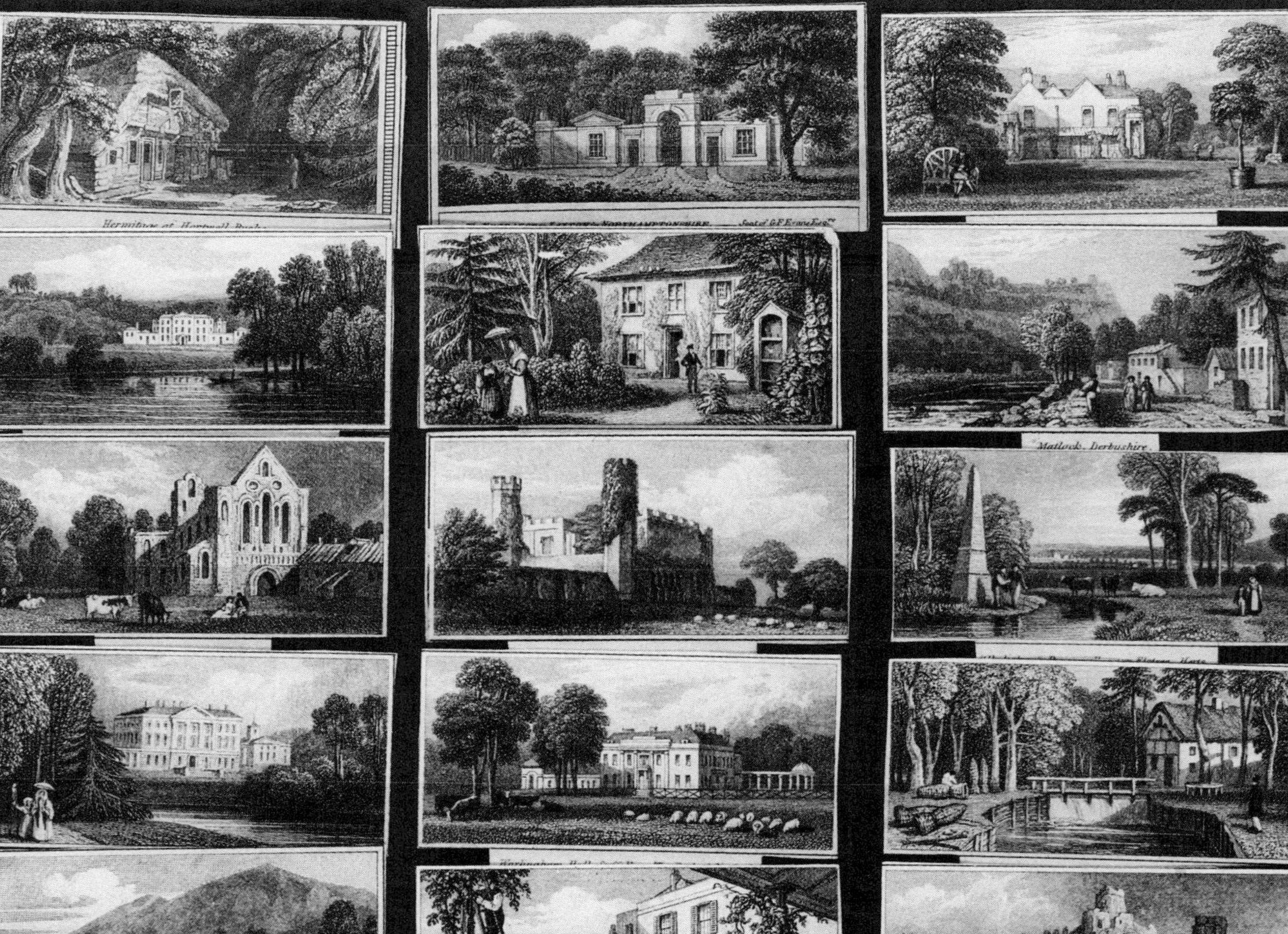
Matlock, Derbyshire

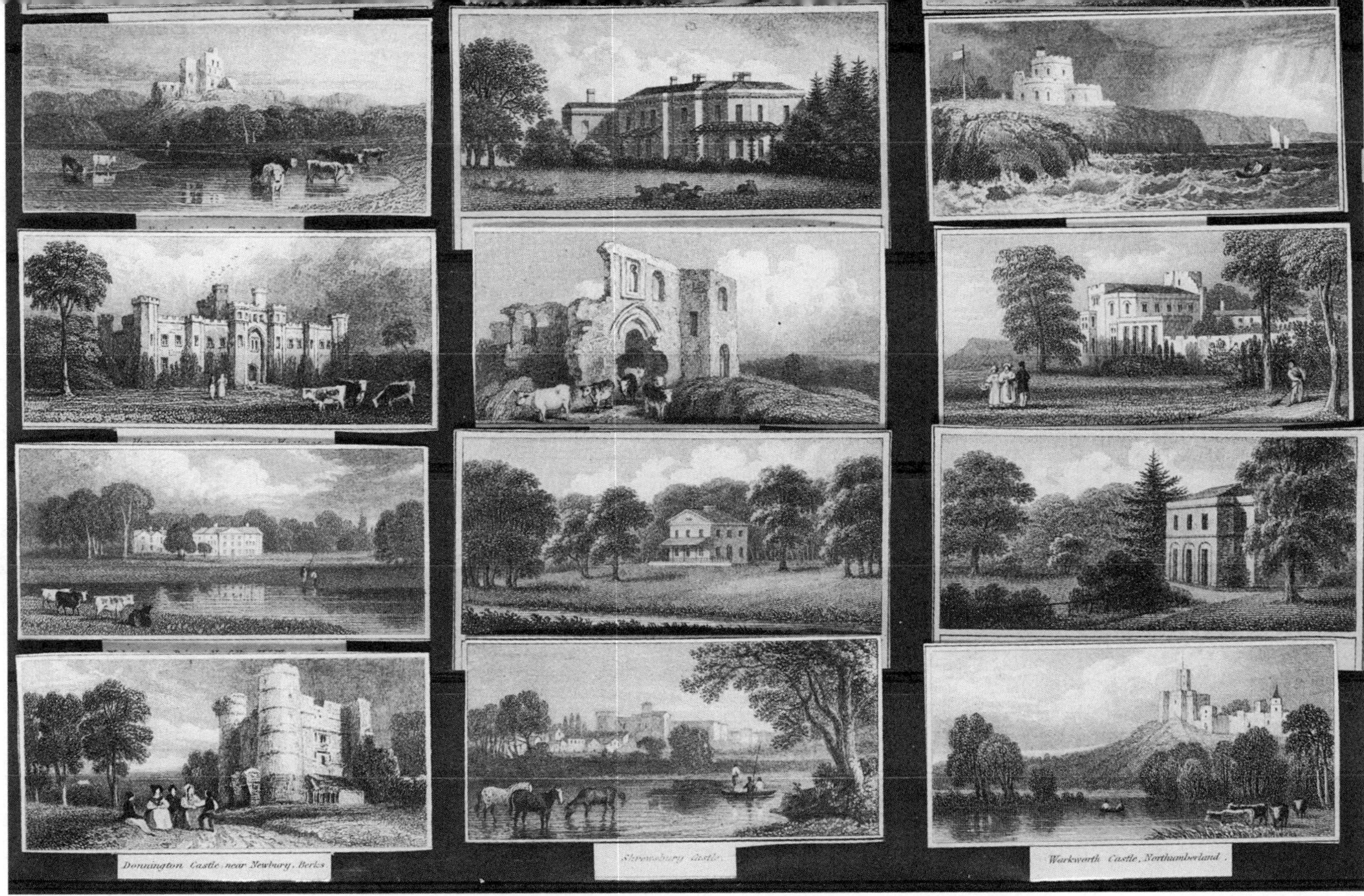

6. Engravings from *Peacock's Polite Repository*. Photograph courtesy of The Lewis Walpole Library, Yale University.

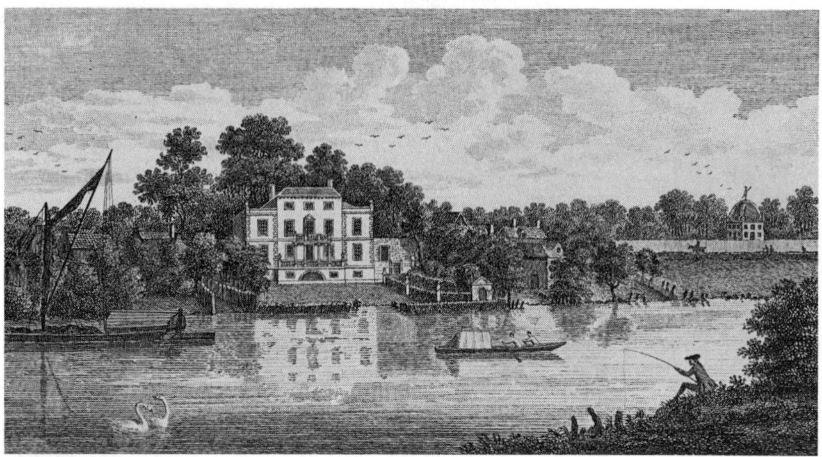

7. Anon., "Mr. Pope's House at Twickenham" (1735). Photograph courtesy of The Lewis Walpole Library, Yale University.

west view of Chatsworth (n.d.), for example, the house dominates the center of the frame and the surrounding landscape (figure 8). In Angus's *Seats*, the first entry, Broadlands in Hampshire (Lord Duncannon, del^t, Wm Angus sculp^t.), we are standing at the edge of the river Test, "a very fine, clear, and copious Stream," with the house across the water, just slightly off center and viewed slightly aslant; in the lower right-hand corner two ladies and some bouncy dogs are approaching us on the estate's approach—it clearly will not take us long to travel the hundred yards or so to the house itself. According to the accompanying text, "The House has been considerably improved by the present noble Possessor [the Right Honourable Lord Viscount Palmerston]" and its "Gardens and Pleasure Grounds are laid out and planted in a neat and elegant modern taste, with a Slope to the River, which has a pleasing Effect, that adds considerably to the View."[57] Brocket Hall (in Hertfordshire, seat of Lord Melbourne, drawn by Paul Sandby) is pushed to the far left and a more considerable distance away; though "elegant and magnificent," it is subordinated to its "most delightful and extensive Park" (Angus Plate II). (This text is one of the few to draw our attention to the lodges, which are generally as bypassed in the *Seats* compendia as they are in other contexts: "*Hatfield* is seen in the Distance; a little to the Right of which are the Lodges seen, which are at the Entrance into the park of *Brocket*." Another lodge features in Hare Hall [Angus Plate XXVIII].) Blenheim ("*From a Drawing by the Right Honourable Lord Viscount* DUNCANNON"), that enormous architectural tribute to England's military power, built by John Churchill, 1st Duke of Marlborough, is tiny in the distance, perhaps a mile away and up a hill, and we have

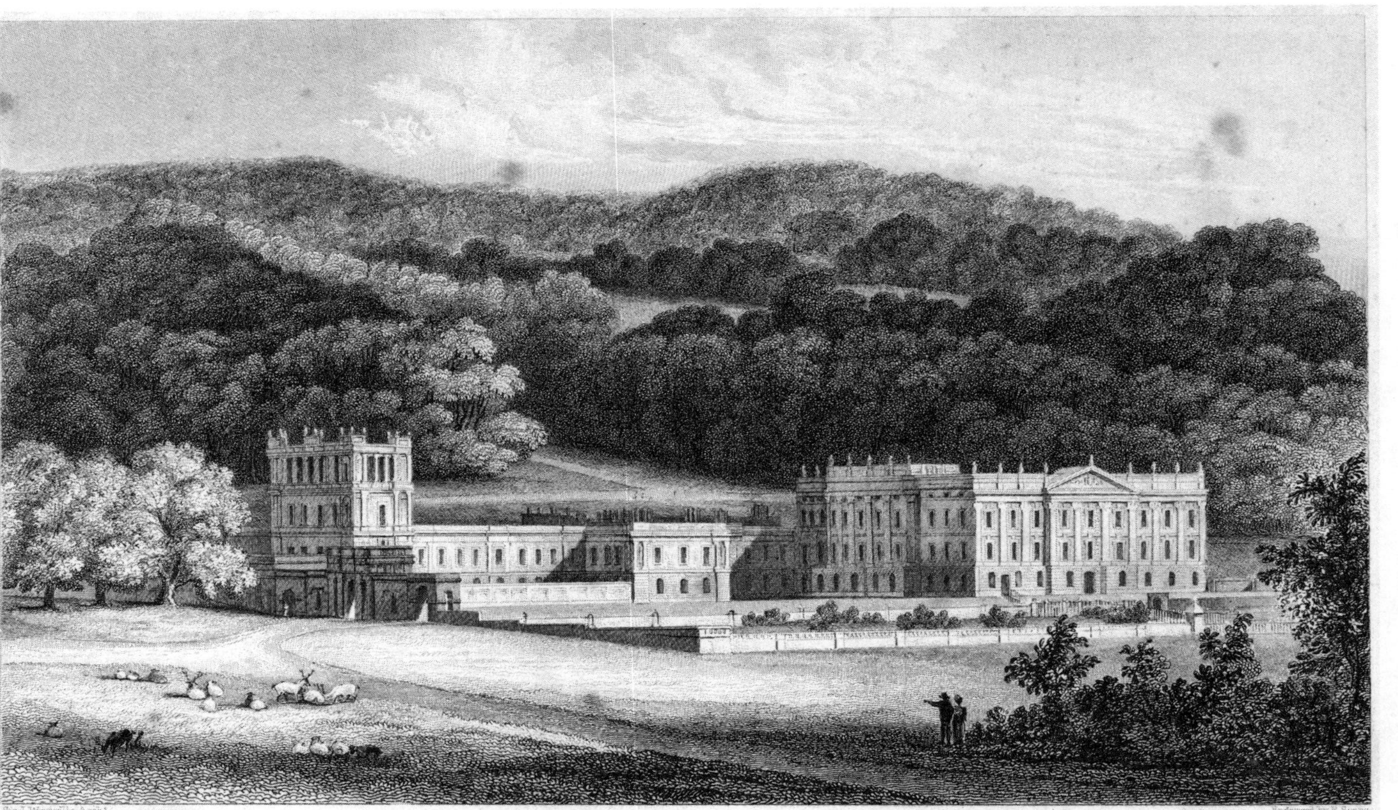

8. Sir J. Wyatville, "Chatsworth," Derbyshire (n.d.). Engraved R. Sears. Photograph courtesy of The Lewis Walpole Library, Yale University.

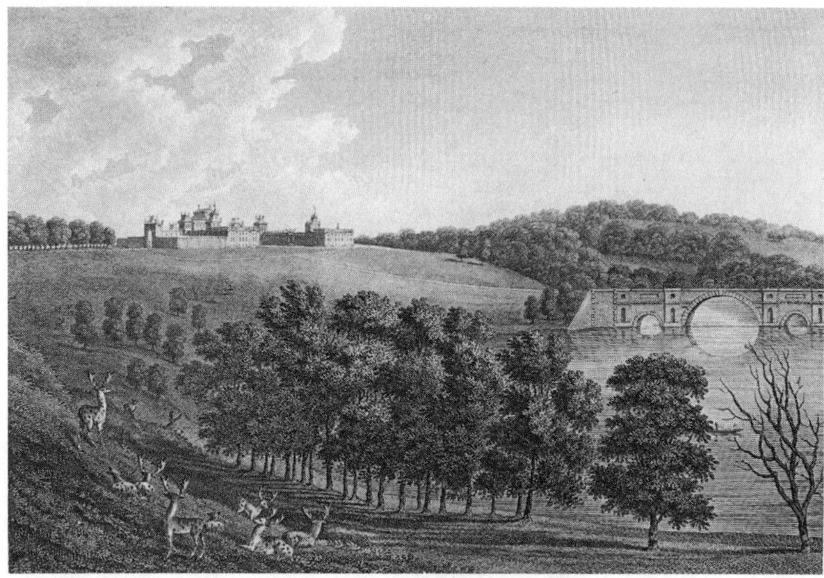

9. Lord Duncannon, "Blenheim," Oxfordshire. Engraved by William Angus. From *Seats of Nobility and Gentry* (1787). Photograph courtesy of The Lewis Walpole Library, Yale University.

to push through all those lounging deer first to get to the approach (figure 9). Dalkeith Palace in Scotland is practically invisible—because, though large, it is "not elegant in its exterior Appearance, otherwise a Front View would have been given" (Angus Plate IX). Longford Castle in Wiltshire is clearly less embarrassing: we are practically at its door, once we cross this bit of the Avon River; presented in "an oblique View of the South Front," the castle dominates the right-hand side of the image (Angus Plate X). Raby Castle in Durham, "a most noble massy Building of its kind, uninjured by any modern Improvements," drawn by E. Dayes ("*Draughtsman to his Royal Highness the* DUKE *of* YORK"), dominates the entire frame, and we are just a few steps away from the group of people strolling on the grass near the entrance (Angus Plate XXV). Sheffield Place in Sussex (drawn by Repton) is clearly "very large" (an understatement), its southeast front aspect sunlit in the left-hand side, otherwise surrounded by large dark trees (with a carriage dimly discerned in their shadows, marking out the approach) in this "picturesque View" (Angus Plate XXVI). Nettlecombe Court in Somersetshire is tucked away in the distance among "exuberan[t]" hills, with two approaches converging in the center of the frame (Angus Plate XXXIII). North Court House on the Isle of Wight (drawn by J. C. Barrow) is back in front: we are just stepping onto the approach, on the very level with the front-and-center house just twenty yards away. And Felbrigg Hall, in Norfolk, the site of Repton's first commission, features Repton himself in the foreground, tending to the details of his composition (plate VII).

The views, the perspectives, vary wildly, but in most cases the house—though the focal point of the engraving—needs to be reached by a visual route, by an approach of sorts, as it wanders into corners and tucks itself behind trees or nestles among hills or essentially retreats from the visual if not the conceptual center. We might almost say it behaves prepositionally. And like their petite counterparts the *Polite Repositories*, the *Seats* views were meant to be "appropriated"—individualized—by their owners. As the compendia were often issued serially, over the course of years, the collector would wait until the final prints appeared before binding the collection to her taste, or he might insert the separate prints into his extra-illustrated travel books. In any of their physical possibilities, the topographical views of country seats gave the country to its people: "*You* command a full view" (Angus Plate XXVIII, my emphasis).

André Rogger argues that the *Seats* compendia of Watts, Harrison, and Angus influenced the format of Repton's Red Books, in which "the house becomes the motor of the argument" (over the landscape), and where the text-and-image format provides "a sequence of perceptions tracking those of a traveler or visitor coming to the estate for the first time" (90, 91). In the *Seats*, each plate has an accompanying text that identifies the owner, situates the seat, and describes the building, its surroundings, sometimes its interior, sometimes bits of its history, and often how it can be seen, and what can be seen from its premises. In the description of Lacy House, home of the playwright Richard Brinsley Sheridan, the villa on the Thames is notable for its command of "picturesque Views both up and down the River" which are characterized by a "Variety of moving Objects that constantly engage Attention" (Angus Plate XXXVI). The concept of approach, in fact, here springs outward from the center, captured by the succession of views out the window (figure 10).

In Watts's volume, the plates and texts face each other, as they do in Repton's Red Books, setting up a visual/verbal dialogue. Repton's Red Books follow but also expand the same narrative pattern as the views books. He describes the topographical situation in terms of its landscaping potential; he then gives a "character" of the estate, its general impression upon the observer (of the owner's taste, wealth, power, &c.); he evaluates or recommends the "approach" from the perspective of the visitor; he then moves inside the house to look back out the windows and describe the new views offered by the improvements. (There may be additional sections devoted

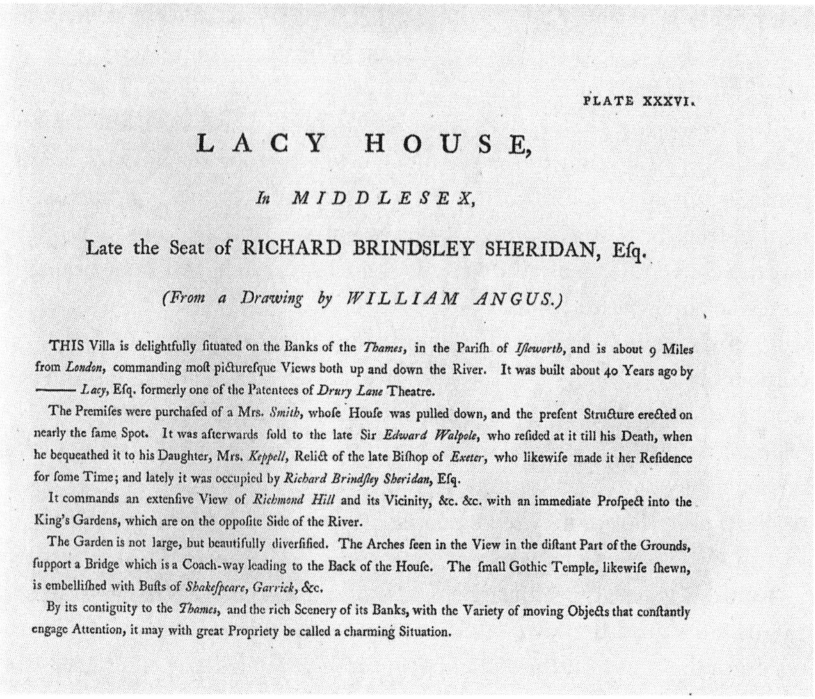

PLATE XXXVI.

LACY HOUSE,

In MIDDLESEX,

Late the Seat of RICHARD BRINDSLEY SHERIDAN, Eſq.

(From a Drawing by WILLIAM ANGUS.)

THIS Villa is delightfully ſituated on the Banks of the *Thames*, in the Pariſh of *Iſleworth*, and is about 9 Miles from *London*, commanding moſt picturesque Views both up and down the River. It was built about 40 Years ago by ——— *Lacy*, Eſq. formerly one of the Patentees of *Drury Lane* Theatre.

The Premiſes were purchaſed of a Mrs. *Smith*, whoſe Houſe was pulled down, and the preſent Structure erected on nearly the ſame Spot. It was afterwards ſold to the late Sir *Edward Walpole*, who reſided at it till his Death, when he bequeathed it to his Daughter, Mrs. *Keppell*, Relict of the late Biſhop of *Exeter*, who likewiſe made it her Reſidence for ſome Time; and lately it was occupied by *Richard Brindſley Sheridan*, Eſq.

It commands an extenſive View of *Richmond Hill* and its Vicinity, &c. &c. with an immediate Proſpect into the King's Gardens, which are on the oppoſite Side of the River.

The Garden is not large, but beautifully diverſified. The Arches ſeen in the View in the diſtant Part of the Grounds, ſupport a Bridge which is a Coach-way leading to the Back of the Houſe. The ſmall Gothic Temple, likewiſe ſhewn, is embelliſhed with Buſts of *Shakeſpeare*, *Garrick*, &c.

By its contiguity to the *Thames*, and the rich Scenery of its Banks, with the Variety of moving Objects that conſtantly engage Attention, it may with great Propriety be called a charming Situation.

10. William Angus, description of "Lacy House, in Middlesex." From *Seats of Nobility and Gentry* (1787).

to planting, water features, stables, and offices.) What with leafing through the pages, comparing the watercolors to the existing views, matching verbal description with graphic depiction, and lifting and replacing the slides for the before and after, the experience of a Repton Red Book is one that forms new combinations in the mind of the viewer at every instant. (Though Repton notes "with some mortification" that the slides seem to be what most capture the attention of "the common observer" [*Sketches* 33]). Repton *textualized* the eighteenth-century approach.

Rogger suggests that the compendia may even have given Repton his idea for the slides: "In several *Seats* compendia, the plates were protected by a semi-transparent paper. [. . .] [T]he weaknesses of a status quo scene were easily visible through the thin, protective sheet, and a light hand could readily sketch corrections directly onto the tissue paper" (90–91). The temporal experience is suggested with the spatial: the reader has a sense of her relation to the house, and the artistically inclined could imagine the house through time, both through the text (historical past) and the invitation to draw the future. The *Seats* pattern of geographical and social positioning, historical ownership, and a few lines about "the general impression that will be gained by someone approaching the house" (91) is appropriated by Repton; Repton adds a section on the approach (or its improvements) he proposes. Although the *Seats* rarely mentions approaches or lodges, most of the views contain at least the former (if, as viewer, we have already entered the estate in the frame, we have presumably already passed the lodges).

"We" are not the only ones to enter the grounds of the *Seats* and the Red Books. "Staffage" is another aspect of drawing and painting that, while part of these arts since the beginning, has, like park gate lodges and prepositions, been often overlooked. The *Oxford English Dictionary* defines staffage (pronounced as in French, /'stafɑːʒ/ /stə'fɑːʒ/ /'stafɪdʒ/, "a pseudo-French formation after German *staffiren*") as the "accessories of a picture" and gives its first usage in 1872. The "accessories" include the animals and human figures with no particular identity or story (if, no matter how tiny the figure, it *does* have an identity, biblical or mythological or historical, the painting leaps a generic fence from a "landscape" to a "history"). As William Gilpin explains in *An Essay upon Prints* (1768): "The last thing included in design is the use of proper appendages. By appendages are meant animals, landskip, buildings, and in general, what ever is introduced into the piece by way of ornament. Every thing of this kind should correspond with the subject, and rank in a proper subordination to it."[58] Staffage figures tended to be decorative, perspectival, or instructional but never central—peripheral and prepositional, in fact. The painters of the Green Frog Service, for example, "were especially fond of adding trees to frame or enrich their compositions. [. . .] [S]ometimes a figure was used to emphasise the emotional atmosphere of a painting, as for example the lonely human silhouette in the view of the Elysian Fields at Stowe" (Voronikhina 10). As Vivaldi says to Schedoni in Radcliffe's *The Italian* (1797): "That arch [. . .] suspended between two rocks, the one overtopped by the towers of the fortress, the other shadowed with pine and broad oak, has a fine effect. But a picture of it would want human figures" (1:120). Staffage figures could contribute to the sense of perspective, as in the early seventeenth-century Dutch landscape artist Pieter Molyn, whose "lively staffage figures [. . .]—usually seen from the back and walking toward or facing the center of the composition, or placed on the top of a dune, silhouetted against the sky—emphasize the illusion of recession into space."[59] Or not: the figures in Kip and Knyff's *Britannia Illustrata* are the same size in the background as in the foreground (Russell 25). Or they could add the flavor of local activity, historical and ideal. In Kip's plate of "Long Leate," for example, as Ronald Russell describes it,

> seven people appear to be playing a form of cricket or bowls; six horses are drawing a coach around a field which is only twice the length of the complete equipage and through whose minute gate it could not possibly have entered,

> while two horsemen trot around. Everything is neat and tidy, trim and organized. [. . . In these plates] Kip found a method of showing everything in the same degree of detail as if the bird was on two or three different levels simultaneously. (28)

As such, staffage could be advertisement. Tim Clayton suggests that in midcentury "the staffage of human figures shown in prints of gardens may not have exaggerated the number of visitors with their children and servants on an open day in the season. Certainly prints encouraged visitors by stressing the amenities offered by the park" (*The English Print* 166–67).

And yet there is relatively little written in art-historical circles about staffage. Presumably the anonymity as well as the ubiquity of staffage figures contributes to that general lack of interest. They were often outsourced: the Bucks, for example, in the 1720s and '30s employed Dutch engravers "skilled in the art of staffage," or later the East Anglian artist Thomas Rosse, who would then "transform" their drawings by supplying "picturesque foregrounds with figures" (Hyde 27). By the nineteenth century pattern books abounded for staffage figures to be copied into drawings and paintings.[60] So in some ways "staffage" equals "Central Casting." Things were worse if the figures in the landscape did *not* behave like Central Casting. William Gilpin criticized "BASSAN" (Jacopo Bassano or Jacopo dal Ponte, 1510–92) for his "scripture-stories": "his method was, to croud his fore-ground with cattle, well painted indeed, but wholly foreign to his subject; while you seek for his principal figures, and at length perhaps with difficulty find them in some remote corner of his picture" (6). In 1800, Goethe had a rather opposite complaint: it is not the misbehaving cattle so much as the human figures themselves. In "Etwas über Staffage landschaftlicher Darstellung," he argued that introducing historical or mythological figures into a landscape disturbs its balance; appropriate staffage might be fishermen at a river or cattle under trees.[61] Staffage figures are "decorative or stereotypical."[62]

But a closer look at staffage figures is more interesting than it might seem. Mark Girouard and Tim Clayton both comment on the ways staffage in a painting or view can index cultural tastes. Clayton notes that the figures in Kip's views "demonstrate the amenities afforded by his seats [. . .] (there is a bowling green in almost every view). Servants are few and tourists are only prominent in the royal palaces" ("Publishing Houses" 58). Jacques Rigaud's (1681–1753) early eighteenth-century views of Stowe, he says, are "almost as heavily populated as his Paris châteaux," but that most likely reflects Rigaud's "compositional requirements and Bridgeman's aspirations rather than observed reality" (58). By the late eighteenth century, observes Mark Girouard, "pictures of country houses no longer showed them thronged with people, as had been the normal way of representing them [. . .] Instead they appeared in idyllic solitude, with perhaps just a single figure—a horseman, or a ploughman with his team—or herds of grazing deer or cattle, to add a touch of life to the scene" (217). That emptying out of the country house scene is even more marked in the nineteenth-century views of gentlemen's seats. In the architectural plates from *Ackermann's Repository of Arts* (published 1809–29) the house occupies much more of the frame, the plates are colored, and rarely is seen an occupant, gardener, dog, or deer. In the image of Belmont House, Devon (1820) (figure 11), the lady at the door has almost vanished inside, while the house itself has marched up to our very feet—quite back to its old seventeenth- and early eighteenth-century habits of behaving like a Noun. And in Francis Orpen Morris's six-volume *A Series of Picturesque Views of Seats of the Noblemen and Gentlemen of Great Britain and Ireland with Descriptive and Historical Letterpress,* published 1880, the perspective of centrality, the sense of immediacy, and yet the equal sense of impenetrability characterize the highly colored and often atmospherically melodramatic prints. Though Morris confesses a certain difficulty in choosing among "the mansions of Old England [. . .] where so many claim foremost attention," the various criteria he lists have in common a quite striking preference for the isolated: one is notable for its "remarkable seclusion," another for its "present desolation"; "This stands on the very margin of a 'glassy clear translucent lake'; that overhangs the sheer cliff"; "here another [. . .] stands out from its nook in the heart of scenery of the wildest and grandest character"; "one abuts on the rock that overhangs the bend of a winding river; another stands on a wooded islet in the middle of an inland lake"; "Another is guarded by an ancient moat, and approached by the drawbridge over it [. . .] and one more rises up in solitary loneliness in its hollow in the centre of the ranges of hill." Splendid isolation, indeed. He concludes with a happy superiority: "In a word, these are the mansions of our country, each and all suited to their various situations, and each and all characteristic of the favoured country in which we have such deep cause for thankfulness that our lot has been cast."[63]

There is another aspect of staffage in the topographical views that relates to the different grammars of approach explored in this book: their narrative possibilities. In his analysis of Goethe's *Wilhelm Meisters Wanderjahre* (conceived 1790s, published 1821), Benjamin Bennett argues that, as Wilhelm is described by the narrator as "'an excellent artist who knows how to decorate watercolor landscapes with ingenious and well-drawn and developed staffage,'" his interest in Mignon is "professional": she is "the theme, the justification, the token of artistic control, in his landscapes." So we as readers, "when we appear to become passionately involved in a literary fiction, are in truth only collecting 'staffage,' making reflective judgments in the develop-

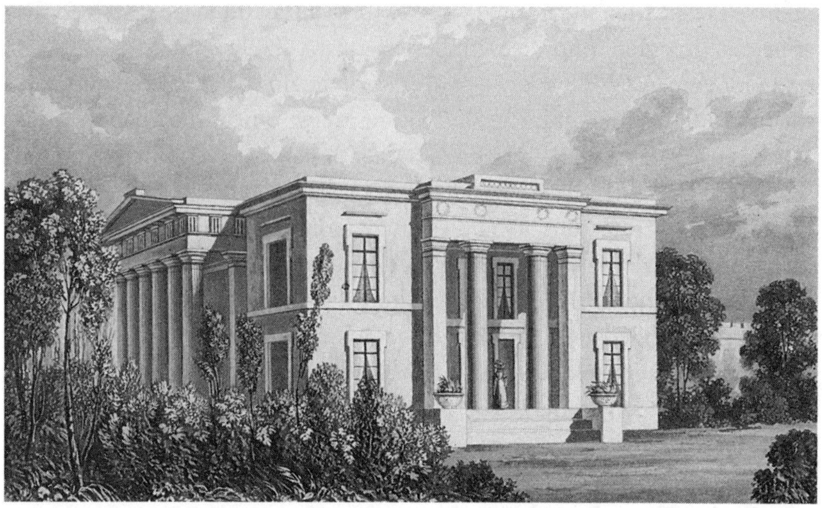

11. Anon., "Belmont House," Devon. From *Ackermann's Repository of the Arts* (1820). Photograph courtesy of The Lewis Walpole Library, Yale University.

ment of our own imaginative concerns."[64] Alison Martin explains that Goethe himself in 1816 described the draughtsman in the foreground of Ruisdael's (1629–82) *Ruined Monastery by a River*, his back to the observer, as not the "so oft mißbrauchte Staffage" [frequently misused] but "als Betrachter, als Repräsentant von Allen" [an observer representative of all observers], who is,"like the spectator, taking stock of the scene. [. . .] Goethe implied that as we beheld the painting, we implicitly projected ourselves into this figure, who acted as our entry point into the scene" (972). Staffage, well handled (well drawn and well placed), can be more than "decorative," "stereotypical," or simply mass-produced; it can be an entry into a narrative. William Gilpin observed: "We often see a landskip well adorned with a story in miniature. The *landskip* here is principal; but at the same time the figures, which tell the story, tho subordinate to the landskip, are the *principal figures*" (6–7). (In Bassan's paintings, he scoffs, the "cattle are the ornament of his pieces. To introduce a story then is absurd" [7].) We have seen how the architectural manuals began to invest the drawings of cottages with pipe-smoking tenants and romping dogs. In the topographical views, the houses are the "*principal figures*," and the "appendages" tell their stories—of coming and going, working and playing, walking and frisking, of performing prepositionally, plunging the observer as well into near, far, under, above, alongside, within, and without.

This section on topographical views opened with Humphry Repton's trade card as something that told a story: the young landscape architect at his theodolite, perhaps instructing his assistant/client, who himself is contemplating fishing, the men working at the shore of the lake below, the "prospect" not just of the current scene but of the improved future. André Rogger shows how Repton "encountered in the *Seats* the motif of a gentleman with outstretched arm describing the beauties of a property to a lady sitting beneath a parasol," of a "gentleman lean[ing] nonchalantly against a tree," of "formally dressed gentlemen with a parasol-shaded lady," of "a carriage—in which potential visitors leafing through the guide could imagine themselves the passenger—approaching a country seat" (96–97). Among other ways we enter the narratives of the *Seats*: in Angus's Longford Castle (Angus Plate X), a gentleman walks his dog toward a gate with two tiny lodges; Coghill Hall (Angus Plate XI) is a friendly place, with a gentleman and three ladies fishing in the river (it looks like mother and father are standing and the two girls have made themselves more comfortable on the grass), while another jolly lady and gentleman are strolling toward us (and the fishing party) down the approach (figure 12) and a gentleman on a horse rides toward the house, and a few docile cows graze nearby. At Armastan in Hertfordshire (Angus Plate XII), the group in the forefront take a break from work; the dogs at Broome, in Kent (the seat of Sir Henry Oxenden, Bart.) (Angus Plate XVIII) are barking and bowing and ready to frisk. (Dogs in general have a grand time in topographical views.[65])

We have seen Repton manipulate the figures in the before and after slides of the approach to Glemham Hall in terms of the carriage full of visitors (plates III, IV). Given all we now know about approaches, we can see how the novelistic conversations occurring during an approach (John Thorpe exaggerating the thrills of Blaise; Henry Tilney exaggerating the mysteries of Northanger; Elizabeth Bennet thinking in Whatelyan rhythms toward Pemberley) are part of the "new combinations" prompted *by* the approach. But Repton in his Red Books does even more for narrative theory. As Rogger argues about Repton's innovations to the *Seats* formats of text-and-image: "Repton combined two voices that had until then been kept apart: his ideas as a garden designer were interwoven with the possible reflections and judgement of future visitors to the property, shaping a compelling alliance that may well have contributed to the Red Books' appeal" (91). Repton says in the Red Book for High Legh in Cheshire (1791), for example:

> By judicious management of the plantation it will not I hope be difficult to cheat a stranger into this description of the Place—viz. 'The turnpike road passes thro' the park and for some distance makes part of the Approach to the house', this will surely be a more favorable description than that which every one must now give—viz. 'The High-Road goes all the way along side of the park; and close by the house.'[66]

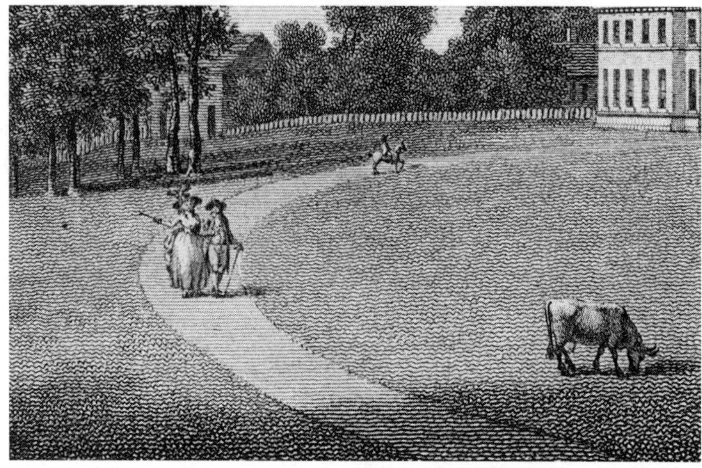

12. N. J. Dall, "Coghill Hall," Yorkshire. Engraved by William Angus. From *Seats of Nobility and Gentry* (1787) (detail). Photograph courtesy of The Lewis Walpole Library, Yale University.

I will expand on this in chapter 5, but for now I want to point out that the visitor, like the viewer, is given a choice of narrative in the choice of approaches; as we have been invited to enter the views of seats and act as semi-omniscient narrator—or perhaps free indirect discourser—for the stories of their staffage (*is one of those women his wife? did she slip or fall off that chair? who's a good boy, then?*), so our own discourse becomes a palimpsest onto Repton's views. Here, our current narrative is the straight line of the high road, with a linearity and predictability parallel to the avenue. With a little "judicious management" of our expectations, the narrative acquires a little more variety, a little something more for the possessive individual, whether owner or visitor: the approach appropriates some of the road to itself. It's not that we take the road less traveled; it's that we take the road of *story*: the Approach.

A Bridge to the next part: "A Village on, or across the River of *Thames*"

> *LONDON-BRIDGE* [. . .] may properly be called a Village on, or across the River of *Thames*; its Number of Houses and Trade far exceeding many Corporations in *England*.
>
> Roger Griffiths, *A Description of the River Thames, &c.* (1758)

For centuries London Bridge was the Approach to London from the south, and by definition a prepositional structure for travel *across* the river.[67] Until

1750, with the building of Westminster Bridge, every traveler to London from the south had to cross the Thames by this arched stone bridge or else by boat.[68] Every important foreign visitor entered London this way (and usually wrote about it); it was the route of every returning monarch, including both Charleses (not to mention Neptune). It was the site of pageants and battles and frost fairs. But London Bridge was also, from the moment master mason Peter de Colechurch built his own house upon it in 1176, a street of houses—a village *on* the river.[69] It became a distinct neighborhood, full of merchants' mansions, hosiers' shops, and the House of Many Windows. It was considered a wonder of the world, greater than the Ponte Vecchio, the Rialto, or the Pont au Change, with "such Massy Walls, such Towers [. . .], such Posts" that Neptune himself "shook his Trident, and astonish'd said; / Let the whole Earth now all the Wonders count, / this Bridge of Wonders is the Paramount."[70]

But between 1757 and 1762 London Bridge was completely destroyed, replaced by a newer, cleaner, houseless, shopless, villageless bridge—a briskly functional means of transport and transition. The preposition of position, "on," was run over by the preposition of direction, "across," after centuries of almost mythological status. Why? I suggest it was a matter of approach. At the same time that what we might call an earlier "gothic" or "picturesque" typography was regularized into Palladian symmetry—common nouns decapitalized, italics uprighted, long *ſ* furled (the subject of chapter 3)—so the gothic, picturesque old bridge was made into something more like an avenue, straight and smooth and unencumbered. But just as the modernized, uniform page allowed *things in-between* more room to see and be seen, and the prepositional park gate lodge announced a different way of approaching the house, so the new bridge, along with its new partner Westminster Bridge, emphasized the *approaches to* the city.

As by definition a structure "across," the bridge served its purpose royally. On 12 November 1501 Catherine of Aragon, bride of Arthur, Prince of Wales, the eldest son of Henry VII, was welcomed at the bridge by an elaborate pageant; she was then "conveied through Southwerk streight over London Bridge, and soo thorough the Bruge strete to Greschurch strete" (qtd. in Home 145, 146). Emperor Charles V entered London across a pageanted bridge with Henry VIII in March 1522. On 29 May 1660 Charles II reached London (on his birthday), and the mayor and aldermen rode across the bridge—"richly adorned for the joyous occasion with tapestries and silk" (Home 229) to greet him in St. George's Fields, where they all refreshed themselves, and then processed back across the bridge to Whitehall.

But in its glory days, London Bridge was celebrated more for its "on-ness" than its "across-ness." John Lyly, in *Euphues and his England* (1578), declares it one of London's greatest "showes":

> among al the straung and beautifull showes me thinketh there is none so notable, as the Bridge which crosseth the Theams, which is in manner of a continuall streete, well replenyshed with large and stately houses on both sides, and situate upoon twentie Arches whereof each one is made of excellent free stone squared. (qtd. in Home 153)

In 1592 Jacob Rathgeb, traveling as the private secretary of Frederick, Duke of Würtemburg, saw as his first glimpse of London "a beautiful long bridge, with quite splendid, handsome and well-built houses, which are occupied by merchants of consequence."[71] In 1598 a German traveler, Paul Hentzner, was impressed by the "wonderful work" of the "bridge of stone [. . .] covered on each side with houses, so disposed as to have the appearance of a continued street, not at all of a bridge."[72] John Norden's colorfully drawn "View of London Bridge from East to West" (1597) describes in an insert: "The howses are on either side so artifically combyned / As the bridge seemeth not only a contynuall strete / But men walke as under a ferme vaute or lofte." He declares that he is publishing "this rude Conterfeite" so that the fame of the bridge "is spred throwgh manie nations So by this picture / It may appear to such as haue heard of it and not reallye / Beheld it."[73]

John Stow tells the bridge's spatial story in *The Survey of London* (1598):

> King Iohn gaue certaine voide places in London to builde vpon, the profites thereof to remaine towardes the charges of building and repayring of the same bridge: a Mason being maister workeman of the bridge, builded from the foundation, the Chaple on London bridge, of his owne propererpences. [. . .] After that example sundry houses were thereupon shortly after erected.[74]

Stow describes the bridge overall as "a worke very rare, hauing with the drawe bridge, 20. Arches made of square stone, of height 60. foote, compact and joyned together with vaultes and sellers: vpon both sides bee houses builded, so that it seemeth rather a continuall streete than a bridge" (23). Its houses had between three and six stories. Various great houses—Nonesuch House, the House of Many Windows, the Chapel of St. Thomas à Becket, and assorted merchants' houses—were interspersed with smaller dwellings and warehouses and as many as 138 shops, with more houses built over them. The ornate Nonesuch House, built in 1577, was made entirely of wood, assembled in Flanders, and transported up the Thames to be erected upon the bridge. The chapel, in the center of the bridge, was

> a beautiful Gothic structure [. . .] paved with black and white marble. [. . .] Clusters of small pillars arose at equal distances on the sides, and, bending over the roof, met in the centre of the arch, where they were bound together by large flowers cut in the same stone; between these pillars were the windows, which were arched, and afforded a view of the Thames on each side.[75]

The larger houses stretched over the edges of the bridge and across it, their upper stories bolted together by several "lofty arches, which were designed to prevent the houses from giving way; [. . .] and being covered with laths and plaister, appeared as if built with stone" (*Curiosities* 76). In 1632 Nehemiah Wallington recorded the names and trades of bridge houses burned in a fire, including haberdashers, hosiers, milliners, glovers, mercers, linen and woolen drapers, grocers, shoemakers, and "Stiller of Strong Waters."[76] There were no inns, apart from the famous Bear at the Southwark Bridge-foot and the Three Neats' Tongues, but plenty of stationers and booksellers.[77]

The bridge-as-village-street is captured in a true story in William Henry Pyne's *Wine and Walnuts* (1823). The antiquarian "Ephraim Hardcastle" records "Crispin Tucker's" reminiscences to Jonathan Swift:

> You must know, reverend sir, that one day, about twelve years ago [April 1722], the drawbridge arch wanted some repairs. It was settled that the bridge should be shut Saturday and Sunday, and the workmen were let in; Saturday was shut up shop; our old street was silent, as I've heard my father say it was in the great plague of sixty-five. But, as we had no other plagues but a fine day and nothing to keep us out of mischief, we agreed to get drunk, and had our tables out in the highway, and kept it up gloriously till Sunday morn.[78]

The year of this bridge party was the year the Lord Mayor attempted to regulate traffic by ordering all vehicles to "keep to the left." The street was notoriously narrow—its width did not exceed twenty feet—barely wide enough for two coaches to pass, and little or no room for foot passengers. Throughout the centuries, three open spaces were kept "that People passing along may take a View of the River East and West, and may also step out of the Way of Carts and Coaches."[79] (The bridge had a number of other notable residents worth mentioning. Jacob Rathgeb was struck by the "thirty-four heads of persons of distinction" stuck on pikes on the Bridge Tower [9]. Paul Hentzner also noticed the tower, "on whose top the heads of such as have been executed for high treason, are placed upon iron spikes. We counted above 30" [5]. See figure 13.)

The bridge suffered a number of fires and was frequently rebuilt. After the Great Fire of 1666, says John Strype in his 1720 edition of Stow, it became once again "the most stately Bridge in the whole World."[80] Until the mid-eighteenth century, that was historically typical praise. In 1645 the new buildings at the north end of the bridge replacing those lost in the fire of 1632–33 were described by Strype as "very substantial and beautiful [. . .] And over the Houses were stately Platforms, with Rails and Ballasters very commodious, and pleasant for walking, and enjoying so fine a Prospect up and down the River; and some had pretty little Gardens with Arbors" (Stow 1720, 1:56–57). (The *Antiquities of London* in 1722 repeated Strype's description and evaluation almost verbatim.) The *New and Compleat Survey of London* (1742) pronounced the new buildings of 1685 additions of "Beauty and Magnificence to this noble Structure" (142). By this time all the medieval houses were gone, apart from the microvillage clustered at the Southwark foot of the bridge (figure 13), and in 1745 George Dance added Palladian fronts to the rebuilt houses on the north end, called the Piazza and much admired. The centuries-old pattern of medieval infilling had been overtaken by Georgian order, "new built in a regular and uniform manner" (*New and Compleat Survey* 143).

But it may be that a front, however Palladian, is sometimes just a front. William Hogarth—a satirist rather than eulogist, a historian of the darker side—gives a glimpse of a dilapidated version of the bridge though a window in the miserly merchant's house of *Marriage à la Mode* (1743–45). Inside, the panes of glass are broken and the starving dog is definitely not a happy *Seats*-staffage dog. London Bridge is falling down, and appears peripheral. Hogarth records the physical dangers and aesthetic drawbacks that finally generated the architectural and cultural reassessment of the bridge. On 25 June 1756 an Act of Parliament authorized exactly that: the removal of all the houses and the widening of the bridge. The committee formed to examine the state of the bridge concluded: "[We are] humbly of opinion that the houses upon London Bridge are a public nuisance, long felt, and universally censured and complained of" (qtd. in Home 265). Though the published descriptions of the bridge before 1750 had neither censured nor complained, for the rest of the century the rhetoric vociferously did both. In 1756 *English Architecture; or, The Publick Buildings of London and Westminster* declared that the houses of London Bridge, which had been "the pride of the time wherein they were raised," were now in such "ruinous condition" that it was "necessary to take a great part of them down; and the bridge has appeared encumbered, not ornamented by them."[81] In 1767 the *Companion to Every Place of Curiosity and Entertainment* cited its hazards:

> The narrowness of the passage over this bridge having occasioned the loss of many lives, from the number of carriages passing and repassing, and the strait-

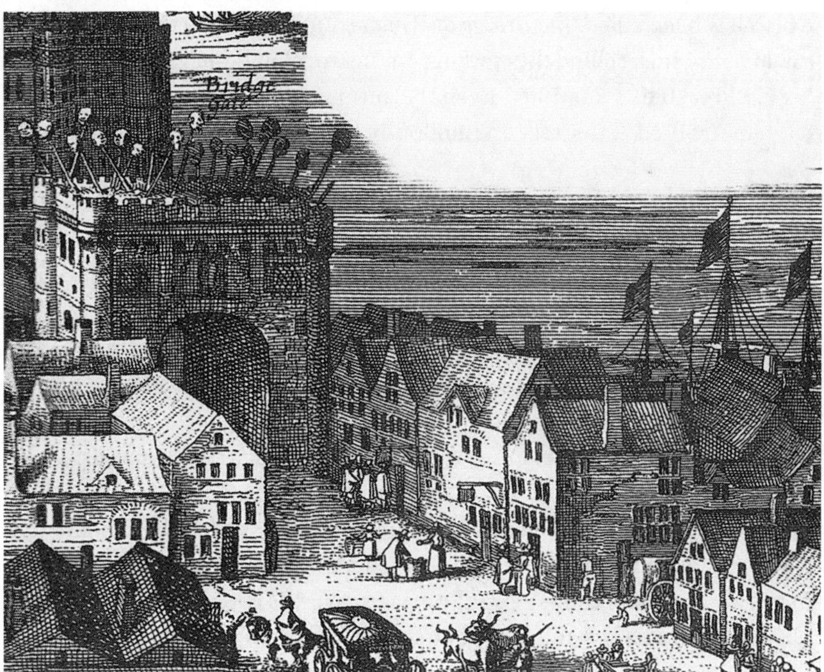

13. Claes Janszoon Visscher, *Panorama of London* (1616) (detail).

> ness of the arches, with the enormous size of the sterlings, having also occasioned many fatal accidents, there passed two acts of parliament in 1756, for removing all these obstacles [. . .] and accordingly the houses, with a great part of the bridge, were demolished.[82]

The invective gets darker as the decades roll on. In 1776 Walter Harrison, in *A New and Universal History, Description and Survey* [. . .] *of London*, tells us that "the view from the water and the quays" of the outside of the bridge was

> exceedingly disagreeable. Nineteen disproportioned arches, with sterlings increasing to an amazing size, by frequent repairs, supported the street above. [. . .] The back part of the houses next the Thames had neither uniformity nor beauty; the line being broke by a great number of closets that projected from the buildings, and hung over the sterlings. This deformity was greatly increased by the houses extending a considerable distance over the sides of the bridge, and some of them projecting farther over it than others.[83]

In 1786 *The Curiosities of London and Westminster*, anxious to "prevent posterity from being deceived by the pompous eulogiums bestowed on this bridge, which has been stiled *The Bridge of Wonders*," repeats the 1767 *Companion*'s catalogue of sins, calling the sterlings "monstrous" and the view of the whole "as disagreeable as possible." Even the antiquarian Thomas Pennant (1726–98) remembered "the street on London-bridge" as

> narrow, darksome, and dangerous to passengers from the multitude of carriages: frequent arches of strong timber crossed the street, from the tops of the houses, to keep them together, and from falling into the river. Nothing but use could preserve the rest of the inmates, who soon grew deaf to the noise of the falling waters, the clamours of the watermen, or the frequent shrieks of drowning wretches. Most of the houses were tenanted by pin or needle makers.[84]

Not until the nineteenth century would London Bridge regain any luster, and then only in nostalgia.[85]

Westminster Bridge, opened in 1750, set out the architectural alternative. It was designed by the Swiss engineer Charles Labelye, with fourteen symmetrical arches and room for four carriages to cross abreast. *English Architecture* rhapsodized (1756): "[It] is at once so massy, and so noble, that it attracts the eye equally, and demands the applause. Perhaps it is not too much to say, that it is the finest bridge in the world" (64). More like an "avenue," in what J. C. Loudon called the "geometrical style" of laying out grounds, Westminster Bridge "advances directly in front of the house"[86]—or rather, the city. It revealed itself immediately as an "*Entrance or Way lying open to a Place,*" the operative word being "open."[87]

London Bridge was therefore "improved" in the Westminster mold. The hanging signs were removed from the last shops in 1761, and the last house was pulled down in 1762. The bridge was widened, a footway was added, and some of the arches were consolidated. Of the new London Bridge, the *Curiosities of London and Westminster* announced triumphantly:

> [A]ll those deformities are now removed. Instead of a narrow street, there is a passage for carriages of 31 feet broad, with handsome raised pavements of stone on each side, seven feet broad, for foot passengers, and instead of houses projecting over the river, the sides are secured and adorned by an elegant balustrade.—It is also guarded at night by a number of watchmen, and handsomely lighted with a great number of lamps. (79)

Not only lamps appeared, but "Prospects": "[The new bridge] has a grand appearance; and affords the passengers on it a delightful prospect of shipping, &c. below it, and an extensive view of buildings both above and below"

(*Companion* 1767, 33). The prepositional view was no longer dominated by the village "on" but by the "extensive" views "above" and "below" and by the readier means "across." What would normally have attracted the 1760s interest in the gothic and picturesque was instead cleared away so that something else could be seen. In this case, the new straight approach to London that was London Bridge revealed how much lay *in between* the Great Stone Gate and the Cityitself. Scraping off the bridge brought the approach into view.

In that massive midcentury architectural clearance on the bridgescape of the city we find a curious analogy with the massive midcentury typographic clearance on the landscape of the page, the subject of the next chapter. "Ephraim Hardcastle" had described the bridge as a "tolerable specimen of the appearance of old London": "Here stands one [house] that aims to be a palace, and next it another that professes to be a hovel; here a giant, and there a dwarf; here slender, and there broad; all most admirably different in their faces, as well as in their height and bulk" (*Wine and Walnuts* 2:74–75). Mr. Hardcastle might as well be describing pre-mid-eighteenth-century typography. In his *General History of Printing* (1729), Samuel Palmer lists a number of "peculiar[ities]" of early printing, such as outsized folios, mixed typefaces, arbitrary orthography, and pages with no pageherds (running titles, catchwords, page numbers, paragraphs). Words were "printed so close to one another, that it was difficult and tedious even to those who were us'd to MSS"[88]—the textual version of Fanny Price's visit to the Portsmouth house. Add to that the fondness for capitalized common Nouns, italicized *Place Names*, and the long *ſ*, and we have palaces and hovels, giants and dwarfs, faces and forms slender and broad, crowded together in a typographical space waiting to be cleared, to make new views, new possibilities, visible.

CHAPTER 3

The Topographical Page

> [W]ithin the foot of the said letter L, the beautiful rising sun peers at dawn, and there remains during most part of the day, instilling sweetness.
>
> Geofroy Tory, *Champ Fleury* (1529)

> Written characters have, in themselves, no sort of virtue, nor the least influence on the mind of man; and the utmost extent of their artificial power can reach no farther, than that of exciting ideas of sounds, which belong to spoken words.
>
> Thomas Sheridan, *A Discourse* [. . .] *on Elocution* (1759)

> An authour's language, Sir, is a characteristical part of his composition, and is also characteristical of the age in which he writes. Besides, Sir, when the language is changed we are not sure that the sense is the same.
>
> Samuel Johnson, Boswell's *Life of Johnson* (1791)

The three epigraphs above capture a debate across time and of space about the power and relevance of the printed page in relation to its content. Printers, of course—at least the innovators and artisanal among them—have always cared.[1] Geofroy Tory (1480–1533), master French designer and typographer, argued that printed letters ought to "be conscious in themselves [. . .] of the art of architecture," and assigns them positions in the house of print (figure 14): *A* is the gable of the house; *H* is its body; *K*, "because of its joint, signifies stairs to ascend in a straight line"; *S* gives us a spiral stair; *I* is a "long straight gallery"; and the *L* is the hall. Anyone who sees in the letter *L* the rising sun distilling sweetness and "receiv[ing] in its face the wind from the north, which is pure and clean & brisk, by reason of the short front within [its] foot," does not need me to point out his happy place in the argument.[2] Thomas Sheridan (1719–88), Irish actor and major proponent of the elocution

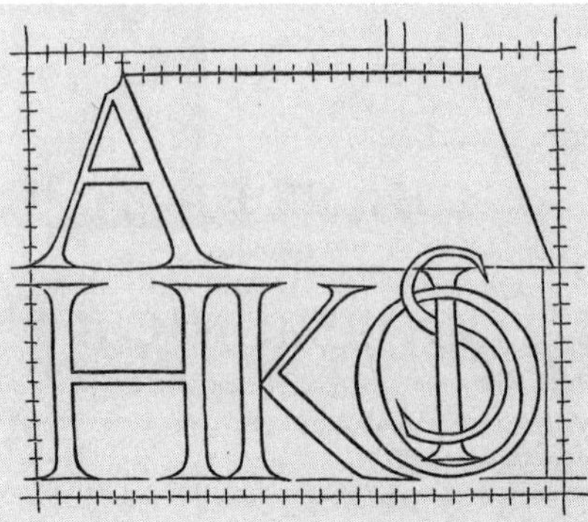

14. Geofroy Tory, house of letters (detail of figure 15). From *Champ Fleury* (1529). Courtesy the Grolier Club of New York. Photograph: Special Collections, University of Virginia, Charlottesville (NK 3615. T62 1927).

movement in England in the eighteenth century, made his living by speaking and acting, through sound and gesture. Print? *Phphphphphht.* He waves it away. (Although naturally he *published* his *Course of Lectures on Elocution and the English Language.*[3]) And Samuel Johnson (1709–84) was criticizing Lord Hailes "for having modernised the language of the ever-memorable John Hales of Eton, in an edition which his Lordship published of that writer's works."[4] As Margaret Doody says of eighteenth-century poets, no one ever "paid more attention to the sound of their words, or their appearance on the page in relation to each other."[5] She argues that to modernize the Augustan poets, to "correct" spelling, expand contractions, and fill in elisions, indeed changes the "authour's language."[6] (Similar arguments have clustered around Shakespeare at least since 1911.[7]) But while a goodly number of critics have recently demonstrated that the minutiae of formatting and punctuation can be as interpretively important for the eighteenth-century novel as they always have been for poetry, this chapter will argue that the ways the *topography* of the page changed over the period—the shape of letters, the contours of line, the patterns of punctuation—were a microcosmic, indeed mimetic, version of the changes in perspective, in the concept of approach, developed through reshaped landscapes. As the architectural approach was designed to wind "through the most interesting part of the grounds" and to "form new combinations on every movement of the spectator,"[8] so burrowing into the historical interstices of word and line and page unearths new combinations of meaning for both literary and nonliterary texts.

The textual topography of the eighteenth-century page (what we might call the endo- or hypotextual complement to Gérard Genette's paratexts) experienced its own relandscaping that was a sort of mirrored obverse of the picturesque movement.[9] That is, where the sweeping lawns and reflecting lakes of Capability Brown had irritated the likes of Gilpin, Knight, and Price into the landscape activism of the picturesque, with its sharp contrasts, broken angles, and "fantastic roots of trees,"[10] so the thickly textured page of the seventeenth and eighteenth centuries, with its capitalized common Nouns, long *ſ*, and italicized *Names* and *Places*, was rather suddenly scraped smooth and spaciously reordered. The Noun was decapitated, the internal *ſ* made to curl into *s*, and *italics* told to straighten up. But that smooth, uniform text, I argue, produced its own underground picturesque.[11] With the dominant Noun no longer looming over the other words in a sentence and the self-dramatizing italics effaced, the things *in between* could be more visible—as, for example, punctuation and prepositions.

Chapter 4 will look at how the linguistic engineering by the energized grammarians of the later eighteenth century brought the "lesser" parts of speech into more prominence (think "fantastic roots of trees"), and how the literature experimented with and codified new prepositional phrasings, new syntactical patterns. This chapter will survey the changing contours of typography, from fonts to formatting to punctuation, and pick out their root systems within literary passages across the century. D. F. McKenzie feared that the eighteenth-century typographic revolution had lost for modernity "the hand-held theatre of the book." "Modern books," he reproves, "are notorious for smoothing the text and dull our sensitivity to space as an instrument of order."[12] But by excavating the in-betweennesses of the reordered "modern" page, we can discover the power of a different spatial—"picturesque"—order, a different avenue of approach toward narrative pattern and meaning. Taking a historicized, three-dimensional approach to the page that lies *beneath* the content dramatizes how changing typographical forms can reshape the possibilities for narrative structures.

The typographical landscape

One common objection to this approach is the assumption that seventeenth- and eighteenth-century authors had little or no control over or interest in the printed appearance of their text, that the (frequently inept or inconsistent) compositors were entirely in charge. Joseph Moxon had outlined the compositor's power in *Mechanick Exercises* in 1683: "As he *Sets* on, he considers how to *Point* his Work, viz. When to *Set* , where ; where . where to make ( ) where [ ] ? ! and when a *Break* [. . .] When he meets with proper Names of Persons or Places he *Sets* them in *Italick* [. . .] and *Sets* the first *Letter* with a *Capital*, or as the Person or Place he finds the purpose of the Author to dignifie, all *Capitals*" (215–16). But this turns out to be something of a literary myth.[13] Various eighteenth- and nineteenth-century printers offer some suggestive counterexamples.[14] Moxon himself had an "Advertisement to Authors," for that "curious" author who will not trust his pointing to the compositor: "*Therefore it behoves an Author to examine his* Copy *very well e'er he deliver it to the* Printer, *and to Point it, and mark it so as the* Compositor *may know what Words to* Set *in* Italick, English, Capitals, &c." (250). John Smith, in his wonderful *Printer's Grammar* (1755), reiterates several times that in matters of punctuation, capitalization, and italics compositors "ought to submit to the method, or even humour, of Authors, and authorized Correctors, rather than give them room to exclaim about spoiling the sense of the subject, because the Points are not put *Their* right way."[15] (It is worth noting that the *Printer's Grammar* was printed by Samuel Richardson, from motives of "enlightened self-interest"; as Richardson wrote to the lawyer William Blackstone in February 1756: "[I]t is far more eligible to deal with those who know something of the Business."[16]) Smith warmly approves of "Gentlemen who have regard to make the reading of their Works consonant with their own delivery, point their Copy accordingly, and abide thereby, with strictness," although he acknowledges that such careful ownership is not universal: "[W]ere it done by every Writer, Compositors would sing, *Jubile!*" (88). Still, they have their chance. The perfectionist printer John Baskerville, in his edition of Congreve's plays, commiserates with Pierre Bayle, who, "in his Preface to the first Edition of his Dictionary, speaks of the Vexation of ineffectual Supervising the Press, in Terms so feeling, that they move Compassion in his Reader; and concludes the Paragraph touching it, in these Words, '*Je l'oublie autant que Je puis, animus meminisse horret*' [I forget it as much as I am able, my soul shudders to remember]."[17] C. F. Partington offers an even more psychologically resonant argument for authorial control in *The Printer's Guide* (1825): "It is a practice, too common with some authors, of keeping their proof-sheets too long in their hands" because the "pleasure arising from beholding, as it were, the 'form and texture' of one's thoughts, is a sensation easier felt than described."[18] I expect every author recognizes the pleasure of beholding the form and texture of one's thoughts in that first set of page proofs. So we should not underestimate the extent to which authors *could* and *might* have influenced the "form and texture" of their texts. I suppose we could call this the "copyediting fallacy," but then, argument-from-design has always been a part of literary criticism, the basis for close reading: sufficiently consistent and formally interpretable typographical patterns in a text can be as important as syntactical or visual patterns in prose as well as in poetry. The "accidental" is quite frequently, in fact, "substantive."[19]

Besides extrapolating from the authorial pleasure of beholding the form and texture of one's thoughts, there are a number of authors for whom we have direct evidence of textual micromanaging. Laurence Sterne is the most immediately obvious eighteenth-century example: not only was it a matter of black and blank and marbled pages, of hyperactive dashes and asterisks; he also wanted short lines and a large Caslon font in a tight duodecimo, and his very catchwords were part of his narrative design. Each page of *Tristram Shandy* is, as one critic puts it, a "'co-existential' verbo-visual whole."[20] McKenzie, David Foxon, and Richard Wendorf have demonstrated the hands-on attention of Congreve, Pope, Gray, and Collins to the appearance of their text. Master printer and master novelist Samuel Richardson pioneered innovations in ornament and punctuation, and bent assiduously over his proof sheets and revisions, as M. B. Parkes, Janine Barchas, Thomas Keymer, Christopher Flint, and others have shown.[21]

None of this is new to the eighteenth century, or to England, of course. Italic was invented in Italy to imitate manuscript hand. Geofroy Tory structured not only his letters but, in one instance, his paragraphs in an architectural form that almost anticipates a George Herbert poem (figure 15).[22]

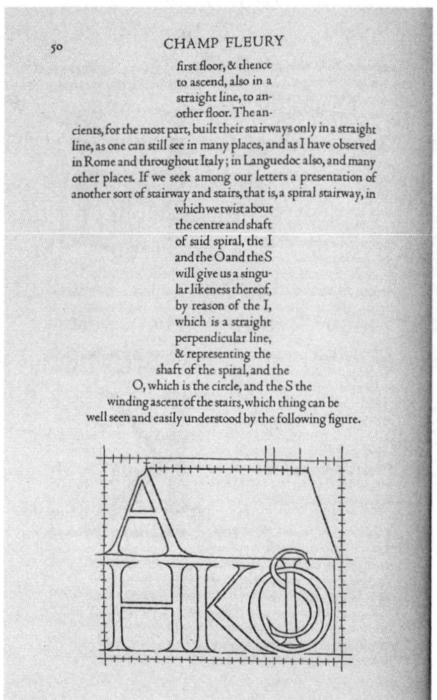

50 CHAMP FLEURY

first floor, & thence
to ascend, also in a
straight line, to an-
other floor. The an-
cients, for the most part, built their stairways only in a straight
line, as one can still see in many places, and as I have observed
in Rome and throughout Italy; in Languedoc also, and many
other places. If we seek among our letters a presentation of
another sort of stairway and stairs, that is, a spiral stairway, in
which we twist about
the centre and shaft
of said spiral, the I
and the O and the S
will give us a singu-
lar likeness thereof,
by reason of the I,
which is a straight
perpendicular line,
& representing the
shaft of the spiral, and the
O, which is the circle, and the S the
winding ascent of the stairs, which thing can be
well seen and easily understood by the following figure.

15. Geofroy Tory, stairway of words and house of letters, from *Champ Fleury* (1529). Courtesy the Grolier Club of New York. Photograph: Special Collections, University of Virginia, Charlottesville, VA (NK 3615. T62 1927).

The architecture not just of the page but also of the very letter (as Tory argues and as the fonts designed by Claude Garamond, William Caslon, John Baskerville, and Giambattista Bodoni display) has always carried interpretive possibilities for content, cultural as well as authorial.[23] Janine Barchas has elegantly supplied a richer understanding of Swift's *Description of a City Shower* (1710) by reading its last regurgitating triplet within its original textual context, amid the mob of frenetic advertisements in the original half-sheet of *Tatler* No. 238.[24] Printing, as much as landscaping and architecture and the novel, "involves the exact placing of forms in space" (McKenzie 96). The ways that poetry carves the space on a page is as obviously luxurious as the pinched pages of a novel are economical.[25] But as familiar as this may be to bibliographers, textual editors, early modern scholars, poets, and novelists, the idea of fonts, spacing, punctuation, and archaic conventions having any significance beyond the general fussiness of manuals-of-style rules is not exactly self-evident to a vast and different swath of modern students and editors. So, rather like Alice, I would like to plunge down the rabbit hole of the eighteenth-century page, into the peculiar biographies and mechanics of spacing, typeface, capitals and italics, catchwords, and punctuation, to trace their changing cultural negotiations with space and contour and motion. Although each of these may most often be printers' rather than authors' provinces—matters of house style—each (even catchwords) can also be shown in some instances to be author-managed. And even when the product of author-editor-printer relationships *is* simply house style, the formatting provides contemporary flavor and texture: this work *looked like this*; it felt like *this* to read it.[26] As John Grice, a printer of our own time, has said of his exquisite book *Punctuation: A Printer's Study* (2001), "I wished to bring forward to others the worth of the text being read as a whole. [. . .] Who would choose to read of punctuation? If made a delight perhaps."[27] I hope here to join the ranks of those who have made the mechanics of print and punctuation a delight. My contribution will be to show how the changes of the eighteenth-century page enact—even dramatize—the events on the surface of the English visual world and in the grammatical expressions of it. I want to make reading the eighteenth-century literary page a consciously three-dimensional experience.

The letters on the page

In the beginning was the page—what we might call the hand-held landscape of the book, to paraphrase McKenzie. From the paper to the positioning of the letters and the spacings of the lines, for the printers and compositors each page is a separate landscape, a drama in miniature.[28] (And as it was an explicit convention in eighteenth-century British printing that punctuation marks other than the comma and period "not only admit, but require, to be separated from the matter" [Smith, *PG* 101], so all my quotations from primary texts from here on will include any "thin Space" between word and point, to demonstrate contemporary textual ventilation—the in-betweenness in the landscape.) "A good *Compositer*," says Moxon, "is ambitious as well to make the meaning of his *Author* intelligent to the *Reader*, as to make his Work shew graceful to the Eye, and pleasant in Reading" (Moxon 211). There is a code of neatness, propriety, and good behavior that governs each page, but codes of print propriety, like tastes in fashion, architecture, landscape, and language, are historical productions. Mark Bland argues that in the very transition from manuscript to print, "space—the physical blanks of type—introduced a precise and ordered structure where previously, with manuscripts, flexibility and sinuous variation had been a necessity."[29] From the early eighteenth-century point of view, the printed page of the early fifteenth century looked like an impenetrable thicket. In his *General History of Printing* (1729), Samuel Palmer lists eighteen properties "peculiar" to early printing, among them size (generally larger folios); pages "without running-title, direction-word, number of pages, or divisions into paragraphs" (flocks without pageherds, as I suggested in the last chapter); typeface that was a mixture of Gothic and Secretary (to imitate manuscript); arbitrary orthography; frequent abbreviations; no use of capital letters to begin sentences or to designate names; no publishing imprints; unidentified quotations; "no intermixture of *Roman* and *Italick*"; a general sense of crowdedness and obscurity, with words "printed so close to one another, that it was difficult and tedious even to those who were us'd to MSS"; and sentences "distinguish'd by no other points than the double and single one, *i. e.* the *colon* and *full stop.*"[30] Partington adds also the "inequality and thickness of the types" (198). Thus, an early seventeenth-century page could present itself like this (figure 16):[31]

CAP. 3, § 4 : Of woords without number :

¶ **1** *Of a Prepositio n.*

And hetherto of woords with number and case. Woords without number and case, ar Preposition, and Adverb.

Prepositions in Apposition are these ; **aboov, about, after, against, amid** or **amids, among** or **amongst, anent, at before, behinde, beside** or **besides, behether, beyond,**
† of the **betweene** or **betixt, †benede, by, concerning, for, from, far-from, in, into,**
Saxon **mauger, nig** or **nig-to, of, on or upon, on this side, on that side, to** or **unto,**
benedden. **touching, toward or towards, through, thorow, thorow-out (or rather throog, thoorrow, thoorrow-out**, as the sound and original reqire vide TT in Incide) **under, until, with, within, without.**

And all these ar set before the Rect cases of Nouns, and the obliqe of Pronouns : as **by a man, without mee.**

*concerning and touching ar forc't to supplie the roome of the forgotten woord anent.

(a) For To, is soomtime used A, especially before Verbals : as I goe a fishing, a hunting, a field.

16. Charles Butler, *The English Grammar* (1633). A seventeenth-century page. Author's transcription.

The implication was that the eighteenth-century printed page behaved like a model of spacious, nuanced, and signposted order. (That eighteenth-century page itself would be overhauled over the course of its century, scraped and leveled and regularized, as the next sections will show.)

Inside the page, the letters themselves can lead a dramatic life. James Watson closes his 1713 *Art of Printing* with a 112-line poem in which God is the Printer and we live the life of those letters:

> G*REAT Blest* MASTER PRINTER, *Come*
> *Into thy* Composing-Room :
> *Wipe away our foul Offences* ;
> *Make, O make our Souls and Senses,*
> *The* Upper *and the* Lower Cases ;
> *And thy large* Alphabet *of* Graces
> *The* Letter, *which being ever fit,*
> *O haste thou to Distribute it* :
> *For there is (I make Account)*
> *No* Imperfection *in the* Fount.
> *If any* Letters Face *be* foul,
> *O* wash *it, ere it touch the Soul* ;
> *Contrition be the* Brush ; *the* Lye,
> *Tears from a Penitential Eye.* (62)[32]

In the Great Composing Room of Life the "accidentals" of printing are our own particularities; the page-of-life cliché takes on a different sort of textual precision and ontological relevance here. God is the COMPOSITOR who does not need a CORRECTOR; the entire printing apparatus is allegorically relocated (the nut and spindle stand for gentleness; the platten affliction; the girts the gift of continence; and so on). We have Majusculed Souls and minusculed senses; if we can be properly cleaned and cut and spaced, we can be read by the world; "*And when this* White-Paper'*s done, / Work a* Reiteration" (64).

Even within the printing manuals themselves we find lettered drama. Kerned letters, for example (which have "part of their Face hang[ing] over" the edge of the type block [Smith, *PG* 33]), face the peril of having "their Beaks broke,"

> especially the Roman f, when it stands at the end of a line, where it is exposed to other accidents, besides those from the lie-brush : but in still more danger are Kerned letters of the Italic ; especially *d ſ l*, when they stand, with their

> Beaks unguarded, at the end of lines ; and at the beginning of lines, *f g j ſ y* run as great a hazard. (34)[33]

Smith's letters live in the Lilliputian version of Watson's Brobdingnag: the lye-brush that threatens the letter *ſ* can bring a penitential tear to the human eye; their beaks unguarded may be broken, and "*f* and *ſ* in particular are most liable to suffer" (34). Our heart's white paper is "*Fit only for the worst* Impression"; if by any chance one of us Letters "batter'd *is, / Being come unto thy View,* / Take it out, put in a new" (Watson 64).

A letter's room in its line can be determined by the genre in which it is thrown. "In Works of Poetry, it will recompense a Compositor's trouble to collect and to pick as many thick Spaces as he can, that he may space his Matter all alike, and not be interrupted by Spaces that are too thin" (Smith, *PG* 115). For work that is "spaced close," such as novels and architectural treatises, it "will be equally convenient to throw out thick Spaces" (116.) Too many spaces used to justify a line—"wide *Whites*"—are, says Moxon, "(in way of Scandal) call'd *Pidgeon-holes*, and are by none accounted good Workmanship" (207). In fact, Smith gives a typographical context for the many-claused sentences of eighteenth-century prose: "where an Author is too sententious, and makes several short periods in one Paragraph," the "many Blanks of m-quadrats will be contemptuously called *Pigeon-holes* ; which, and other such trifles, often betray a Compositor's judgment, who may be a good workman else" (*PG* 113). A single printed page can be read as a dramatic spatial production, an ontology unto itself.

i. fonts

The history of type design is itself a historical drama, and fonts have their own ontologies. Typographical historians know well the ferocious aesthetic battles over the tiny variations in letter shapes; now, "thanks to technology and the gadgets we use," says Sarah Hyndman (a "typography consultant") in *Why Fonts Matter* (2016), "more people than ever before are aware of them—from gateway fonts like Comic Sans to the superstar typefaces like Helvetica and Gotham."[34] She analyzes the emotional and psychological responses to different kinds of fonts and tracks their history in advertising, business, and education. (One student mapped his rising grade averages to his changed use of fonts, from Trebuchet, in which his average grade for eighteen essays was B–, to Times New Roman, eleven-essay-average A–, to Georgia, which earned him an A average over twenty-three essays [Hyndman 50].) I prefer Garamond for its delicate, assured elegance; I find things printed in

Times New Roman to be duller, and in Courier, practically infantile. Most of my students, however, graduate as well as undergraduate (with some notable exceptions, particularly among those inclined toward the eighteenth century) even today go with their default font, either having no relationship with their page or unaware of its fontic possibilities.

I would like to help bring an awareness of fonts, along with everything else on the page, back into the reading experience of the text. Fontlove is an ancient and honorable phenonmenon. According to Stanley Morison, authorities in typography have pronounced the type brought out by Nicholas Jenson (1420–81) "the most perfect type ever cut"[35]; known as the Venetian type family, it is "highly sought for its wider letterforms, lighter tone and even texture of black strokes."[36] (Its modern software heirs include Centaur and Hightower.) But alas, Jenson's capitals "are unnecessarily self-assertive, a fault that was avoided in most of the work of Aldus" (Morison 30)—his successor Aldus Manutius (1450–1515), who "astonished the world" in 1501 with the *cancelleresca,* or Chancery—the italic.[37] Meanwhile in 1524 Geofroy Tory and the printer Simon de Colines freed France from the black letter with an edition of Horace printed in roman type possibly cut by Claude Garamond (c. 1510–61), who created "the second great family type—the *old face*" (Morison and Jackson 48). The Garamond letter soon became the dominant European model.

In England, gothic type persisted until 1572, when John Day introduced the first roman type copied from a design by Robert Granjon in 1565 for the printing house of Plantin in Antwerp. For the most part, Elizabethan and Jacobean printers had to purchase their type from abroad, usually Dutch adaptations of Garamond. Well after the Restoration the Dutch letter was the English letter of choice. Joseph Moxon declared them the best in the world for "the commodious Fatness they have beyond other *Letters,* which easing the Eyes in Reading, renders them more Legible ; As also the true placing their Fats and their Leans, with the sweet driving them into one another, and indeed all the accomplishments that can render *Letter* regular and beautiful, do more visibly appear in them than in any *Letters* Cut by any other People" (22–23). To the printer's eye, each different letter has its own form of visibility, a distinctive identity over which the printer may wax rhapsodic.

But back to our potted history. France was more accommodating to its printers—François I had appointed Geofroy Tory "printer to the king"; Louis XIV created the Royal Printing House in 1640. And it was in France that the self-styled "modern" letter appeared, from Pierre Simon Fournier-le-jeune, who purchased the Le Bé foundry (established 1552) in 1736. (In 1693 Philippe Grandjean had created a new face, "Romain de roi," which was arguably the first "modern" type, although it was Fournier who first employed the term.) "Modern" type uses a "serif that is thinner, longer and more refined than in the old face. There is a marked difference of weight between stem and hairline and qualities of extreme precision and emphatic perpendicularity dominate the design. As a rule the body of the modern letterform is less round and open than old face" (Morison 46).

By the early eighteenth century, English printers were retaking their place on the world printing stage. The restrictions imposed by the Star Chamber in the late sixteenth and early seventeenth centuries and by Cromwell, as well as the vise grip of the Stationers' Company, were relaxed or repealed. William Caslon (1692–1766) was the first to cut an English type (still based on Dutch baroque models) in 1720, and in 1734 issued his first specimen sheet, which has since been reproduced in virtually all printing histories. Caslon's font became so famous (it was used for the Declaration of Independence) that it generated a slogan: "When in doubt, use Caslon." Samuel Richardson used Caslon types:

> Our Printers are engaged mostly with a Letter-founder of our own (Caslon) who gives a good deal of satisfaction ; [. . .] Every Printer here, being furnished with *his* Types, the Booksellers, in a large Work, can for Dispatch-Sake, put it to several Printers, and print on the same Type. Let me observe for the Sake of this worthy Gentleman, that in his Text Romyn, the Capital Letters are thought rather too large for the rest, and too gross ; [. . .] But on the Whole, both that and the Gar[a]mond are very pretty Letters.[38]

Caslon's success meant that the English paid little attention to type innovation on the Continent (by Grandjean and Fournier, for example), and dominated the English print landscape until the mid-eighteenth century, when John Baskerville's designs changed the English taste in printing.

Baskerville (1706–75) had been a writing-master in Birmingham and a painter and japanner (lacquerer) before he turned to printing in 1750: "Having been an early admirer of the beauty of Letters, I became insensibly desirous of contributing to the perfection of them. I formed to my self ideas of greater accuracy than had yet appeared."[39] Like Humphry Repton in the previous chapters, Baskerville is for me an emblem of "grammars of approach," inventing new turns and "expressing the Relation of Things in Construction" within the "fundamental principles or rules" of a variety of arts and sciences.[40] The nineteenth-century print historian John Nichols observed: "Taste accompanied him through the different walks of agriculture, architecture, and the fine arts."[41] In a letter describing Baskerville's house to the Earl of Cork in 1760, one Mr. Derrick rolls Baskerville's accomplishments, interests, perceptions, and creations into a seamless paragraph:

> His house stands at about half a mile's distance, on an eminence that commands a fine prospect. I paid him a visit, and was received with great politeness, though an entire stranger. His apartments are elegant ; his staircase is particularly curious ; and the room in which he dines, and calls a smoaking room, is very handsome. The grate and furniture belonging to it are, I think, of bright wrought iron, and cost him a round sum.——He has just completed an elegant Octavo Common Prayer Book ; has a scheme for publishing a grand Folio edition of the Bible ; and will soon finish a beautiful collection of Fables by the ingenious Mr. Dodsley. He manufactures his own paper, types, and ink ; and they are remarkably good. This ingenious Artist carries on a great trade in the japan way, in which he shewed me several useful articles, such as candlesticks, stands, salvers, waiters, bread-baskets, tea-boards, &c. elegantly designed and highly finished. (Nichols 3:450n)

Baskerville's house, Easy Hill, commanding that fine prospect, recalls the topographical views in chapter 2; the narrator's eye follows the tourist's track into the house, surveying the taste and price of the interior. Baskerville as artist, literary printer, print innovator, creator, and collector are all assembled here into a phenomenological whole: from the commanding house on the eminence to the highly finished tea board within, Baskerville unites the large picture and small detail, the topographies of land and print.

Bertrand Bronson specifically ligatures Baskerville to the landscape movement in eighteenth-century Britain. Using Horace Walpole's phrase for landscape gardener William Kent, Bronson declares:

> Baskerville "leaped the fence" and saw that his problem was really one of learning how to manipulate the space around the letters. The letters themselves are very beautiful, especially the Roman capitals, so suggestive of lapidary depth. But they are the more gracious because they are so open in feeling and treated so openly that air seems to flow through them and around them.[42]

The sense of air "flowing through and around" Baskerville's letters is a product of greater contrast between the thick and thin strokes, a sharper, tapered serif, and a more perpendicular axis for the round characters.

Baskerville declared in the preface to his edition of Milton's *Paradise Lost* (1758) that he did not desire to print many books: "but such only, as are *books* of *Consequence*, of *intrinsic merit*, or *established Reputation*, and which the public may be pleased to see in an elegant dress, and to purchase at such a price, as will repay the extraordinary care and expence that must necessarily be bestowed upon them." He hopes that "persons of judgment and penetration" will find the edition to excel in its "*Paper, Letter, Ink* and *Workmanship.*" His beautification of Congreve is more modestly cast as "the least faulty Impression, which has yet been printed ; in which, Care has been taken both to Revise the Press, and to Review and Correct many Passages in the Writing."[43] Reading these editions grounds Bronson's soaring description in a meta-readerly reality, a typographical experience. A shift to a less perfectionist page is almost tactile in its grittiness.

Baskerville was not entirely successful in his own time. The printers' and typefounders' world was not one he was born into, and his perfectionism exacerbated and threatened them. "The London Booksellers preferred the sterling types of Caslon and his apprentice Jackson" (Nichols 3:460). They declared he was too expensive, even though, as he wrote to Benjamin Franklin on 7 September 1767, "I offered the London booksellers to print for them within five percent as low as their common currency, but cannot get from them a single job."[44] Others insisted that his sharp contrasts were too hard on the eyes. One gentleman complained to Franklin that Baskerville "would be a means of blinding all the Readers in the Nation, for the strokes of [his] Letters being too thin and narrow, hurt the Eye, and he could never read a Line of them without Pain."[45] (Franklin, suspecting both the eye and the agenda of this gentleman, brought him a specimen-sheet of Caslon's, with Caslon's name removed, and the gentleman, thinking it Baskerville's, triumphantly went over the letters and pointed out the distortions.) Baskerville continued his complaint: "After having obtained the reputation of excelling in the most useful art known to mankind, of which I have your testimony, is it not to the last degree provoking, that I cannot even get bread by it. I must starve, had I no other dependence" (Franklin 781). He retired from printing in the last years of his life.

But his admirers, from Benjamin Franklin to Bertrand Bronson, in the end outvoiced the detractors, agreeing in assessments of lapidary clarity and lasting innovation. His work was greatly admired abroad, particularly in France and America. His most popular successor, Giambattista Bodoni, then working at the Vatican printing office, traveled to Birmingham to meet him. Pierre Simon Fournier wrote of him that he was "plus moderne" and "il n'a épargné ni soins ni dépenses pour les porter à la plus haute perfection: les caractères sont gravés avec beaucoup de hardiesse, les italiques sont les meilleures qui'il y ait dans toutes les Fonderies d'Angleterre ; mais les romains sont un peu trop larges. [He has spared neither pains nor expense to bring [his types] to the utmost pitch of perfection. The letters are cut with great daring and the italic is the best to be found in any English foundry, but the roman is a little too wide.]"[46] After his death, no one in Britain would buy his types, not even the press at Cambridge, for which he had printed his greatest work, a folio bible, considered today "one of the finest books not just of the eighteenth century, but since William Caxton established the first English press, five centuries ago."[47] The French dramatist Beaumarchais bought the Baskerville equipment for a seventy-volume octavo edition of Voltaire's works (ninety-two volumes duodecimo); in a letter from Paris, 8 August 1780, he wrote: "Baskerville's types, which were bought it seems for a trifle, to the eternal disgrace of Englishmen, are to be made use of for the purpose of propagating the English language in this country" (Nichols 3:460–61n). Nichols indignantly snorted, "We must admire, if we do not imitate, the taste and œconomy of the French nation, who, brought by the British arms in 1762 to the verge of ruin, rising above distress, were able, in seventeen years, to purchase Baskerville's elegant types, refused by his own country" (3:460–61).

Baskerville type was revived by the American typographer Bruce Rogers in 1917 when he worked as an adviser to Cambridge University Press and came across a Baskerville specimen in a bookshop (Lawson 192). And a 2012 experiment conducted by documentary filmmaker Errol Morris concluded, after polling about forty-five thousand readers on NYTimes.com, that "subjects were more likely to believe a statement when it was written in Baskerville than when it was written in Computer Modern, Georgia, Helvetical, Trebuchet, or Comic Sans."[48]

ii. CAPITALS *and* Italics

Your Poem finish'd, next your Care
Is needful, to transcribe it fair.
In modern Wit all printed Trash, is
Set off with num'rous *Breaks* — — and *Dashes*— —

To Statesman wou'd you give a Wipe,
You print it in *Italick Type.*
When Letters are in vulgar Shapes,
'Tis ten to one the Wit escapes ;
But when in *Capitals* exprest,
The dullest Reader smoaks the Jest.

Jonathan Swift, *On Poetry: A Rapsody* (1733)

Swift's poem exhibits as well as addresses the endotexts (to play on Genette) of late seventeenth- through mid-eighteenth-century English printed pages, with capitalized common nouns and italicized proper ones.[49] The text must speak; Swift satirizes the nudgenudge winkwink lack of subtlety generally employed. The text speaks in its typographical energies; common, ordinary ("vulgar"), unemphasized letters let meaning sieve through. (As today's email, Twitter, and online comment section users know, CAPITALS and other typographical aids seem to be required for the "dullest Reader" to "smoak" a satire—or even a basic point.) The poem is also another argument for authorial oversight: the text was corrected to "CAPITALS" in the 1734 Dublin edition.[50] As John Smith says, while some authors "give themselves no concern about capitaling, but leave that to the Printer's discretion ; yet there are others who shew themselves more acquainted with Printing ; and, in order to avoid intermixtures of Letter, of their own accord distinguish no Substantives by Capitals, but prefix them to names of persons and places," while still others "also denote their emphatical expressions, by beginning them with Capitals" (*PG* 51).

Capitalized nouns (and occasionally adjectives) had been commonplace in English texts at least since the Elizabethan period. It was an inheritance from what Samuel Johnson considered the language's "*Teutonick* character"[51] (and indeed the practice lived on much longer in Germany), but it was also practiced in Holland and to a lesser extent in France.[52] John Jones notes in 1701 that in print "they generally put *great* or *capital Letters,* in the Beginning of the common Names of Things, to adorn it ; but that it is not yet become customary in Writing, tho' it daily gains ground."[53] Thomas Dyche, in his 1736 *Guide to the English Tongue,* explains that "'Tis esteem'd Ornamental to begin any *Substantive* in the Sentence with a *Capital,* if it bear some *considerable Stress* of the Author's *Sense* upon it, to make it the more *remarkable* and *conspicuous,*" and indeed that "*'Tis grown Customary in Printing to begin every* Substantive *with a* Capital."[54] Benjamin Franklin argued that this imitation "of our Mother Tongue, the German" made it "particularly useful to those, who were not well acquainted with the English; there being such a prodigious Number of our Words, that are both *Verbs* and *Substantives,* and spelt in the same manner, tho' often accented differently in Pronunciation."[55] Smith, who didn't approve of the "intermixtures of Letter" (roman with italic, upper with lower case) thought that the "noble figure" of Large Capitals "would hardly have a chance to shew themselves, were it not for their being put at the front of nouns substantives, to distinguish them from Verbs, Adverbs, or other parts of Grammar" (*PG* 50). Capitalized nouns thus literally *do* overlook the other parts of speech ("commanding a noble view," in the common architectural phrase). That accords with the theory promoted by the School of Languages in Lagado, in Swift's *Gulliver's Travels* (1726), which was working mightily to "shorten Discourse by cutting Polysyllables into one, and leaving out Verbs and Participles; because in reality all things imaginable are but Nouns."[56] Nouns are capitalized because they are ontologically superior. Nouns stand for Things. (More on this in the next chapter.)

Italics for proper nouns was another feature of the seventeenth- and early eighteenth-century English page. Introduced by the Venetian Aldus Manutius in 1501, it held down a number of jobs. Joseph Loewenstein argues that it reproduced "the aesthetic freedoms of scribal handicraft, even of nonprofessional handwriting."[57] The 1855 *History of Printing* declares it was designed to "get rid of the great number of abbreviations used in printing."[58] Smith insists that the "chief, and almost only use" for which it was originally designed was to "distinguish such parts of a book as may be said not to belong to the Body thereof, as Prefaces, Introductions, Annotations, congratulatory Poems, Summaries, and Contents" (*PG* 12). Italics can suggest "either instructing, satyrizing, admiring, or other hints and remarks" (14). The italic has also had a quasi-gendered life of "particular delicacy"; roman type, "being always of a bolder look than Italic of the same Body, takes advantage of the soft and tender face of Italic" (16, 13). Loewenstein argues that italics "fracture the English body type, so to print other, more highly authored words. *Thus* do we make the muffled authority of mere impression give way to authentic inscription" (224). But *thus* with a combination of studded capitals and oblique italics, we have, I would say, not so much a "fractured" English body type as a *textured* one.

The hand-held landscape of the early eighteenth-century book declaims through these textures in this haunting passage from Daniel Defoe's *A Journal of the Plague Year* (1722):

> Passing thro' *Token-house-yard* in *Lothbury*, of a sudden a Casement violently opened just over my Head, and a Woman gave three frightful Skreetches, and then cry'd, *Oh! Death, Death, Death!* in a most inimitable Tone, and which struck me with Horror and a Chilness, in my very Blood. There was no Body to be seen in the whole Street, neither did any other Window open; for People had no Curiosity now in any Case; nor could any Body help one another; so I went on to pass into *Bell-Alley*.[59]

The italicized place names have iconic reverberations; it is no accident that Defoe placed his narrator H. F. in London streets that gesture from the tokens of the plague to the Donnean tolling bell. The faceless woman's cries do indeed fracture this text, and capitalization draws attention to "no Body," which has a chillness of its own: H. F. has already recounted (counted) for us the dead bodies in the streets. And when H. F. recaps the various surges of the plague in the city, the parish names lean together in a dense urban-textual crush:

> It began at St. *Giles*'s and the *Westminster* End of the Town, and it was in its Height in all that part by about the Middle of *July, viz.* in St. *Giles* in the *Fields*, St. *Andrew's Holborn*, St. *Clement-Danes*, St. *Martins* in the *Fields*, and in *Westminster*: The latter End of *July* it decreased in those Parishes, and coming East, it encreased prodigiously in *Cripplegate*, St. *Sepulchres*, St. *Ja. Clarkenwell*, and St. *Brides*, and *Aldersgate*; while it was in all these Parishes, the City and all the Parishes of the *Southwark* Side of the Water, and all *Stepney, White-Chapel, Aldgate, Wapping,* and *Radcliff* were very little touch'd; so that People went about their Business unconcern'd, carryed on their Trades, kept open their Shops, and conversed freely with one another in all the City, the East and North-East Suburbs, and in *Southwark*, almost as if the Plague had not been among us. (179)

Where the plague is raging in the paragraph, the italics crowd in a parataxis of urban boundaries. Where places are "very little touch'd," the lines, like the people, open up, and in simple regular clauses go about their unemphasized business.

Not everyone in the eighteenth century (or in our time, for that matter[60]) appreciated such a typographically textured text. Objections to these practices of typographical emphasis mounted early on, although as Foxon notes, printers may not have always practiced what the grammarians preached (180). Ephraim Chambers's *Cyclopædia* of 1728 protests, with palpable textual irony:

> CAPITALS, in Printing, are the *Majusculæ*, or initial Letters, wherein Titles, &c. are compos'd, and all Periods, Verses, *&c.* commence ; call'd also *uncial* Letters. See UNCIAL. All proper Names of Men, Countries, Kingdoms, Terms of Arts, Sciences, and Dignities, are to begin with *Capitals*. The *English* Printers have carried *Capitals* to a pitch of Extravagance ; making it a Rule, to begin almost every Substantive with a *Capital* ; which is a manifest Perversion of the Design of *Capitals*, as well as an Offence against Beauty and Distinctness. Some of 'em begin now to retrench their superfluous *Capitals*, and to fall into the Measures of the Printers of other Nations. See LETTERS, CHARACTERS, and PRINTING.[61]

And indeed, a glance at a paragraph from William Stow's *Remarks on London* (1722) suggests a kind of typographical street brawl of Capitals vs. *Italics* (the prepositions nearly squeezed to death):

> Some People are so ignorant, especially in the Country, as to think *London, Westminster,* and *Southwark,* is all *London,* because contiguous to one another ; which is a grand Mistake ; for if you should send a letter to a Friend in *King-Street,* which is in *Westminster,* but write at the bottom of the Superscription, *London* ; how should the Postman know, whether you mean *King-street* by *Guildhall, King-street* on *Great tower-hill, King-street* in *Spittle Fields, King-street* in *Prince's street* near *St. Anne's Church, King-street* near *Golden Square, King-street* in *Dean-street* by *Soho-square, King-street* in *Covent-garden, King-street* by *Hay's court* near *Newport Market, King-street* in Upper *Moor-fields, King-street* by *Old-street Square, King-street* by *Bloomsbury Square, King-street* by *St. James's Square, King-street* near the *Six Dials* [*sic*], or *King-street* in the *Mint* ?[62]

It may be that some in the early eighteenth century were finding their typographical exertions resembling those Lagadoan philosophers who, "since Words are only Names for *Things*," decided to

> carry about them, such Things as were necessary to express the particular Business they are to discourse on [. . .] which hath only this Inconvenience attending it; that if a Man's Business be very great, and of various Kinds, he must be obliged in Proportion to carry a greater Bundle of Things upon his Back, unless he can afford one or two strong Servants to attend him. (*Gulliver's Travels* 177–78)

Italics, too, though they have that "particular delicacy," have also a "troublesome nature": they are "not of the same good-natured disposition" as roman letters but "*will* be humoured by Spaces, or else they make but an aukward and unsightly appearance" (Smith, *PG* 16, 17, 52). In short, the eighteenth-century page, which had seemed to early eighteenth-century print historians a model of clarity and coherence compared to its sixteenth- and seventeenth-century ancestors, began to be perceived as a sort of typographical chaos that needed spatial ordering, cotemporaneous with the great moves to straighten and pave the roads of Britain and level the lines of London Bridge (discussed in the previous chapters).

The move to cleanse the text was pushed by authors, grammarians, and printers alike. As early as 1717 Alexander Pope abandoned the use of capitals for common nouns in his folio *Works* and imposed the new rules on his contributors in *Poems on Several Occasions* (1722).[63] William Collins revised his 1742 *Persian Eclogues* in 1757, "abandoning the capital" and much of its "distinctive styling," in Richard Wendorf's words (73). Richardson's *Pamela* (1739) had capitalized common nouns and italicized propers; *Clarissa* (1747–48) did not. The modernizing printer Robert Dodsley declared that "pointings," including italics and capitals, are "like false Guiding-Posts, [. . .] perpetually turning out of the High Road of Common Sense."[64] Smith describes "the more modern and neater way" as that in which printers "pay no regard to put any thing in Italic but what is underscored in our Copy : neither do we drown the beauty of Roman Lower-case Sorts by gracing every Substantive with a Capital ; but only such as are Proper names, or are words of particular signification and emphasis" (as "Italic," "Copy," "Lower-case," "Substantive," "Capital," and "Proper" so clearly must be [*PG* 202]). Thus the italics were straightened up and the nouns decapitated, which made the letters "shew themselves more neatly" (51). By 1786 Joseph Robertson, in his *Essay on Punctuation*, could say with satisfaction: "It was usual with our ancestors, both in writing and printing, to begin every noun with a capital. But this custom, which was always troublesome, and not in the least useful or ornamental, is now entirely discontinued ; and small letters are used in all common words."[65] Robertson is a little too quick on the draw here; the practice was not "entirely discontinued": as the expanded 1787 version of Smith's *Printer's Grammar* explains, when "Authors r*evise* [their copy . . .] they first agree with themselves, which way they would have their Work done ; whether the common way, with Capitals to Substantives, and Proper names in Italic ; or whether without Capitals and nothing in Italic."[66]

The transition, thus and of course, was neither clean nor complete. Novels and expensive folios of poetry are the most conspicuously modernized in terms of their capitals and italics by the second half of the eighteenth century, but the older forms lingered in manuscripts, in poetry for the masses, and in a good many nonliterary publications. Just as Jones had noted in 1701 that the habit of capitalizing common nouns had not quite filtered into handwriting, at the other end of the century, Jane Austen's manuscripts retain the older forms of capitalization, spelling, and punctuation (see "Of a COMMA" below). But the Brownscaping of the textual landscape meant, in fact, that people *did* begin to see the comma below. In both the reaction to and consequences of the typographical relandscaping lies an underground picturesque, a response to the uniform and the linear that favors more "the winding paths of sheep" and the angling of the approach.

Benjamin Franklin provides one example of the inverse picturesque of print. In a vocabulary parallel to that of Gilpin, Price, and Knight, he deplores the loss of visual power and character and direction. In a letter to his son William Franklin (6 October 1773) he complains of the change in terms that could be described by the very title of his piece published in London in the *Chronicle* which suffered the fate of modernization: *Rules by which a great empire may be reduced to a small one*. The essay had been "stripped of all the capitalling and italicing [*sic*], that intimate the allusions and marks the emphasis of written discourses, to bring them as near as possible to those spoken: printing such a piece all in one even small character, seems to me like repeating one of Whitfield's sermons in the monotony of a school-boy" (886). In the letter to Noah Webster (26 December 1789) he articulates the advantages of the older print customs for reading aloud, in providing something for the eye to clutch:

> In so doing the Eye generally slides forward three or four Words before the Voice. If the Sight clearly distinguishes what the coming Words are, it gives time to order the Modulation of the Voice to express them properly. But, if they are obscurely printed, or disguis'd by omitting the Capitals and long *ſ's* or otherwise, the Reader is apt to modulate wrong; and, finding he has done so, he is oblig'd to go back and begin the Sentence again, which lessens the Pleasure of the Hearers. (1177)

The modern line is so slick you skid right over it. In fact, he declares, the more uniform line is actually *less* legible, "as the paring all Men's Noses might smooth and level their Faces, but would render their Physiognomies less distinguishable" (1177). Clearly, like Gilpin, Franklin would just as soon take a mallet to the too-regular Tintern Abbey of type.

iii. catch-
words

> CA'TCHWORD, [phon.] *s.* The word at the corner of the page under the last line, which is repeated at the top of the next page.
>
> Samuel Johnson, *Dictionary* (1755)

One of the aids to the eye as it slides forward is the catchword, carrying the last line of one page up to the first of the next. It was sometimes called the "direction"—as in Moxon's *Mechanick Exercises* (1683): "*Direction,* the word that stands alone on the Right Hand in the bottom *Line* of a *Page*" (338). Not a great deal of attention has been paid to this almost ubiquitous feature of eighteenth-century British texts. Its history is briefly repeated by bibliographers: scribes inserted them in medieval manuscripts to guide the binder in arranging the sections; by the mid-sixteenth century they were common in printed books, although use varied among countries. In France they did not appear until the sixteenth century (and then only sporadically) and disappeared again in the eighteenth. In England they were not used by Caxton, but then held strong from about 1530 to the end of the eighteenth century. McKerrow and Gaskell both describe the use of catchwords in printed books as similar to the scribal aim: "as guides to the printer in imposing the pages," "to help the compositor to get the pages in the right order for printing."[67] Such a description is digested from printers' manuals; Smith, for example, explains: "The first page being made up to the length of the number of lines of which it is to consist, we set the Direction line, that shews the first word of the next page" (205). It was important for the composing and assembling of pages that the catchword have a distinct identity; otherwise, it could happen "that a *Compositor*, by having two or more *Pages* in his *Sheet* with the same *Direction-line* [. . .] *Transposes* two *Pages*, or more, in his *Sheet*" (Moxon 237–38). The catchword was, then, primarily a convenience for the printer or compositor, apparently of little interest to the reader. In any event, given later technological advances in assembling books, the demise of the catchword was unmourned:

> STOWER: Direction words at the bottom of the page are not now generally used ; the omission of them does not injure the appearance of the work, but saves time and expense where overrunning occurs in the proof. (*The Printer's Manual* [1817], 16)

> JOHNSON: Catchwords [are] now generally abolished. (*Typographia* [1824], 1:68)

> DE VINNE: For more than three centuries printers of books appended at the foot of every page the first word or syllable of the next page [. . .] but the catchword is now out of use, and it is not missed. (*Practice of Typography* [1901], 142–43)

> GASKELL: [A]lthough the full use of catchwords was general in English and in most continental printing until the later eighteenth century, they were not always considered necessary. (*New Introduction to Bibliography* [1972], 53)

Yet under the microscope the catchword can be a curious wee beastie. The German name for it is *Kustode* (custodian, keeper, curator) and the French *réclamé* (advertisement; claim) (McKerrow 82n). It shepherds the line as it leaps over the page; it heralds the immediate future. Is it possible catchwords had more *caché*, so to speak, than they usually get credit for? *Notes and Queries* of 1882 features a brief but patriotic exchange on this point between two Victorian gentlemen. WILLIAM PLATT of Callis Court, St. Peter's, Isle of Thanet, wrote in: "It is unaccountable that the use and convenience of the catchword did not occur to the Parisian printers until the year 1520." ALFRED WALLIS responded:

> These were not in use by the celebrated French printer Johan Petit so late as February, 1520. I have a book, *Cathena Auria supoer Psalmos,* most beautifully executed in red and black by him [. . .] which has signatures, but neither numerals nor catchwords. The Rev. W. P. Greswell observes, almost in MR. PLATT's words (*vide Annals of Parisian Typography*, 8vo. 1818, p. 6):— ' The printers of Paris did not adopt them till a period so late as 1520 : though they are found in the *Tacitus,* printed at Venice by Spira, *circa* 1468').[68]

Clearly Messrs. Platt and Wallis took pride in the good old English catchword.

The catchword indeed seems occasionally to play a more interesting role than simply the visual connector for the printer or compositor setting and assembling the pages. An alert reader *sees* the catchword. Theodore De Vinne asserted in 1901 that the catchword "was supposed to be needed by the reader to make clear the connection between the two pages."[69] Some books set in double columns had catchwords at the foot of each column, suggesting an aide to the reader (rather than the pressman) in navigating back up to the top.[70] For someone reading aloud—whose eye, as Franklin pointed out, "generally slide[s] forward three or four Words before the Voice"—catchwords also "clearly [distinguish] what the coming Words are" and "[give] time to order the Modulation of the Voice to express them properly" (1177).

Manuel Portela has convincingly demonstrated that "Sterne (with the collaboration of his printers) [. . .] shaped the typography of his narrative at the line and page levels as well."[71] At one point Portela looks closely at the catchwords of the first edition of *Tristram Shandy* (1759–67); in the scene describing the death of Le Fever (6:45–46), he argues, the page break, catchword, line break, and dashes combine "to recreate in image and rhythm the last palpitations of Le Fever's dying heart":

> Notice how the catchword gets a sound value on its own; how the long dash is used both as visual marker and as notation of cardiac arrest; how a long dash is introduced at the beginning of the second line of page 46 so that the word 'moved' can be hyphenated into two syllables and the word 'No' can go to the

last line by itself. Notice the symmetry between text segments (2 × 3) × 3. Even the apostrophes at the verb's past endings achieve the same synthesis of sound and visual meaning.

Nature instantly ebb'd again,——the
film returned to its place,——the pulse
flut-

[46]
fluttered——stopp'd——went on——
——throbb'd——stopp'd again——mo-
ved——stopp'd——shall I go on ?——
No.

C H A P. XI.

John Kristensen, a proprietor of the Firefly Press in Boston, has practical doubts about my arguments for reading catchwords as part of the text (or at least looking to see if anything comes out of it): "What raises the greatest doubt in my technical rather than literary mind is that the catchword is an interruption of the text; if it is read as part of the text rather than ignored, then there is a jarring repetition of words."[72] Portela's example demonstrates how that repetition can be mimetic rather than jarring. The "catchword gets a sound value on its own"—"fluttered" visually flut-flutters. Franklin's reminder of the oral reader aligns the catchword functionally with punctuation: the performer would not voice the catchword, but the catchword gives a chance to breathe and modulate. Like eye-rhymes, the catchword can perform with or without "sound value."

But that, we might say, is Sterne just being Sterne. Richardson, who had the same typographical opportunities, doesn't seem as invested; *Pamela* ("Printed for C. RIVINGTON, in St. Paul's Church-Yard ; and J. OSBORN, in Pater-noster Row. M DCC XLI") has nothing particularly catchy among its catchwords. In volume I, they are typically Lovelace's "little words"—pronouns, conjunctions, auxiliary words, exclamations ("O !"), and so forth.[73] But things do not look quite so utilitarian in, say, Ann Radcliffe's *The Mysteries of Udolpho* ("PRINTED FOR G. G. AND J. ROBINSON, PATERNOSTER-ROW. 1794").[74] In volume 1, roughly 175, or about one-third, of the catchwords are the "little words"—articles, pronouns, prepositions. The remaining 252 are full-fledged significant words, many of them comparatively long—exhibiting, pleasure, softened, fever, affliction, comfortable, vallies, thunder, past !, a stranger, chamber, flowers, following, terrific, condition, chateau, Emily—though many are hyphenated, to be or not to be reunited on the next page (melan / melancholy, resi / dence, neigh / bouring, ten / derness, wood / wood-walks). As a preview of the next page, a Radcliffean catchword can be a visual cliffhanger:

and foaming amidst the dark rocks in its
descent, and then flowing in a limpid lapse
to the brink of other precipices, whence
again it fell with thundering strength to the
H 6 abyss[75]

Yet surely positing an argument-from-design for catchwords in most cases is doomed from the start. Kristensen warns me (as have others), "compositors were journeymen, not artists," and as "type was set in galley-length proofs to begin with and only paginated after correcting, it would be hard to control where exactly the pages broke. I find it difficult to believe that a compositor on his own, who would initially be setting galley-length proofs rather than page-length ones, would take upon himself such subtlety." His take is that any deliberate effects would have been made at the direction of the author. He echoes Gaskell, who asserts that both compositor and corrector "worked more or less automatically, and did not necessarily take in the general sense of what he was reading" (113).[76] But he *could*; what if he *did*?

Think of the way any of us might subversively entertain ourselves within menial tasks (C. S. Lewis famously entered "Rabbit, Peter" in an index). Could a compositor, apart from any authorial directions, manipulate the direction-line to make it more interesting? What would that entail? Kristensen suggests investigating whether "the conventions of straight matter typesetting were distorted at all in order to achieve a telling result. Do facing pages have a different number of lines when paragraph breaks do not call for them? Is the word spacing of the last or last few justified lines of a page other than as conventionally even as would be the case if no special effect were intended?"[77] Some preliminary work I have done—setting some *Udolpho* pages myself with the typesetting furniture of the University of Virginia's Rare Book School, and checking the last lines of pages in the first edition suggests the possibility of some small conscious patterns (e.g., *lots* of "pigeonholes" that accommodate the longer catchwords). I cannot yet make a definitive argument. But I am a firm believer in the value of suggestiveness itself.[78]

Of course, often more than one compositor would set pages for any one work. Trying to identify individual patterns would be like trying to identify medieval pew-carvers who leavened their manual labor with idiosyncratic variations on the given pattern. But then, archaeologists and historians have identified similarities among pew-carvings in particular geographic regions, suggesting the possibility that "one carver might have done the work in one area, a second in another area, etc."[79] (East Anglia, apparently, inspired quite a few carvings of its birds.)

Consider the monks who painted fetching little cats in the margins of their illuminated manuscripts.[80] Catchwords were regularly decorated in medieval manuscripts; in Paul Gehl's words, they could "elaborate, pun upon, call attention to, or distract and detract from the text altogether."[81] Both scribe and decorator would have had "a large literary repertoire of images to choose from in any text to hand" (68). Early print practices often replicated scribal ones (although according to McKerrow the earliest printed books had no catchwords [83]). Printer's manuals themselves articulate all that is involved in choosing and positioning the catchword, and the difference between the intelligent, careful workman and the indifferent journeyman.

The printers' grammars spell out, step by step, the assembling of the page. When the compositor gets to the end of his page, "being made up to the length of the number of lines of which it is to consist, we set the Direction line, that shews the first word of the next page" (Smith, *PG* 205). Moxon explains that the compositor "*Sets* a *Line* of *Quadrats* and at the end of it the first word of the next *Page*, or if the Word be very long and the *Line* very short, two *Syllables*, or sometimes but one of that *Word*" (338). That is, under the last line of the page text, he inserts chunks of faceless type (quadrats or quads) to create empty spaces until he gets to the end of the line and then inserts the word (or the first part of a word) that begins the next page. Both the grammars and the printing manuals of the age have very specific directions about the division of words (although they do not always agree with each other). John Smith articulates the basic code of honor: "In dividing words [. . .] very few Printers suffer a syllable of a single letter to be put at the end of a line ; as, *a-bide, e-normous, o-bedient,* &c. [. . .] In the same manner that neat Workmen prevent a division of a single-letter syllable at the end of lines, they contrive that the short remains of a word shall not appear at the beginning of lines ; and therefore avoid, as often as they can, to put the final syllables *al, on, ny, en, ly, er,* &c. at the head of them" (*PG* 97, 98).

Note the "neat Workmen"; Moxon had said parenthetically but pointedly that it was "but seldom through too *much* care" that compositors transposed their pages by not paying close enough attention to the direction line. Smith and his successor in the 1787 *Printer's Grammar* both underline the point that "tho' it is very common with the French to begin a page with a Break-line whose major part consists of matter, it does not suit an English eye ; for in such case we make a page either longer, or shorter, rather than see a piece of a line at the Head of a page" (211–12). Over and over, Smith and others will emphasize the "good judgment in a Compositor" (99) in the matter of divisions and spacings of words on each line of each page. "True Spacing [. . .] recommends a Compositor greatly for a good workman" particularly when he performs "for neatness sake, what is prejudicial to his present interest" (112). The presumption is that (a) the good compositor cares what he does with his page and (b) he therefore knows what he is doing when he is doing it. *Could* a "neat Workman" do more than simply "prevent"?

It seems unlikely, even to me, that any but the most micromanagerial (and commercially successful) authors would have much say in the placing of catchwords in their printed text. But in a sort of historical parallel to the Shakespearean punctuation debates of the twentieth century (as in McKenzie's argument that "Compositor B" punctuated more heavily than "Compositor A" in the quartos of *The Merchant of Venice*[82]), I think it is plausible to suggest—where patterns warrant—that the compositor could well be taking part in McGann's "socialized text" if he was paying attention to what he was reading while he was spacing it: within certain spatial parameters, he could choose the catchword to emphasize a moment, to augment suspense, to mimic a feature, to carry the reader's eye across the abyss. The catchword manages expectations—the reader's as well as the printer's.

John Baskerville supplies an interesting test case. He was, in his own words, "desirous of contributing to the perfection of Letters." He intended his edition of *Paradise Lost* (among other "*books* of *Consequence*," "*intrinsic Merit*," and "*established Reputation*") to appear in "an elegant dress" and hoped "in the *Paper*, *Letter*, *Ink* and *Workmanship* to excel." And yet he manages to sever his publisher-patron's name in a Preface of otherwise luxuriant and presumably malleable spaciousness:

> [. . .] And I embrace with pleasure the opportunity of acknowledging in this public manner the generosity of *Mr. Ton-*
>
> *son;*
>
> *son*; who with singular politeness complimented me with the privilege of printing an entire Edition of that *Writers Poetical Works*.[83]

The compositors of *The Mysteries of Udolpho* generally reunited a divided word at the top of the next page: "wood-/ wood-walks" (1:21); "fishing / fishing-house" (1:22); "Rousil / Rousillon" (1:77); "moun / mountain-ash" (1:109); "disem / disembodied" (1:180). Tonson's name is thus doubly divided, not given the courtesy of re-memberment on the next page. De Vinne placed Baskerville in the camp of derelict hyphenators: "Not much attention seems to have been paid to a systematic division of words even by good printers of the eighteenth century. In Baskerville's edition of Paradise Lost, I find these divisions in the preface by Milton : e-specially and o-therwise, and they appear in lines where there was no real need for a division of these long words on the single letter" (143n1). But as Smith says, it is occasionally allowable to hyphenate a single-letter syllable at the end of a line in certain "narrow measures, where sometimes the getting in of *one* letter will save the trouble of over-running several lines, especially in large Letter. It is also allowed of by such as love to see Matter spaced close, and even" (97). One could argue that, since Baskerville's edition of Congreve frequently divides characters' names in the catchwords (as "BELL-", "VAIN-", and "HEART-" in *The Old Batchelor*), that Tonson is not being specially disrespected. But such a division in characters' names simply indicates who speaks next—it points the reader toward the next move of the conversation. It does not divide the name in the middle of its own first appearance, and for only three small letters. Baskerville is the perfectionist; he is using large letter here, and he likes things spaced well. And after all, one's name is one's name. It would have been a "singular politeness" to have kept that name intact. I do not know of any reason why Baskerville sliced up "Tonson"; I only suggest (slightly maliciously, perhaps) that it *is* a matter of choice, and *could* have been otherwise.

The first edition of Radcliffe's *The Italian,* printed by a house as illustrious as *Udolpho*'s ("T. CADELL Jun. and W. DAVIES / (Successors to Mr. CADELL) in the STRAND. /1797."), displays a similar range of interesting catchwords when compared to, say, Richardson's *Pamela.* The sheer number of long, unhyphenated, and suggestive words sustain a sort of underground narration—rather like a horizontal *Bouts-Rimés* (in which only the last rhyming words of the lines are printed[84]): *agony, longer, " I guessed, Inquisition, Altogether, grandeur, understood, observed, A faint, cruelty, Inquisitor, guilt, science, particularly, pastoral, chestnuts, forests, Happily, appeared, fancy, cliffs, prison, inferiority, submit, ruling, " Sordid, Spalatro, Schedoni, yielded, smile, " Answer, voice, " Reproach, willing, designed, perplexity, discover, alarmed, endurable, Schedoni's, emotions* (from 2:169–337). The catchwords give decided story signs, affecting the speed of narration if the reader actually pays attention to them. Like Gaskell and Kristensen, Vivian Salmon is skeptical of the idea that "an author *or compositor* was consciously aware of what he was doing when he marked off the structural limits of the sentence," but her own explanation is rather different: "He was doing so unconsciously in accordance with a linguistic 'feeling' which was in fact made articulate by some scholars especially concerned with language" ("Early Seventeenth-Century Punctuation" 360, my emphasis). Yet a number of scholars (Foxon, Parkes, Wendorf, Portela, Sutherland) have shown that some authors were indeed consciously aware of marking off the structural limits of their sentences. There is no way to prove that the compositors for Radcliffe's novels were actually pew-carvers or margin-illustrators. But for me, the emergence of visible patterns, in catchwords that catch the story as much as the line, gives a special McGannian radiance to this textuality. In some cases, reading is energized by watching the *Kustode* looking toward the next line, keeping watching over the leap, laying claim to the next page, advertising the bend in the road, curating a social text. The "direction" is not always a "smaller particle":

> *Let these Letters make a* Word,
> *Let these* Words *a* Line *afford,*
> *Then of* Lines *a* Page compose,
> *Which being brought unto a Close,*
> *Be Thou the* Direction, *L O R D* ;
> *Let Love be the fast-binding* Cord.
> (James Watson,
> *The Art of Printing*, 1713)

iv. ☞ *Pointing*

"YOUNG people should be early taught to distinguish the stops, commas, accents, and other grammatical marks, in which the correctness of writing consists ; and it would be proper to begin with explaining to them their nature and use." So declares the advertisement to Joseph Robertson's *An Essay on Punctuation* in 1786. Nearly fifty years later, John Harris published his charming pamphlet "by Mr. Stops," featuring young Robert and his sisters, Counsellor Comma, Ensign Semicolon, and a gallery of other Perspicuous Points (please look *right now* at plate VIII).[85] Both volumes suggest that by the late eighteenth century the practice of "pointing" had settled into a theory of punctuation. Robertson certainly thought so. "Some imagine," he says in his preface, "that punctuation is an arbitrary invention, depending on fancy and caprice. But this is a mistake. It is founded on rational and determinate principles" ($A5_v$). He was responding to complaints by those such as Ephraim Chambers, who in 1728 finds the rules for pointing "impertinent, dark, and deficient ; and the Practice, at present, perfectly capricious ; Authors varying not only from one another, but from themselves too" (2:911). John Smith agreed: "Pointing is become a mere humour, which is sometimes deaf to rule and reason, it is impossible for a Compositor to guess at an Author's manner of expressing himself, unless he shews it in pointing his Copy" (86). The usual story is that punctuation shifted from the rhetorical to the logical, from *telling* the reader how to read aloud, to *showing* the reader how the sentence is constructed. Language became defined more as a spatial structure than a spoken one, ordering the visual landscape of the page.[86] This story is essentially correct; there is a sense of order from confusion sprung. But it is more correct to say that the two strands of theory and practice were intertwined, both early on and into the nineteenth century, and order and confusion—or the classical and the picturesque—in different ways produced, if not gaudy tulips, a punctuation that sprang out more dramatically as both a busy little architect of the page and the creator of an even more vivid sonic landscape.[87]

The author of *Some Rules for Speaking and Action; To be observed At the Bar, in the Pulpit, and the Senate, and by every one that Speaks in Public* (1716) puts the earlier elocutionary practice succinctly: "A *Comma* stops the Voice while we may privately tell One, a *Semicolon* Two, a *Colon* Three, and a *Period* Four."[88] "Every one that Speaks in Public" includes everyone from the maidservant Pamela and the heiress Clarissa in Richardson's novels, to Thomas Sheridan and his elocution pupils, to Willoughby reading to Marianne in *Sense and Sensibility,* and the members of Dickensian reading circles in the nineteenth century.[89] (In the 1780s, Elizabeth Hamilton commented that the best prose style was "always that which could be longest read without exhausting the breath."[90]) Such practice emerged in the seventeenth century, in works such as Simon Daines's *Orthoepia Anglicana* (1640) or Christopher Cooper's *English Teacher* (1687). But just as the capitalized common noun and italicized proper name lingered in manuscripts and nonliterary texts well into the early nineteenth century, so the two contrasting theories of punctuation were intertwined almost in the same breath from very early on. As John Brightland instructed in 1711: "The Use of these Points, Pauses, or Stops, is not only to give a proper Time for Breathing ; but to avoid Obscurity, and Confusion of the Sence in the joining Words together in a Sentence."[91] Says Thomas Dyche (1736): "THE *Stops* are used to shew what *Distance* of *Time* must be observ'd in *Reading*. And they are so absolutely necessary to *the better Understanding* of what we *write*, and *read*, that without a strict *Attention* to them, all *Writing* would be *confused*, and liable to many *Misconstructions*" (*Guide* 105). In 1775 William Cockin is still telling the counts of commas and colons, as well as "the marks of interrogation (?) and admiration (!)" and the dash (albeit in a footnote).[92]

On the one hand, order and consistency visibly emerge, as even John

Smith observes, warmly approving those "Gentlemen who have regard to make the reading of their Works consonant with their own delivery, point their Copy accordingly, and abide thereby, with strictness" (88). James Buchanan promises in 1767 that the proper arrangement of words and "Members of a Period," or clauses of a sentence, "contribute to a Sense of Order, Elegance, and Perspicuity."[93] But the "confusion" also persisted into the nineteenth century. In *Northanger Abbey* (1818), Mr. Tilney describes to seventeen-year-old Catherine Morland the proper young lady's journal as having "a general deficiency of subject, a total inattention to stops, and a very frequent ignorance of grammar."[94] Jane Austen's own punctuation (and formatting) in manuscript was very different from the more orderly (if still very lively) punctuation of the early editions. Lord Byron simply refused to do his own punctuating amid the early nineteenth century's "mounting weariness and confusion of what the 'correct' use of stops may be" in the rise of "high or dense marking."[95] By 1850 it was still both/and, says William Chauncey Fowler: "The current practice is generally more in accordance with the grammatical than the rhetorical view."[96]

Confusion—or, more cheerfully, invention—bubbled within the emerging order. Novelistic discourse was reorganized on the page as novelists "imposed new conventions of layout and punctuation upon the printer to make it as clear to the reader as possible that the representation of spoken language was intended."[97] The functions of comma and semicolon and colon were more clearly defined and more expressively used. Authors such as Richardson, Sterne, Radcliffe, and Austen developed a particular facility with what Nicholson Baker calls the dash-hybrid.[98] The rest of this chapter will devote itself to the staffage of punctuation peopling the changing landscapes of eighteenth-century texts and their increasing interpretive agility.

Of a COMMA.

> *Comma,* g. (section, cutting,) the smallest of our stops (,).
>
> Elisha Coles, *An English Dictionary* (1685)

"The smallest of our stops" had a tiny little existence in the early days of punctuation and the spaces of the dictionary.[99] In 1658 it is merely "a point in a part of a sentence, without any perfect sense."[100] "*Punctuation* is a modern Art," says Ephraim Chambers in 1728; "the Antients were entirely unacquainted with the Use of our Commas, Colons, &c. and wrote not only without any Distinction of Members, and Periods, but also without Distinction of Words : [. . .] during which time, the Sense alone divided the Discourse" (2:911).[101] Its definitions gradually acquired a little more length, a little more gravitas during the century. In 1704 it is still "*the least note of distinction in writing or printing, marked thus (,)* ," but between 1715 and 1730 its etymology, its secondary meanings, and its ontology of implication muscled up:

> **Comma**, (G a cutting, or paring off from any thing: In *Grammar*, the shortest Point of Distinction, thus marked, (,). In *Musick*, the ninth Part of a Tone, or the Interval whereby a Semi-tone, or a Perfect Tone exceeds the Imperfect.[102]

> **Comma**, (Gr.) A cutting, a little piece or paring cut off from any thing : In *Grammar*, the shortest Point of Distinction, set on part of a Sentence, which only implies a small Rest, or little Pause, and is thus marked (,)

> CO'MMA [κόμμα, *Gr.*] one of the points or stops used in writing, thus marked (,) implying only a small rest or little pause, *L.*[103]

Its "character" in Thomas Dyche's *Guide to the English Tongue* (1736) is that of "a circular Dash at the Foot of a Word"; in his *New General English Dictionary* of 1740 he combines both the elocutionary and the grammatical properties of the comma'd clause: "CO'MMA (S.) one of the most usual marks or stops used in writing or printing, intimating, that the reader should make a small pause or stop, wherever he sees it, in order to collect the sense the more easily, and to fetch breath, marked thus, (,)."[104] Fetching the breath is, for Dyche, "a kind of *Musical Proportion* of *Time*," so that "a *Comma* stops the Reader's Voice, while he may privately, with Deliberation, tell One" (*Guide* 105). (The practice of meditating over each comma we read is not, I diffidently suggest, a current one.) In his *Dictionary* (1755), Samuel Johnson gives a very brief (and entirely grammatical) definition of the comma, with the imprimatur of Pope:

> CO'MMA. *n. s.* [κόμμα]
> 1. The point which notes the distinction of clauses, and order of construction in the sentence, marked thus [,].
>
> *Comma's* and points they set exactly right. *Pope.*
>
> 2. The ninth part of a tone [. . .][105]

James Buchanan, as a grammarian rather than a lexicographer, is at the front of the great wash of works obsessively analyzing the English language (discussed in the next chapter); his chapter "Of STOPS or POINTS, and MARKS or NOTES," in *A Regular English Syntax* (1767), offers richly suggestive descriptions about its variety, about sentence length, and about the reader's experience. He grants more than a full paragraph to the comma. Its primary duties are to "[distinguish] the smallest Members of Sentences" and to follow "every distinct Noun and Verb" (180–81).[106] The "happy Arrangement" of the words in a sentence by means of its pointing "has this Beauty, that by a natural Transition of Perception, it is communicated to the very Sound of the Words, so as in Appearance to improve the Music of the Period" (180). The sheer *appearance* of the punctuation on the page contributes to the sense of rhythm—the "Music"—of the sentence ("Period"). The "natural Transition of Perception" is a particular grammatical approach.

By 1786 Joseph Robertson would list *forty separate uses* for the comma (18–73).[107] He gives the usual brief definition ("a Greek word, which properly means a segment, or a part *cut off* a complete sentence"), as well as its grammatical function ("the POINT, by which a period is subdivided into its least constructive parts") and its rhetorical one ("In reading, it requires a small rest, or a short pause") (18). And then, over the next fifty-five pages, he lists all its glorious possibilities. For example, Rule No. 40 permits the following: "A simple sentence, however, when it is a long one, and the nominative case is accompanied with inseparable adjuncts, may admit of a pause immediately before the verb," as in "THE good taste of the present age, has not allowed us to neglect the cultivation of the English language" (73). He goes on at length about the length of clauses and then notes: "An ingenious writer has observed, that not half the pauses are found in printing, which are heard in the pronunciation of a good reader or speaker ; and that, if we would read or speak well, we must pause, upon an average, at every fifth or sixth word" (75). *Every fifth or sixth word.* This demonstrates the "high or dense marking" that crowds into late eighteenth and early nineteenth-century texts. (The 1877 edition of William Fowler's *English Grammar* gives a mere fourteen rules for the comma.)

We thus have a historical and linguistic context for Ann Radcliffe's well-known penchant for (or frenzy of) commas, displayed to perfection in the opening paragraph of *The Mysteries of Udolpho* (1794) (figure 17):

> ON the pleasant banks of the Garonne, in the province of Gascony, stood, in the year 1584, the chateau of Monsieur St. Aubert. From its windows were seen the pastoral landscapes of Guienne and Gascony, stretching along the river, gay with luxuriant woods and vines, and plantations of olives. To the south, the view was bounded by the majestic Pyrenées, whose summits, veiled in clouds, or
>
> VOL. I B exhibiting
>
> exhibiting awful forms, seen, and lost again, as the partial vapours rolled along, were sometimes barren, and gleamed through the blue tinge of air, and sometimes frowned with forests of gloomy pine, that swept downward to their base. These tremendous precipices were contrasted by the soft green of the pastures and woods that hung upon their skirts ; among whose flocks, and herds, and simple cottages, the eye, after having scaled the cliffs above, delighted to repose.[108]

THE

MYSTERIES

OF

UDOLPHO.

CHAP. I.

"——home is the reſort
Of love, of joy, of peace and plenty, where,
Supporting and ſupported, poliſh'd friends
And dear relations mingle into bliſs."

THOMPSON.

ON the pleaſant banks of the Garonne, in the province of Gaſcony, ſtood, in the year 1584, the chateau of Monſieur St. Aubert. From its windows were ſeen the paſtoral landſcapes of Guienne and Gaſcony, ſtretching along the river, gay with luxuriant woods and vines, and plantations of olives. To the ſouth, the view was bounded by the majeſtic Pyrenées, whoſe ſummits, veiled in clouds, or

VOL. I. B exhibiting

(2)

exhibiting awful forms, ſeen, and loſt again, as the partial vapours rolled along, were ſometimes barren, and gleamed through the blue tinge of air, and ſometimes frowned with foreſts of gloomy pine, that ſwept downward to their baſe. Theſe tremendous precipices were contraſted by the ſoft green of the paſtures and woods that hung upon their ſkirts; among whoſe flocks, and herds, and ſimple cottages, the eye, after having ſcaled the cliffs above, delighted to repoſe. To the north, and to the eaſt, the plains of Guienne and Languedoc were loſt in the miſt of diſtance; on the weſt, Gaſcony was bounded by the waters of Biſcay.

M. St. Aubert loved to wander, with his wife and daughter, on the margin of the Garonne, and to liſten to the muſic that floated on its waves. He had known life in other forms than thoſe of paſtoral ſimplicity, having mingled in the gay and in the buſy ſcenes of the world; but

2 the

17. Ann Radcliffe, *The Mysteries of Udolpho* (1794). Chapter 1, opening pages. First edition Radcliffean commas. Author's transcription.

Radcliffe's narrator takes her time, winding slowly and luxuriantly through her short-lined paragraph, stretching its attention, giving the reader's eye small quick glimpses of river, woods, clouds, mist, summits, precipices, and pastures. The "awful forms" are seen, and lost again, among the mist of commas. "The eye" is isolated; the reader, after scaling all those clauses with her own eye, is likewise delighted to repose at the full stop. The clauses are glances; the paragraph is the winding of the visual approach. The plethora of commas throughout Radcliffe's work directly contributes both to the almost dreamlike rhythms of her prose in the "picturesque" scenes and to the fast-paced terror of the moments of suspense (as when Catherine Morland and Isabella Thorpe in *Northanger Abbey* cannot stop turning pages).

Austen herself, as Kathryn Sutherland has shown, preferred a "lighter" and more "rhythmical" punctuation "distinguished by an overwhelming reliance on commas, full stops, and long dashes."[109] She compares the first edition of *Mansfield Park* (1814) with the second edition of 1816 (the basis for the Oxford standard edition of 1923 by R. W. Chapman) to show the increasing editorial standardization of spelling, capitalization, italicization, and punctuating by grammatical rather than speaking units. The manuscript alternate ending of *Persuasion* illustrates these rhythmical patterns. Anne Elliott has just learned from her invalid friend that her cousin Mr. Elliott, a charming man and would-be suitor, is actually a cold-hearted, scheming predator (which she had rather suspected all along):

> With all this knowledge of M^{r} E—& this authority to impart it, Anne left Westgate Build^{gs}—her mind deeply busy in revolving what she had heard, feeling, thinking, recalling & forseeing everything; shocked at Mr Elliot—sighing over future Kellynch, and pained for Lady Russell, whose confidence in him had been entire.—The Embarrassment which must be felt from this hour in his presence !—How to behave to him?—how to get rid of him?—what to do by any of the Party at home?—where to be blind? Where to be active?—It was altogether a confusion of Images & Doubts–a perplexity, an agitation which she could not see the end of—and she was in Gay S^{t} & still so much engrossed, that she started on being addressed by Adm^{l} Croft, as if he were a person unlikely to be met there.[110]

The commas here largely partition Anne's external actions while the dashes display the flutter of interior thought, which does not settle down until she runs into the Admiral and so must come out of herself. The "confusion of Images & Doubts" is reproduced textually, one thought caught instantly by the next with what Nicholson Baker calls a dash-hybrid ;—.[111] (See the later section "*Of a* DASH.")

Of a COLON *and a* SEMI-COLON.

> *Semicolon*, a half Colon, or Member, being a point in writing, or printing, thus marked (;)
>
> *Colon*, (Greek) a mark or pause of a sentence not fully ended, also one of the three great guts.
>
> Edward Phillips, *The New World of Words*, 1658

While the comma had us musically, privately, and deliberately telling "One," for the semicolon we tell "Two," and the colon, "Three" (Dyche, *Guide* 105). Both have a dictionary history similar to the comma's, acquiring a little more heft through the decades. The semicolon is "a greater Portion of a Sentence than a Comma ; and carries in it an incomplete Sense"; "It is always used when several Nouns, with their different Epithets, equally relate to the same Verb"; and it is "generally used in a Contrast, and in distinguishing Nouns of a contrary Signification" (Buchanan 183). For Robertson, as for the lexicographers, it is "half a member," "used for dividing a compound sentence into two or more parts, not so closely connected, as those, which are separated by a comma ; nor yet so independent on each other, as those, which are distinguished by a colon" (77). Fowler has only three rules for the semicolon.

Edward Phillips's 1658 definition of the colon as "a mark or pause of a sentence not fully ended" is brief and yet poetic, almost a tiny narrative in itself, with a sense of an ending in the lack of an ending, except for its association, after the interstitial comma, with the intestines. Coles's *English Dictionary* (1685) describes it as "half a period." (And "also one of the three great guts.") Kersey's 1715 definition makes it even more corporeal:

> **Colon**, a Member of the Body, especially the Foot, or Arm : In *Grammar*, the middle Point of Distinction, between a Comma and a Period, which is mark'd thus (:) In *Anatomy*, one of the thick Guts, and the largest of all.

Johnson's *Dictionary* is quite skeptical about this point, finding it functionally rubbery:

> CO'LON. *n. s.* [κωλος, *a member.*]
>
> 1. A point [:] used to mark a pause greater than that of a comma, and less than that of a period. Its use is not very exactly fixed : nor is it very necessary, being confounded by most with the semicolon. It was used before punctuation was refined, to mark almost any sense less than a period. To apply it properly, we should place it, perhaps, only where the sense is continued without dependence of grammar or construction ; as, *I love him, I despise him : I have long ceased to trust, but shall never forbear to succour him.*
>
> 2. The greatest and widest of all the intestines, about eight or nine hands breadth long.

Buchanan and Robertson do not share Johnson's doubts; for Buchanan, the colon "marks a perfect Sense ; yet, so as to leave the Mind in Suspense and Expectation of what is to follow" (184). Robertson tells us that a colon is "used with propriety, where a CONJUNCTION is not expressed, but UNDERSTOOD" (86).

I would like to show the semicolon and colon in sophisticated action with three examples from across the eighteenth century. The overall argument is not teleological: the different typographical landscapes have different topographical effects. The footprint scene in Daniel Defoe's *Robinson Crusoe* (1719) demonstrates the visual power of the early textured page, its premodernized special effects. Samuel Richardson employs the punctuational pair with rhetorical effectiveness in a mother-daughter argument in *Clarissa* (1747–48). And Thomas Whately's "Approach to Caversham" in *Observations upon Modern Gardening* (1770), revisited in a new palimpsest from chapter 1, shows how the punctuated page attempts to enact the visual experience of the approach.

Defoe's novels in the early eighteenth century would seem to fulfill Johnson's low expectations for the colon, that its use is not very fixed and that it marks almost any sense less than a period. Defoe's narrators' paragraphs are almost always single complex sentences connected by a series of semicolons and colons, which made Victorian editors apoplectic.[112] But they consistently enact a Robertsonian parataxis—conjunction understood. Ian Gordon, in *The Movement of English Prose* (1966), includes Defoe in a discussion of two of the most common methods in Old English for linking clauses, which persist through the twentieth century: coordination (statements linked by conjunctions) and parataxis (where linking words are absent, replaced by "a firm pause or juncture" [29]). He emphasizes Defoe's "effective paratactic series" in the Footprint scene, where Crusoe sees the imprint of a single foot on the beach of his apparently not-so-deserted island:

> I stood like one thunderstruck, or as if I had seen an apparition: I listened, I looked around me, I could hear nothing, nor see anything. I went up to a rising ground to look further; I could see no other impression but that one. (qtd. in Gordon 30)

Gordon uses modernized punctuation, which has its own prose rhythms, but they are markedly (pun intended) different from the Defovian original:

> I stood like one Thunder-struck, or as if I had seen an Apparition ; I listen'd, I look'd round me, I could hear nothing, nor see any Thing, I went up to a rising Ground to look farther, I went up the Shore and down the Shore, but it was all one, I could see no other Impression but that one.[113]

In a way, this passage could be produced as a counterexample to my point: at least for me, the punctuation in the modernized version is *less* visible than in the textured text. But other visual and oral impacts disappear beneath its surface as well. In the modernized passage, the punctuation allows Crusoe to sit down (rhetorically) several times; it is as if he really is privately and with deliberation telling the counts between clauses and periods. This is a *calm* little paragraph of two sentences, relieving him of what presumably was considered repetitive pacings. The whole typographical apparatus of the 1719 version, on the other hand, is far more mimetic of this mind-gob-smacking moment, beyond the fact that there are two additional clauses: the capitalized and hyphenated "Thunder-struck" bangs louder in the head; clause follows clause follows clause as Crusoe searches up, farther, up, down, listening and looking and hearing nothing and seeing nothing. And although this passage looks like one sentence with ten clauses, all hurrying faster with the one-count comma, it is actually part of an even longer sentence that is the first of two in a paragraph that hinges between wandering around the footprint and running from it.

Samuel Richardson (1689–1761), master printer as well as master novelist, was a textual stylist and punctuational innovator. As M. B. Parkes argues, he "drew upon his taste for the drama, and his experience of printing plays, to introduce marks like the em-rule, or dash, and a series of points to indicate those hesitations and sudden changes in the direction of thought associated with spoken discourse" (92). *Clarissa* was especially influential for later authors. While excellent attention has been paid in recent years to the aesthetic and dramatic effectiveness of Richardson's dashes, his colons and semicolons have received less attention.[114]

The colons employed by Richardson's Clarissa (and she is, after all, the penwoman here, presumably in charge of her point choices) are not the nineteenth-century kind that introduce "after-thoughts"[115] but rather eighteenth-century points marking "a perfect Sense ; yet, so as to leave the Mind in Suspense and Expectation of what is to follow" (Buchanan 184). In a scene early on, where Mrs. Harlowe is urging her to please her father and go back into the parlor to receive the addresses of the repellant Mr. Solmes, Clarissa responds to her mother with emotive punctuation:

> I turned my face to her : My officious tears would needs plead for me : I could not just then speak ; and stood still. [. . .]
>
> She flung from me with high indignation : And I went up with a very heavy heart ; and feet as slow as my heart was heavy.[116]

As we have seen, it was a fairly universal convention in seventeenth- through early twentieth-century books for semicolons and colons to be detached from their clauses; as Smith explains in *The Printer's Grammar*, the "Full-point [. . .] may join to the matter of the closing period ; whereas the other Points not only admit, but require, to be separated from the matter" (101).[117] To choose a colon or semicolon over a comma is thus to choose a clear space on the page between clauses (and this spacing and punctuation *do not change* across at least the first five editions and into Barbauld's 1810 *British Novelists* series); Clarissa and her mother would be textually closer together with commas and full stops. (Though Smith adds: "Even the Comma (we presume) is not under a necessity to clinge to the Matter so close as it always does, in England" [101]). In the first sentence, the two colons balance perfectly poised six-syllable clauses on either side of a decasyllabic one: one holds Clarissa's face, the other her voice, and the middle combines the visual and verbal. "I turned my face to her" makes a "perfect Sense"; the tiny pause is followed by the sight of her tears; another tiny pause for the equally weighted silence—we are "in Suspense and Expectation of what is to follow." But then we have a more deflated pause with the two-count semicolon: things aren't going well. The right response is not called forth. The second sentence is more causal: the mother flings away, where Clarissa had turned toward; the colon pushes out the conjunction; the sad little semicolon again marks an anticlimax. Clarissa's colons and semicolons mark and weight the physical and psychological spaces between mother and daughter.[118]

The last example for this section on overachieving semicolons and colons returns to the approach to Caversham in Thomas Whately's *Observations upon Modern Gardening* (1770) (plate V is my highlighted transcription of this remarkable paragraph). This time, we pay attention to the punctuation rather than to the sentences: here, as in *Clarissa*, those punctuational dividers are not marking Meiklejohn's "after-thoughts," but, rather, clustering related views on the route while "leav[ing] the Mind in Suspense and Expectation of what is to follow" (Buchanan 184). The second sentence marks the stages of the approach, from the entrance, through its "winding in natural easy sweeps," to its rise to the mansion; each new clause presents "some new scene to the view" (Whately 140). The many-claused seventh sentence finds delight in a subtle variety: while "a similarity of style may be said to prevail," the view has a well-planned order of "open plantations" distinguished variously by "a grove," "clumps," "single trees," and plantings on the brow. The eighth sentence sorts the trees. Note again that a sentence can describe not only its subject (landscape) but also itself (punctuation): "The ground, without being broken into diminutive parts, is cast into an infinite number of elegant shapes, in every gradation from the most gentle slope, to a very precipitate fall" (143). The paragraph *is* rather broken into diminutive parts by its commas, but it *does* present a great number of elegant bits, and it *does* create an impressive view at the end of its long avenue. The punctuation of the page does its best to mimic the diversity of the landscape.

Of a PARENTHESIS.

> A PARENTHESIS [from παρεντιςημι, interpono sive obiter insero] is a clause, containing some necessary information, or useful remark, introduced into the middle of a sentence obliquely, which may be omitted, without injuring the construction.
>
> Joseph Robertson, *An Essay on Punctuation*, 2nd ed. (178)

This section will be a parenthetical example, containing some useful information, inserted into the middle of this chapter, obliquely. It may be omitted, without injuring the construction, because parentheticals in general "have a disagreeable effect, being a sort of wheels within wheels, sentence in the midst of sentences, a perplexed method of disposing of some thoughts, which the writer has the art to introduce in its proper place."[119] But it just so happens that Robert Lovelace, the charming rake-villain of *Clarissa*, has a way with parentheses as well as women, as in this letter to his friend "John Belford, *Esq. Cocoa-tree, Saturday, May* 27":

> What ! How ! When !—And all the monosyllables of surprize.
>
> [Within parenthesis let me tell thee, that I have often thought, that the little words in the republic of letters, like the little folks in a nation, are the most significant. The *trisyllables*, and the *rumblers* of syllables more than *three*, are but the good for little *magnates.*] (4:206)

(Later eighteenth-century editions turn the brackets into parentheses.) Robertson allows that "On some occasions parentheses may have a spirited appearance, as prompted by a certain vivacity of thought, which can glance happily aside, as it is going along" (116). Lovelace preens himself on the spirit and vivacity of his letters. But although Robertson warns that "Elegant writers will endeavour to avoid the frequent use of parentheses" (116), and Lovelace considers himself an elegant writer, his entire nature, if not his entire prose, is cast in obliquity, "a sort of wheels within wheels, sentence in the midst of sentences," plot within plot. (He adds three other parentheticals in this letter.[120]) He himself may be described by a line in Maurya Simon's poem "Parentheses: A Bestiary": "A scythe smiling sideways to itself in the mirror."[121]

Of a DASH, *or a short horizontal line, in writing.*

The language police have long fretted over the overuse of the dash. Henry Fielding edited out his sister Sarah's dashes from her novel *David Simple* (1744). Joseph Robertson accused "hasty and incoherent writers" of substituting the dash "in a very capricious and arbitrary manner" for "the regular point" (129). And in 1888 Henry Beadnell "permits himself a wail as just as it is pathetic," according to H. W. and F. G. Fowler in *The King's English* (1908): "The dash is frequently employed in a very capricious and arbitrary manner, as a substitute for all sorts of points, by writers whose thoughts, although, it may be, sometimes striking and profound, are thrown together without order or dependence."[122] The Fowlers go on to blame Sterne's *Tristram Shandy* for the "realms of chaos": even the "modern newspaper writer who overdoes the use of dashes is seldom as incorrect" (275). Nicholson Baker declares that "the single most momentous change in twentieth-century punctuation" was in fact the disappearance of what he calls "the great dash-hybrids."[123] "All three of them—the *commash* ,– , the *semi-colash* ;– , and the *colash* :– (so I name them, because naming makes analysis possible)—are of profound importance to Victorian prose, and all three are now [. . .] extinct" (82). (According to the *Chicago Manual of Style* §5.5, he says, they're actually illegal in the U.S.) He points to their ubiquity in "Dickens, Wilkie Collins, Charlotte Brontë, and

George Meredith. They are on practically every page of Trollope [. . .] They are in Thackeray—[. . .] And in George Eliot—[. . .] The toniest nonfictional Prosicrucians—De Quincey, Carlyle, Ruskin, Newman—also make constant use of dashtards, often at rhetorical peaks" (82–83).[124]

And yet just as many others put the dash firmly back in place. M. B. Parkes showed how Samuel Richardson "drew upon his taste for the drama, and his experience of printing plays, to introduce marks like the em-rule, or dash, and a series of points to indicate those hesitations and sudden changes in the direction of thought associated with spoken discourse"(92). Janine Barchas recovered the dash for Sarah Fielding. Sterne really had no need of all his twentieth- and twenty-first-century defenders to know that he knew exactly what he was doing with his flamboyant punctuation. Baker blazons for us the Victorian splendors of the dash-hybrid. And in her current dissertation, Laura All shows how the marks representing lacunae in Radcliffe's *The Romance of the Forest* (1791) "contribute to creating a Gothic ambience just as much as the secret rooms, locked drawers, crumbling towers, and distant figures dimly seen."[125] In this section I will revisit the *Clarissa* passage from which the colon and semicolon samples were lifted, as well as a passage from Austen's *Northanger Abbey*, to show how expressively and "picturesquely" the dash emerged from the otherwise more uniform typographical landscape of the later eighteenth century. Just when nouns are quieter and the italics are sitting up straight, the dash makes a dash for it.

In the fuller passage (figure 18) where Mrs. Harlowe implores Clarissa to be dutiful to her family's wishes (and Clarissa implores the family to recognize her duty to herself), the dash-hybrids combine emotive punctuation with temporal dilation to create a powerfully charged visual space between the spoken (written, typographical, material) words. Richardson makes full use not just of the colon and semicolon but also of dramatic dashes to give the rhythmic soundscape of deliberation, pause, expectation, hesitation, division (this passage will be revisited yet again for its prepositional energies in chapter 4). The mother's dashes reach out like hands, looking for connection, offering "further opportunity," attaching endearments, gesturing, tying possibility to possibility (go in again, go in again), and holding out that last bait for the Dutiful Daughter: the image of her papa finding her together with Mr. Solmes and behaving herself. But as Clarissa's dashes continually push her mother away, refusing the connection between them, inserting space as she turns to go upstairs, as she ties impossibility to impossibility (what can I do, what can I do). Her mother finally commandeers the dash-as-separator: "go up !—But stir not down again."[126]

We see the taming of the dash in the Anna Lætitia Barbauld's 1810 edition

LETTER XXI.
Miss CLARISSA HARLOW, *To Miss* HOWE.
Sat. Night.

But, Clary, this one further opportunity I give you— Go in again to Mr Solmes, and behave discreetly to him ; and let your papa find you together, upon *civil* terms at least.

My feet moved (of themselves, I think), farther from the parlour where he was, and towards the stairs ; and there I stopp'd and paused. [. . .]

I was moving to go up—

And *will* you go up, Clary ?

I turned my face to her : My officious tears would needs plead for me : I could not just then speak ; and stood still.

Good girl, distress me not thus !—Dear, good girl, do not thus distress me !— holding out her hand ; but standing still likewise—

What can I do, Madam ?—What *can* I do ?—

Go in again, my child—Go in again, my *dear* child !—repeated she ; and let your papa find you together !— [. . .]

Obstinate, perverse, undutiful Clarissa Harlowe ! with a rejecting hand, and angry aspect ; then take your own way, and go up !—But stir not down again, I charge you, without leave, or till your papa's pleasure be known concerning you.

She flung from me with high indignation : And I went up with a very heavy heart ; and feet as slow as my heart was heavy.

❁ ❁ (I:145-6)

18. Samuel Richardson, *Clarissa* (1748). Letter XXI to Miss Howe. Clarissa, dashed and prepped. Author's transcription and highlighting.

of *The British Novelists*, which collection is introduced by the eight volumes of *Clarissa Harlowe*, along with an extensive and influential essay on the genre of the novel. In the same passage, almost half of the dash-hybrids disappear, replaced by single punctuation marks:

> But, Clary, this one further opportunity I give you— Go in again to Mr Solmes, and behave discreetly to him ; and let your papa find you together, upon *civil* terms at least.

My feet moved [of *themselves*, I think], farther from the parlour where he was, and towards the stairs ; and there I stopp'd and paused. [. . .]

I was moving to go up—

And *will* you go up, Clary ?

I turned my face to her : My officious tears would needs plead for me : I could not just then speak ; and stood still.

Good girl, distress me not thus !—Dear, good girl, do not thus distress me ! holding out her hand; but standing still likewise.

What *can* I do, Madam ? What *can* I do ?

Go in again, my child—Go in again, my *dear* child !—repeated she ; and let your papa find you together. [. . .]

Obstinate, perverse, undutiful Clarissa Harlowe ! with a rejecting hand, and angry aspect ; then take your own way, and go up !—But stir not down again, I charge you, without leave, or till your papa's pleasure be known concerning you.

She flung from me with high indignation : And I went up with a very heavy heart ; and feet as slow as my heart was heavy.[127]

The italicized "themselves" and the first "can" of appeal take over some of the job of emphasis. A different house style, a different century; but at more or less the same time that reaction against the picturesqued landscape was setting in, the violently broken lines (the fantastic roots of trees) are pruned a little smoother. Barbauld, who saw *Clarissa* as a textual monument best approached by the old-fashioned, long, straight avenue ("which, without ever losing sight of the object, has more of simplicity and grandeur than the most cunning labyrinth that can be contrived by art"[128]), oversees a small typographical straightening of the text.

In Ann Radcliffe's *The Italian* (1797), the dash is used both within and outside of discourse to choreograph (usually ominous) emphasis. In the scene where the Machiavellian mother of the hero Vivaldi, the Marchesa, is plotting with her confessor-consiglieri Schedoni how best to get rid of the beautiful but literally ignoble Ellena, the dash-play between them looks more like sword-play. (I will reproduce line lengths as well—the rhythms of interruption stand out more violently.)

[Marchesa:] " [. . .] She ought to suffer"—
" Not nearly, but quite equal," inter-
rupted the Confessor, " she deserves—
death !"

[lots of pauses while Schedoni suggests and insinuates and the Marchesa hesitates]

> The Marchesa mused, and remained
> silent.
> " I have done my duty," resumed Sche-
> doni, at length. " I have pointed out the
> only way that remains for you to escape
> dishonour. If my zeal is displeasing—
> but I have done."
> " No, good father, no," said the Mar-
> chesa ; you mistake the cause of my emotion.["]
> *[and into the next chapter:]*
> " This confidence with which you have
> thought proper to honour me," said Sche-
> doni, at length, and paused ; " This affair,
> so momentous"—
> " Ay, this affair," interrupted the Mar-
> chesa, in a hurried manner,—" but when,
> and where, good father ?[" . . .]
> " No matter," said Schedoni, in a stifled
> voice— " she dies !" (2:109, 111, 128, 130)[129]

Radcliffe, as we have seen above, is Very Fond of Punctuation. In this scene, each dash can be read as a separate dramatic marker. Both the Marchesa and the monk think they are manipulating the other. They trade dashes back and forth. The dash can function outside the quotation mark, signaling a pregnant silence between them and an invitation to fill it; it can mark a dramatic pause within the speech leading to the climax; it can signal an aboutface; it can suggest, when combined with the right adjective, a doubt, or a determination over doubt. In short, the dashes operate as shorthand for the two fundamental speechplays here: remaining silent, and resuming at length. ("At length" will feature prominently in the last chapter.)

Catherine Morland, in Austen's *Northanger Abbey* (1797; 1818), has gorged a little too greedily on Radcliffe's novels, and we can see another level of parody in Austen's typography. Catherine, the awed guest of General Tilney, proud owner of Northanger Abbey, and his son and daugher, has just been surprised by young Henry Tilney in the act of investigating his late mother's bedroom, convinced in her heart of hearts that the General had murdered his wife:

> " I have been," said Catherine, looking down, " to see your mother's room."
>
> " My mother's room !—Is there any thing extraordinary to be seen there ? "

> " No, nothing at all.—I thought you did not mean to come back till to-morrow."
>
> " I did not expect to be able to return sooner, when I went away ; but three hours ago I had the pleasure of finding nothing to detain me.—You look pale.—I am afraid I alarmed you by running so fast up those stairs. Perhaps you did not know—you were not aware of their leading from the offices in common use ? "
>
> " No, I was not.—You have had a very fine day for your ride."
>
> " Very ;—and does Eleanor leave you to find your way into all the rooms in the house by yourself ? "
>
> " Oh ! no ; she shewed me over the greatest part on Saturday—and we were coming here to these rooms—but only—(dropping her voice)—your father was with us."
>
> " And that prevented you ; " said Henry, earnestly regarding her.—"Have you looked into all the rooms in that passage ? "
>
> " No, I only wanted to see—Is not it very late ? I must go and dress."[130]

Austen's great early twentieth-century editor R. W. Chapman, whose collations of all early editions comprise the standard Oxford text, argues that Austen's punctuation is "less regular and less logical than the punctuation now in general use, and often resembles the looser 'rhythmical' pointing found in books of the seventeenth century"; he concludes that "to modernize is—in however small a degree—to falsify."[131] But in some ways it is also the *regularity* of her punctuation that is illuminating. These dash-hybrids, like Clarissa's, both push away and pull toward. (In the next chapter I will argue that they behave, in fact, prepositionally: they are both pre-positional and post-positional in that pushing away and pulling toward). Catherine's dash-hybrids urgently try to separate and distract, turning the sentence and Henry's attention *away* from what she's doing in his mother's room and *toward* his ride, his visit, dinnertime, *anything.* But a few desperate punctuation marks are no match for Henry Tilney; he reemploys them to reconnect Catherine back to the moment and the issue at hand. These dash-hybrids, like Clarissa's and the Marchesa's, are lexical markers that quite literally manage relationships in the spaces between the abstract and the concrete. Clarissa, poised between upstairs and downstairs, between family and Lovelace, between heaven and hell, bounds prepositionally upward; the Marchesa and the monk, locked in a duel of wills, perform a duel of dashes; Catherine, poised between upstairs and downstairs, between Tilney and Tilney, between a rather different set of heavens and hells, bounces punctuationally sideways.

Of a PERIOD.

> In English, a sentence of any sort, which is complete in itself, or independent on every other, is called a period ; and the point, distinguished by that name, is always placed at the conclusion.
>
> Joseph Robertson, *An Essay on Punctuation*, 2nd ed. (1786)

And so to bed: I will close this chapter with a period—"The end of a perfect sentence," as Robert Cawdrey put it in *A Table Alphabeticall* (1604). Vivian Salmon, punctilious scholar of punctuation, states that "[f]undamentally, all punctuation is a method (albeit a very crude one) of conveying meaning which is not expressed lexically" ("Seventeenth-Century Punctuation" 347–48). I hope to have shown that the marks on the page, punctuation in particular , can be quite sophisticated and deliberate constructors of nonlexical meaning—grammatical, logical, emotional, *and spatial.* "Written characters" in fact, Mr. Thomas Sheridan notwithstanding, have all sorts of virtues. "Period" marks the end of a sentence; a "period" *is* a kind of sentence popular in the eighteenth century. Robertson describes it as a circuit where the meaning is pending closure; a periodic sentence is, in fact, the syntactical version of THE APPROACH. In both cases expectations are managed with a particular sort of experience in mind. The period, as Hugh Blair says, depends on the "proper arrangement of the words and members" in order to make those members "go on rising and growing in their importance above one another."[132] For the approach, the proper arrangement of drive and landscape leads up to the conclusion of the house. The picturesque landscape of syntax and grammar, of the fantastic roots and winding paths of the prepositional phrase, of the periodic sentence, is the subject of the next two chapters.

CHAPTER 4

The Grammar in Between

> Grammar is the Art of Expressing the Relations of Things in Construction.
>
> Richard Johnson, *Grammatical Commentaries* (1706)

> In the immense field of [. . .] knowledge, innumerable are the paths, and GRAMMAR is the gate of entrance to them all.
>
> William Cobbett, *A Grammar of the English Language* (1819)

In 1762 James Buchanan politely critiques "the judicious Mr [Richard] Johnson" for suggesting that grammar expresses the relation of "Things" in construction; his gentle correction defines it instead as "the Art of expressing the Relations of *Words* in Construction."[1] The linguistic historian of prepositions Tom Lundskær-Nielsen is similarly concerned with the conflation; Anne Fisher, who repeats the construction in her 1759 *A Practical New Grammar* (and all later editions through the eighteenth century), "is open to the same attack for confusing 'things' and 'words.'"[2] "Elsewhere," Lundskær-Nielsen assures us, Johnson "seems to understand that the relations are between words, not things" (162).[3] But throughout the seventeenth and eighteenth centuries there seemed to be a rather notable number of grammarians who have a more allegorical than evidentiary take on the rules of grammar. James Harris, for example, concludes his philosophical discussion of certain parts of speech with the declaration that "THOSE PARTS OF SPEECH UNITED OF THEMSELVES IN GRAMMAR, WHOSE ORIGINAL ARCHETYPES UNITE OF THEMSELVES IN NATURE."[4] That, Lundskær-Nielsen argues, completely "confuses the level of reality with that of linguistic representation" (192). William Ward uses poetry to define the parts of speech, and argues that prepositions, for example, "do not appear in random order, but rather reflect the natural (or, as we might say, unmarked) order of processing spatial relations." That, the modern linguist says, seems "dubious": "it is presumably open to experimental evidence but, to my knowledge, none exists" (233). The linguistic philosophers in Lagado in book III of Swift's *Gulliver's Travels* (1726) literalize the metaphor: "Words are only Names for *Things*"; thus Things may be carried around in sacks and pulled out as needed for conversation.[5] The eighteenth century had its own versions of phenomenologists and logical positivists—the former much more comfortable inhabiting a porous reality, where metaphors might be more substantive than figures of speech. "For all things imprint their forms and shapes in the Mind," says H. C. in his translation of Aristotle's *Rhetoric* in 1686, "and leave certain footsteps of themselves behind, which are imprinted by Nature."[6] As late as 1886 J. M. D. Meiklejohn follows his definition of the preposition as "a word which connects a noun or a pronoun with a verb" with the parenthetical "(It thus shows the relation between things, or between a thing and an action").[7] Some grammarians list the rules; others name the possibilities.

This book is concerned with the Grammars (as in the "fundamental principles or rules of an art or science" [*OED* 6a]) of the Relations between the Things of architecture, landscape, typography, grammar, and narrative patterns, as they are in overlapping or interlocking Construction across the eighteenth century, particularly as the shifting of the older dominant forms permitted newer takes on the things in between. And so, keeping in mind Sir Joshua Reynolds's caveat that it is "a delicate and hazardous thing [. . .] to carry the principles of one art to another, or even to reconcile in one object the various modes of the same Art, when they proceed on different principles,"[8] this chapter will continue the conflation, or at least the systematic alignment, of the figurative and literal, historical and allegorical, architectural and conceptual, physical and psychological, in identifying connections between approaches on the levels of landscape, literature, and the linguistic.

Chapter 1 ended with the avenue turning into the approach, and the approach leading us to the lodge as well as to the house; chapter 2 led into chapter 3 with the prepositional reordering of Old London Bridge, the southern approach to London; chapter 3 closed down the topographical and punctuational page with a section on the "period" as not only the mark at the end of the sentence but also a kind of sentence, "a *circuit* [. . .] in which the meaning is suspended, till the whole is finished"—the syntactical version of THE APPROACH. As the approach depends on the proper arrangement of drive and landscape to lead up to the conclusion of the house, so the period, according to Hugh Blair, depends on the "proper arrangement of the words and members" in order to make those members "go on rising and growing in their importance above one another."[9] The closer analysis of the rhetorical and narrative "period" will be taken up in the last chapter, among the patterns of the narrative and psychological picturesque; here we will investigate the eighteenth-century landscape of grammar itself: the fantastic roots and winding paths of the preposition and "lesser parts of speech." In this chapter we come back with renewed intensity to the words of Robert Lovelace in Richardson's *Clarissa*: "I have often thought, that the little words in the republic of letters, like the little folks in a nation, are the most significant" (4:206).

The rise of grammar

We begin with GRAMMAR as Cobbett's "gate of entrance" to the innumerable paths of (in our case) narrative approach. The history of grammar includes the grammars of every period evaluating their own historical positions even before the field of linguistics erupted in the nineteenth century. Here I want to describe a topography of grammar in the eighteenth century, mapping the changes in its rhetoric onto its changing status, its cultural perceptions.

Before 1700 thirty-four grammars were published in English about English;[10] between 1700 and 1750 another thirty-four appeared; between 1750 and the end of the century, over two hundred.[11] Carol Percy has studied the contemporary reviews of midcentury grammars and noted their excited, if a bit exaggerated, exclamations on the phenomenon:

> According to some reviewers, grammar books "multiply *every month*" (Anon 1765g:389; emphasis added) along with "dictionaries, spelling-books, reading and pronouncing essays, and other *daily* treatises of the same kind" (Anon. 1765e: 138–140; emphasis added), culminating in 1771 with what one reviewer claimed was "an *infinite number* of English grammars" (Anon. 1771c: 314; emphasis added).[12]

The English language underwent a kind of "linguistic engineering," as Laurel J. Brinton and Leslie K. Arnovick explain.[13] That is, the grammatical changes were not "natural" but *designed*. This shift is generally regarded as moving from commodification to prescriptivism (Lundskær-Nielsen 276; Tieken-Boon van Ostade 6); as Andrew Elfenbein argues: "Eighteenth-century standardizers of English let it be known that, whatever had happened in the past, for the future, standardizers, not great writers, would determine the language. As a result of their work, great poetry no longer defined English, but manuals, handbooks, dictionaries, and other guides to usage did."[14] The eighteenth-century commodifying grammars, beginning with Robert Lowth's *A Short Introduction to English Grammar* (1762), culminated in Lindley Murray's definitive ("prescriptive") 1795 *English Grammar*, which went into over three hundred editions during the nineteenth century.[15] But my reading of eighteenth-century grammars finds them much quirkier and more interesting than the "prescriptivist" label suggests.

The latter decades of grammatical explosion are the very years of the architectural approach; of the modernization of the page; of the gothic novel. The interest in vernacular languages as worthy of analysis in their own right, with the possibility of internal rules or grammars distinct from Latin or Greek, or indeed from each other, began in the sixteenth century; the eighteenth century in England witnessed what Lundskær-Nielsen describes as a "zigzag course" between the two poles of the Latin tradition and the national one (96), producing a number of what Otto Jespersen called "squinting grammars," or "grammar squinting at translations in other languages or at other constructions in the same language—instead of looking straight before one, as one should always try to do."[16] This book is all about squinting, in the sense of "To look with the eyes differently directed; to glance obliquely or in other than the direct line of vision" (*OED* 2a). We can argue that the "zigzag course" of delatinizing English was itself a kind of linguistic approach that paralleled the decapitation of the common noun and the complicating of the topographical view: removing or eclipsing the dominant model, the Towering Thing, and discovering what is underneath and in between. Elfenbein surveys the various resistance movements to standardization, including some by the standardizers themselves, and offers some brilliant close readings of grammar, syntax, and punctuation in Chatterton, Coleridge, Wordsworth, Burns, Blake, and Hemans (all of whom could plausibly be identified as purveyors of the linguistic picturesque). I want to argue that even in "standardization"—even in the Capability Browns of grammars—there was more interest shown in the fantastic *roots* of trees, in the substrata of substantives, so to speak.[17] Bishop Lowth himself, with the reputation for proscribing "preposition stranding," described preposition stranding with a stranded preposition: it is, in fact, "an Idiom which our language is strongly inclined to."[18]

The very definitions of "grammar," as with the definitions of punctuation marks we saw in the last chapter, generally acquire more weight, nuance, and interest over the eighteenth century. In 1640 Ben Jonson simply called it "the art of true, and well speaking a language."[19] The seventeenth- and early eighteenth-century definitions continue the concision:

> *Grammatical*, (Greek) belonging to the art of Grammar, *i.e.* the Method of attaining to any language by certain Rules. (Phillips, *The New World of English Words*, 1658)[20]

> *Grammar*, g. the Art of Speaking, Reading, and Writing. (Coles, *An English Dictionary*, 1685)[21]

> Grammar, *the Art of Speaking, Reading, and Writing.* (Cocker, *Cocker's English Dictionary*, 1704)[22]

The art of speaking, reading, and writing begins to acquire a moral or ontological authority: Richard Johnson, in *Grammatical Commentaries* (1706), asserts: "The True Definition of Grammar is this, *Grammar is the Art of Expressing the Relations of Things in Construction, with due Accent in Speaking, and Orthography in Writing, according to the Custom of those, whose Language we learn.*" John Kersey confirms that "**Grammar**" is "the Art of Speaking and Writing truly" (*Dictionarium Anglo-Britannicum*, 1715, 1721). (It is also "a Book which contains the Rules of that Art.") Edward Phillips's 1658 definition (quoted above) is expanded in the eighteenth century: "**Grammar**, (according to *Cicero*'s Definition) is the Art of Speaking and Writing truly, established by Custom, Reason and Authority"; like Kersey, this edition adds its objective correlative, the grammar-book; and also inserts an etymology: "'Tis so call'd from the *Greek* Word *Gramma, i.e.* a Letter, because it shews in the first place how to form articulate Sounds, which are represented by Letters" (*The New World of Words*, 1720).[23] Chambers's 1728 *Cyclopædia* also defines grammar as "the Art of *speaking* rightly," with "rightly" glossed as "expressing one's Thoughts, by Signs mutually agreed on for that purpose."[24] From enabling one to reach out and "[attain] to any language" in the mid-seventeenth century, grammar became a way of delivering from within. It is almost spatial.

That sense of spatial, three-dimensional relationship is concretized by Richard Johnson (1706) and Anne Fisher (1759) in the phrase that so irks James Buchanan in 1762 and Tom Lundskær-Nielsen in 2011: grammar as "*the Art of Expressing the Relations of Things in Construction.*"[25] Fisher determinedly retained her hold on "Things" throughout her many editions beyond Buchanan's objection, and she is not the only one to employ a material metaphor (if metaphor indeed is what it is). In 1728 Ephraim Chambers reports:

> Some have called *Grammar* the Door, or Gate of the Arts and Sciences ; by reason none of these are attainable, but by means hereof. *Grammar*, according to *Quintilian*, is that to Eloquence, which the Foundation is to the Building : They who despise it, as only dealing in low, trivial Things, are exceedingly mistaken : It has, really, more Solidity than Shew. (1:177)

Ninety years later William Cobbett wrote to his son that in "the immense field of [. . .] knowledge, innumerable are the paths, and GRAMMAR is the gate of entrance to them all."[26] And as we will see in the next section, somewhere in between Johnson, Fisher, and Cobbett, the sense of grammar as dealing with *things* in relation to each other will transfer some of that sense of materiality to one of its minuter parts, the preposition—the little lever of spatial and temporal relations between things.

By the middle of the eighteenth century, grammar acquires the gravitas of a science. Thomas Dyche, in the third edition of *A New General English Dictionary* (1740), argues that "the science, as such, is the same all over the world, and the difference between the *grammar* and system of one language and another is purely accidental, the essence being universally the same."[27] Anne Fisher's first grammar of 1745 claims the field is "truly accounted the Basis of Literature, being the Source from which all the other Sciences proceed"; Lundskær-Nielsen comments on the boldness of this claim for its time.[28] The definition in Samuel Johnson's *Dictionary* (1755) also adds "science" to "art" and adds the signature literary exemplars:

> GRA'MMAR. *n. s.* [*grammaire,* French; *grammatica,* Latin; γραμματκη.]
> 1. The science of speaking correctly ; the art which teaches the relations of words to each other.
>
> To be accurate in the *grammar* and idioms of the tongues, and then as a rhetorician to make all their graces serve his eloquence *Fell.*
>
> We make a countryman dumb, whom we will not allow to speak but by the rules of *grammar*. *Dryden's Dufresnoy.*
>
> Men, speaking language according to the *grammar* rules of that language, do yet speak improperly of things. *Locke.*[29]

It was in a scientific vein that James Buchanan corrected Richard Johnson (and implicitly Anne Fisher) for mistaking "Things" for "Words" in 1762; grammar is repeatedly characterized as a science in the later eighteenth century:

> *Grammar* is the Science of Letters. (1751)[30]

> Gram'mar (*s. from* gramma) The science of letters, the act of speaking and writing correctly, correctness of speaking and writing, a book which treats of the various relations of words to each other. (1775)[31]

> Gram-mar, *s.* the science of writing correctly. (1777)[32]

From a science, grammar moves into manners, increasingly becoming a matter of propriety. Samuel Johnson's second definition asserts that grammar is "[p]ropriety or justness of speech ; speech according to grammar." Bishop Lowth, who would be held up as the monitor of mannered propriety through the centuries, and whose influence lingers into the present, did *not* actually define grammar as the "proper" way of speaking but as "the Art of rightly expressing our thoughts by Words" (17). His term "rightly" seems more embedded in the early eighteenth-century world of "truly," of rules of a system rather than codes of conduct. Lowth was *made into* the image of proper English for more than a century. It was other grammarians who picked up Johnson's notion of "propriety." *The Female Miscellany* of 1770 defines "ENGLISH GRAMMAR" as "the Art of speaking and writing English in a proper manner; that is, according to the pervailing [*sic*] Custom."[33] Dilworth's "Science of Letters" adds: "the Art of Writing and Speaking properly and syntactically." And Duncan Mackintosh ("and His Two Daughters"), in *A Plain, Rational Essay on English Grammar* (1797), turns propriety itself into a science (figure 19):

2
1 4 3 21 1 3 1 1 21 1 2 243
GRAM'MAR is the a'rt *of* spe*a*k'ing and *w*rit'ing with propri'ety.

19. Duncan Mackintosh, "Gram'mar" (1979). Mackintosh, plain and rational. Author's transcription.

Art itself, Mackintosh claims, is "a rational method—a system of rules and examples, digested into convenient order, for the teaching and learning of something : and the methodical collection of rules and observations made on the genius of a nation, in the institution, order and use of their words, is what is meant by Grammar."[34]

Rather as for Henry Tilney it was an easy step from politics to silence, so the gravitas of grammar could easily slip into pedantry: "GRAMMATICA'STER, a Smatterer in Grammar ; a paltry School-Master" (1730).[35] *See also*: "GRAMMATICA'STER (S.) a pretender to, or a smatterer in the art of grammar, without being really skilful" (1740); "Grammaticáster. n. s. [Latin.] A mean verbal pedant; a low grammarian" (Johnson, *Dictionary*, 2nd ed., 1755–56).

Yet certainly by the end of the eighteenth century, those who despise grammar "as only dealing in low, trivial Things" are mistaken indeed. The proliferation of grammars, and the increased interest in the internal workings of the vernacular per se, enabled other low, trivial Things to come into view. As Carol Percy says, variations in the emerging grammatical standards "could be used for quite nuanced stylistic effects."[36] The so-called lesser parts of speech—like the typographical forms of punctuation—became more visible, acquired new interest, and began to form their own new combinations of rhetorical and visual patterns. The perceptual experiences of changing perspectives—these designed "approaches" in architecture—find a common linguistic denominator in a changing grammatical landscape, away from objects and things (those capitalized common Nouns) to the spaces in between (prepositions). The move to standardize grammar brought what George Dalgarno in 1661 had called the "nerves and ligaments" of written text into surface visibility.[37]

The rise of the preposition

THE prepositions are as marks design'd
Of modes of thought exerted, when the mind
By substantives so circumstantiates,
Or objects nam'd by nouns, or verbal states,
That sev'ral things unite in diff'rent views,
And no encrease of number thence ensues.
William Ward, *An Essay on Grammar* (1765)

What better way to open a section on the rise of the preposition than with a poem in its honor?[38] In fact, Ward's poem—intended as a mnemonic, she said doubtfully—is one of *three* poems in honor of the preposition in this chapter. While this particular little ditty may not be as helpful in remembering the function of the preposition as it hopes, the bare fact that the preposition earned itself a poem in the eighteenth century is certainly something to mark. Toward the end of the eighteenth century the linguistic perspective, like the architectural, typographical, and literary, swerved away from previous formal models—away from the avenue, the direct view, the capitalized common noun, from objects and things and it-narratives—and began to pay attention to the different relations *between* them—to the prepositional relation of prepositions, we might say.[39] In effect, the trend reversed the efforts of the School of Languages in *Gulliver's Travels*. Now the Nouns were *not* the only Things "necessary to express the particular Business they are to discourse on."[40] Or to put it obversely, as the print world was pushing against the "oblique inclination" of the italic in the name of smoothing and paving the topography of the page, and the smoothing and leveling of Old London Bridge opened up a new sense of approach to London, so the grammatical attention began to "squint" less at classical languages, "looking straight" at the idiosyncracies of its own vernacular. Richard Wendorf argues that the typographical debate "involved not just writers and printers but grammarians and encyclopedists as well" because "what is at stake [. . .] is not just the 'proper' function of various typographical conventions but the necessity of employing these mediating modes of pointing, distinction and emphasis in the first place."[41] I suggest that the typographical leveling allegorically cleared the spaces between nouns; the typographical made room, as it were, for the grammatical.

The "lesser parts of speech" had, until the late eighteenth century, a fairly ignominious history, at least in English—the Italians had been interested in the preposition since the sixteenth century. Indeed, ignominy persisted even among linguists in the twentieth century; as Ray Jackendoff complained in a groundbreaking article of 1973:

> People seem never to have taken prepositions seriously. One proposal in print (Fillmore (1968)) treats prepositions as case markers, having equal status with the case inflections of Latin or German. Another proposal (Postal (1971)) treats them as realizations of features on noun phrases. Still another (Becker and Arms (1969)) tries to reduce prepositions to a subclass of the category "verb." What all these proposals have in common is that they deny that the category "preposition" has any real intrinsic syntactic interest other than as an annoying little surface peculiarity of English.[42]

By the end of his argument he will claim with deep satisfaction: "Our rather simple observations make it far more difficult to treat prepositions merely as features of verbs or nouns, phonologically realized through trivial transformations. Prepositions must instead be accorded the right to a small but dignified syntactic category of their own" (355).

The linguistic reformations of the School of Lagado left out "Verbs and Participles; because in reality all things imaginable are but Nouns" (*Gulliver's Travels* 177). Swift may have thought that was silliness, but a more complex version of the concept was held by a number of early linguists. As Charles Coote speculated in 1788, "It is highly probable, that, in the first formation of language, only the noun and the verb were for some time in use ; as these contain in themselves the essence of speech, and can form, without the assistance of other words, a perfect affirmative sentence, which the other parts of speech, unaided by these, are incapable of effecting."[43] Prepositions were sometimes treated as subclasses of particles, sometimes as their own part of speech, sometimes as cases, and for one seventeenth-century grammarian, as a kind of noun. (And as Lundskær-Nielsen puts it, "There is as little consensus among grammarians nowadays regarding the number and constitution of word classes, and the definition of prepositions, as there was during the more than two centuries of English grammars" [22].) Ian Michael explains: "The function of the preposition was traditionally 'to be set before' another word; the grammarian's eye was fastened not on the preposition itself but on the word it governed" (454). Like that prepositional building the park gate lodge, the preposition itself was literally over-looked. But as English grammarians began to take more interest in English grammar on its own terms rather than as derived from Latin, the preposition (like other "little words") was recognized as giving "a peculiar *Beauty*, *Fluency*, and *Elegancy* to our Language ; by the Help of which we do all that the *Greeks* and *Latins* did" (Fisher 1759, 89n). Or as Margaret Doody says of Augustan poetry: "Grammatical elements, themselves lucid and glassy, take on the bright colours of what they support: 'Die *of* a Rose, *in* aromatic pain'; 'Slow rose a form *in* Majesty *of* Mud.'"[44]

In the eighteenth century we witness the rise of the Allegorical Preposition, along with the other "lesser parts of speech"—Robert Lovelace's "little words." My approach is more historical and rhetorical than strictly linguistic: I am interested in the ways that prepositions are *described* as a preparation for the ways they are then differently employed. My preposition will stand in for all the little spaces in between Noun and Verb, for what is seen from the oblique perspective, as the little words came to play a more emphatic, self-advertising role in narrative patterns of the later eighteenth century, forming new combinations on the page and in the mind via new grammatical approaches. Prepositions, like punctuation, became interesting in their own right as "lynchpins of contingency," as Jayne Lewis has said. They emerged as yet another set of Clifford Siskin and William Warner's mediating toolbox of "everything that intervenes, enables, supplements, or is simply in between."[45] The overlooked preposition is unearthed and acknowledged as a powerful lever of literary meaning.

William Clare's 1690 definition of the preposition as "an undeclined part of Speech, which is put before other parts of Speech either in *composition*, or else in *apposition*,"[46] was itself a figuratively undeclined definition "since the Roman grammarians" (Lundskær-Nielsen 153). The early definitions were spare, the early appreciation dim. The preposition was a "Woord without number and case" (1633);[47] "a part of speech set before other parts; either in apposition, or composition" (1654);[48] "A putting before, also one of the eight parts of Speech in Grammar, so called because it is set before a Noun or Verb" (Phillips 1658, 1720); "*a word, or part of speech placed before other parts*" (Cocker 1704); "one of the 8 Parts of Speech, so call'd, because it is set before a Noun, or Verb" (1715);[49] "Parts of Speech in *Grammar*, so called because set before a Noun" (1730);[50] they are "Fore-placed Words" (1711, 1735).[51] Prepositions did not get much dictionarial attention because they did not seem to do much work compared to nouns and verbs. As the author of the 1708 *Compleat Guide to the English Tongue* snorts about adverbs, conjunctions, and prepositions: "I Shall speak of these three Parts of Speech under one Head, because I han't [*sic*] much to say of any of them; and leave out the *Interjections,* as the most barren of 'em all."[52] Ephraim Chambers's *Cyclopædia* (1728, 1738, 1751) notes that "F. Buffier does not allow the *preposition* to be a part of speech, but merely a modificative of a part of speech ; *viz.* of the noun ; serving only to modify or circumstantiate it."[53] And in 1819 William Cobbett said of prepositions, "[O]f what *use* [is it] to us to enter on, and spend our time in, inquiries of mere curiosity? It is for monks, and for Fellows of English Colleges, who live by the sweat of other people's brows, to spend their time in this manner, and to call the result of their studies *learning.*"[54]

As with the punctuation marks and the term "grammar" itself, prepositions and other little words began to get slightly thicker definitions toward the middle of the century. Thomas Dyche elaborates on the basic definition ever so slightly: "PREPOSI'TION (S.) a placing or putting before any thing; and particularly spoke of those small particles in a language that are put or set before others" (Dyche 1740). By the middle of the eighteenth century more roles for the preposition were identified. A certain kind of prepositional *power* emerges, as in Chambers's *Cyclopædia* of 1752: "The *preposition* is an indeclinable particle, which yet serves to govern the nouns that follow it. Such are, *per, pro, propter, in, with, through, from, by,* &c. They are called *prepositions,* because *præpositæ,* placed before the nouns they govern" (2:416). "Govern" appears with increasing regularity; in John Marchant's 1760 *New and Complete English Dictionary,* the preposition is "so called because it serves to govern the noun that follows it ; such as *through, for, with, by,* &c."[55] By 1751 Thomas Dilworth brings in the concept of analogical relationships: "*Analogy* teaches us how to know distinctly all the several Parts of *Speech* in the *English Tongue*" (97). *Relationships* become central to the perception of prepositions. The preposition, Dilworth embellishes, is "a Part of Speech regularly set before a Word of another Part of Speech, either separated from it or joined to it, to signify its *Rest, Alteration,* and *Manner of Motion*" (114). Lowth's *English Grammar* (1762) adds to the standard definition of prepositions as "so called because they are commonly *put before* the words to which they are applied" (note his emphasis); their function is "to connect words with one another, and to shew the relation between them" (113). The *Vocabulary, or Pocket Dictionary* printed by John Baskerville (1765) explains that prepositions "express the Relation which one Word has to another ; such as, *of, with, from, to* &c. as, *He bought the Book* WITH *Money* ; *He went* FROM

York TO *London*."[56] John Ash's *New and Complete Dictionary* (1775) defines a preposition as "a word set before *nouns*, or *pronouns*, to express the relation of persons, places, or things to each other: as, he came *to*, and stood *before* the city" (14). And Coote's 1788 *Elements of the Grammar of the English Language* sets the relational definition historically: "PREPOSITIONS are words of very frequent use. The generality of them originally denoted the relation of place ; but they are now used to express other relations. The following is a list of them, *viz. Of, to, from, for, by, in, into, at, with, within, without, up, down, on* or *upon, off, over, through, above, below, beneath, under, before, after, behind, beyond, till, about, against, among, between, toward*, &c." (152).

Although the preposition was for the most part sparely defined and generally under-regarded before the middle of the eighteenth century, there was a line of philosophical interest in and materialist expression of these "ligaments" of grammar from the seventeenth century that swells in the late eighteenth and finds a Greek chorus in the nineteenth. In 1661 George Dalgarno declared in *The Art of Signs* that "particles" (which include prepositions)

> are to speech what the soul is to man, what the nerves and ligaments are to the body, or what cement is to the building. For, if particles are taken away from speech, what remains? What else but a dead body without the form of man? Or unconnected limbs without the form of a body? Or a pile of stones without the form of a house? And just as the particles constitute the formal and most primary part of speech, and indeed likewise the most difficult one (the whole practice of logic and grammar residing in their correct use), so they also constitute the most important part of speech. It is for that reason that I call the analysis of the particles, and their reduction to rules of art, the key to the invention. (241)

The linguistic and the metaphoric abstractions rhetorically materialize in one breath as body and building; piles of stones are emphatically Things (and distinctly not "low, trivial Things") in need of Construction.

For John Wilkins, in *An Essay Towards a Real Character, and a Philosophical Language* (1668), prepositions are those "*Connexive* Particles" that express the "*Construction of word with word*" (adverbs and conjunctions express the "*Contexture of sentence with sentence*"); they "joyn Integral with Integral" in the service of "*Cause, Place, Time*."[57] Although he describes them as "having a Subserviency to Nouns" to such an extent that some grammarians obliterate their nominal identity—"by some stiled *Adnomia*, or *Adnomina* and *Prænomia*"—Wilkins himself not only retains their names, he constructs and illustrates a sort of galaxy for them: "There are thirty six Prepositions

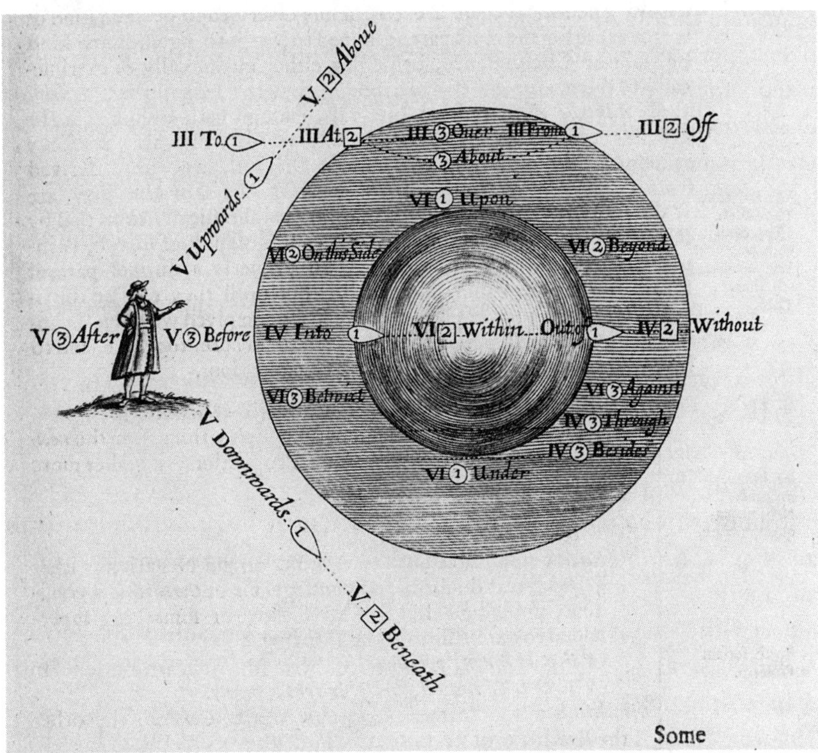

20. John Wilkins, "Preposition Man." From *An Essay Towards a Real Character, and a Philosophical Language* (1668). Figure 1, p. 311. Photograph courtesy of The Newberry Library (Case folio X 186. 974), Special Collections.

or eighteen paires of them, or six Combinations, which may, with much less equivocalness then [*sic*] is found in instituted Languages, suffice to express those various respects, which are to be signifyed by the kind of Particle" (309). He then refers the reader to the "diagram" (figure 20). He explains that the "*Oval Figures*" represent "*Prepositions determined to Motion*" while the "*squares*" signify "*rest* or the *Terms* of *Motion*" and the "*round* [. . .] may indifferently refer either to *Motion* or *Rest*" (311). The whole engraving has a rather cosmic narrative quality, with the grammatical surveyor, in cloak and cap, standing on a floating patch of earth, poised between a suggestive "Before" and "After," "Upwards" and "Downwards," and pointing toward his brave new world, in which (rather like the allegorical characters in John Bunyan's *The Pilgrim's Progress* [1678]) the abstract is infiltrated by the material; the allegorical is absorbed into the real.

John Locke, in *An Essay Concerning Humane Understanding* (1690), also recognized the rich possibilities of the preposition. Nouns, "which are names of *Ideas* in the Mind," get the most attention, but the study of "*Particles*" has been, "perhaps, as much neglected, as some others over-diligently cultivated." The words that "signifie the *connexion* that the Mind gives to *Ideas, or Propositions, one with another*" are what, with "right use," determine "the clearness and beauty of a good Stile." Thus,

> he who would shew the right use of Particles, and what significancy and force they have, must take a little more pains, enter into his own Thoughts, and observe nicely the several Postures of his Mind in discoursing. [. . .] They are all *marks of some Action, or Intimation of the Mind* ; and therefore to understand them rightly, the several views, postures, stands, turns, limitations, and exceptions, and several other Thoughts of the Mind, for which we have either none, or very deficient Names, are diligently to be studied.[58]

The body of our mind, so to speak, is sculpted by prepositions; or in another sense, the approach of the mind—its views and turns, its pauses and motions—is shaped by prepositional acts, and if we *enter* our mind and *observe* its "Postures," rather like a psychological Capability Brown, we would discover the "significancy and force" of those bits of grammatical landscape that so unjustly escape "cultivation."

A few early eighteenth-century grammarians answered the call of Dalgarno, Wilkins, and Locke. James Greenwood, in *An Essay Towards a Practical English Grammar* (1711) offers a sort of "contexture" of Dalgarno and Locke:

> The *Prepositions* of which we shall now treat, and the *Conjunctions*, of which we shall speak hereafter, are as it were, the *Nerves* and *Ligaments* of all Discourse ; and we cannot attain to a right Knowledge of any Language, without a good Understanding of these two Parts of Speech. The other Parts of Speech are Materials prepared for the Building ; but the *Prepositions* and *Conjunctions* are the *Mortar* and *Lime* which are to cement and join those Materials together.[59]

He too, like Locke, will "shew you their Significancy and Force" (he has the grace then to quote Locke); while "some" call particles the "little Parts of Speech," *he* will "treat of the Doctrine of Prepositions, next to that of *Noun Substantives*," since these "little Words, being rightly understood, the whole *Syntax*, or *Construction* of *Substantives* is learnt at the same time." And he promises that "if this shall meet with any Encouragement, [he] may be excited to make farther Improvements in these Matters, by taking more Pains to observe nicely the several Postures of the Mind in Discourse" (72). Greenwood apparently did not get enough encouragement to excite him into further postural explorations, but the root system of a picturesque preposition continued to spread underground.

As Thomas Dilworth said, "*Analogy* teaches us how to know distinctly all the several Parts of *Speech* in the *English Tongue*" (97). Analogy and allegory mark the rise of the preposition, the roots beginning to gnarl above the grammatical ground by mid-century. In 1751 James Harris in *Hermes; or, a Philosophical Inquiry Concerning Language and Universal Grammar* observes that "tho' the original use of Prepositions was to denote *the Relations of Place*, they could not be confined to this Office only. They by degrees extended themselves to Subjects *incorporeal*, and came to denote Relations, as well *intellectual*, as *local*" (268). Prepositions early burst their bounds—in Harris's view, moving from the concrete to the abstract, but in a Lagadian sense: "the *first Words* of Men, like their *first Ideas*, had an immediate reference to *sensible Objects*, and that in after Days, when they began to discern with their *Intellect*, they took those Words, which they found *already* made, and transferred them by metaphor to *intellectual* Conceptions" (268–69). That is, Things in Construction became things of construction. And the preposition, though "devoid it self of Signification," is actually the force that unites "*two Words that are significant, and that refuse to co-alesce or unite of themselves*" (261; original emphasis). The preposition wrestles the obstinate nouns into a meaningful relationship. As Anne Fisher puts it, "by the Help of little Words called *Prepositions*," the English language is able to express the "*Affections* of Things to one another" (1759, 65n). And by their help, English is every bit as good as Greek and Latin, to quote her note in full:

> *Besides the *separate Use* of *Prepositions* they have *another*, which is to be joined in Composition with a vast Number of Words ; and by this Means, they create a great *Variety*, give a peculiar *Beauty*, *Fluency*, and *Elegancy* to our Language ; by the Help of which we do all that the *Greeks* and *Latins* did, partly by Prepositions, and partly by the Diversity and Difference of Cases. (1759, 89n)

The underground particle gets the help of the underground subtext to push its way into view. Philip Dormer Stanhope, 4th Earl of Chesterfield, wrote to his son in 1751 about the critical importance of some other "little words": "Our pronouns and relatives often create obscurity or ambiguity; be therefore exceedingly attentive to them, and take care to mark out with precision their particular relations."[60] By 1765 James Elphinston recognizes the "numberless elegancies" of which "every particular preposition" is "susceptible"; they are "directives of motion or exhibitives of situation" that "in their vast variety of literal and figurative service, [. . .] become happy instruments of the most delicate combinations, whether of noun and noun, verb and verb, or of noun and verb together."[61]

The 1775 edition of Lowth's *A Short Introduction to English Grammar* treats the preposition extensively, its own footnote root system in some places overtaking the page's main text, bulging with the energy of subterranean growth—the *visual* effect is of Substance (figure 21):

3] The Particle *a* before Participles, in the phrases *a* coming, *a* going, *a* walking, *a* shooting, &c.; and before Nouns, as *a*-bed, *a*-board, *a*-shore, *a*-foot, &c. ; seems to be a true and genuine Preposition, a little disguised by familiar use and quick pronunciation. Dr. Wallis supposes it to be the preposition, a*t.* I rather think it is the Preposition *on* ; the sense of which answers better to the intention of those expressions. *At* has relation chiefly to *place : on* has a more general relation, and may be applied to a*ction*, and many other things, as well as *place.* "I was *on* coming,, *on* going," &c ; that is, employed *upon* that particular *action :* so likewise those other phrases above-mentioned, *a*-bed, &c. exactly answer to *on* bed, *on* board, *on* shore, *on* foot. Dr. Bentley plainly supposed *a* to be the same with *on* ; as appears from the following passage : "He would have a learned University make Barbarisms *a* purpose." Dissertation on Phalaris, p. 223. "The depths *on* trembling fell." J. Hopkins, Ps. Lxxvii.16. That is, as we now say in common discourse, "they fell *a* trembling."And the Preposition *on* has manifestly deviated into a in other instances : thus the Saxon compounded Prepositions [. . .] Much in the same manner, John *of* Nokes, and John *of* Stiles, by very frequent and familiar use, became John *a* Nokes, John *a* Stiles : and one *of the* clock, or perhaps *on the* clock, is written, one *o*'clock, but pronounced, one *a* clock. The phrases with *a* before a Participle are out of use in the solemn style ; but still prevail in common discourse. They are established by long usage, and good authority: and there seems to be no reason, why they should be utterly rejected.

[1] " *Who* servest thou *under ?*' Shakespear, Hen. V.
" *Who* do you speak *to?*" As you like it.
I'll tell you, w*ho* Time ambles *withal, who* Time trots *withal, who* Time gallops *withal*, and *who* he stands still *withal.*
"I pr'ythee, w*hom* doth he trot w*ithal*?" Ibid.
"We are still much at a loss, w*ho* civil power belongs *to.*" Locke.
In all these places, it ought to be *whom.*
" Now Margaret's curse is fall'n upon our heads,
When she exclaim'd *on* Hastings, you, and *I.*"
Shakespear, Rich. III.
It ought to be *me.*

21. Robert Lowth, *A Short Introduction to English Grammar* (1775), 114–15n3, 163–64n1. Author's transcription.

William Scott, an Edinburgh schoolmaster, was one of the first to recognize "the adjectival and adverbial function of the phrase formed by a preposition" (Michael 455). The preposition "always requires another part of speech after it, with which it expresses a circumstance of some word or words preceding it."[62] As Ian Michael notes, "To have such a flexible view of the preposition was not, in the 1770s, an entirely trivial achievement" (455). Before this, although the early grammarians were aware of the backward-reference possibilities of the preposition (and its consequent similarity to the adverb), it was given no prominence "partly because the change of case kept their attention on the noun" (Michael 454). But as we are seeing, attention was beginning to shift from the major parts of speech to the spaces in between.

Hugh Blair argued in his *Lectures on Rhetoric and Belles Lettres* (1783): "Prepositions and conjunctions, are words more essential to discourse than the greatest part of the adverbs. They form that class of words, called connectives, without which there could be no language, serving to express the relations which things bear one to another, their mutual influence, dependencies, and coherence ; thereby joining words together into intelligible and significant propositions."[63] They are, in fact, "the foundation of all reasoning" (Blair 85). In 1788 Charles Coote devotes a good seventeen pages to the preposition. His speculative history of the grammatical origin of language sounds rather like the origin story in Genesis:

> Of these two essential parts of speech, the noun and the verb, the former, in all probability, first suggested itself to the inventors of language. The utility of giving names to the various objects that presented themselves, was too obvious not to strike them on the first view of the subject. Hence arose that part of speech which grammarians style a *noun*, that is, a *name* expressive of any substance that exists either in nature, or merely in the imagination. This is also called a *substantive*, from it's [*sic*] being appropriated to the designation of *substances*. (7)

He takes issue with James Harris, who in *Hermes* "considers the definitives and connectives, that is, the articles, conjunctions, and prepositions, as having no signification of themselves." But since, he argues, prepositions et al. were originally constructed from nouns and verbs, "they may well be supposed to have a meaning of themselves," though they cannot form a sentence on their own (Coote 6n*(b)*). He brings them to life, with detailed examples that are refreshingly mix-gendered and semi-narrativized:

> *At (q)* is annexed to the place or time in which any thing is said to have happened, or to be likely to happen ; as, *they are now* at *the same place ; he departed from England* at *the beginning of the year ; he will be here* at *ten o'clock* at *night.* Sometimes it merely intimates nearness ; as, *he is standing* at *the front door.* It also refers to a particular action or state of being, &c. as, *they are* at *study* ; *he is* at *enmity with her ; she frequently plays* at *cards ; he pillaged the province* at *discretion ; that house was sold* at *a great price.* (156)

By the middle of the nineteenth century, the preposition bursts into linguistic and allegorical glory in William C. Fowler's *English Grammar: The English Language in its Elements and Forms* (1850). It is worth giving a *glimpse* of the extent and depth of attention he grants the preposition and contrast it to Charles Butler's 1633 definition in *The English Grammar,* "Woord without number and case." For Fowler, prepositions are striking analogies between the "external or sensible world with the internal or intellectual"; much like C. F. Partington's 1825 view of page proofs expressing "the form and texture of our thoughts" (chapter 3), Fowler's prepositions express "the form of our ideas." Fowler's system, like Wilkins's two centuries before, is a beautiful, *spatial* one, connecting the physical and intellectual worlds, capturing an "almost infinite" set of relations within the "wonderful economy" of a few small words (figure 22):[64]

THE NATURE AND OFFICE OF PREPOSITIONS.

§ 328. 1. Prepositions, although a secondary and less important part of speech, deserve more attention than is usually paid to them in our common grammars. They exhibit in a striking manner the analogy of the external or sensible world with the internal or intellectual. [. . .]

3. Prepositions express neither essences, (like substantives,) nor activities, (like verbs and adjectives,) but only their relations. They express not the substance, but the form of our ideas. Hence they are ranked by Becker with form-words.

4. Prepositions are indeclinable, as the relations of things are external to the things themselves, and are not affected by the changes which take place in them.

5. Prepositions express relations between verbs whose original nature consists in activity or motion, or some other parts of speech involving the verbal idea, and a noun expressing an essence. Of course, with very few exceptions, they denote local relations, or other relations conceived of as local relations by the mind.

6. The relations expressed by prepositions are either external or internal to the human mind. The external relations are of a physical nature, and obvious to the senses. The internal relations belong to the province of the intellect. As these higher relations are subject to the same analysis as the sensible relations, and the mind supposes a close resemblance between the physical and intellectual worlds, so prepositions denoting the external relations are also employed to express the internal.

7. Physical relations are for the most part local. Activity is motion. Relations of activity are directions of motion. These relations arrange themselves in antitheses, forming a beautiful system; as, *In* and *out*, the only absolute relation of space; Latin *cis* and *trans*; *before* and *behind*; *above* and *below*, relative relations of space; *to* and *from*, relations of direction; *into* and *out of*, a compound relation, etc. This system is too little regarded in our common grammars.

8. Intellectual relations are conceived of as physical, and are expressed by prepositions denoting physical relations. They are exhibited to others, as they strike our own minds. [. . .]

9. Prepositions thus exhibit a wonderful correlation between the intellectual and physical worlds; a correlation which shows that both worlds proceeded from the same Author.

10. Prepositions exhibit the wonderful economy of language. The number of relations is almost infinite; yet they are all expressed by a comparatively small number of prepositions, and this without any confusion or danger of mistake. We are guided in the meaning by the nature of the ideas between which the relation exists; but if one local relation were used for another, confusion would immediately arise. [. . .]

22. William Fowler, "The Nature and Office of Prepositions" (1850). Fowler and the wonderful preposition. Author's transcription.

Jo Rubba argues that over time the preposition acquired an increasing "semantic independence" in its "freedom to combine with dependent predications" as, for example, body-part terms shifted via metonymy and metaphor "from a THING profile to a RELATIONAL profile" and that cognitive grammar can "bring us closer to an understanding of the nature and features of this particular kind of linguistic change."[65] A linguist's approach to historical change is different from a literary critic's; my effort here has been to demonstrate how the *language* of language—the descriptions of prepositions—changed across the eighteenth century and into the nineteenth, tracking the linguistic landscape from an attitude of treating adverbs, conjunctions, and prepositions "under one Head" because one "han't much to say of any of 'em," to a sense that the "higher relations" of the "intellect" and the sublunary relations of the "sensible" are subject to the same analytical process and can turn on the same prepositions (acting temporally, spatially, literally, allegorically). Eve Kosofsky Sedgwick has noted the affinity of what she calls "periperformative sentences" with "the mobile proscenium, the itinerant stage, the displaceable threshold";[66] in my parallel spatial analogies of the approach, the preposition, too, constitutes the linguistic turn in the road that shifts the eye and creates the space for what Uvedale Price called the "charm of expectation."

Clarissa and the little words: the avenue and the approach

Within the tract of changing eighteenth-century grammatical land Samuel Richardson employs the preposition in *Clarissa* in simultaneously temporal, spatial, literal, and allegorical ways. His work makes the preposition (and the other "little words") vividly visible in midcentury—out from the in-between. As we saw in chapter 1, Anna Lætitia Barbauld was perhaps the first to explicitly poise Samuel Richardson *between* ways of looking at things. Unlike the modern approach, from which "we are made to catch transiently a side-view of [the mansion] through an opening of the trees, or to burst upon it from a sudden turning in the road," *Clarissa* (Clarissa) is of the Avenue: "We do not come upon unexpected adventures and wonderful recognition, by quick turns and surprises : we see her fate from afar, as it were through a long avenue," where the old mansion stands full and yet grows "larger and more distinct every step" the traveler and reader advance.[67] And yet Richardson, master printer as well as master novelist, in every way looks forward as well as draws back; or rather, explores the side ways, the words between the nouns as well as the punctuation between the words. In this section, we will look at how some aspects of Richardson's practices as a printer underlie his play with the little words to design a narrative approach rather than an avenue.[68]

i. Richardson as printer

"My Business, Sir, has ever been my chief Concern," Richardson wrote to Johannes Stinstra in 1753.[69] The way he entered his business and the ways he managed it are intricately part of the landscapes of his texts. As Keith Maslen notes, "The study of Richardson as printer and writer combined came about once editors and textual critics began seriously to consider how texts were transformed in the printing house"[70]—about two hundred years *after* Richardson's novels entered the canon. The cast of Richardsonian textual scholars have combined to dislodge the assumption that, as Stephanie Fysh puts it, "Samuel Richardson became a novelist in spite of being a printer."[71] It is worth spending a little time here recalling the printerly contexts of Richardson's literary works—how his attention to detail in business is a context for his approach to detail in the literary.

As Richardson tells it to Stinstra, he early learned (at age thirteen) the exquisite power of the little words from the young ladies whose love letters he wrote, "directing *this* Word, or *that* Expression, to be softened or changed" (*Richardson-Stinstra* 27). He went into the business of being a printer when his father could no longer afford to educate him for "the Cloth": "I chose that of a Printer, tho' a Stranger to it, as what I thought would gratify my Thirst after Reading" (24). His father was, he said, "a joiner, then more distinct from that of a carpenter than now it is with us. He was a good draughtsman, and understood architecture."[72] That is, like John Baskerville (chapter 3), Richardson's father understood shape; he understood the fine lines, the causal connections, the mortise of material design, we might say—the same requirements for a master printer and a master novelist (and a master gardener). They are all concerned with "the exact placing of forms in space" (McKenzie 96), with "the Relation of Things in Construction" (Fisher 1759, 1).

After seven years' apprenticeship, Richardson continued for five or six years "working as a Compositor, and correcting the Press," and then "began for my self, married, and pursued Business with an Assiduity that, perhaps has few Examples" (*Richardson-Stinstra* 25). John Smith, whose *Printer's Grammar* of 1755 was printed by Richardson, describes his "Printing-house" as "the most compleat," which "afforded means to grace [*The Printer's Grammar*] with particulars that otherwise could not have been expected."[73] Maslen suggests that the "particulars" included ornaments and founts—those accessory details that embed so much meaning in Richardson's own novels. Richardson prided himself on "improv[ing] a Branch of [printing], that interfered not with any other Person ; and made me more independent of the Booksellers (tho' I did much business for them,) than any other Printer" (*Richardson-Stinstra* 25–26). That improvement consisted of the indexes, prefaces, dedications, abridgements, abstractions, compilations, and opinions he would compose for booksellers. He half-apologizes to Stinstra: "These, Sir, are little things to trouble you with : But my Circumstances were little, and your Enquiries are minute" (*Richardson-Stinstra* 25). Yet indexes, prefaces, dedications, abridgements, abstractions, and compilations are complex works defined by and dependent upon detail and intricate networking. Richardson's works, as printer and as novelist, are directed toward those "little things."

The famous legal case regarding the printing of *Sir Charles Grandison* demonstrates Richardson's care for control on every level.[74] He had heard a Dublin bookseller boast he could obtain the sheets of any book in any printing house in London before publication, which made him fear an Irish piracy of *Grandison*. He had at the time three of his own printing houses and so had the sheets "composed, and wrought, by different workmen, and at his different houses" (Nichols 4:589–90n). He posted written notice of precautions to be taken:

> I hope I may depend upon the care and circumspection of my friends, compositors and press-men, that no sheets of the piece I am now putting to press be carried out of the house ; nor any notice taken of its being at press. It is of great consequence to me. Let no stranger be admitted into any of the work-rooms. Once more, I hope I may rely on the integrity and care of all my workmen— And let all the proofs, revises, &c. be given to Mr. Tewley [his foreman] to take care of.' [. . .] Yet, to be still more secure, as he thought, he ordered the sheets, as they were printed off, to be deposited in a separate warehouse. (Nichols 4:587–89n)

To no avail: the piracy sailed through. Nichols quotes "The Editor" (Richardson) who, as he "had also great reason to complain of the treatment he met with in his 'Pamela,' on both sides the water, cannot but observe, that never was work more the property of any man, than this is his. *The copy never was in any other hand :* he borrows not from any other author : The paper, the printing, entirely at his own expence, to a very large amount" (4:590–91n, my emphasis). Richardson critics tend to agree with Joe Bray that "though he may not have stood over his compositors while they were working, it does seem likely that, in Greg's words, Richardson 'took responsibility . . . in respect of accidentals no less than substantive readings' for all the revised editions of his works published in his lifetime."[75] Biographers T. C. Duncan Eaves and Ben D. Kimpel note that "Richardson, who read little else, read his own works constantly and seldom read them without changing something."[76] John Mullan confirms that he was a "most fastidious editor of his own works."[77] Bray notes that in all Richardson's revisions of the ten lifetime editions of *Pamela*, the four of *Clarissa*, and the five of *Sir Charles Grandison*, the "accidentals" receive as much attention as the "substantives" (107). Fysh has shown that "Richardson's control over the material text of *Clarissa* was so complete that he was able to interrupt the normal patterns of printing in order to obtain the unusual typographic layout of Paper X, which could have been more easily accomplished with an engraving" (124). Christopher Flint records his attention to type size, "marginal 'Dots or inverted Full-points'" and countless other changes testifying to the ways that "the text's mutability mattered to Richardson as a way of shaping reader response, enhancing aesthetic pleasure, and promoting sales."[78] And Peter Sabor has pointed out that "Richardson, as his own printer, was in a position very different from that of his fellow novelists—either in the eighteenth century or today—because he was able to alter the texts of his novel at will, without facing financial penalty or having to gain the approval of a recalcitrant publisher."[79]

In some cases the meaning of a minute change in emphasis might be difficult to declare, but that in a way would simply underscore the magnitude of Richardson's attention to the tiny. As Bray argues in the case of *Pamela*, changes in emphasis—particularly italicization—indicate a real difference in shading. He argues that as italics underwent their shift in function in the mid-eighteenth century, "their new, emerging role was [. . .] a driving force behind Richardson's considerable addition of italics in his final revision of his first novel, *Pamela*. With characteristic attention to the '*minute*,' Richardson lends these italics, in the context of other changes, a substantial meaning which, far from being accidental, is carefully plotted and designed" (105). The argument works as well for *Clarissa*. Consider, for example, Lovelace's "little words" passage across editions:

> First edition (1748):
>
> LETTER XXXVI. / *Mr.* LOVELACE, *To* JOHN BELFORD, *Esq. / Cocoa-tree, Saturday, May* 27.
>
> What ! How ! When !—And all the monosyllables of surprize.
>
> [Within parenthesis let me tell thee, that I have often thought, that the little words in the republic of letters, like the little folks in a nation, are the most significant. The *trisyllables*, and the *rumblers* of syllables more than *three*, are but the good for little *magnates*.] (4:206)
>
> Third edition (1750):
>
> LETTER XLV. / *Mr.* LOVELACE, *To* JOHN BELFORD, *Esq. / Cocoa-tree, Saturday, May* 27.
>
> What ! How ! When !—And all the monosyllables of surprize.
>
> [*Within Parentheses* let me tell thee, that I have often thought, that the little words in the republic of letters, like the little folks in a nation, are the most sig-

nificant. The *trisyllables*, and the *rumblers* of syllables more than *three*, are but the good for little *magnates*.] (4:275–6)

Barbauld's edition (1810):

LETTER XLV. / *Mr.* LOVELACE, *To* JOHN BELFORD, *Esq.* / *Cocoa-tree, Saturday, May* 27.

What ! How ! When !—And all the monosyllables of surprise.

[*Within Parentheses* let me tell thee, that I have often thought, that the little words in the republic of letters, like the little folks in a nation, are the most significant. The *trisyllables*, and the *rumblers* of syllables more than *three*, are but the good-for-little *magnates*.] (4:294)

"*Within Parentheses*," turned italic in the third edition, turns more inward, feels more secret. ("A scythe smiling sideways to itself in the mirror."[80]) After all, this is the scene where Lovelace self-administers ipecacuanha to vomit blood and pretends to hide his "illness" from Clarissa; the monosyllables of surprise are hers to the "maid" Dorcas. The changes in the posthumous 1810 edition, on the other hand, seem more purely technical—a change in the accepted spelling of "surprise," of hyphenating the adjectival phrase.[81]

For Richardson as printer, whose business had "ever been [his] chief Concern," it is all about the incidentals, the little things in between. As Lovelace himself says, "I never forget the *minutiæ* in my contrivances. In all *doubtable* matters the *minutiæ* closely attended to, and provided for, are of more service than a thousand oaths" (*Clarissa* 3:192).[82] He finds the advice worth repeating to "Captain Tomlinson": "I have always told you the consequence of attending to the *minutiæ*, where art (or *imposture*, as the ill-manner'd would call it) is designed—" (5:363). Printing is in practice the art of positioning the *minutiæ* to do their hermeneutic service.

ii. Clarissa *and prepositions*

Gaston Bachelard has said that *words* "are little houses, each with its cellar and garret," where "common-sense lives on the ground floor."[83] (This recalls Geofroy Tory's sixteenth-century House of Letters; see figure 14.) One can go upstairs in the "word house" and withdraw, "while to go down to the cellar is to dream, it is losing oneself in the distant corridors of an obscure etymology" (146). We have been burrowing in this book under the surfaces of text and grammar and page, feeling for the impress of the invisible, for what makes the shape of the land change, for the Bachelardian "new environment" that with its "syncretism of sensitivity keeps words from crystallizing into perfect solids" (147). In chapter 3 we looked at the hermeneutics of punctuational *minutiæ* in *Clarissa* and its sustained patterns of organization, emphasis, and subtle shifting of the undergrowth. Here, as part of the emerging "linguistic picturesque" of the grammatical minute, I want to examine prepositions in *Clarissa* and, ultimately, Clarissa *as* preposition. For Bachelard, staring closely at a word discovers "[u]nexpected adjectives collect[ing] about the focal meaning of the noun" (147); in this book we find the preposition and other "little words" and "lesser parts of speech" destabilizing the prominence of the noun, shifting the landscape view to the in-between.

Clarissa has a different grammatical undergrowth from *Pamela* or *Sir Charles Grandison*, positioned, in fact, between them. Where *Pamela* initially broke through the linguistic boundaries of "Requisite Style and Form" (as Richardson had characterized proper style in *Familiar Letters* [1741]) with what Margaret Doody calls the "forceful earthiness" of her language,[84] *Clarissa* turns on the "little words," on the grammar in between. *Sir Charles Grandison* (1753) returns to a much smoother grammatical field. Richardson's novelistic texts, that is, anticipate the picturesque but then return to (or are reshaped into) their contemporary midcentury landscape.

Pamela's language in the first edition is part of an intentionally rough linguistic terrain, as Thomas Keymer explains:

> The opening letter introduces such colloquialisms as 'a Clog upon my dear Parents', 'wrapt close in a Paper, that it mayn't chink', and 'I did nothing but curchee and cry' (pp. 11–13), thereby setting a trend that can still be seen in the closing letter's phrase 'a Power of pretty Things' (p. 498). It is obvious enough that these usages (all colourlessly standardized in 1801: 'a burden to my dear parents'; 'wrapped close in paper, that they may not chink'; 'I did nothing but curt'sy and cry'; 'many pretty presents') sharply distinguish the Bedfordshire servant of *Pamela* from the bland stylistic exemplars of *Familiar Letters*. [. . .] If her style occasionally brings Bunyan to mind, it is not only because of its vigorous blending of scriptural cadence with practical rustic speech, but also because of the specific locality that the rusticisms evoke. (*Pamela* 2001, xvii)

Throughout the revisions, however, Richardson would sand the edges off Pamela's prose in what Keymer calls "a series of culturally determined reinscriptions, improving the novel only in the meagre sense of bringing its language and actions more closely into line with polite eighteenth-century taste" (*Pamela* 2001, xxxii). Upon the ageing *Pamela*, Richardson performs a sort of Capability Brownian resculpting for smoothness and gentility, excising the "picturesque" of earthy impertinence.

The well-bred Clarissa is, of course, more well-spoken than her country cousin Pamela; but just as the regularization of typography allowed more of the linguistic undergrowth to emerge into view, Clarissa's clear elegance actually exposes her unusual grammatical emphases. *Clarissa*, the novel that would influence so many later novelists from so many different directions—psychologically, narratively, typographically, grammatically—balances its vast weight on the obscurities and ambiguities of the little words of surprise. Like the Sedgwickian periperformatives, whose "rhetorical force does not diminish along an even gradient from performative center to periperformative edge" (Sedgwick 75), so the Clarissian preposition delicately leverages our attention from the center of noun and verb to the spaces in between.

Lord Chesterfield advised his son to pay close attention to "the address, the [arts], and the manners of those *qui ont du monde*" because it is "much oftener owing to little causes" that they own that world; the "little causes" are "volatile" and can have more "sudden an affect" (260; 30 April 1752). Lovelace knows this; we readers of Richardson know this. Keymer has said that in "Lovelace's hands words are not incarnations but contrivances" (*Richardson's "Clarissa"* 179); in Richardson's hands, and the hands of *all* of his characters in subtly different ways, the little words are careful contrivances. Sometimes they can foil even Lovelace: "THEM, and BOTH, and THEY !—How it goes against me to include this angel of a creature, and any man on earth, but myself, in *one* word!" (*Clarissa* 5:152).

One contemporary reviewer pointed out that "[t]he style of *Clarissa* is peculiar to itself ; that of *Lovelace* is full of new words, arbitrarily formed in his own manner."[85] Yet well before we hear Lovelace's voice and parse Lovelace's syntax we get a range of little words batted around, shaped and reshaped, turning characters and situations on their heels, "directing *this* word, or *that* expression" (Nichols 4:579n). Clarissa's father, not usually the most linguistically subtle, wrings the fine tensual distinctions of past, present, and future from Clarissa's incomplete verb phrase as she tries to remind him of her lifelong filial obedience:

> LETTER VIII. / *Miss* CLARISSA HARLOWE, *To Miss* HOWE. / *Feb.* 24.
>
> Sir, you never had reason, I hope—
>
> Tell me not what I never *had*, but what I *have*, and what I *shall* have.— (1:49)

Clarissa herself, responding indignantly to Anna Howe's close reading of her early thoughts on Lovelace, flicks away the insinuations about her fluttering heart with a small-capped, sharp-pronged demonstrative adjective and definite article that slap the little face of the lower-cased noun:

> LETTER XI. / *Miss* CLARISSA HARLOWE, *To Miss* HOWE. / *Wednesday, March.* 1.
>
> Indeed, my dear, THIS man is not THE man. (1:64)

Clarissa reports on how she overheard her siblings muttering their grievances and plotting their plots with their own compound nonce-verbs, yoking the adverb "out" ("from one's possession, control or occupation into the hands of another" (*OED* 1f) with the most important nouns of all, at the moment:

> LETTER XIII. / *Miss* CLARISSA HARLOWE, *To Miss* HOWE. / *Wedn. March* 1.
>
> ' See how it is !—You and I ought to look about us !
>
> ' — This little Syren is in a fair way to *out-uncle*, as well as *out-grandfather* us both ! ' (1:78)

These odd little "*Obs. Nonce-wd[s]*" make their exemplary debut in the *Oxford English Dictionary* under "out, adv., prep., and int. 5c": "out-grandfather" ("to do out of a grandfather") and "out-uncle" ("to do out of an uncle"). Lovelace performs a similar grammatical act when he recounts to Belford the effect Clarissa has on "Captain Tomlinson," who has been past-tensed by a proper noun:

> LETTER XII. / *Mr.* LOVELACE, *To* JOHN BELFORD, *Esq.* / *Sat. Night, June* 10.
>
> And then she burst into tears, which even affected that dog, who, brought to abet me, was himself all *Belforded* over. (5:114)

After the rape, Lovelace employs "that" like a fist to punch in certainty:

> LETTER XXXI. / *Mr.* LOVELACE, *To* JOHN BELFORD, *Esq.* / *Sunday Afternoon, 6 o'Clock* (*June* 18.)
>
> She knows the worst. That she cannot fly me ; that she must see me ; and that I can look her into a sweet confusion. (5:248)

Later, Clarissa uses the same little word to produce the same—or rather, in this case, a *real*—certainty, when she writes to Lady Betty Lawrance her reasons for why she will not marry Lovelace. Note how the clauses, flung down in hypozeuxis (paralleling of a number of clauses) with the "thats" adding conjunctive force, are reinforced by the colons, emphasizing reintroduction, reiteration:

> LETTER XIII. / *Miss* CL. HARLOWE, *To Lady* BETTY LAWRANCE. / *Monday, July* 3.
>
> When your Ladyship shall be informed of the following particulars ;
>
> That after he had compulsatorily, as I may say, tricked me into the act of going off with him, he could carry me to one of the vilest houses, as it proved, in London :
>
> That he could be guilty of a wicked attempt, in resentment of which, I found means to escape from him to Hamstead :
>
> That, after he had found me out there (I know not how), he could procure two women, dressed out richly, to personate your Ladyship and Miss Montague ; who, under pretence of engaging me to make a visit in town to your cousin Leeson (promising to return with me that evening to Hamstead), betrayed me back again to the vile house : Where, again made a prisoner, I was first robbed of my senses ; and then (why should I seek to conceal that disgrace from others, which I cannot hide from myself ?) of my honour :
>
> When your Ladyship shall know, That, in the shocking progress to this ruin, wilful falshoods, repeated forgeries (particularly of one letter from your Ladyship, another from Miss Montague, and a third from Lord M.), and numberless perjuries, were not the least of his crimes :
>
> You will judge, That I can have no principles that will make me worthy of an alliance with Ladies of yours and your noble sister's character, if I could not from my soul declare, that such an alliance can never *now* take place. (6:29–30, my emphasis)

The repeated little words build a linguistic and logical fortress with the temporal progression from "when" to the emphatic italicized "*now*." This is, in fact, a cumulative periodic sentence (to be discussed more fully in chapter 5), "unfold[ing] gradually, so that the thought contained in the subject/verb group" is held "in suspense before its final revelation"—a syntactical approach, in fact.[86]

But at least for me, the most compelling little words throughout *Clarissa* are the prepositions, the words between the nouns and verbs that "exhibit in a striking manner the analogy of the external or sensible world with the internal or intellectual" (Fowler 323). Prepositions are extraordinary word-houses in this novel, reiterated, pulled from their contexts and revolved into view, with cellars and garrets full of syncretic meaning. Even the headers of the over five hundred letters house a prepositional world of direction, relation, position, implications—as when volume II closes with the shocking revelation that in the space between letter XLIV, written in the "*Ivy summer-house, Eleven o'Clock*" when Clarissa has resolved to see things through with her family, and letter XLV, "*Miss* CLARISSA HARLOWE" is now writing "*To Miss* HOWE" from "*St. Alban's, Tuesday Morn. past One*" (2:298, 306).

In the passage from volume I where Clarissa's mother tries to persuade her to rejoin her father and Mr. Solmes in the parlor, analyzed for dash-hybrids and colons in chapter 3, the prepositions have an equally active and allegorical life of their own, here as prepositional adverbs:

> LETTER XXI. / *Miss* CLARISSA HARLOWE, *To Miss* HOWE. / *Sat. Night.*
>
> But, Clary, this one further opportunity I give you—Go in again to Mr Solmes, and behave discreetly to him ; and let your papa find you together, upon *civil* terms at least.
>
> My feet moved (of themselves, I think), farther from the parlour where he was, and towards the stairs ; and there I stopp'd and paused. [. . .]
>
> I was moving to go up—
>
> And *will* you go up, Clary ? [. . .]
>
> What can I do, Madam ?—What *can* I do ?—
>
> Go in again, my child—Go in again, my *dear* child !—repeated she ; and let your papa find you together !— [. . .]
>
> Obstinate, perverse, undutiful Clarissa Harlowe ! with a rejecting hand, and angry aspect ; then take your own way, and go up !—But stir not down again, I charge you, without leave, or till your papa's pleasure be known concerning you.
>
> She flung from me with high indignation : And I went up with a very heavy heart ; and feet as slow as my heart was heavy. (1:145–46)

The prepositions—repeated, reversed, placed perpendicularly to each other—spin the scene narratively and emotionally; these lesser parts of speech are part of Richardson's larger "*refusal* to impose closure," in the words of Thomas Keymer and Peter Sabor.[87] Throughout the novel it seems as if *everyone* surrounding Clarissa is pushing her in one direction or another, "*above, about, after, against, among, amongst, at, before, behind, beneath, below, between, beyond, by, through, beside, for, from, in, into, on, upon, over, out of, to, towards, under, with, of, within, without*" (Fisher 95). Or as the poet Mark Bibbins puts it: "Prepositions: that's where we all get sucked / under. Prepositions: the San Andreas / fault of meaning."[88] Pushed and pulled between duty and honor, upstairs and downstairs, home and away, Clarissa's prepositions are as metaphorical as they are locational.

Early on, she goes "down into the garden" and strikes "into an oblique path, and g[ets] behind the yew-hedge" to avoid her father, her uncle Antony, and James and Arabella. She is pathetically comforted "seeing my papa so near me.—I was glad to look at him thro' the hedge, as he passed by"—until she hears her father hand all the authority over her to her brother and sister: "You cannot imagine what my emotions were behind the yew-hedge" (2:225–26). What she hears from *down* in the garden, *behind* (and looking *through*) the hedge in the oblique walk is how she is going to be obliquely levered into submission.

What I have elsewhere called the implied spaces of *Clarissa*, beyond the bounds of her visual perception,[89] is also prepositional space: "ALL is in a hurry below-stairs. Betty is in and out like a spy. [. . .] Doors clapt to : Going-out of one apartment, hurryingly, as I may say, into another" (2:227). When Lovelace contrives the panic of her escape, she recounts her flight in a prepositional collapse: "Now behind me, now before me, now on this side, now on that, turned I my affrighted face, in the same moment ; expecting a furious brother here, armed servants there" (3:15). Lovelace recounts the same scene with prepositions expanded, italicized, leaping up from the page: "But seest thou not now [as I think I do] the wind-outstripping fair-one flying *from* her love, *to* her love ?—Is there not such a game ?—Nay, flying from friends she was resolved not to abandon, to the man she was determined not to go off with ?" (3:55). He baits her with the "inner-house" in "Dover Street," with its series of secure-seeming betweennesses: it is the "genteelest," it has access to the "outer-house, if [she] choose[s] to look into the street," it has a "little garden," and most fetching and comforting of all, it has, *in parentheses*, "([. . .] a pretty light closet in it, which looks into the little garden)" (3:185). (This letter itself is *enclosed* from "Thomas Doleman.") Lovelace likes an "approach" to a lady: "What, as I have often contemplated, is the enjoyment of the finest woman in the world, to the contrivance, the bustle, the surprizes, and at last the happy conclusion of a well-laid plot ?—The charming *roundabouts*, to come the *nearest way home* ;—" (5:289). As Keymer rightly notes, even his "speeches" are "crooked."[90] Clarissa indeed seems to be the pretty little miss at the fair, "in the One go up, the Other go down picture-of-the-world vehicle" (6:4).

iii. Clarissa as *preposition*

—*Except* that Clarissa herself behaves textually and psychologically like a preposition in its most powerful sense: as the "indeclinable particle, which yet serves to govern the nouns that follow it." She is like a preposition "because *præpositæ*, placed before the nouns [she] governs" (Chambers

1752, 2:[416]). As her uncle John Harlowe cries, "How can you be so unmov'd yourself, yet be so able to move every-body else ?" (2:86). It was Clarissa who so affected that dog Tomlinson, he was *Belforded* all over (5:114). After her escape to Hampstead, the manservant Will gives Lovelace an account of his search for her, in which he tries to recover her prepositionally: "'They shewed her up to the very room where I now am. She sat at the very table I now write upon ; and, I believe, the chair I sit in was hers.' O Belford, if thou knowest what Love is, thou wilt be able to account for these *minutiæ*" (5:3). In that letter announcing the rape, note how Lovelace ends his sentences adverbially: "And now, Belford, I can go no farther. The affair is over" (5:222). The euphemistic noun "affair" is embedded in a grammatic ambiguity that is semantically all too clear. The rape is not recounted but implied by the deceptive littleness of "no farther" and "over." And in that self-justifying and self-promising letter quoted earlier, that "She knows the worst" and "That she cannot fly me" have their preposition "from" implied, pushed out, as Clarissa herself has been vanquished: what can she do but be looked into "a sweet confusion," or "rave and exclaim"? Lovelace is used to raving and exclaiming, so anticipates: "Here she comes !—" (5:249). But his anticipation of confusions and ravings is thwarted; the space between that exclamash (to riff on Nicholas Baker's dash-hybrids) and the opening of the next letter reveals Clarissa behaving indeclinably and governing from her pre-position *before* Lovelace (the line lengths reproduced here for a fuller sense of textual shape):

> LETTER XXVI. / *Mr.* LOVELACE, *To* JOHN BELFORD, *Esq.* / *Sunday Night.*
> NEVER blame me for giving way to have Art
> used with this admirable creature. All the
> princes of the air, or beneath it, joining with me,
> could never have subdued her while she had her
> senses. (5:248–49)

Whether of the air or beneath it, in the end, Clarissa always takes her own way, and goes up. Barbauld notwithstanding, we "*are* made to catch transiently" various emotional and psychological "side-view[s] through an opening of the [linguistic] trees, or to burst upon [them] from a sudden turning in the road." *Clarissa* explores the grammatical approach.

Of course, everyone everywhere, inside and outside of literature, lives a prepositional life by definition. As the speaker in Sharon Olds's "The Prepositions" says, of learning her list of forty-five prepositions in the seventh grade,

my
eyes followed the line of the arches
up and over, up and over, like
alpha waves, *about, above,*
across, along, among, around, an
odd calm began in me,
before, behind, below, beneath,
beside, between, I stood in that sandstone
square and started to tame.[91]

But I contend that there is nothing quite like *Clarissa*'s prepositional emphasis in either *Pamela* or *Sir Charles Grandison*, or in other early contemporary novels. Richardson's linguistic innovations in all his novels were in fact remarked—often disapprovingly—by some of his contemporary reviewers. The "Lover of Virtue," for example, comments sourly:

> Our language, though capable of great improvements, has, I imagine, been for some time on the decline, and your works have a manifest tendency to hasten that on, and corrupt it still farther. Generally speaking, an odd affected expression is observable throughout the whole, particularly in the epistles of Bob Lovelace. His many new-coin'd words and phrases, Grandison's *meditatingly*, Uncle Selby's *scrupulosities*, and a vast variety of others, all of the same Stamp, may possibly become current in common Conversation, be imitated by other writers, or by the laborious industry of some future compiler, transferred into a Dictionary, and sanctioned by your great Authority.[92]

Richardson's "new-coin'd words and phrases" did indeed transfer into dictionaries (as in the citations for "out-uncled" and "out-grandfathered" in the *Oxford English Dictionary*). And all of his novels have a linguistic as well as typographic playfulness. But the coinages and linguistic emphases play out differently in *Pamela, Clarissa,* and *Sir Charles Grandison*. For all of *Pamela*'s emphasis on the little words ("*I* ashamed to see *you!* thought I: Very pretty indeed!—But I said nothing,"[93] for all that Pamela's is, as Keymer puts it, "unmistakably a voice from below" (*Pamela* 2001, viii), for all the typographical innovation of Mr. B's proposals and Pamela's answers, for all of Pamela's recognition of the sideways movement of the mind ("*Love,* did I say!—But, come, I hope not!—At least it is not, I hope, gone so far, as to make me *very* uneasy; for I know not *how* it came, nor when it begun" [*Pamela* 2001, 248]), Pamela and *Pamela* plunge more forthrightly into (or retreat more directly from) their textual world.

In *Samuel Richardson: Printer and Novelist* (1936), Alan McKillop has a chapter titled "The Approach to *Grandison*."[94] It records, indeed, a long and twisty path of correspondence between Richardson, his supporters, and his detractors. At the beginning point—the publication of *Clarissa*—Richardson was, he says, "successful in getting friends in the great world" (159). But by the time of *Sir Charles Grandison*, in the mid-1750s, he "preferred [. . .] to withdraw into his own little world of cotton-wool and compliments" (189). McKillop finds fault with the Grandisonian universe of "a polite benevolence, a favorable view of human nature, the conception of the feelings as materials to be arranged in order, an approval of that order which is at once aesthetic and rational" and argues that because of a "guarded" treatment of the hero, "the story does not move steadily to a conclusion, but is dragged along intermittently. It is *Grandison*, rather than *Clarissa*, that we may call with Tennyson a 'great still book'" (208, 210). Without commenting on McKillop's aspersions on the best of men and his great good book, I (along with most other readers) agree there is a different sense of movement and direction and impact in *Grandison* that is felt from the level of plot to the level of prose. Being dragged along intermittently is not the same as following a winding path. Although there is language play (the "meditatinglys" and "scrupulosities" that so irritated the Lover of Virtue), the perspective is more full-frontal, even Palladian. Sir Charles is always in front of us; we could use Barbauld's words against him: "We do not come upon unexpected adventures and wonderful recognition, by quick turns and surprises : we see [his] fate from afar, as it were through a long avenue, the gradual approach to which never loses sight of the object" (lxxxiii). Sir Charles is, as I have written elsewhere, a superb spatial negotiator—as a kind of indeclinable preposition himself, he moves himself and others into specific places and positions within rooms, and so creates different social orders, different axes of power.[95] But neither he nor Harriet is quite prepositional in the way Clarissa is, always poised *between* spaces, persons, duties, plots, and events. Grandison and Harriet are emphatically *central*. The very scene where Harriet arrives at Grandison Hall gives us a topographical view of the country estate with herself as anything but staffage:

> LETTER V. / *Lady* GRANDISON, *To Mrs.* SHIRLEY. / *Grandison Hall, Saturday 12 o'clock, Dec.* 9.
>
> O My dearest, dearest Grandmamma ! Here I am ! The declared mistress of this spacious house, and the happiest of human creatures ! This is all at this instant I can write.[96]

This spacious house is antecedent to—the premise of—her happiness, both emotionally and syntactically. The other characters are dimly lit in this scene; Dr. Bartlett, for example,

> was approaching to welcome us ; but drew back till our mutual congratulations were over. He then appeared. I present to you, my dear Dr. Bartlett, said the best of men, the lovely friend, whom you have so long wished to see mistress of this house. He then offered my hand to the Doctor. (*Grandison* 7:18)

We then get the long, inexhaustibly detailed description of the interior and the exterior of "this large and convenient house" with its "several fine avenues" (7:23[a]). It is "*your own* house," says Sir Charles to Harriet, underlining the possessive pronoun for her; and then, in case he hadn't been clear, adds, "The whole house, my dear [. . .] and every person and thing belonging to it, is yours" [7:19]). As Alistair Duckworth argues, "[F]or the linguistic structuralist the interest of Richardson's descriptions [of Grandison Hall] lies [. . .] in the opportunity they provide for a structured praise of the owner through a series of metonymic displacements."[97] Harriet is in fact the lucky reader of the topographical view who actually, *really and truly and not just imaginatively*, absorbs the elements of the country house, view, narrative, guide, metonymic displacements, and all. It is all, all *mine*: the "noble" dining room (7:18); her own special drawing room "elegantly furnished" and "hung with a light green velvet" (7:19) ("EVERY-BODY admires the elegance of this drawing-room" [7:20]); "Your Oratory, your Library, my Love" (7:20); the "fine suite of rooms on the same floor" (7:20); back to the "noble and well-proportioned dining-room" (7:22); the "best bed-chamber [. . .] hung with fine tapestry" (7:22); and, of course, the "gardens and lawn seem from the windows of this spacious house to be as boundless as the mind of the owner, and as free and open as his countenance" (7:23). And still to come: the gallery, the music-parlor. Lucy's description of "*the Situation of the House, and the Park, Gardens, Orchard, &c.*" is then appended as an extensive footnote that takes up most of page 23 and spills over onto page 24 of the third edition, in a really small font. In that, we have perhaps a glimpse of the picturesque approach embedded in a Brownian landscape, the view sweeping from "the north side of the park" with its "winding stream" and "noble cascade, which tumbles down its foaming waters from a rock [. . .] in a ledge of rock-work rudely disposed"; the "remarkable [. . .] prospects, lawns, and rich-appearing clumps of trees"; the "neat, but plain villa, in the rustic taste," on the south side of the river ("on a natural and easy ascent"); the gardener's house, "a pretty little building"; the gardens, vineyards, orangery, orchard, lawns, grass-walks, alcoves, temples, and seats are all "beautifully laid out" and "the whole being bounded only by sunk fences, the eye is carried to views that have no bounds"; the view from the top of the rustic villa "commands the whole" of the orchard with its concentric circles of pears, apples, cherries, plums, and apricots, with the "neat stone bridge [. . .] thrown over the river" in its center; outside the orchard are rows of pines, cedars, and Scotch firs all "at proper distances from each other" (7:23–24[a]). Jocelyn Harris points out that Sir Thomas Grandison's design for the park was "a significantly close copy of God's landscaping in Eden (cf. *Paradise Lost*, iv.139–49)";[98] it is also a proper midcentury landscape looking back to formalism with avenues and statues and ahead to rocks and cascades. (See plate I.)

As an epistolary novel, *Grandison*'s letters have none of the devious, adventure-filled life of *Pamela*'s or *Clarissa*'s. Far from words and meanings sewn into petticoats, hidden in poultry-yards, buried under bricks, or themselves pocketing allegories and ambiguities, every moment and every waking thought of Harriet's life is read by Grandmamma and the whole Selby contingent. Her very psychological machinations are on public display, as when she coaxes Sir Charles to relieve her mind for the umpteenth time about that "dear girl" Clementina, the elegant Italian aristocrat with whom he was in marriage negotiations when he first met Harriet Byron: "I fear, I fear—/ What fears my Love ? — That the happiest of all women cannot say, that her dear man loved her first !— He folded me in his kind arms" (7:38). Despite this reassuring hug, the characters in *Sir Charles Grandison* do not seem as "deeply embodied" as Pamela and Clarissa.[99] Clarissa's embodiment turns on her prepositions, while she herself behaves indeclinably, "unmov'd [herself], yet [. . .] so able to move every-body else" (*Clarissa* 2:86). *Sir Charles Grandison*, for all its goodness and excellence, indeed for all its adventures and subtleties, seems to retreat from the precariousness of the prepositional.

Clarissa as a grammatically experimental model is poised between Richardson's own experimentalism and his century's. Clarissa was searching for the "*hortus conclusus*, where / everything had a place," where she could be "*in / relation to, upon, with*" (Olds, "The Prepositions"). *Clarissa*—both avenue and approach—is also an approach between two avenues. Between the linguistic smoothings of the revised *Pamela* and the revisited formalities of *Sir Charles Grandison* lives *Clarissa*, the novel of the in-between.

CHAPTER 5

The Narrative Picturesque

Period (gr) The end of a perfect sentence.

Robert Cawdrey, *A Table Alphabeticall* (1604)

A PERIOD properly signifies a *circuit*, or a sentence, in which the meaning is suspended, till the whole is finished.

Joseph Robertson, *An Essay on Punctuation* (1786)

I have been arguing that changes in landscape and architectural design are more than a metaphor for contemporary changes in text and grammar; the landscapes of page and prose are shaped by some of the same formal perceptions. In the argument for various grammars of approach, chapter 3 closed with the combined meanings of a "period" as the punctuation mark defining the end of a sentence, and a "period" *as* a kind of sentence popular in the eighteenth century. Chapter 4 saw from the newly cleared typographical field the vigorously sprouting "little words." The "point" delimiting lexical content, or the period closing the period, and the increasingly self-conscious prepositional play, supply two of my surveyor's chains for the linguistic picturesque in the topography of the page.[1] That topography is the three-dimensional effect of its typography, punctuation, and syntactical structures. This is not a historically changing point in itself. As Ian Gordon puts it, "A field may be under crops one season and pasturing cattle the next. The change is considerable—to the casual onlooker. But it is the same field. Nothing has altered its contours or its subsoil or its basic geomorphic structure. The change is on the surface and many other similar changes will follow."[2] The basic geomorphic structures of type, punctuation, and syntax remain while their historical surfaces change. But the surface changes matter. If we look *at* the page rather than *through* it, as Richard Lanham urges, we can see how changes to its surface texture, whether designed by author or enacted by printer, original or modernized, can affect interpretation.[3]

This chapter gathers up the various patterns of eighteenth-century architectural, typographical, and linguistic approaches of the previous chapters into an analysis of the changes in narrative patterns and their new "affordances" in Levine's sense of "uses or actions latent in materials and designs."[4] Typographically, the works of Bunyan, Defoe, and Haywood occupy the older landscape of the page; here I want to show not only the significant differences between the topographical fields of earlier and later printed works but also how in each case their contemporary textual markers are *part* of their interpretational resonance.[5] The typography of the earlier works *looked* picturesque in its irregularity, with something like Price's "cluster of low thorns, a furze-bush, a tussuck, a large stone, forc[ing] the wheels into sudden and intricate turns" in the very navigation of the page.[6] But in the general spirit of both/andedness in this book, remember that Benjamin Franklin found that the older typographical furze-bushes and tussocks of the capitalized common Noun, the italicized proper *Noun*, and the long *ſ*, rather than forcing wheels in new directions, actually gave the reader something like a steering wheel to head straight:

> If the Sight clearly distinguishes what the coming Words are, it gives time to order the Modulation of the Voice to express them properly. But, if they are obscurely printed, or disguis'd by omitting the Capitals and long *ſ's* or otherwise, the Reader is apt to modulate wrong; and, finding he has done so, he is oblig'd to go back and begin the Sentence again, which lessens the Pleasure of the Hearers.[7]

The later eighteenth-century topographical page, to borrow phrases from Uvedale Price, is "so regularly sloped, so regularly planted," "so uniformly levelled" and "so nicely edged" (*Essays* 1:24), that its linguistic picturesqueness must emerge elsewhere: above ground, in what George Saintsbury calls its "highly coloured" style, or in something like the sweep of free indirect discourse, and below ground, in a "buried magnificence" of prepositional windings.[8] That is, the regularization of typography visually and then conceptually opened up the spaces *between* nouns, and the lesser parts of speech acquired more dignity in the eyes of the grammarians and were employed in new ways by what Robert Southey called the "prosemen"—the "weigher[s] of words and sentences."[9]

Syntactically, as Virginia Woolf has pointed out, all great novelists write "a natural prose" that is based "on the sentence that was current at the time."[10]

Elizabeth Traugott has studied the ways that "cultural, including philosophical, changes may affect the particular syntactic realization of a pattern."[11] Traugott argues that "simplification in one part of the grammar may result in elaboration elsewhere" (17); I argue that the "simplification" of the Brownian landscape, which eventually provoked the picturesque landscape (with the parallel shift from straight avenue to winding approach, from the focus on the house to a focus on the perceiver of the house), had its narrative as well as typographical corollaries. Early eighteenth-century writers are more traditionally associated with the "loose" or "running" style, a paratactic, incremental, "syntactic democracy" (Lanham 33). The mid- to late eighteenth century buffed and polished the Ciceronian periodic sentence; as a form "in which the meaning is suspended, till the whole is finished"[12] and the effect of which is "to keep the mind in a state of uniform or increasing tension until the *dénouement*,"[13] its structure often functioned like the modern architectural approach. And yet, as we will see, there can be as much formal precision and architectural sculpting in the "running" style as in the periodic sentence—and equally as much *running about* in the latter. In representational cases that follow, both early and late, syntactic style behaves allegorically, its form illustrating its meaning. Each has sentences built, in Stanley Fish's phrase, of "words so precisely placed that in combination with other words, also precisely placed, they carve out a shape in space and time."[14] And in each case, that allegorical performance becomes ever more radiantly visible through the textual medium in which it was first created—in the typographical performance of its page.

Syntactical architecture in textual landscapes

There is often a teleological whiff in critical comparisons of early and later eighteenth-century prose styles (more like a snort from the nineteenth and early twentieth centuries); although the Battel of the Antients vs. Moderns never seems won, the presentists tend more often, and perhaps by definition, to *think* they've won. (After all, the Antients are always looking to what's been lost.) We certainly saw Horace Walpole and Thomas Whately privileging the modern style of gardening in the 1760s and 1770s. The prose analysts of the late eighteenth century clearly styled themselves victors. Bishop Lowth, for all his urges to correct and improve, believed that the English language had by his time noticeably changed, and for the better: "its bounds have been greatly enlarged ; its energy, variety, richness, and elegance, have been abundantly proved, by numberless trials, in verse and in prose, upon all subjects, and in every kind of style."[15] Hugh Blair and the "prescriptivist" grammarians did their very best to relandscape early eighteenth-century prose (Blair, for example, fiddles with the positions of Addison's adverbs, and then proceeds to show how Shaftesbury, Swift, and Bolingbroke also transgress the rules of clearness and precision, unity, strength, and harmony).[16] The style of writers outside the circle of "Augustans," even when appreciated, tends to be considered a fortunate accident. John Bunyan's style is "homely," though "just and natural"; Daniel Defoe is *not* "a careful builder of sentences" but has a "nervous" style, its "strength arising from variety, copiousness, and vigorous fitness of plain words"; Eliza Haywood's "amatory clichés" have "the logic of a mathematical demonstration," even if they also devolve into "hysterical romantic fustion."[17] As Carey McIntosh wonders, "[H]ow often in the history of any of the Western languages have school texts been filled with quotations from the major authors of fifty or seventy-five years earlier as examples of *bad* writing?"[18]

But much of the recent critical work on early eighteenth-century literature (particularly its prose) has uncovered not just cultural or political value but formal sophistication. Here I will look at the topographical pages of Bunyan, Defoe, and Haywood on the interconnected planes of formatting and syntax—of page patterns (connecting back to chapters 1 and 3) and word patterns (chapter 4)—to survey where the angles shift, the shadows move, the lines are redrawn, and the landscape is reshaped later in the century. Bunyan's "homely" prose lies in the power of his metaphors to incarnate, and of his words to "open and set abroade those thinges" included within them.[19] Defoe's paratactic sentences model, in Lanham's formulation, "the mind in the act of coping with the world" through "small-scale, minute-to-minute tactics" (54). His narrators, known for their digressions, have their own ways of bringing themselves back to the point: Roxana's is "in a word" and "in short." Haywood's narrators prefer the daintier "in fine"; her sentences display a hypotactic control that belies their erotic exuberance, while her pages enact both.

i. Bunyan: "thinges . . . included in one word"

> *So situate* it is, *so* roomthy fair,
> *So* Warm, *so* Blessed, with such wholsome Aire ;
> That 'tis enticing : who so wishes well
> To his Souls health, should covet here to dwell.

So John Bunyan describes the "House of God" in *A Discourse of the Building, Nature, Excellency, and Government of the House of God* (1688).[20] The repeated, italicized intensifier encloses the warm and well-situated pronoun for the House of God in a four-walled syntactical structure. Words, for Bunyan, are microworlds, and roomthy fair. Pragmatographia, according to Henry Peacham in 1577, "open[s] and set[s] abroade those thinges which were included in one word" ($Oiiii_v$). Bunyan's simple nouns, verbs, and adjectives imaginatively expand in the alchemy of reading. His "homely style" serves up sentences with protein. His typography ventriloquizes his multiple narrative voices. The topography of his page is the map of his message.

Opening and setting abroad those things included in one small word is one of the most remarkable rhetorical feats of Bunyan's prose. One of the first things readers have noticed about his works throughout the centuries is their powerful sense of visual immediacy. And yet descriptions in *The Pilgrim's Progress* are actually quite spare, their language plain:[21] "*I saw a Man cloathed with Raggs, standing in a certain place, with his face from his own House, a Book in his hand, and a great burden upon his Back*" (19); "they drew near to a very *Miry Slough* that was in the midst of the Plain" (15); "On either side of the River was also a Meadow, curiously beautified with Lilies; And it was green all the year long" (86); Giant Despair throws them into "a very dark Dungeon, nasty and stinking to the spirit of these two Men" (89). Elsewhere I have discussed the cultural and generic contexts for the spareness of the visual descriptions;[22] here I want to probe their syntactical power. What makes those spare descriptions, comprising simple nouns and adjectives, so pragmatographically powerful, opening and setting abroad so many images for so many readers?

The plainness and simplicity of Bunyan's language has been (usually) praised since its first appearance. The *Gentleman's Magazine* in 1741 remarked that the "Expression" of *The Pilgrim's Progress*, "if it be homely, is at the same time so just and natural, and so exactly of a Piece with the Structure of his Tale, that, take it all together, there never was an Allegory better designed or better supported."[23] Samuel Taylor Coleridge admired the irony of how "the Bunyan of Parnassus had the better of the Bunyan of the Conventicle": though the "lowest style of English," it was "without slang or false grammar"; in fact, "if you were to polish it, you would at once destroy the reality of the vision."[24] Scott commended Robert Southey's recovery, in his edition of *The Pilgrim's Progress*, of Bunyan's "masculine and idiomatic English" from successive "careless, or unfaithful, or what is as bad, conceited correctors of the press" (qtd. in Sharrock 60). William Cowper thought the "humorous vein, strong sense, and simple style / May teach the gayest, make the gravest smile."[25] Sir Charles Firth said in 1898 that Bunyan "addressed the unlettered Puritan in a speech which unlettered Puritans could understand [. . .] the every-day language of the seventeenth century workman or shopkeeper."[26]

And C. S. Lewis grants him "a perfect natural ear, a great sensibility for the idiom and cadence of popular speech."[27] They all mean such moments as "*Tush,* said *Obstinate*" (*TPP* 13); "So *Pliable* sat sneaking among them" (17); "*Apollyon* strodled quite over the breadth of the way" (48); "*Pope* [. . . was] grown so crazy, and stiff in his joynts, that he can now do little more then sit in his Caves mouth, grinning at Pilgrims as they go by, and biting his nails, because he cannot come at them" (53); "that Lock went *damnable* hard" (92); and, of course, Giant Despair talking comfortably in bed with his wife, as she counsels him to beat the prisoners' brains out: "And, sayest thou so, my dear" (91–92). "The first lines" of the work, Dorothy Van Ghent splendidly declares, "launch us with great swift strides" into its world; "the brief past-tense forms of the verbs, with their clear Anglo-Saxon vowels and serried ranks of consonants—'I walked,' 'I lighted,' 'I dreamed,' 'I looked,'—have the energy and hard feel of reality, and hurry us to that cry, 'What shall I do?'"[28]

The "hard feel of reality" in Bunyan's words takes its energy from his own Bedford landscape. Presumably for every visually powerful writer the given landscape shapes the page to some extent, but for Bunyan, the physical world is often *overpresent*, its reality *really hard*. Literally. In *Grace Abounding* (1666) he recounts the first days of his conversion; when he began to consider his love of bell-ringing an irreligious vanity, he finds himself drawn to the steeple house just to watch, not to ring—until the bells suddenly loom with an allegorically physical (*physigoricall?*) and highly detailed threat:

> But I thought this did not become Religion neither, yet I forced my self, and would look on still : But quickly after, I began to think, *How if one of the Bells should fall ?* Then I chose to stand under a main Beam, that lay overthwart the Steeple, from side to side, thinking there I might stand sure. But then I should think again, Should the Bell fall with a swing, it might first hit the wall, and then rebounding upon me, might kill me, for all this Beam : This made me stand in the Steeple-door ; and now thought I, I am safe enough ; for if a Bell should then fall, I can slip out behind these thick walls, and so be preserved notwithstanding.[29]

Until, that is, he asks himself, "How if the Steeple it self should fall ?" (16, §34). Just so will Christian look askance at the high hill on the way to the house of Legality: "but behold, when he was got now hard by the *Hill*, it seemed so high, and also that side of it that was next the way side, did hang so much over, that Christian was afraid to venture further, lest the *Hill* should fall on his head" (*TPP* 19). The everyday world presses threateningly upon writer and character, too thick, too close, too hostile, too much: "me thought

I saw, as if the Sun that shineth in the Heavens did grudge to give light ; and as if the very stones in the Street, and tiles upon the houses, did bend themselves against me ; me-thought that they all combined together, to banish me out of the World" (*GA* 91–92, §188). As Henri Talon has argued, "If space and horizons and free air are to be conjured up before us, landmarks on a road such as a gate, a slough, a cross and a palace are not enough. No, a feeling of muscular exertion must be induced in the reader by the movement of the prose."[30] The muscle that moves the prose begins with the words.

Van Ghent said that Bunyan's words have that "hard feel of reality" for *us*, but *Grace Abounding* makes it clear that words and sentences assaulted Bunyan himself with a material punch. His grammar *is* Richard Johnson's and Anne Fisher's "Art of Expressing the Relations of *Things*"—not simply words for things—"in Construction."[31] Words as microworlds attack him as if from outside: "one day, after I had been so many weeks oppressed and cast down therewith, as I was now quite giving up the Ghost of all my hopes of ever attaining life, that sentence fell with weight upon my spirit, *Look at the generations of old, and see : did ever any trust in God, and were confounded?*" (*GA* 28–29, §62). He then searches for the phrase in his bible, "for it was so fresh, and with such strength and comfort on my spirit, that I was as if it talked with me" (29, §63). Scripture follows him around, calling so loudly that he turns his head to listen (43, §§93, 94). Satan is always physically and vocally proximate, pulling at his clothes (50, §108) or whispering savagely, "*Sell Christ for this, or sell Christ for that ; sell him, sell him*" (50, §136). Actual *sentences* articulate themselves in the air around Bunyan, fall on him with their weight, kindle in his spirit, weigh like brass fetters on his legs, sound in his ear, fall like thunder-bolts, cloud and darken, and appear unexpectedly, stingingly, fittingly (§§62, 92, 144, 146, 164, 174, 189). The sentences pass sentence upon him: "all those Scriptures fore-named, in the *Hebrews*, would be set before me, as the only Sentences that would keep me out of Heaven" (103, §209); "those Sentences [. . .] stood against me (as sometimes I thought they every one did) more, I say than an Army of forty thousand men that might have come against me" (123, §247). So he looks for "a word, a word to lean a weary soul upon, that [he] might not sink for ever ! 'twas that [he] hunted for" (125, §251).

Bunyan attempts to capture and contain those words in the air, in his head, within the dense, numbered paragraphs of his text. Spiritual autobiography is a textual space to write about self, but "self" as prismed, dissected for meaningful and translatable moments of crisis and conversion, for ordinary detail with transcendent implication—to use words to find the Word. And in Bunyan's version, the separately numbered aphorisms become their own little worlds of order and ordering on the page, self-contained yet cumulative, linked by numerical and temporal progression as if to bind in the frequent spiritual regressions—with limited success. Within those self-contained sections, the physical and biographical expand and spill over their own borders:

> But upon a day, the good Providence of God did cast me to *Bedford*, to work on my Calling ; and in one of the streets of that Town, I came where there were three or four poor women sitting at a door, in the Sun, and talking about the things of God ; [. . .] And me-thought they spake as if joy did make them speak ; they spake with such pleasantness of Scripture-language, and with such appearance of Grace in all they said, that they were to me as if they had found a new world. (17–18, §§37, 38)

A doorstep becomes a doorway, and words create worlds.

Bunyan's typographical structures, from the numbered sections of *Grace Abounding* to the vivid textual topography of *The Pilgrim's Progress*, bristle with asterisks, italics, manicules, and vociferous marginal voices. Although, as Roger Sharrock argues, "there is no evidence that [Bunyan] was interested in the exact preservation of the minutiae of his original copy,"[32] the thirteen editions of *The Pilgrim's Progress* (1678) in his lifetime preserve in the main its particular typographic peculiarities. "For the faithful reproduction of his message [Bunyan] put his trust in Ponder"—Nathaniel "Bunyan" Ponder, his Nonconformist publisher, whom he appointed ("But no other") to "Print this Book."[33] Bunyan's text had been "corrected" and "improved" throughout the eighteenth and nineteenth centuries (and even in some of the lifetime editions[34]), but Wharey (and Sharrock) argue for the importance of the original spelling, punctuation, capitalization, and italicization of the first edition (and earliest additions): "it is only in the first edition that a less officious printer allows us to see the English of Bunyan as it was in his copy" (Wharey xcv). As early as 1829 Robert Southey agreed, as he prepared his own edition: "A *correct* text has appeared to me (who, both as a verseman and a proseman, am a weigher of words and sentences) of so much consequence since I undertook the collation, that I should like to correct the proofs myself."[35] The text we choose, as Southey implies, affects the weight of words and sentences. The *look* of a text in its time has experiential and thus potentially interpretive value; I want to say, with William Cobbett, "What an odd taste that man must have who prefers a turnpike-road to a lane like this"; he prefers the "flinty, and very flinty" path to the smooth paved road.[36] I suggest that "a *correct* text"—or at least, the flintier typography of the time—gives us a fuller visual as well as syntactical rendering of Bunyan's textual landscapes.

In *The Pilgrim's Progress*, for example, the marginalia were from the outset a defining typographical feature, as Nathaniel Ponder indignantly insists in his Advertisement to the fourth edition, warning against piracies:

> *Thomas Bradyl* a Printer [. . .] I found Actually printing my Book for himself, and five more of his Confederates [. . .] but in truth he hath so abominably and basely falcified the true Copie, and changed the Notes, that they have abused the Author in the sence, and the Propriator of his right [. . .] You may distinguish it thus, The Notes are Printed in Long Primer a base old letter, almost worn out, hardly to be read, and such is the Book it self. Whereas the true Copi is Printed in a Leigable [*sic*] fair Character and Brevier Notes as it alwaies has been [. . .] ——*N. Ponder.*
>
> *This is Brevier, and the true Copy.*
>
> *This is Long Primer Letter.* (qtd. in Wharey xlix)

The notes, in their Brevier type, live a different textual life in the margins.[37] They demand a more difficult setup from the compositor than do footnotes or endnotes, for one thing. And that position *alongside*, rather than *below, underneath,* or *at the back*, grants them a kind of typographical equality. Contrast, for example, the footnotes in Pope's *Dunciad*, which boil furiously down in the sewers of the text, threatening to explode into the poetic surface, and in fact squeezing the lines of poetry up to the ceiling of the text. Or think of Pamela's responses to Mr. B's naughty proposals: she assembles his numbered proposals in a column on the left, and faces them with her own responses on the right. Hers are insistently and consistently longer—bigger—than his, with her last voice textually overwrapping his. Size, as well as position, matters. And (also rather like Pamela herself), while Bunyan's marginalia mostly behave as quiet little signposts to biblical reference, their special typographical status seems to give them a sense of impertinent freedom: "*He that sleeps is a loser*" (*TPP* 36); "Apollyon *pretends to be merciful*" (47); "By-ends *loth to tell his name*" (77); "*The Giant sometimes has fits*" (89) and the oddly diary-like entry "On Thursday Giant Despair beats his Prisoners" (89); Ignorance saying one thing, the marginalia pointing out another: "*He saith to everyone, that he is a fool*" (96); "Christian *snibbeth his fellow for unadvised speaking*" (99); "Hopeful *swaggers*" (100); and best of all, the running sarcasm on Talkative: "Talkatives *fine discourse*," "*O brave* Talkative," "*O brave* Talkative," "Talkative *flings away from* Faithful," "*A good riddance*" (61–67).

The marginal voices can *stalk* the page, layering the horror of the gothic moments. In part II, when Christiana's group crosses the Valley of the

Shadow of Death, they hear "a groaning as of dead men: a very great groaning"; they feel "the Ground begin to shake under them, *as if* some hollow place was there"; they hear "a kind of hissing *as of* Serpents; but nothing as yet appeared" (189, my emphasis). The threat is implicit, lurking, still at one remove; the similes create hollow places—and snakes—doubling the terror. And then with a most chilling economy of horror:

> *Christiana* said, Methinks I see something yonder upon the Road before us, a thing of a shape such as I have not seen. Then said *Joseph*, Mother, what is it? An ugly thing, Child; an ugly thing, said she. But Mother, what is it like, said he? 'Tis like I cannot tell what, said she. And now it was but a little way off. Then said she, it is nigh. (189)

In the margins: "*The* Fiend *appears.*" The indeterminacy, the "as ifs," the relentless rhythm of approach—*and now . . . then*, with the paragraph breaking off with "it is nigh"—keeps the ugly thing in darkness and full horror; young James is "*sick with Fear.*" It is only when Greatheart confronts it head on that it vanishes; it feeds on being partially seen, but cannot exist when really seen. The power of such scenes creates what C. S. Lewis described as "the flames of Hell [. . .] always flickering on the horizon" (152), *haunting* with semi-ness, with displaced space, with textual as well as syntactical hollows.

And in a final little exercise of typographical power, the marginal note glosses the Dreamer himself—with a manicule, or printer's pointer, no less: "☞ *The Dreamers note*" (*TPP* 106).

The marginalia (like the other paratexts of prefaces and conclusion) are italicized. As we saw in chapter 3, John Smith in *The Printer's Grammar* (1755) notes that italics were designed for "varying the different Parts and Fragments, abstracted from the Body of a work—for passages which differ from the language of the Text—for literal citations from Scripture—for words, terms, or expressions which some authors would have regarded as more nervous; and by which they intend to convey to the reader either instructing, satyrizing, admiring, or other hints and remarks."[38] Or as Joseph Loewenstein puts it, "To print in italics is to fracture the English body type, so to print other, more highly authored words. *Thus* do we make the muffled authority of mere impression give way to authentic inscription."[39] *Thus* the varied voices chirping in the margins do more than signpost biblical references—they obtrude and assert, pronounce and denounce, in the position and font of privileged discourse.

In "The AUTHOR's *Apology* For His BOOK," Bunyan records the ease and pleasure with which he wrote *The Pilgrim's Progress* in words that recall C. F.

Partington's acknowledgment of the "pleasure arising from beholding, as it were, the 'form and texture' of one's thoughts":[40]

> *Thus I set Pen to Paper with delight,*
> *And quickly had my thoughts in black and white.*
> *For having now my Method by the end;*
> *Still as I pull'd, it came; and so I penn'd*
> *It down, until it came at last to be*
> *For length and breadth the bigness which you see.* (*TPP* 5)

His own pleasure in the black and white of pen on page, and Ponder's spirited defense of his (consistent) formatting, underscore the pleasures of the topographical page. As much as the flatlands of Bedfordshire defined or delimited Bunyan's conception of mountains (as Coleridge said, "A wide field full of mountains and of dark mountains, where Hypocrite stumbled and fell!" definitely "requires a comment"[41]), so the energy and hard reality of stones and tiles bending against him and Satan plucking at his cloak and words and sentences pelting his brain and the landscapes of imprisonment, physical and psychological, impress the simple, vivid economy of adjective + noun into an equation powerful enough to open in the reader's imagination the scene in full. Words would upon the lightest touch perform pragmatographia and render worlds.

ii. Defoe: "in a Word"

In 1881 William Minto summarized the view of Defoe as a prose writer that was characteristic in the nineteenth and for most of the twentieth centuries:

> *Sentences and Paragraphs.*—In this mechanical part of composition our author is singularly negligent, especially in his hurried political tracts. Had he been, like Temple, a careful builder of sentences—studious of the arts of arrangement—he could not have produced one-tenth of what he wrote. His ungrammatical laxity would not be allowed in any modern writer. (352)

But Samuel Taylor Coleridge argued that in fact "De Foe was a first-rate master in periodic style,"[42] and W. R. Owens and P. N. Furbank demonstrate that "Defoe, when he wanted, was very capable of constructing sentences and paragraphs on this plan" of the periodic, or "'teleological' or Ciceronian idea of a sentence."[43] Defoe's prose style in general has received more nuanced appreciation in the last few decades, and features such as digression, repetition, and even apparent mistakes have been shown to be more consistently designed than they appear.[44] Defoe, we might say, was one of the earliest practitioners of the linguistic approach. I want to argue that Defoe is indeed a careful builder of sentences *and* paragraphs, and the patterns of those sentences and paragraphs are monadic representations of the shape of plot itself. George Saintsbury, in his *History of English Prose Rhythm* (1912), finds a structural rhythm in Defoe's novels: "in *Robinson* rather specially, [in] set passages of description or otherwise, he advances this style, by the aid of balance, quite after the general fashion" (240–41). Defoe builds and balances his sentences, his paragraphs, his pages, with as much care as (or rather, with as much intensity but rather *more* care than) his characters build their physical and narrative fortifications. The topography of Defoe's eighteenth-century page can be extraordinarily helpful in reading his text.

We saw in chapter 3 how Defoe's novels typically employ coordination (statements linked by conjunctions) and parataxis (where linking-words are absent, replaced by "a firm pause or juncture"), reading the Footprint scene as an "effective paratactic series" (Gordon 29, 30), as well as a punctuationally powerful one, particularly in the original version. In *Robinson Crusoe* (1719) generally, Crusoe's syntax is integral to his architecture. He describes the building of his "Retreat" (a.k.a. his "Castle," his "Habitation," his "Fortification") at least eight separate times. The first (*extremely* detailed) description uses coordinative parataxis to create a syntax that seem intended to psychologically reinforce the fortification. "*Then* I took the Pieces of Cable which I had cut in the Ship, *and* laid them in Rows one upon another"; "*and* this Fence was so strong"; "*and* so I was compleatly fenced in, and fortify'd," "*and* consequently slept secure in the Night."[45] The rest of the descriptions themselves function paratactically in that their very repetition reinforces the walls. Repetition is comfort, after all: think music and prayers. The second description acknowledges the existence of the first but still redescribes its central features, calling it and raising it, for now he adds a turf wall and a camouflage of trees. The third appears in his transcribed journal, which makes it the originary description, but he interjects a retrospective Nota Bene that promises to omit what was described before. He then promptly repeats all the essential details of time and space. The next version stakes out the whole point: "if any People were to come on Shore there, they would not perceive any Thing like a Habitation." And hammering the point home yet once again: "As for my Wall made, *as before*, with long Stakes or Piles, those Piles grew all like Trees, and were by this Time grown so big, and spread so very much, that there was not the least Appearance to any one's View of any Habitation behind them" (179). Crusoe wants above all things in this world domestic security—as much as or more than the grace of God.

We saw in chapter 3 how Defoe could reproduce urban density on the textual page with crowds of italicized place names (p. 107). The linguistic pattern I want most to emphasize here, however, is a particular narrative tic in *Roxana* (1724) as a rhetorical contrast to and context for a different kind of prepositional phrase emerging later in the century (around the time of the approach), particularly in the works of Ann Radcliffe: "at length." Roxana habitually concludes a paragraph or intensifies a train of thought with the summative prepositional phrases (or linking adjuncts) "in a Word" or "in short."[46] She uses the former at least 32 times (it appears on about 7.76% of the total number of pages), and the latter 45 (10.9%). Roxana intensifies this particular speech pattern: Moll Flanders, for example, uses "in a Word" 29 times (6.65%) and "in short" 22 (5%); H.F. uses "in a Word" only 12 times (4.1%), and "in short" 4 (1.7%); Crusoe "in a Word" 23 (6.1%) and "in short" 3 (0.8%). (We will see in the next section that Eliza Haywood's preferred summative is "in fine.") Google Books Ngram Viewer shows that all three phrases, "in short," "in a word," and "in fine," had peak usage in about the 1720s, with "in short" most frequent (at nearly 0.00500% around 1730, and down to 0.00150% in 2000); "in a word" peaks at about 0.00355% in about 1725, and drops to something like 0.00020% in 2000; and Haywood's "in fine" reaches 0.00155% in about 1720 but is virtually invisible at 0.000010% by 2000. The decline of all three across the nineteenth century and into the twentieth is dramatic.[47]

Both summatives are spatial as well as temporal. They roll up rather than unroll, contain rather than extend, compress rather than connect, and, in short, conclude within a different temporality.[48] For Roxana, the phrase "in a Word" usually concludes one full paragraph, itself often one long sentence:

> The Truth was, there was no Need of much Discourse in the Case, the Thing spoke it self ; they saw me in Rags and Dirt, who was but a little before riding in my Coach ; thin, and looking almost like one Starv'd, who was before fat and beautiful : The House, that was before handsomely furnish'd with Pictures and Ornaments, Cabinets, Peir-Glasses, and every thing suitable, was now stripp'd, and naked, most of the Goods having been seiz'd by the Landlord for Rent, or sold to buy Necessaries ; in a word, all was Misery and Distress, the Face of Ruin was every where to be seen ; we had eaten up almost every thing, and little remain'd, unless, like one of the pitiful Women of *Jerusalem*, I should eat up my very Children themselves.[49]

Obviously, the summation never *is* in *a* word, but the capitalized nouns "Rags and Dirt," balanced by the uncapitalized adjectives "fat and beautiful," the solid successive list of pictures, ornaments, cabinets, and pier glasses opposed by the long sustained clause of removal, are syntactically caught up in the nouns of "Misery and Distress" and the clauses of utter consumption. "In a word," for Roxana, is more than summative; it is superlative.

Sometimes the summative is the center of the paragraph, long or short, as when she describes her first husband, the Brewer, in a short paragraph that, "in short," "cut[s] short a dull Story" (10). Other times, as in the two paragraphs detailing her sexual capitulation to her landlord, the summatives appear in the center of paragraphs as pivots to action or of reaction: "in a Word, he conquer'd all the little Resistance I intended to make" (43). At other times, the center of a paragraph is more satisfyingly convex, with the darkness or anxiety on the fringes, and the summative becomes a wax seal of approval—particularly when it comes to money. For example, when she discovers, on the murder of her Landlord-Jeweller "Husband," that she is suddenly wealthy, "in a Word" is itself an heiress, syntactically acquiring "ten Thousand Pounds":

> These things amaz'd me, and I was a good-while as one stupid ; however, after some time, I began to recover, and look into my Affairs ; I had the Satisfaction not to be left in Distress, or in danger of Poverty ; on the contrary, besides what he had put into my Hands fairly, in his Life-time, which amounted to a very considerable Value, I found above seven Hundred Pistoles in Gold, in his Scrutore, of which he had given me the Key ; and I found Foreign-Bills accepted, for about 12000 Livres ; so that, in a Word, I found myself possess'd of almost ten Thousand Pounds Sterling, in a very few Days after the Disaster. (55)

This one paragraph begins with shock and ends with the reference to "Disaster," but by the third clause it becomes a veritable duvet of layered "Satisfactions." "In a Word," in fact, is a number: £10,000. When her affair with the Prince is drawing to a close, and she is "not only well supply'd, but Rich, and not only Rich, but was very Rich ; in a word richer than I knew how to think of," the paragraph only frays at the edges "for fear of losing it all again by some Cheat or Trick, not knowing any-body that I could commit the Trust of it to" (110).

Sometimes the summative must introduce its own full paragraph, as when Roxana insists that "no-body" should "conclude from the strange Success [she] met with in all [her] wicked Doings" that she was either "happy or easie"; she had a "secret Hell within":

> *In a word* , it never Lightn'd or Thunder'd, but I expected the next Flash wou'd penetrate my Vitals, and melt the Sword (Soul) in this Scabbord of Flesh ; it

> never blew a storm of Wind, but I expected the Fall of some Stack of Chimneys, or some Part of the House wou'd bury me in its Ruins ; and so of other things. (260)

And sometimes "In a Word" or "in short" riddle the paragraph in much the way events or motives are often concealed *under* Roxana's narrative. When Roxana's daughter Susan has been stalking her to the point of discovery, Roxana's maid-companion-doppelgänger Amy steps in:

> *Amy* was so provok'd, that she told me, *in short*, she began to think it wou'd be absolutely necessary to murther her: That expression fill'd me with Horror ; all my Blood ran chill in my Veins, and a Fit of trembling seiz'd me, that I cou'd not speak a good-while ; at last, What is the Devil in you, *Amy, said I* ? Nay, nay, *says she*, let it be the Devil, or not the Devil, if I thought she knew one tittle of your History, I wou'd dispatch her if she were my own Daughter a thousand times. (270)

"*In short*" is followed by Roxana's (shocked or pondering?) silence and at last met by "at last." Then Roxana says she wants to kill Amy just for "your but *naming* the thing" (271, my emphasis)."Well however, I was not for killing the girl yet" (298). (*Yet?*) Again and again, *naming* and *mentioning* and *the thought* of the deed smother the possible appeal of the deed itself: "I cou'd not bear the Mention of her murthering the poor Girl"; "I cou'd not bear the Thought of it, much less the Mention of it" (313). And need she imagine in quite such specific detail the death of that daughter? "Sometimes I thought I saw her with her Throat cut ; sometimes with her Head cut, and her Brains knock'd-out ; other-times hang'd up upon a Beam ; another time drown'd in the Great Pond at *Camberwell* : And all these Appearances were terrifying to the last Degree" (325). On the one hand, Susan threatens to destroy the life of pleasure and prosperity built up over "six and twenty Years" of what she retrospectively calls "Wickedness." On the other hand, Roxana remembers very vividly, and with apparent satisfaction, that in the moment she "went on smooth and pleasant" and "wallow'd in Wealth" (188). One way or another (or on both hands) Amy "effected all afterwards" (302). Amy, "*in a word*, did all [her] Business" (318).

iii. Haywood: "In fine, she was undone"

George Saintsbury accuses "this whole period and department of [eighteenth-century] prose" as "curse[d]" with a "fatal lack of variety" (288).

Certainly Eliza Haywood has been frequently underestimated, considered a mere purveyor of repetition and cliché.[50] (John Richetti declared that it was "one of the more appalling and therefore interesting facts of literary history that the three most popular works of fiction before *Pamela* were *Gulliver's Travels, Robinson Crusoe*, and . . . *Love in Excess*."[51]) But recent work has uncovered much more art and wit and pattern, not to mention politics, in her "flimsy" and "formulaic" early amatory fiction.[52] In this section I want to reconsider Haywood's prose, the typographical patterns of her early fiction, and her own variation on the summative prepositional phrase "in fine," as another example of the *exuberant* variety of early eighteenth-century prose and page.

Haywood's first successful novel, *Love in Excess* (which went through three London and one Dublin editions, several reissues, and was included in her first collected *Works*) experiments in lavishly different forms of excess: physical (there are forty swoonings and forty-three rendings of hair); verbal ("a thousand" is a favorite epithet); emotional (we are first introduced to Alovisa as someone who regularly "sigh'd," "burn'd," "rag,'d" and fell "into Ravings" [1:2] when thinking about Count D'elmont); descriptive (or refusing to describe, as each character is more beautiful than the last); plot (Alovisa, for example, "had by Accident run on her Husband's Sword" [2:109]; Ciamara "swallow'd Poyson, and in the raving agonies of Death, confess'd [3:122]); names: Alovisa, Amena, Ansellina, Anaret; Brillian, Bellpine; Ciamara, Charlotta, Camilla, the Chevalier, the Count; Melliora, Melantha. The waves of excess are so, er, excessive, the melodrama so fervid, the plot and language so "outrageously unreal," as Richetti puts it, that it is not surprising that there is often little taste for lingering, for lifting up the flap of surface prose (along with its "transparent ideology" and "technical ineptitude" [xxv]) to look underneath, at its structure.

The genre of amatory fiction has had the same critical trajectory as the gothic, and for the same reasons. The outside is so visually *noisy*—self-covered in apparent stereotypes and clichés and stage props, with predictable formulas and special effects. And certainly for some—perhaps many—of the peddlers of those genres, the accusations are accurate, the contempt earned. But the originators of the genre—like the originators of clichés—generate audiences, imitators, and critical histories precisely because they are cleverer than they appear.[53]

Levels of cheeky irony lurk in the arrangement of words in all of Haywood's works, perhaps most cleverly in *Fantomina* (1725), where, for example, the sexually enthusiastic Lady is "punished" by being sent to a monastery (not a "convent") in France. *France*. In *Love in Excess* we first glimpse the inner Count D'elmont as "he consider[s] his own Perfections" (1:5). The novel seems to enjoy putting its hero in ridiculous situations, as when he is surprised in bed and discovers the woman with him is not the virtuous Melliora but the minxish Melantha (1:88); or when he trips over a rug into two ladies' laps, moments after they have been discussing "With what an Air he walk'd !" and "how graceful was his Bow !"(3:19). And, of course, the real sweetness of his nature is revealed in "the fatal enquiry" he puts to the Baron about seducing Melliora: " — But O her Father's Memory ! My Obligations to him ! Her Youth and Innocence are Daggers to my cool Reflections — Wou'd it not be pity ESPERNAY (continu'd he with a deep sigh) even if she shou'd consent, to ruin so much sweetness ?" (2:43–44). Ha ha ha, they laugh, and "it was soon Concluded betwixt them, that on the first opportunity, MELLIORA shou'd fall a Sacrifice to Love" (2:44). He is every inch the chivalric equal to Beauplaisir, who when he thinks he is helping a newly grieving widow "began to think he should have but a dull Journey, in the Company of one who seem'd so obstinately devoted to the Memory of her dead Husband" (*F* 272). In fine, the Haywoodian hero is usually shredded by his own clichés.

Haywood shapes a sort of hypotactic rather than paratactic *plot* structure, keeping tight control over the ordering and balance of events. Syntactically as well she displays "balance, quite after the general fashion," as Saintsbury would say (241). At least two recent critics have addressed this. David Fairer, commenting on a passage in *Lasselia* (1724), argues that the "shapeliness of Haywood's sentence is indicative of a narrative that retains its balance, complete with a rhetorical *tricolon auctum*":[54]

> IT wou'd have been impossible for *Lasselia*, had she endeavoured it, to conceal the swift Vicissitudes of her rolling Thoughts while reading ; alternate Joy and Shame, Surprize and Fear, and sometimes a Start of virtuous Pride and Indignation, sparkled in her Eyes-----a thousand different Passions succeeded on another in their turns-----all too fierce to be restrain'd, and too sudden to admit Disguise.[55]

Fairer makes us see the *position* of "Joy" and "Shame," "Surprize" and "Fear," "Pride" and "Indignation," pushing us past the meaning of the words to the meaning of their structure. The last pair of clauses (not quoted by Fairer) confirms that balance with a Ciceronian period, the verbs neatly if dramatically concluding the thoughts. Fairer describes this as a "staple narrative style of earlier 'amatory fiction'" where "the well-behaved *Passions* pair up before forming an orderly queue" (148).

Richetti himself is struck by the structural balance in the following passion-soaked paragraph from *Love in Excess*:

> What now could poor AMENA do, surrounded with so many Powers, attack'd by such a charming force without, betray'd by tenderness within : Vertue and Pride, the Guardians of her Honour fled from her Breast, and left her to her Foe. [. . .] [H]e found her panting Heart beat measures of consent, her heaving Breast swell to be press'd by his, and every Pulse confess a wish to yield ; her Spirits all dissolv'd sunk in a Lethargy of Love, her snowy Arms unknowing grasp'd his Neck, her Lips met his half way, and trembled at the touch ; in fine, there was but a moment betwixt her and Ruine ; when the tread of some body coming hastily down the Walk, oblig'd the half-bless'd Pair to put a stop to farther Endearments.[56]

Richetti argues: "[T]he balanced phrases and clauses just about contain the rushing participles which do the actual describing ('surrounded . . . attack'd . . . betray'd . . . panting . . . heaving . . . press'd . . . dissolv'd . . . grasp'd . . . trembled'). The construction matches the erotic tension of guilty and illegal lovers on dangerous ground" (188). The level of syntactic order over erotic content is even higher: these participles actually pair up with prepositions to "just about contain" themselves: poor yielding Amena is "attack'd" from "without," "betray'd" from "within"; her Honour flees *from* her breast; and then her panting heart beats, her heaving breast swells, her every pulse confesses as that second sentence swells towards its rhythmic orgasm until the final twist, "in fine."

"In fine" is in fact the Haywoodian narrator's preferred summative. It is a daintier version of Roxana's brisk and businesslike "in short" or euphemistic "in a Word."[57] Though not as frequent as the various summatives of Defoe's narrators, "in fine" appears consistently throughout her early fiction ("in short" shows up only once or twice, and "in a word" not at all); no other major novelist in the eighteenth century makes much use of the phrase at all.[58] It is not a simple equivalent of "in short";[59] the phrase is based on the noun "fine" in the sense of "a cessation, termination, end, or conclusion of something" (*OED* 1a), and carries a whiff of its adjectival counterpart, "Characterized by or affecting refinement or elegance" (*OED* 11). (And perhaps even "Of printing: intended for display as much as for reading; decorative, 'ornamental'" [*OED* 3b].) "In fine" is a romantic, ladylike version of bringing something near or to a close. "In fine" had stepped in to rescue Amena; for Fantomina, no such luck: "— *He* was bold ; — he was resolute : *She* fearful, — confus'd, altogether unprepar'd to resist in such Encounters, and rendered more so, by the extreme Liking she had to him. [. . .] In fine, she was undone."[60] And occasionally, "in fine" can link a series of clauses to make a match, as between the doomed lovers Anadea and the Count Blessure in *The Fatal Secret: or, Constancy in Distress* (1724): "— He had an uncommon Delicacy in his Nature ; so had she : — A grave Chearfulness, or, if you will, a gay Solidity in his Behaviour ; so had she. — In fine, never were two Persons of different Sexes so alike, so fram'd to please each other."[61] Paired balances again, though here with a built-in imbalance that makes its own structural point: *he* gets the long clauses; *she* syntactically nods.

In Haywood, as in Defoe and Bunyan, the conventions of early texts—typography as cultural medium—flavor the content. Narrative extravagance is given more vivid voice by "the hand-held landscape of the page" (in my paraphrase of D. F. McKenzie). Ironically, David Oakleaf's argument for modernizing his Broadview edition of *Love in Excess* makes for me an eloquent, even novelistic argument for *not* modernizing:

> [The text] bristles with initial capitals, routinely marshals italics or large and small capitals to dignify proper nouns like *Paris* or MELLIORA, and regularly marks with italics quoted letters and a few other brief quotations. Flocks of apostrophes silence letters we never pronounce. [. . .] Direct speech merges unmarked into the surrounding prose. [. . .] Capitalization, typefaces, and punctuation were seasonings stirred liberally into the prose by the printer just before serving hot to an eager public.[62]

Oakleaf's description offers a little amatory plot-on-the-page, letters and punctuation bristling, marshalling, dignifying, flocking—spicing up the visual dish. Although we have no evidence that Haywood pointed her own proofs (Oakleaf assumes all is done at the printer's[63]), Oakleaf himself only modernizes so far, because "[s]uch variations may reveal early readers trying to capture the rise and fall of Haywood's voice. [. . .] Excessive modernization would spoil the flavour" (26). Although he adds quotation marks to clarify discourse, he also argues that the convention of "shift[ing] from one character's speech to another's within a single sentence" is something that "suit[s] Haywood's intersubjectivity and deliberate blurring of boundaries" (25). And although Haywood's printers for *The Works of Mrs Eliza Haywood* (1724) and *Secret Histories, Novels and Poems* (1725) Dan. Browne Jun. and S. Chapman are not, perhaps, the most persnickety of their trade (they now and then "make *Botches*," as Moxon says: a title page of *Secret Histories* declares itself printed "at the in *Angel Pallmall*"[64]), there is enough consistency in capitalization, italicization, and punctuation, and enough correspondence between textual and typographical excess, to sustain a distinctive sense of voice. Haywood herself became a publisher in the 1740s, and Patrick Spedding says she "is known to have corrected proofs for the press on at least one occasion and to have revised at least two works that were published posthumously" (89).[65] Even if she didn't regularly correct her proofs, she well knew and thus could depend upon (automatically exploit) the bristling capitals, the vehement italics, the flocking apostraphes, the breathless "thin spaces" between ! ! !s. I propose we follow Virginia Woolf on the best method of a first reading:

> To begin with, I ran my eye up and down the page. I am going to get the hang of her sentences first, I said, before I load my memory with blue eyes and brown and the relationship that there may be between Chloe and Roger. There will be time for that when I have decided whether she has a pen in her hand or a pickaxe. So I tried a sentence or two on my tongue.[66]

A passage in volume III of *Love in Excess*, which erupts passionately about passion and also neatly shoves D'elmont into deliberate cliché, reads very differently in the modernized edition compared to the first:

> *Love* creates intollerable torments! unspeakable joys! raises us to the highest heaven of happiness, or sinks us to the lowest hell of misery.
>
> Count D'elmont experienced the truth of this assertion; for neither his just concern for the manner of Alovysa's death could curb the exuberance of his joy, when he considered himself beloved by Melliora; nor any diversion, of which Rome afforded great variety, be able to make him support being absent from her with moderation. [. . .] He preferred a solitary walk, a lonely shade, or the bank of some purling stream, where he undisturbed might contemplate on his beloved Melliora, to all the noisy pleasures of the Court, or the endearments of the inviting fair. In fine, he shunned as much as possible all conversation with the men, or correspondence with the women; returning all their *billet-doux*, of which scarce a day past, without his receiving some, unanswered. (Broadview *LE* 170–71)

❧

> *Love* creates intollerable Torments ! unspeakable Joys ! raises us to the highest Heaven of Happiness, or sinks us to the lowest Hell of Misery.
>
> C O U N T D' E L M O N T experienc'd the Truth of this Assertion ; for neither his just concern for the manner of A L O V Y S A's death cou'd curb the Exuberance of his Joy, when he consider'd himself beloved by

> M E L L I O R A ; nor any Diversion, of which *Rome* afforded great Variety, be able to make him support being absent from her with Moderation. [. . .] He prefer'd a solitary Walk, a lonely Shade, or the Bank of some purling Stream, where he undisturbed might contemplate on his Belov'd M E L L I O R A, to all the noisy Pleasures of the Court, or the endearments of the inviting Fair. In fine, he shun'd as much as possible all Conversation with the Men, or Correspondence with the Women ; returning all their *Billet-Doux*, of which scarce a Day past, without his receiving some, unanswer'd. (3:5–6)

The bristlings *enact* the Torments ! and Joys ! as well as typographically highlight the already clichéed (by Pope and others) solitary Walk, lonely Shade, and "*some*" purling Stream. Thomas Keymer notes that for the 1732 edition of Haywood's works, Richardson's printing house made "strategic use of printers' ornaments—throbbing hearts, simpering Cupids—to highlight the erotic identity of the text."[67] (And as Richetti notes, Richardson imported much of Haywood's rhetorical art into *Pamela*, though he never acknowledged his debt [188].[68]) Those ornaments simply *ornament* a vocabulary, a syntax, and a typography that already throb. Richetti agrees that the "dashes, exclamation points, and ersatz cadences of the swelling prose are the real content of the scene and drive the reader along to the near-climax with which it ends" (201).[69]

David Fairer outlines a stylistic "divide" between the writing of Eliza Haywood and Laurence Sterne that in imagery as well as argument supports the syntactical distinctions I am making at both ends of this chapter. Fairer quotes Tristram Shandy's diatribe against prefaces: "'tis one of the silliest things in one of them, to darken your hypothesis by *placing a number of tall, opake words, one before another, in a right line, betwixt your own and your readers conception,* ———" (*TS* III.xx; Fairer's emphasis). The difference between Sterne's "poetically alive writing" and the earlier "staple" emerges in the passage where the Widow Wadman is wooing Uncle Toby:

> [I]n following my uncle Toby's forefinger with hers, close thro' all the little turns and indentings of his works—pressing sometimes against the side of it—then treading upon it's nail—then tripping it up—then touching it here—then there, and so on—it set something at least in motion. (VIII.xvi; qtd. in Fairer 145)

Fairer focuses on the "electricity," the "sentimental conductivity" of the passage. For my purposes, the syntax and punctuation of Sterne enact the linguistic picturesque of the approach, wandering close through little turns, prepositionally against and upon and here and there, predicated on motion. In Haywood's prose, says Fairer, everything "is decorously composed. The *opake words* unroll, with subordinate clauses in place and everything successively ordered, *one before another, in a right line*" (149). Haywood's prose often creates a hypotactic avenue. And as we have seen, a close analysis of that unexpectedly formal control uncovers something of the art of those "old gardeners" who created the pleasures of the "old-fashioned long perspectives" of the avenue.[70] In all those Fatal Enquiries, Fatal Secrets, Fatal Curiosities, and Fatal Fondnesses, there is, in fine, none of Saintsbury's "fatal lack of variety."[71]

The narrative picturesque

The prose patterns of Ann Radcliffe, Frances Burney, and Jane Austen, as with any set of writers in any given spot of time, are distinctively, emphatically different from each other—as are the syntactical architectures of John Bunyan, Daniel Defoe, and Eliza Haywood. But as cohabitors of a particular set of decades and particular fashions in landscapes, they share cultural matrices with their contemporaries. The following sections will survey how the changing perceptions and representations of landscape, typography, and grammar in the second half of the eighteenth century relate to changes in narrative—specifically, how prose fiction developed what George Saintsbury described in 1912 as a "taste for the picturesque" as seen in its "more gorgeous and highly coloured—which necessarily means a more variously and intricately rhythmed—style," and its conscious return to the "buried magnificence" of Elizabethan and seventeenth-century prose. In short, he argues, "the same movement against monotony, uniformity, convention, which was breaking up the tyranny of the heroic couplet in verse, almost necessitated the return to complicated values and irregular outlines in prose" (294). More recently, Richard Lanham has also compared the two basic prose styles that have typically characterized the earlier and later eighteenth century—the periodic and the running, or the hypotactic and paratactic—to different garden patterns:

> Styles in prose then are rather like styles in gardens. The periodic style is like the vast formal garden of a Baroque palace, all balanced squares and parallel paths. The land is rearranged in ways that the visual cortex can easily sort out. The running style, on the other hand, is like the informal garden which shapes nature without seeming to. Nature is not dominated and reformed but simply

> helped on the way it wanted to go anyway. We can wander—since there is no beginning, middle, and end—but again without fear of getting lost.[72]

The periodic style, he argues, is basically hypotactic, the clauses ordered by "balance, antithesis, parallelism, and careful patterns of repetition"; the loose or running style is paratactic, a "syntactic democracy" (33). This simile at first appears to entirely subvert my metaphor. But just as real gardens, real prose, and real swaths of history are much more complicated than their labels, so my metaphor of "approach" in prose as well as in landscape architecture can accommodate this piffling objection. The periodic sentence revived and flourished in the late eighteenth century, and its contemporary definitions could equally describe the architectural approach.[73] For Joseph Robertson, we recall, "A PERIOD properly signifies a *circuit*, or a sentence, in which the meaning is suspended, till the whole is finished."[74] Lanham points out that "[t]he secret of a periodic structure is *pacing*, slowly building up steam for a thundering climax. [. . .] If the secret is pacing, the center is drama, the suspense as the syntactical spring is wound tighter and tighter and finally—ah, got him! released" (56). In this sense the periodic sentence behaves as a kind of syntactic approach, where the mind is kept in a state of increasing tension (forming new combinations) until the *dénouement*, when "it bursts upon the house, the water, and the opposite bank in an interesting point of view.[75] And like the approach, when the subject matter of the sentence is "easy and familiar," says Minto, "the reader, finding the sentence or clause come to an end as soon as his expectations are satisfied, receives an agreeable impression of neatness and finish"; when difficult or unfamiliar, "or when the suspense is unduly prolonged, the periodic structure is intolerably tedious, or intolerably exasperating" (5). In the wrong kind of approach, according to Uvedale Price (as well as Repton), "the charm of expectation" is defeated (1:250). The well-wrought period is "vigorous and lively"; the "sense being suspended, keeps the attention awake until the close of the sentence" (Fowler 636). We saw this kind of hypotactic period in chapter 4 (p. 163), when Clarissa outlines her reasons for not marrying Lovelace, poising each cumulative clause upon successive "thats" until she unmistakably, resoundingly closes the door: "such an alliance can never *now* take place" (*Clarissa* 6:29–30). On this reading, the period is closer to the approach than to the formal baroque garden. Period and approach are *both* both/and: in the winding approach, *the land is* also *rearranged* in visibly ordered ways but, as in the running style, *helped on the way it wanted to go anyway*—at least if it is a sensible approach. We wander in the approach because it is designed to begin at the beginning and end at the house, but within the middle, it pretends otherwise—yet we never fear getting lost. In the middle of the well-wrought periodic sentence, too, we are lusciously poised, gathering the points (in both senses) as we go, suspended until we arrive.[76]

i. Radcliffe and the prepositional phrase

In a review of *The Mysteries of Udolpho* in the *Critical Review* (August 1794), Samuel Taylor Coleridge describes the novel as if it were a burlesque approach:

> She delights in concealing her plan with the most artificial contrivance, and seems to amuse herself with saying, at every turn and doubling of the story, ' Now you think you have me, but I shall take care to disappoint you.' This method is, however, liable to the following inconvenience, that in the search of what is new, an author is apt to forget what is natural ; and, in rejecting the more obvious conclusions, to take those which are less satisfactory.[77]

Humphry Repton had remarked on overzealous "improvers" who "seem to have mistaken the most obvious meaning of an *approach*, which is simply this—A ROAD TO THE HOUSE. If that road be greatly circuitous, no one will use it when a much nearer is discovered."[78] However, Repton adds: "if there be two roads of nearly the same length, and one be more beautiful than the other, the man of taste will certainly prefer it" (*Sketches* 91). And so Coleridge lets escape: "the reader, when he is got to the end of the work [*Udolpho*], looks about in vain for the spell which had bound him so strongly to it" (*Critical Review* 362). *Where has all this turning and doubling taken me?* But William Enfield in the *Monthly Review* (November 1794) points to an answer: Radcliffe has "as powerful an effect as if the invisible world had been obedient to her magic spell" in part because of *Udolpho*'s ability "to hold curiosity in pleasing suspence."[79] The arc of the novel as a whole is that of the periodic sentence, "in which the meaning is suspended, till the whole is finished" (Robertson 90), or of the approach, which depends on Price's "charm of expectation" (1:250). Or as Richard Payne Knight declared, "The best approach to ev'ry beauteous scene" is

> To lead, with secret guile, the prying sight
> To where component parts may best unite,
> And form one beauteous, nicely blended whole,
> To charm the eye and captivate the soul.[80]

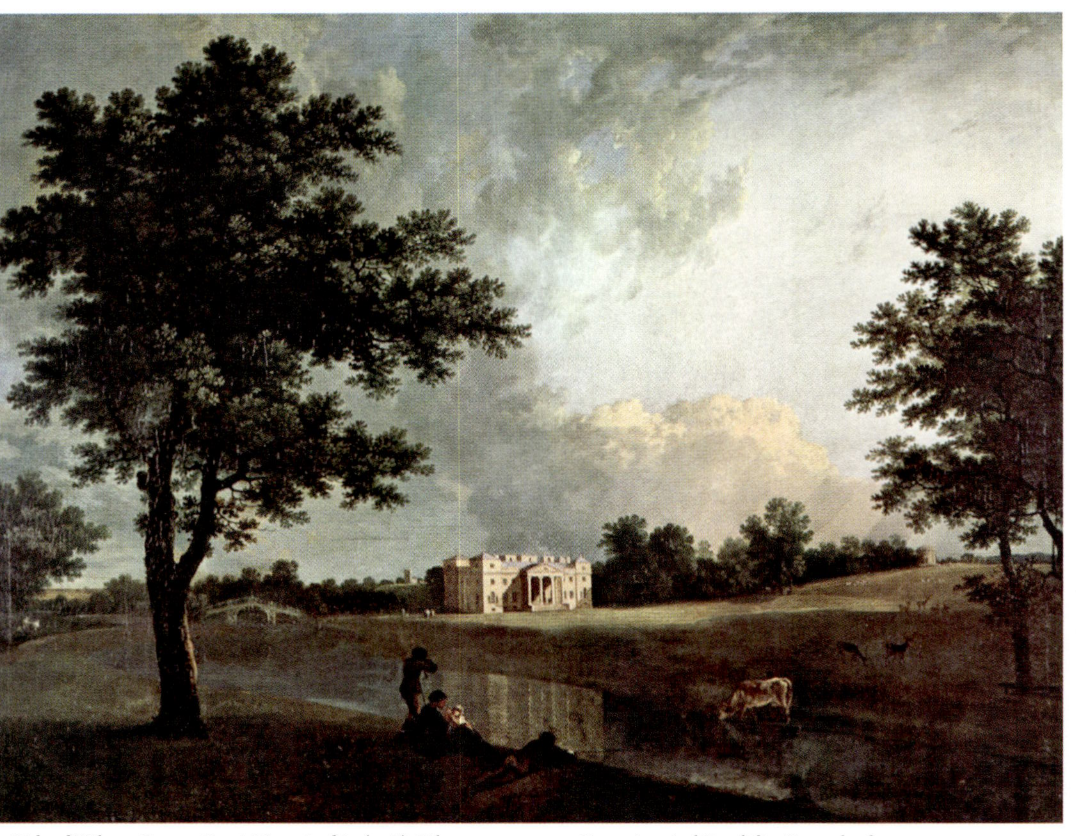

1. Richard Wilson, *Croome Court, Worcestershire* (1758). Oil on canvas. 122 × 168 cm. A typical Capability Brown landscape.

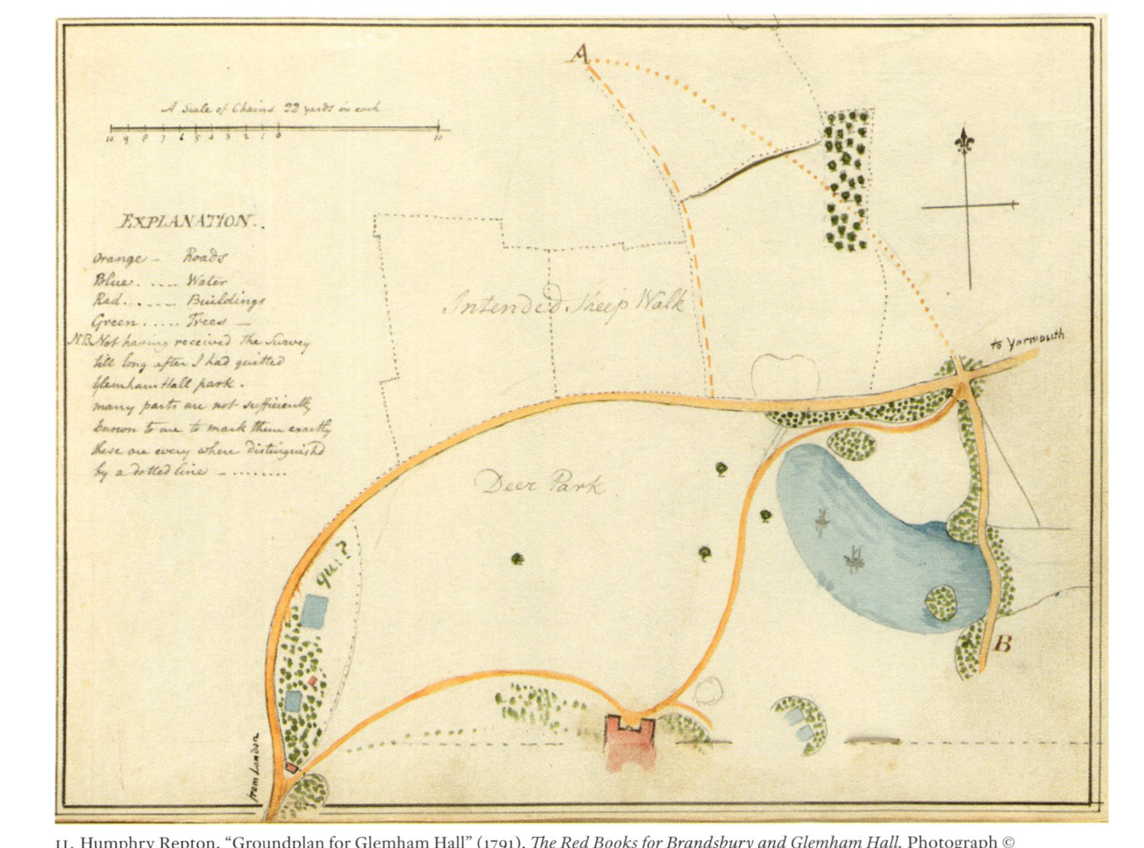

11. Humphry Repton, “Groundplan for Glemham Hall” (1791). *The Red Books for Brandsbury and Glemham Hall.* Photograph © Dumbarton Oaks Research Library and Collection, Rare Book Collection, Washington, DC.

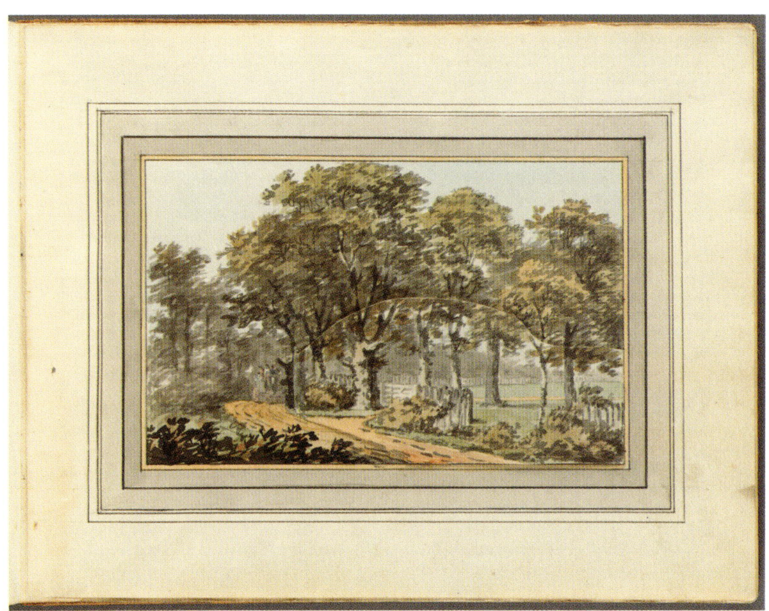

III. Humphry Repton, “Approach to Glemham Hall” (1791) (before). *The Red Books for Brandsbury and Glemham Hall.* Photograph © Dumbarton Oaks Research Library and Collection, Rare Book Collection, Washington, DC.

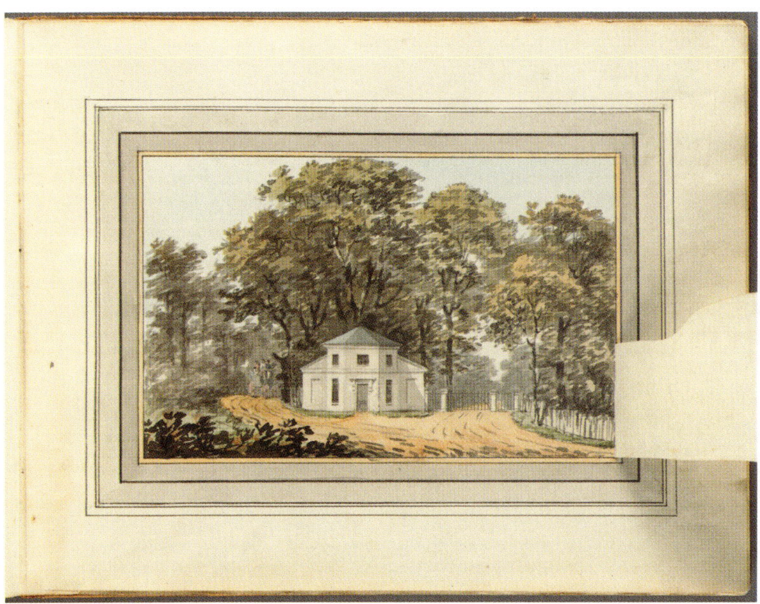

IV. Humphry Repton, “Approach to Glemham Hall” (1789) (after). *The Red Books for Brandsbury and Glemham Hall.* Photograph © Dumbarton Oaks Research Library and Collection, Rare Book Collection, Washington, DC.

[140]

a narrow vista. A mere line of perspective, be the extent what it may, will seldom compensate for the loss of that space which it divides, and of the parts which it conceals.

The approach to *Caversham, though a mile in length, and not once in sight of the house, till close upon it, yet can never be mistaken for any other way than it is ; a passage only through a park is not introduced with so much distinction, so precisely marked, or kept in such preservation. On each side of the entrance is an elegant lodge ; the interval between them is a light open palisade, crossing the whole breadth of a lovely valley ; the road is conducted along the bottom, continually winding in natural easy sweeps, and presenting at every bend some new scene to the view ; at last it gently slants up the side of a little rise to the mansion, where the eminence, which seemed inconsiderable, is found to be a very elevated situation, to which the approach, without once quiting the valley, had been insensibly ascending all the way. In its progress, it never breaks the scenes through which it passes ; the plantations and the glades are continued without interruption, quite across the valley ; the opposite sides have a relation to each other, not answering, not contrasted, but

* The seat of lord Cadogan, near Reading.

connected

[141]

connected ; nor does the disposition ever seem to have been made with any attention to the road ; but the scenes still belong purely to the park ; each of them is preserved entire ; and avails itself of all the space which the situation will allow. At the entrance the slopes are very gentle, with a few large hawthorns, beeches, and oaks, scattered over them ; these are thickened by the perspective as the valley winds ; and just at the bend, a large clump hangs on a bold ascent, from whence different groupes, growing gradually less and less till they end in single trees, stretch quite away to a fine grove, which crowns the opposite brow : the road passes between the groupes, under a light and lofty arch of ash ; and then opens upon a glade, broken on the left only by a single tree ; and on the right by several beeches standing so close together as to be but one in appearance : this glade is bounded by a beautiful grove, which in one part spreads a perfect gloom, but in others divides into different clusters, which leave openings for the gleams of light to pour in between them. It extends to the edge, and borders for some way the side, of a collateral dale, which retires slowly from the view ; and in which the falls of the ground are more tame, the bottom more flattened, than in the principal valley ; the banks of this also near the junction, are more gentle than

before

[142]

before ; but on the opposite side, the steeps and the clumps still continue ; and amongst them is a fine knole, from which descend two or three groupes of large trees, feathering down to the bottom, and by the pendency of their branches favouring the declivity. To these succeeds an open space, diversified only with a few scattered trees ; and in the midst of it, some magnificent beeches crouding together, overshadow the road, which is carried through a narrow darksome passage between them : soon after it rises under a thick wood in the garden up to the house, where it suddenly bursts out upon a rich, and extensive prospect, with the town and the churches of Reading full in sight, and the hills of Windsor forest in the horizon. Such a view at the end of a long avenue, would have been, at the best, but a compensation for the tediousness of the way ; but here the approach is as delightful as the termination : yet even in this, a similarity of style may be said to prevail ; but it has every variety of open plantations ; and these are not confusedly thrown together, but formed into several scenes, all of them particularly marked : one is characterised by a grove ; the next by clumps ; and others by little groupes, or single trees : the plantations sometimes cover only the brow, and retire along the top from the view ; sometimes they seem to be suspended on the edge, or the sides, of the descents ; in one place they leave the bottom clear ; in another they overspread the whole valley : the intervals are often little less than lawns ; at other times they are no more that [*sic*]

narrow

[143]

narrow glades between the groves; or only small openings in the midst of a plantation. The ground, without being broken into diminutive parts, is cast into an infinite number of elegant shapes, in every gradation from the most gentle slope, to a very precipitate fall : the trees also are of several kinds, and their shadows of various tints ; those of the horse-chesnuts are dark ; the beeches spread a broader but less gloomy obscurity ; and they are often so vast, they swell out a succession of such enormous masses, that, though contiguous, a deep shade sinks in between them, and distinguishes each immense individual : such intervals are in some places filled up with other species ; the maples are of so extraordinary a size, that they do not appear inconsiderable, when close to the forest trees ; large hawthorns, some oaks, and in one part many, perhaps too many limes, the remains of former avenues, are intermixed ; and amongst all these often rise the tallest ash, whose lighter foliage only chequers the turf beneath, while their peculiar hue diversifies the greens of the groupes they belong to. After enumerating the beauties of this approach, and reflecting that they are confined within a narrow valley, without views, buildings, or water, another can hardly be conceived so destitute of the means of variety, as to justify the sameness of an avenue.

v. Thomas Whately, "The approach to Caversham," from *Observations on Modern Gardening* (1770). Author's transcription and highlighting.

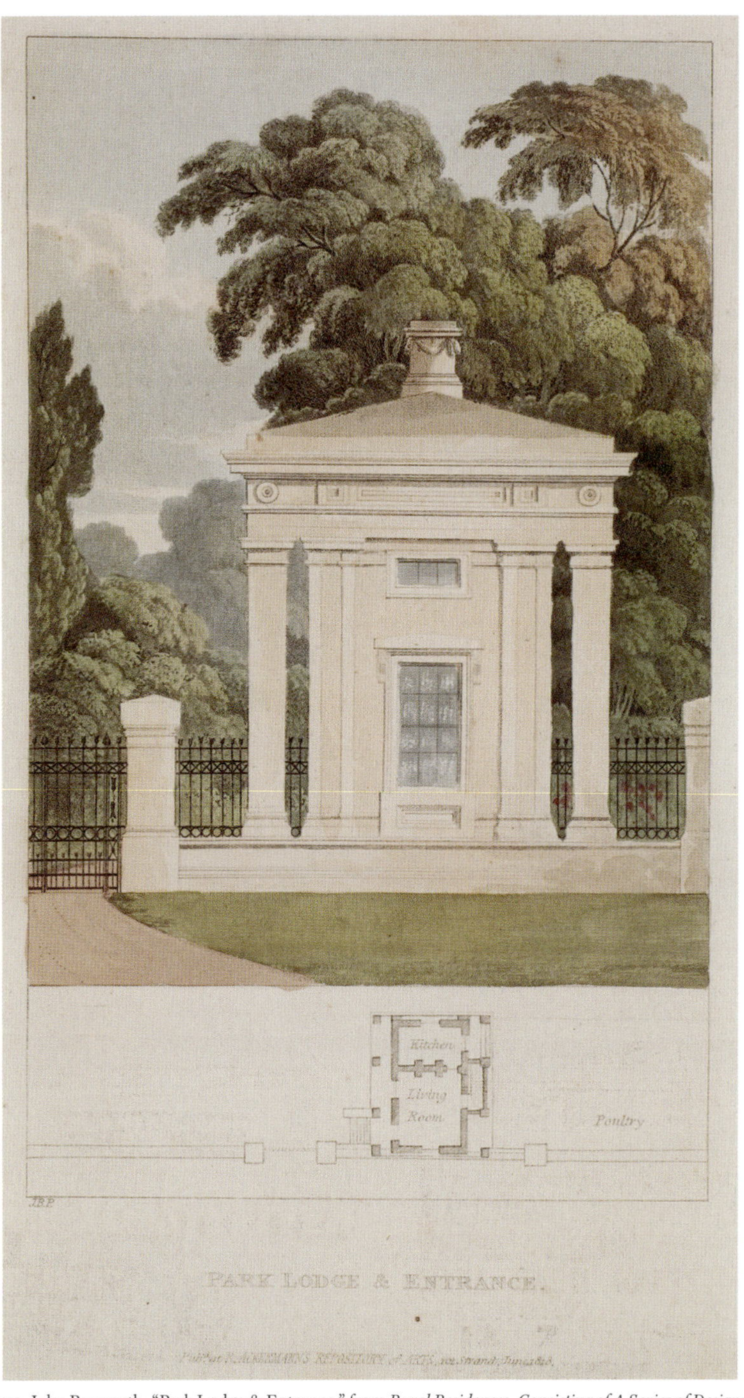

VI. John Papworth, "Park Lodge & Entrance," from *Rural Residences, Consisting of A Series of Designs for Cottages, Decorated Cottages, Small Villas, and other Ornamental Buildings* (1818). Plate XIX. Photograph: Special Collections, University of Virginia, Charlottesville, VA (NA7132 .P2 1818).

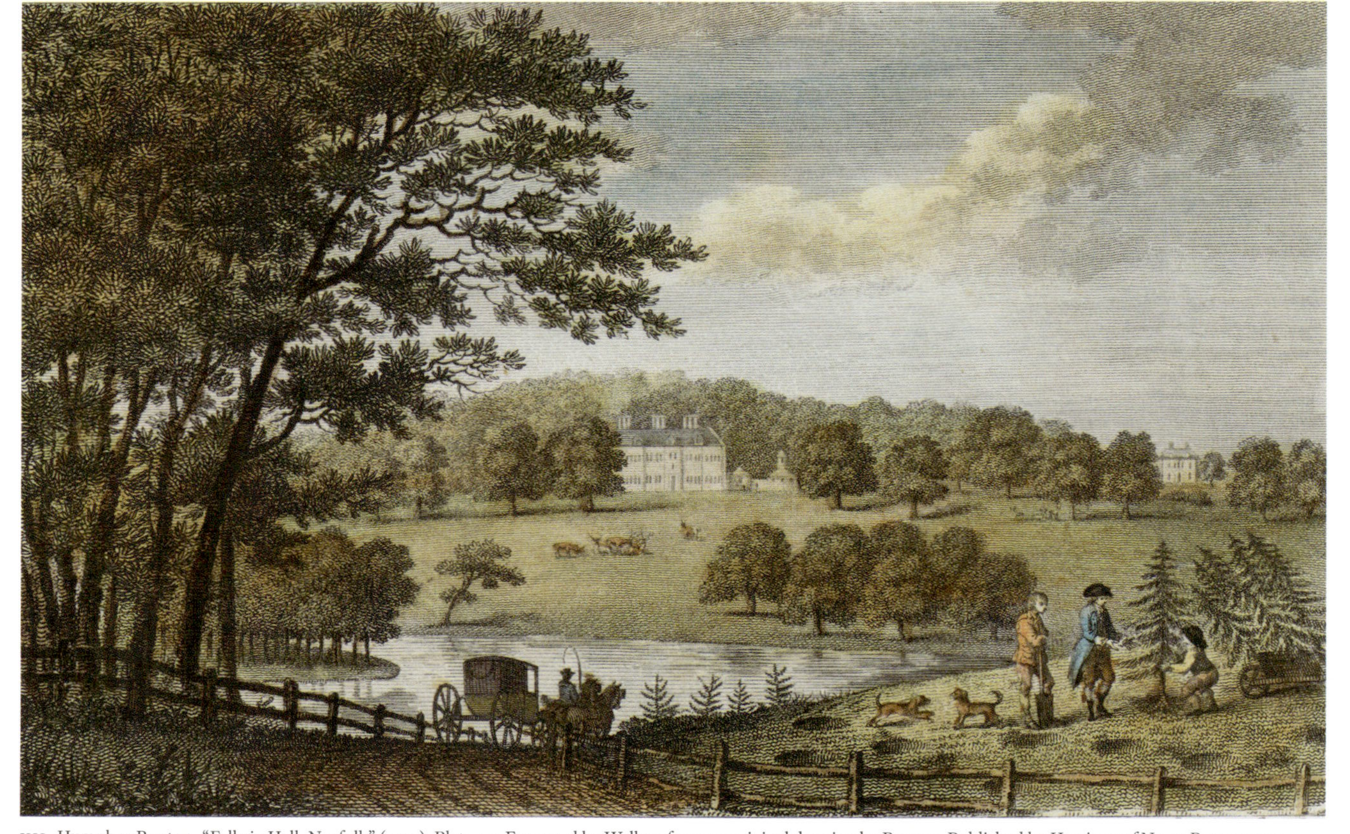

VII. Humphry Repton, "Felbrig Hall, Norfolk" (1793). Plate 40. Engraved by Walker, from an original drawing by Repton. Published by Harrison of No. 13 Paternoster Row, London. Humphry Repton surveying his first commission. Photograph: Courtesy of The Lewis Walpole Library, Yale University.

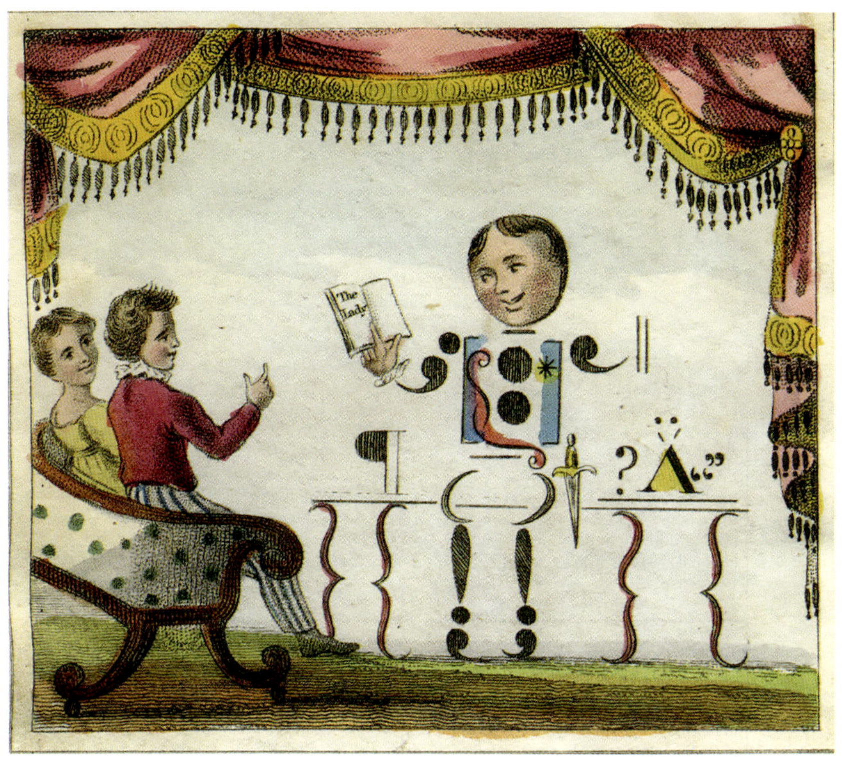

viii. John Harris, "Mr. Stops Reading to Robert & his Sister," from *Punctuation Personified* (London, 1824). Plate 2. Photograph courtesy the Winterthur Library: Joseph Downs Collection of Manuscripts and Printed Ephemera (838 Box 54).

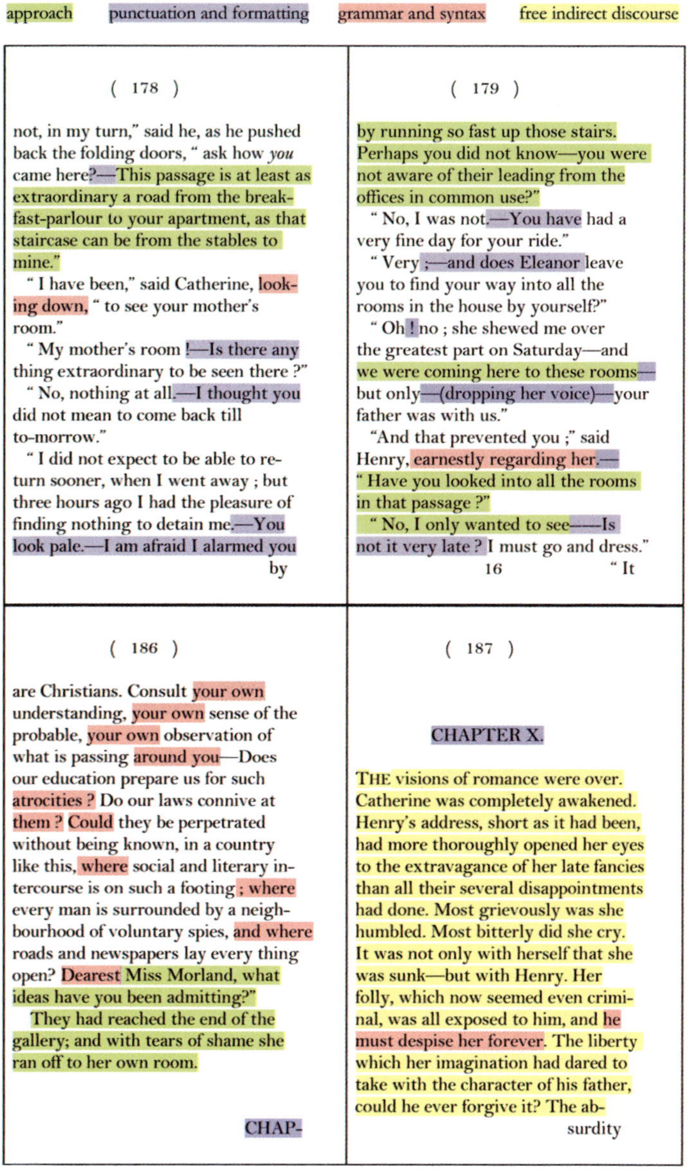

approach punctuation and formatting grammar and syntax free indirect discourse

(178)

not, in my turn," said he, as he pushed back the folding doors, " ask how *you* came here?—This passage is at least as extraordinary a road from the break-fast-parlour to your apartment, as that staircase can be from the stables to mine."

" I have been," said Catherine, look-ing down, " to see your mother's room."

" My mother's room !—Is there any thing extraordinary to be seen there ?"

" No, nothing at all.—I thought you did not mean to come back till to-morrow."

" I did not expect to be able to re-turn sooner, when I went away ; but three hours ago I had the pleasure of finding nothing to detain me.—You look pale.—I am afraid I alarmed you

by

(179)

by running so fast up those stairs. Perhaps you did not know—you were not aware of their leading from the offices in common use?"

" No, I was not.—You have had a very fine day for your ride."

" Very ;—and does Eleanor leave you to find your way into all the rooms in the house by yourself?"

" Oh ! no ; she shewed me over the greatest part on Saturday—and we were coming here to these rooms—but only—(dropping her voice)—your father was with us."

"And that prevented you ;" said Henry, earnestly regarding her.—" Have you looked into all the rooms in that passage ?"

" No, I only wanted to see——Is not it very late ? I must go and dress."

16 " It

(186)

are Christians. Consult your own understanding, your own sense of the probable, your own observation of what is passing around you—Does our education prepare us for such atrocities ? Do our laws connive at them ? Could they be perpetrated without being known, in a country like this, where social and literary in-tercourse is on such a footing ; where every man is surrounded by a neigh-bourhood of voluntary spies, and where roads and newspapers lay every thing open? Dearest Miss Morland, what ideas have you been admitting?"

They had reached the end of the gallery; and with tears of shame she ran off to her own room.

CHAP-

(187)

CHAPTER X.

THE visions of romance were over. Catherine was completely awakened. Henry's address, short as it had been, had more thoroughly opened her eyes to the extravagance of her late fancies than all their several disappointments had done. Most grievously was she humbled. Most bitterly did she cry. It was not only with herself that she was sunk—but with Henry. Her folly, which now seemed even crimi-nal, was all exposed to him, and he must despise her forever. The liberty which her imagination had dared to take with the character of his father, could he ever forgive it? The ab-

surdity

IX. Jane Austen, *Northanger Abbey* (1818). Author's transcription and highlighting.

Radcliffe's "secret guile" (Coleridge's "Now you think you have me!" or Lanham's "ah, got him! released") does bring the reader "through every turn and doubling" to a whole in which nearly every component part unites. While for some readers that unity means that "the interest is completely dissolved,"[81] for others, the spell remains: "curiosity is kept upon the stretch from page to page" (*Critical Review* 361). Even William Hazlitt, who was was frequently scathing about Radcliffe's works (her descriptions are "vague and wordy," her characters are "insipid," "her story comes to nothing"), admits that it is due to "repeated perusal[s]" of *The Romance of the Forest* and *The Mysteries of Udolpho* that he in fact "survey[s] the full-orbed moon shining in the blue expanse of heaven," "hear[s] the wind sighing through autumnal leaves," and "walk[s] under the echoing archways of a Gothic ruin" (note the prepositional experience). Repton had warned that "[a]s soon as the house is visible from the approach, there should be no temptation to quit it; which will ever be the case, if the road be at all circuitous; unless sufficient obstacles, such as water, or inaccessible ground, appear to justify its course" (*Sketches* 92). In Radcliffe, readers do *not* see the end until the end; there is no temptation to quit the narrative; there are sufficient obstacles in "the strange luxury of artificial terror" (*Monthly Review* 280) to justify its circuitousness. And, like the approach, it retains enough interest for "repeated perusals."

Chapter 1 of this book tracked various images of approaches (and "deproaches") in *The Italian*, and chapter 3 paid attention to the catchwords and commas of *The Mysteries of Udolpho*. In this section I will look at the most famous of Radcliffe's approaches—to the castle of Udolpho—as a narrative approach, applying its syntactical architecture to its architectural imagery. I argue that one reason critics such as Coleridge "look[ed] about in vain for the spell which had bound" them to Radcliffe's novels lies in the ways in which she replays time and space. Ian Gordon has argued that "in the late eighteenth century something quite new was being created, a prose directed towards manipulating the feelings of the reader." Edmund Burke, he argues, "achieves his effects" through "the use of evocative imagery and of a sentence made up of short co-ordinated elements," which also happen to be "the common property of a group of his contemporaries, notably the writers of the sentimental and terror novel" (148). We saw how Radcliffe's many-comma'd sentences could produce the paragraphical equivalent of a winding visual approach; her short coordinated clauses create the rhythms of both dream and terror. But she uses another little coordinating element to particular effect: the prepositional phrase "at length," a very differently effective summative from Roxana's "in a Word" or Haywood's "in fine."

"At length" turns out to be a regular marker of temporal and spatial progression throughout the novel. Words most associated with Radcliffe's affective prose would include, say, "sublime." "Sublime" appears thirty-four times in *Mysteries*. Other likely candidates include:

"pensive," 47;
"horror," 85;
"terror," 140;
"melancholy," 193;
and "tears," 227.

The apparently insignificant "at length" appears a surprising 281 times, or about 70 times per volume over four volumes. For some context: *The Romance of the Forest* (1791, 3 vols.) has 143 instances; *The Italian* (1797, 4 vols.), 120. For other later eighteenth-century authors: "at length" shows up 16 times in Sterne's *Tristram Shandy* (1759–67, 7 vols.); 65 times in Smollett's *Roderick Random* (1748, 2 vols.), 29 times in *Humphry Clinker* (1771, 3 vols.); 30 times in Burney's *Evelina*, 53 in *Cecilia*, 40 in *Camilla*; 92 times in Charlotte Smith's *The Old Manor House* (1793, 4 vols.); 31 in Sophia Lee's *The Two Emilys* (1798, vol. 2 of the *Canterbury Tales*); 9 in Maria Edgeworth's *Belinda* (1801). Radcliffe's is a remarkable insistence.[82]

The phrase itself was most popular around 1650 and then again in the later eighteenth century, peaking about 1800, and then plummeting after 1850 into near disuse in 2000.[83] In the early eighteenth century, for example, Defoe uses it relatively rarely in his novels compared to "in short" or "in a Word."[84] It will show up occasionally in Haywood and Fielding, but its appearances are sparse. While more common in later literature, it is a particularly distinctive feature in Radcliffe's prose, "manipulating [. . .] feelings," as Ian Gordon puts it, through her particular combination of "evocative imagery" and the "short co-ordinated elements" of prepositional phrases (148).

What exactly is "at length," anyway? A prepositional phrase poised on both spatial and temporal axes. In the entry for "at, prep." the *Oxford English Dictionary* places the phrase under section IV, "Time, order, consequence, cause, object," definition 33: "Of order: e.g. at first, at last, at length, at the conclusion, etc." ("At," the *OED* apologizes, "denote[s] relations of so many kinds, and some of these so remote from its primary local sense, that a classification of its uses is very difficult. Only a general outline can be here given; its idiomatic constructions with individual words must be looked for under the words themselves.") Under the phrases for "length, n." we have III.14: "at length. a. To or in the full extent; fully, in full; without curtailment. Also *at full, great, some* etc. *length.* †Rarely, *at the length.* [. . .] b. After a long time; at or in the end; in the long run. †Also *at the length.*"[85]

As prepositional phrase or as noun phrase, "at length" in *Udolpho* plays with all the possibilities, managing the ordering and perception of both time and place. Where Defoe's "in a Word" or "in short" compressed the sense of a paragraph, and Haywood's "in fine" engraved a flourish, Radcliffe's "at length" extends and spins out the reading experience of time and place. The most prolonged and vivid use of "at length" as a narrative device is during the long approach of Emily St. Aubert, her aunt, and her brooding guardian Signor Montoni to his castle in *The Mysteries of Udolpho*. That textual approach exerted immediate power: contemporary reviewers frequently quoted it in full.[86] The narrative approach to Udolpho is precisely a "winding line" that "form[s] new combinations on every movement" for the reader as well as the spectator, not only in its imagery but also in its language. The paragraphs are fenced by frequent repetitions of the phrase "at length" to mark the windings and plateaux. The approach begins: "At length, the travellers began to ascend among the Apennines."[87] The imagery of the approach covers all the architectural approach-ground, so to speak. The road winds *between* the mountains; the eye catches a "momentary glimpse of the country below" through an opening in the woods. Particular sentences capture a Whatelyan topography:

> The gloom of these shades, their solitary silence, except when the breeze swept over their summits, the tremendous precipices of the mountains, that came partially to the eye, each assisted to raise the solemnity of Emily's feelings into awe ; she saw only images of gloomy grandeur, or of dreadful sublimity, around her ; other images, equally gloomy and equally terrible, gleamed on her imagination. She was going she scarcely knew whither. (2:164)

What Emily sees is fragmented; her own journey is turning and doubling. The next paragraph has the travelers "still ascend[ing]"; "steep" rises over "steep" and, like the nouns, the mountains "multiply, as they went." Each summit becomes a new base, with "at length" itself a linguistic summit that becomes a base for the next. "At length," the travelers reach a "little plain" (2:165) where the drivers rest and the prose *intends* to—as soon as it properly admires the "extent and magnificence" of the scene opening below. Then follows the full page of description of that scene. The next paragraph has the "travellers continu[ing] to ascend" (and still "among the pines") into a narrow pass, the paragraph choked with tremendous crags, scathed branches, and strong roots (2:167). This pass "at length opened to day" and to a "long perspective" of more mountains (2:167). The scene's characteristic feature virtually quotes J. C. Loudon (or perhaps, given their dates, Loudon is consciously or unconsciously invoking Radcliffe): "The scene seemed perpetually changing, and its features to assume new forms, as the winding road brought them to the eye in different attitudes" (2:167–68). Shifting vapours partially conceal; "sometimes an abrupt opening presented a perspective of only barren rocks" and "sometimes pastoral scenes exhibited their ' green delights' in the narrow vales" (2:168). A few paragraphs later "the road wound into a deep valley" with another "long perspective of retiring summits, rising over each other"; here the travelers pause and Montoni pronounces on the castle below (the original line-lengths preserved to demonstrate the compact intensity of the paragraph):

> " There," said Montoni, speaking for
> the first time in several hours, " is Udol-
> pho." (2:170)

This is perhaps the shortest paragraph in the entire novel, and it is powerfully effective, visually its own brief opening within the solid, claustrophobic, typographical mountains of text. Structurally, as a bit of syntactical architecture, it is perfect. The sentence itself is a miniature periodic sentence and a miniature approach. It begins with the demonstrative adverb "There" and ends with the proper noun of the spatial center of the novel, the "house" of the approach. With only four short coordinated clauses, the paragraph seems brief, but after all, a summit is *pointed* (multiple puns intended). Montoni is paragraphically poised between his own spoken discourse, his own words, his own quotation marks; as gothically implied metonym for his own castle, he employs the little words magnificently: "said Montoni" = "is Udolpho." The little nondescript verbs anchor the proper nouns. His speech (and speech-marks) contain his landscape. He appears to state the obvious but actually acquires something of a visual deep voice from the surrounding silences—not only his own but that of all the other travelers, who have not had recorded conversations in several page-hours. The travelers appear to stand "there" an extraordinary while, as "the light died away on its walls," as "the rays soon faded," as "the twilight deepened" (2:170–71); the text holds us in this moment, at this view, on this approach, *for ten duodecimo pages*, until "the carriage-wheels rolled heavily under the portcullis" (2:173), and the gothic equivalent of the park gate lodge has been passed. We have crossed many mountains, witnessed many hours, and turned many pages, levered along by "at length."

Radcliffe employs "at length" in multiply supple ways throughout the novel. As an ordering function, it can serve as a kind of enclosure, bounding certain kinds of fraughtnesses—rather like Bertrand Bronson's description of the double rules on eighteenth-century title pages, which are "architecturally and psychologically" important: "there is order here: the matter is held within its appointed bounds, and given due emphasis and proportion."[88] In the first two chapters of the fourth volume, for example, when Emily has agreed to an interview with the disgraced Valancourt (who has by now Been to Paris), the interviews are introduced by the phrase: "In the evening, when Emily was at length informed, that Count De Villefort requested to see her, she guessed that Valancourt was below" (4:1). The next day, the second "hour of interview, at length, arrived" (4:21). The interviews themselves are marked by Valancourt's extraordinary petulance; he is continually hedged in and betrayed by the telling phrase, as it creates a small space that points to his guilt, his weakness, his general selfishness: "At length, in a tremulous voice, he said" (4:2). Emily points out that his own conduct has made their separation necessary—he is not, frankly, very promising husband material. He is at first passive-aggressive: "returning to the chair beside her, at length, [he] said [. . .] 'No, Emily—no—you would not do this, if you still loved me. You would find your own happiness in saving mine'" (4:8). She weeps, but it doesn't work; he then grows violent, giving Emily "new reasons for fear" (4:9). He finally cries out that he will leave her forever—then "[throws] himself again into the chair. [. . .] 'My fortitude is gone,' said Valancourt at length" (4:14). The histrionic choreography repeats itself the next day, until he finally leaves. Then it is Emily herself who passes into the complicated linguistic bounds of "at last," "finally," "fully," "extensively" *exhausted*. The chapter ends with Emily, "at length, roused by the voice of the Countess in the garden"; a bit later "she was, at length, sufficiently composed to return to her own room" (4:25–26). In this typical segment the phrase plays a role as psychological marker, a creator of silences, pauses, hesitations, doubts, of not quite being in one state or the other, of passing uncertainly from one more certain state to another.

Radcliffe puts "at length" to good narrative use in her other novels as well, though not as intensely. In *The Italian* (1797), when Vivaldi waits to meet Signora Bianchi, the mother of his beloved Ellena, to plead his case, the phrase piles weight upon the previous sentences of expectation:

> Every object, on which his eyes rested, seemed to announce the presence of Ellena ; and the very flowers that so gaily embellished the apartment, breathed forth a perfume, which fascinated his senses and affected his imagination. Before Signora Bianchi appeared, his anxiety and apprehension had encreased

> so much, that, believing he should be unable to support himself in her presence, he was more than once upon the point of leaving the house. At length, he heard her approaching step from the hall, and his breath almost forsook him.[89]

"At length" here signals the last turn in the temporal approach, the last twist of anxious suspense. It comes to his aid twice in the enfolding scene, once expanding the sense of his "ingenuous manner" and then signalling his leave. The breathless escape from the convent in volume II, visited in chapter 1 as a "deproach" of long perspectives and remote windings, and in chapter 3 for its agitated punctuation, resurfaces here for its closure: "Released, at length, from immediate apprehension, Ellena listened to the mattin-hymn of the pilgrims, as it came upon the still air and ascended towards the cloudless heavens" (2:44). Perhaps the most significant use of "at length" in this novel is when the monk nudges Vivaldi's mother, the Marchesa, into pronouncing a death-sentence on Ellena. In this long-drawn-out scene (first visited in chapter 3, p. 133), the dashes start to appear as shorthand for "at length," signaling a pregnant pause, but watch "at length" as well:

> " The woman who obtrudes herself upon a family, to dishonour it," continued the Marchesa, " deserves a punishment nearly equal to that of a state criminal, since she injures those who best support the state. She ought to suffer"—
>
> " Not nearly, but quite equal,["] interrupted the Confessor, " she deserves—death!"
>
> He paused, and there was a moment of profound silence, till he added—" for death only can obliviate the degradation she has occasioned ; her death alone can restore the original splendor of the line she would have sullied."
>
> He paused again, but the Marchesa still remain[ed] silent[.]
>
> [. . .]
>
> " Hah !" exclaimed the Marchesa, in a low voice, " What is that you mean ? You shall find I have a man's courage also."
>
> " I speak without disguise," replied Schedoni, " my meaning requires none."
>
> The Marchesa mused, and remained silent.
>
> " I have done my duty," resumed Schedoni, at length. " I have pointed out the only way that remains for you to escape dishonour. If my zeal is displeasing— —but I have done."
>
> " No, good father, no," said the Marchesa ; " you mistake the cause of my emotion. New ideas, new prospects, open !—they confuse, they distract me !" (2:109–12; my underline)

Suggestion; pause (typographical); suggestion; pause (verbal); more pauses and more suggestions, until Schedoni has at length done his twisted duty and opened up new prospects to the Marchesa. After another "at length" and several more typographical at-lengths, the scene concludes: " No matter," said Schedoni, in a stifled voice— — " she dies !" (2:130).

This syntactical framing of the psychological interior is in my view one of the most spectacular of Radcliffe's narrative achievements. This powerful turn is the psychological counterpart of the architectural parallax. The eighteenth century loved to carve out various perspectives through experiments with obliquity, and interior spaces were multiplied by mirrors or windows or angles, arranged so that the occupant of a room would see "not enclosing walls, but a series of open arcades through which architectural spaces extended in an infinite parallactic sequence beyond the confines of the room."[90] The interior of Udolpho continues the array of visual parallax: "a light, glimmering at a distance through a long perspective of arches" (*Udolpho* 2:174) renders the gothic hall more striking; as Emily "approached a marble stair-case," the arches "opened to a lofty vault, [. . .] and the rich fretwork of the roof, a corridor, leading into several upper apartments, and a painted window, stretching nearly from the pavement to the ceiling of the hall, became gradually visible" (2:175). She and the maid Annette "wandered about through other passages and galleries, till, at length, frightened by their intricacies and desolation" (2:185) they call for help. Radcliffe's narrative rhythms enact—as her imagery describes—the gothic version of approach in the parallax of multiplied perspectives. Even inside, the circuit is held in suspense.

The psychological fold of the parallax—the early instance of free indirect discourse—we can resee in the approach to Udolpho. In that approach scene, the text clearly, in Dorrit Cohn's words, casts the language of the character into that of the narrator: "she saw only images of gloomy grandeur, or of dreadful sublimity, around her; other images, equally gloomy and equally terrible, gleamed on her imagination. She was going she scarcely knew whither" (*Udolpho* 2:164). Although the use of "at length" in the approach to Udolpho seems primarily topographical, in that each use marks another elevation, these posts of ascension also capture telling psychological moments in between. That first paragraph of approach, beginning with "At length, the travellers began to ascend among the Apennines," ends with the really *not* rhetorical question "why else did she shudder at the idea of this desolate castle?" (2:164, 165). In the second level of "at length," Emily loses for a moment her sorrows. (As I have argued elsewhere, Udolpho is a *good* thing for someone who, though she likes the "soft and glowing landscape" well enough, loves more "the wild wood-walks," and "still more the mountain's stupendous recesses" [1:16]; Emily gazes and gazes and gazes upon Udolpho [literally; the word is used three times in one paragraph].[91]) Although critics from 1794 to the present have thought that Radcliffe's descriptions "sometimes partake too much of uniformity," are "minute even to tedious prolixity" and of "too great frequency," and display too much "similarity of expression" (qtd. in Rogers 19, 21, 25), this approach to Udolpho—appearing well into volume II, when we should have been glutted—still makes most readers linger in the stretches of time created by that prepositional description.

Radcliffe plays with elegant adroitness on the temporal and spatial axes of the phrase "at length" to add emotional and psychological weight to a scene, to spin time and distance out or to roll them neatly up, as a kind of metronomic pace, rhythmically dreamy or breathlessly hurried. She approaches the psychological interiors of her protagonists with syntactical subtlety. Under the microscope, the approach of this almost invisible prepositional phrase can cast a spell to catch even a Coleridge.

ii. Burney and the psychological interior

As if to underscore the point that for Radcliffe "at length" really is a state of mind, Frances Burney is *not* such a keen employer of the phrase, sprinkling it very sparely among her novels.[92] Burney builds different sentences. It strikes me as a matter of pacing; Evelina is, shall we say, a bit sprightlier than Emily. I want to investigate a different narrative approach in Burney, one contemporary with the usage-peak of "at length" at the end of the eighteenth century and beginning of the nineteenth.

We saw in chapter 2 how *Camilla* (1796) featured park gate lodges as literal and psychological markers of approach. In this section I will show how Burney enters and illuminates interiors in that same novel in the context of changes in country house guides and architectural manuals. Like the design books of park gate lodges, Burney makes visible the homely details of a cottage interior, complete with staffage come alive. She does this by having the principal, upper-class characters enter—move *within*—and observe, their different psychological perspectives refracted in their direct discourse.

The social approach more generally was turning toward (increasingly working-class) interiors, as represented in the guides and manuals, and perhaps culminating in Henry Mayhew's *London Labour and the London Poor* (1851). New combinations of "inside" were forming, and the practical methods for visualizing, creating, and entering domestic interiors were soon adapted by novelists for visualizing, creating, and entering psychological interiors.[93] Humphry Repton explicitly analogizes the approach to the house and the entrance to its interior:

> The road by which a stranger is supposed to pass through the park or lawn to the house is called an approach ; and there seems the same relation betwixt the approach and the house externally, that there is internally betwixt the hall or entrance and the several apartments to which it leads. If the hall be too large or too small, too mean or too much ornamented for the style of the house, there is a manifest incongruity in the architecture, by which good taste will be offended ; but if the hall be so situated as not to connect well with the several apartments to which it ought to lead, it will then be defective in point of convenience: so it is with respect to an Approach ; it ought to be convenient, interesting, and in strict harmony with the character and situation of the mansion to which it belongs.[94]

Architects as well as novelists in the later eighteenth and early nineteenth centuries were increasingly interested in creating convenient, interesting, and architecturally harmonious dwellings below the category of mansion. The laboring staffage of the topographical views had comfortable new lodges and cottages built (or at least drawn) for them.

In *Essays on the Picturesque*, Uvedale Price recounts an anecdote that captures the artistic sensibility of the time:

> Sir Joshua Reynolds told me, that when he and [Richard] Wilson the landscape painter were looking at the view from Richmond terrace, Wilson was pointing out some particular part ; and in order to direct his eye to it, " There," said he, " near those houses—there ! Where the *figures* are." — Though a painter, said Sir Joshua, I was puzzled : I thought he meant statues, and was looking upon the *tops* of the houses ; for I did not at first conceive that the men and women we plainly saw walking about, were by him only thought of as figures in the landscape. (1:338–39; see plate I for Wilson's painting of the Brownian-landscaped Croome Court)

The adverb "only" is interesting here, implying a little moral shock on the part of Reynolds; in another sense, it is Richard Wilson who *sees* the "figures," or staffage. I suggested in chapter 2 that the anonymity as well as the ubiquity of staffage figures contributed to the general lack of art-historical interest in them, but that the popular topographical views, as well as the decorative architectural treatises, helped make visible the figure in the landscape as encapsulated narrative—as in William Gilpin's "landskip well adorned with a story in miniature," where "the figures, which tell the story, tho subordinate to the landskip, are the *principal figures*."[95] The laboring poor, as many critics have explored, in their own anonymity and ubiquity, were rarely visible in earlier eighteenth-century novels.[96] J. C. Loudon believed in 1806: "The part acted by the cottager in the great drama of life, though important when viewed collectively, is nevertheless, as to the operations of the individual, scarcely discernible. The first and last time that we see him is in the field or in the highway at hard labour ; when he is no longer capable of toil, he retires under the shelter of his cottage, and leaves the world as obscurely as he came into it."[97] But just as cottage design books by T. D. W. Dearn and Thomas Frederick Hunt populate their illustrations with relaxed gardeners and frisking dogs, works such as Loudon's *Encyclopædia of Cottage, Farm, and Villa Architecture and Furniture* increasingly inserted live-action figures into their textual fields. Where painters saw "figures," architects began to see human stories. As the chapter from *Camilla* I will focus on below explores, it is "Two Ways of looking at the same Thing." From the other side, *Camilla* will open up the interior of a respectable cottage, the sort argued for by John Papworth in *Rural Residences* (1818), where "the porch in which [the labourer] rests after the fatigues of the day" is "ornamented by some flowering creeper," and "neatness and cleanliness [. . .] bespeak that elasticity of mind, and spring of action, which produce industry and cheerfulness."[98]

Country house guides, travel narratives, and design manuals increasingly brought the reader into domestic interiors across the eighteenth century.[99] The professional guides were concerned almost exclusively with upper-class interiors, but they began the prepositional turn *within*. In the mid-eighteenth century George Bickham adopted a cheery second-person approach, inviting us directly into the text's spaces in *The Beauties of Stow* (1750): "From *Buckingham* Town you pass through a little Village called *Chatmore*. [. . .] This charming Garden you enter by Steps that lead to a superb Terras, which is carried cross-ways the whole Length of the Ground."[100] In 1763 he and P. Norbury printed *A Short Account of the Principal Seats and Gardens in and about Richmond and Kew*, which opens up to us the private houses of this "KINGDOM" on "the Banks of the *Thames*," formerly ruled by "the Terror of Fools and Knaves, and the Darling of the Learned and Virtuous" (Alexander Pope), and now by "Mr. Cambridge" (Richard Owen Cambridge [1717–1802], poet and essayist).[101] *A Short Account* captures in discrete paragraphical sections the intimacy of neighborhood interiors, opening little windows on individual tastes and choices. In Horace Walpole's seat Strawberry Hill, for example, our guide brings us into the Library, which "contains a fine Collections of Books." He predicts: "You are struck with an Awe [. . .] proceeding from *The high embowed Roof, / And antique Pillars massy Proof, / And storied Windows richly dight, / Casting a dim, religious Light*" (9). Although our guides find "*Claremont*, belonging to the D. of *Newcastle*," an "old fashion'd ungraceful

Building" with most of its rooms "very small, and very ill furnish'd," it is well worth pushing farther in:

> [T]hat which is most remarkable, is the top Room of all, for the House lessening to a Point, finishes with a pretty good Apartment, with Windows backwards and forwards : when you look down from the Front you see the Lawn and Avenue below, but when you turn to the back Window, you are astonish'd to find yourself on a Level with the Garden, into which you enter by a large Glass Door that reaches to the Ground. (13)

Each brief narrative paragraph is enchanted by prospects and perspectives and the forming of new combinations to the eye; the reader is brought in to see, to turn, to see again. We seem to have *access* to everything. In the octagonal summer house at Esher, home of the Pelham family, each of its windows commands "a Prospect so rich, so various, and so unbounded, that the Gazer's Eye is opprest by the Profusion of Beauties, and knows not where to fix" (12). At "Mrs. PRITCHARD's House at *Twickenham*, called *Ragman's Castle*, from its original Builder,"[102] we agree that

> [t]he Front of the House is very pretty, being covered with Gravel, and the best Room (with a handsome Bow Window) forms a very uniform Appearance : This Appartment is hung with India Paper, dispos'd in a most elegant Taste. It represents a Chinese Pavilion supported with Lilac Pillars. In several Parts there are Looking Glasses so artfully placed in the Chinese Houses, that the Prospect is seen by every Person, from every different Part of the Room, which in the Afternoon, when the Barges are coming up, presents the most beautiful moving Picture imaginable. (7)

This paragraph offers another textual topography: each sentence supplies a different perspective, and the multiplied perspectives *move*, literally and participially. In a sense, this is the approach seen *from within*, as when Humphry Repton explains that the "view [taken] from the Centre window of the drawing room" at Glemham Hall will show the approach from Yarmouth from the inside, revealing "a handsome Lake" and a lodge "so constructed as to appear like a tower rising above the wood."[103] Both Repton and Bickham are here positioning what David Marshall calls "the frame of art," turning nature—or at least the view from the window—into "a series of living tableaux."[104] But where Marshall sees a discomfiting consequence of "turning people into figures," as Reynolds witnessed Wilson doing, it strikes me as more narrative than fixative: the descriptions notice (or create) the motion, the detail, the stories, the inside as well as outside. The reader *moves* through the paragraph, starting from the outside, as if from a barge on the Thames, admiring that handsome bow window; we are then suddenly inside, dutifully noting the India Paper; we are then pointed to the Looking Glasses "so artfully placed"; and then we—every Person of us—experience from within the prospect we had been part of without: the barge we arrived on. The mirrors, the window, the narrative all create the "moving Picture[s]," the variegated prospects, the new perspectives, the new combinations, of the new sense of approach.

Typographically, *A Short Account* has a rich and vivid texture. One of the smallest entries becomes a miniature portrait of dweller-in-dwelling (figure 23):

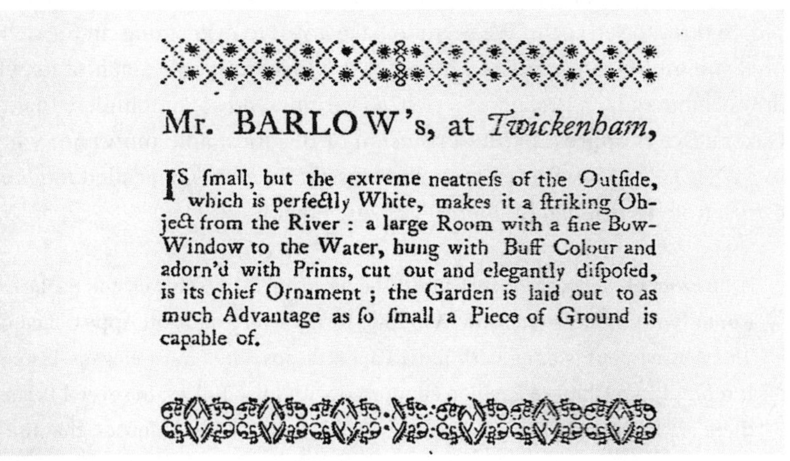

Mr. BARLOW's, at *Twickenham*,

IS ſmall, but the extreme neatneſs of the Outſide, which is perfectly White, makes it a ſtriking Object from the River : a large Room with a fine Bow-Window to the Water, hung with Buff Colour and adorn'd with Prints, cut out and elegantly diſpoſed, is its chief Ornament ; the Garden is laid out to as much Advantage as ſo ſmall a Piece of Ground is capable of.

23. George Bickham, "Mr. Barlow's, at Twickenham," from *A Short Account of the Principal Seats and Gardens in and about Richmond and Kew* (1763).

Our Mr. Barlow is a fastidious man, a Dickensian man, keeping everything just so; even the ornaments surrounding his cunning little world evoke the "Prints, cut out and elegantly disposed." Typographically and syntactically, as well, much can be done with the "so small a Piece of Ground" within this tiny topo-paragraph: the variety of printers' ornaments thickly hedging—but graciously spaced—above and below the description; Mr. BARLOW's name in the same proud capitals as the Duke of Newcastle's; the first sad fact of the dwelling's modest size immediately qualified by the parataxes of exquisiteness; and the periodic finality of advantage found in that "so small a Piece of Ground."

Details of color, fabric, texture, ornament, and furnishings began to emerge in architectural publications toward the middle of the eighteenth century. Earlier, someone like Batty Langley (1696–1751), who published a number of popular trade books for builders and their clients, outlined a more generalized spatial theory about the importance of proportion in relation to human habitation and gesture.[105] (He underscores, for example, the importance of always being able to end a flight up or down a staircase with the same foot that began it.) William Kent (1684?–1748) first regarded furniture "as an essential part of interior decoration" and believed that "each room should be a separate individual work of art." Without Kent, according to Elizabeth Burton, "the English interior might have remained an uncoordinated hodge-podge."[106] For each room to be perceived as a separate work of coordinated art, each needs a proper observer. The diaries of Caroline Lybbe Powys (1756–1808), visited in chapter 1, give us the perspective of that observer. In her first visit to Houghton Hall in 1756, for example, she found Kent's rooms "very superb; [. . .] more especially as the rooms are, instead of white, painted dark green olive."[107] With the houses featured in the topographical views open to visitors and readers, each of whom is presumed to have her own aesthetic judgment and human curiosity at play in observation, we might say that the figures in the landscape are very much alive and entering interiors. We are the staffage. The views *need* us to enter the landscape; the narratives *need* us to enter the story.

John Papworth's *Rural Residences* (1818) is concerned with the interiors of the middle and laboring classes. In "Plate XV. A VILLA, DESIGNED AS A RESIDENCE FOR A SMALL FAMILY," Papworth designs a "dining-room [. . .] decorated by niches and statues"; the "drawing and music-room, communicating with a small conservatory, would form a very agreeable suite of apartments, wholly unconnected with the dinner room," and the "library is arranged for a tasteful disposition of the books; and, as being a room of business, it is entered immediately from the small hall" (64). The pleasures and businesses of the future family are architecturally and narratively imagined; the very arrangement of the rooms anticipates the motions of the occupants, entering from the small hall or out of sight and sound of the dining room.

For the laborers' cottages, he gives specific architectural directions for their comfort:

> Cottagers suffer greatly by the expense of fuel, whether it be of wood or of coal, it is therefore highly important that the fireplaces should be so constructed that the apartments may be sufficiently heated with the least possible quantity of supply. To effect this, the fire-place should be so formed that the heat may readily pass into the apartment from the front, ends, bottom, and top of the stove or grate in which the fuel is placed, and that the draught shall be sufficient to keep the smoke from issuing into the apartment. (24)

He then recommends the reader to the "observations on these subjects, published by Dr. Franklin and Count Rumsford" as of both practical and theoretical interest (24).

By 1833 Loudon's massive and popular *Encyclopædia of Cottage, Farm, and Villa Architecture and Furniture* was imagining the interiors of both the simplest cottages and the most magnificent of villas in exhaustive detail and actually *peopling* them with characters, as if the staffage of the topographical views has come alive. Directions for materials are precise, down to their manufacturing labels: "*Without a Cornice no Room can have a finished Appearance*, therefore we recommend cornices to be introduced into the living-rooms and principal bed-rooms of even the humblest cottages"; plaster ornaments for the ceilings of cottage parlors "have recently been manufactured by Messrs. Bielefelds and Haselden, at a very low price, of a description of papier maché."[108] Varieties of paint colors and contrasts, stenciling and wallpaper patterns, are carefully considered: "*Papering the Walls of Rooms* is a very general practice in Britain. [. . .]. [I]t gives a clothed, warm, and comfortable air to bed-rooms, and an enriched finish to the better description of living-rooms" (279).

In a section entitled "*The Beau Ideal of an English Villa*," the narrator, even more chummy than Bickham, links arms with us and confides his innermost aesthetic wishes:

> Entering our drawing-room from the saloon, at the end opposite would be a square or circular bay window, commanding a view of the park and the distant country beyond it. On the right side would be the fireplace, and on the opposite side two windows looking over the terrace and parterre. In this room I would have a splendid white marble chimneypiece. (796)

After discussing the apple-green, rose-colored, and mulberry effects in the drawing room at Earlstoke Park, the narrator moves into a delicious discussion of *our* color choices: "As I am reserving crimson for the colour of the dining-room furniture, I really do not know what to choose for the drawing-room ; suppose, at a venture, we fix upon blue satin ; I mean a pale blue, which is a good candlelight colour. [. . .]. The next difficulty is, what should be the colour of the walls : perhaps buff would do" (796–97). (Harriet Byron would have vastly enjoyed this tête-à-tête.) After furnishing the room with pictures ("a small Claude," perhaps), a few busts, a large looking glass, a marble slab, a bookcase filled with handsomely bound works of "the best poets and novelists" (Baskerville's Congreve, perhaps?), "some curious specimens of old china," an Axminster carpet, and an assortment of flowers, carvings, and fringes, the narrator prepares the interior—stage setting—for its figures:

> [A]s nothing gives a room a more dismal effect than an appearance of idleness, every thing should be so arranged [. . .] as if the persons using the rooms had been employed in some way or other. This effect would be produced by the daily papers, and some periodical works, and open letters received in the morning, on the principal tables ; and, on other tables, some of the blotting books might be open ; the inkstands not thoroughly in order, with some unfinished writing and open books or portfolios. (798–99)

Rather like the Dennis Severs House in Spitalfields, the figures slowly become visible, taking up hypothetical positions and occupations, acquiring sentence by sentence a sort of novelistic identity:

> [T]he library would be the morning sitting-room for the gentlemen, who might here read the papers and new publications, write and answer letters ; and thus, with a stroll round the garden or farm, and a look into the stables and kennels, employ the time till luncheon, after which some would join the ladies in an excursion on horseback while others rode with their host to see some improvements upon the farm or estate. (799)

A story begins to emerge—a flirtation, perhaps even a romance:

> [I]n summer evenings, the doors of the living-rooms would be thrown open. [. . .] [I]n the library, a gentleman may, perhaps, be referring to a book, while he explains [mansplains?] something to the ladies with whom he had conversed during the morning ride. In the saloon a lady is, perhaps, playing a lively air, while the young ladies and some of the gentlemen are lounging about the room engaged in playful conversation. (799)

At this moment our friend the Fieldingesque narrator whispers in our ear:

> While we have them in these positions, let me ask what you think of the general effect of the sitting-rooms now seen together through the open doors. Stand for a moment near the bay window at the end of the library, and look at the perspective view of the whole, terminating in the distant prospect seen through the opposite bay window in the drawing-room. I hope the effect is not disagreeable. (799)

The narrator and the reader have become the staffage, *not* "mißbrauchte [misused]" in Goethe's sense but "als Betrachter, als Repräsentant von Allen [an observer representative of all observers]," who is, as Alison Martin argues, "taking stock of the scene. [. . .] Goethe implied that as we beheld the painting, we implicitly projected ourselves into this figure, who acted as our entry point into the scene."[109] The narrator in this case is our entry point into the scene, and we enter the buff-walled, blue-satined room along with the rest of the staffage. The motion of narration catches us all up: as "the half-hour bell has rung," we join the narrator to peep into the dining room while "the ladies are hurrying to their dressing-rooms ; and the gentlemen slowly follow" (799). As Peter Collins argued, "It was the desire to live the experiences of a novel which constituted the original essence of architectural romanticism" (39).

As novels adapted the descriptive practices of nonliterary genres such as country house guides and design manuals, so they began to enter newly detailed, visualized domestic interiors. We have seen a glimpse of Harriet Byron, now Lady Grandison, delighting in her light-green-velvet drawing room in Grandison Hall (chapter 4, p. 169); here I would like to look at a moment in Frances Burney's third novel, *Camilla* (1796), where narrator and characters enter—and see in different ways—"a new little cottage."[110] The cottage has been "just fitted up" by the hero Edgar Mandlebert for "the wife of the poor prisoner" for whom Camilla had interceded. Edgar wants to take a friendly group to witness his happy benevolence (as one does in the eighteenth century): his cousins Camilla and Indiana, Indiana's governess Miss Margland, and Edgar's watchful mentor Dr. Marchmont. The cottage is "not above a mile from the parish church," and "the weather was fine" (1:299). They have several chapters' worth of adventures on the one-mile journey, but when they eventually arrive, book II, chapter XIII reveals "Two Ways of looking at the same Thing" (1:354). Indiana, the first observer, is "in the most sprightly spirits she had ever experienced" because she believes she is "on the verge of becoming mistress of a fine place and a large fortune"—Edgar's (1:359–60). Hers is the first view. Even before she syntactically enters the cottage she disparages it (the line lengths are reproduced in their compact originals for this cottage-sized paragraph):

> " Dear ! is this the cottage we have
> been coming to all this time ?" cried In-
> diana, upon entering ; " Lord ! I thought
> it would have been something quite
> pretty." (1:360)

In that small paragraph it is as if Indiana simply sweeps in, not bothering with the niceties of a door. Edgar responds: "' And what sort of prettiness,' said Edgar, ' did you expect from a cottage ?'" The narrator supplies no adverb or adjective giving us a clue to his tone, but by this point we know him well enough to imagine it carefully blank. "' Dear, I don't know—but I thought we were come on purpose to see something extraordinary ?'" (1:360). She then prattles on with no indication that she recognizes the existence of the cottager, despite her second-person address. She prowls the room,

> amusing herself with an inspection more minute, taking up and casting down everything that was portable, without any regard either to deranging its neatness, or endangering its safety :— exclaiming, as she made her round of investigation, " Dear! Crockery ware ! how ugly !— Lord, what little mean chairs !— Is that your best gown, good woman ?— Dear, what an ugly pattern !— Well, I would not wear such a thing to save my life !— Have you got nothing better than this for a floor-cloth ?— Only look at those curtains ! Did you ever see such frights ?— Lord ! do you eat off these platters ? I am sure I could sooner die ! I should not mind starving half as much !" (1:364)

Indiana seems to view the modest cottage as the sort of desperate, sordid interior of the eviction scenes studied by Ruth Perry, where "the minimum space required for the comfort of the body is an oblong the size of a grave or a mattress" (448). If it were not for the occasional direct address to its inhabitant, the "good woman" seems invisible from Indiana's perspective—the figure of staffage, barely quaint. Indiana's blithe insults performed in those second-person interjections suggest an ugly obverse of free indirect discourse: she cannot (or certainly will not) enter into the mind of the cottager, however much she barges into the cottage.

Camilla, naturally, demonstrates the second way of seeing the same thing. Already grave at her cousin's behavior, Camilla ("who, by nature, was gay") makes an "exclamation far different" from Indiana's the moment she "crossed the threshold," when she recognizes the woman she had tried to help (*Camilla* 1:361). "' How I rejoice to see you !' cried she," and then meets "the husband, now in decent garb." Camilla compliments Edgar on his well-bestowed generosity; "' You see,' answered he, *gratefully*" (1:362, my emphasis). She sees. She "seat[s] herself on a stool" and proceeds to see more, and with pleasure: "' How neat is this ! How tidy that !' were her continual exclamations; ' How bright you have rubbed your saucepans ! How clean every thing is all round ! How soon you will all get well in this healthy and comfortable little dwelling !'" (1:365). The narrator never gives us a description of the interior; instead, the characters' conflicting observations light up the floor-cloths (which, as Loudon notes, "are not only cheap, but in many cases look remarkably well" [*Encyclopædia* 345]) and curtains and dishes of the cottage. And more crucially, their comments also reflect light back from the well-rubbed saucepans into the interiors of the observers themselves.

iii. Austen and the psychological approach to the interior

> She was a warm and judicious admirer of landscape, both in nature and on canvass. At a very early age she was enamoured of Gilpin on the Picturesque ; and she seldom changed her opinions on either books or men.
>
> Henry Austen, "Biographical Notice of the Author" (1817)[111]

> Upon the whole, the turn of this author's novels bears the same relation to that of the sentimental and romantic cast, that cornfields and cottages and meadows bear to the highly adorned grounds of a show mansion, or the rugged sublimities of a mountain landscape.
>
> Sir Walter Scott, unsigned review of *Emma* (1816)[112]

Austen's novelistic landscapes do not situate "show mansions" at their centers; she foregrounds what to Lady Catherine de Bourgh would be the staffage in the "cornfields and cottages and meadows." She perfects a new form of psychological and narrative approach. Austen knew the works of Walpole, Whately, Gilpin, Repton, Price, and Knight; she knew the debates over the Brownian emparkments and the picturesque craze; she admired the strengths and relished the absurdities of each. She may have been enamoured of Gilpin at a very early age; yet from a very early age, "ironic allusions to Gilpin are frequent."[113] She may have satirized Repton in *Mansfield Park*; yet many scholars "believe his ideas of improvement were close to her own" (Duckworth 283). The grounds of Pemberley have been tastefully modernized; Sotherton is poised to be trendily so; Donwell Abbey is beautifully old-fashioned. I do not intend to use this section to weigh in on the matter (although I must say I would align her early and last views with Edward Ferrars's and Humphry Repton's, in favor of uniting beauty with utility and preferring troops of tidy villagers to the finest banditti). Rather, I would like to argue that Austen's famous innovations in free indirect discourse are grounded in the same aesthetic and psychological shifts that were reshaping landscapes, typographies, and grammars.

Free indirect discourse has at least as long a bibliography as landscape gardening and linguistic change, but although it has a "history" (in that Austen is cited as the primary English practitioner, with Flaubert, James, and Woolf to follow), that history tends to be descriptive rather than analytical or material.[114] But narrative strategies, along with any other conceptual practice, can find a material, cultural ground. I agree with Julie Park, who has argued that Austen's narrative strategies "evoke and collude with period landscape design."[115] More specifically, I think that Austen's use of free indirect discourse maps onto the theory, practice, and description of the architectural approach, which itself has its basis in the fundamentals of the picturesque: Gilpin's "peculiar kind of beauty" which requires a foreground, middle distance, and background, parts contributing to the whole, careful distribution of light and shade, varied textures and animated expressions, and moods of place and time" (*Essay upon Prints* x).

In 1978 Dorrit Cohn described the nature of free indirect discourse (which she called narrated monologue; the English term for *style indirect libre* or *erlebte Rede* had not yet been settled) in terms that themselves suggest the eighteenth-century architectural approach: "By leaving the relationship between words and thoughts latent, the narrated monologue casts a peculiarly penumbral light on the figural consciousness, suspending it on the threshold of verbalization in a manner that cannot be achieved by direct quotation."[116] The narrative form is suspended on a threshold; it is poised "grammatically *between* the two other forms, sharing with quoted monologue the expression in the principal clause, with psycho-narration the tense system and the third-person reference" (105, my emphasis). It is "more oblique" than quoted monologue, though more direct than "psycho-narration." It casts the language of the character "into the grammar" of the narrator.

Narratologists often speak of free indirect discourse as "double-voiced discourse," "dual," or "two-in-one,"[117] which happens to echo Loudon's description of the "modern style" as "showing two fronts at once" (*Encyclopædia* 769). Humphry Repton's own narrative strategies involve a kind of proto-FID. André Rogger has noted that Repton's Red Books, like the *Seats* compendia examined in chapter 2, narratively describe the properties visited, but with a difference:

> In the role of a guide, he pointed out the felicities and infelicities that may have been obscure to gentleman owners possibly lacking experience and unable to look at their estates with the detachment required to make unbiased assessments. The difference lies in the fact that Repton combined two voices that had until then been kept apart: his ideas as a garden designer were interwoven with the possible reflections and judgement of future visitors to the property, shaping a compelling alliance that may well have contributed to the Red Books' appeal.[118]

In this instance, the voice of the narrator blends with the "character" of the imagined visitor; we do not find ourselves in *their* minds so much as the narrator anticipates *our own*. Rogger offers an example from the Red Book for High Legh in Cheshire, a seat of George John Legh (1791, fol. 6):

> By judicious management of the plantation it will not I hope be difficult to cheat a stranger into this description of the Place—viz. 'The turnpike road passes thro' the park and for some distance makes part of the Approach to the house', this will surely be a more favorable description than that which every one must now give—viz. 'the High-Road goes all the way along side of the park; and close by the house.' (Qtd. in Rogger 249n34)

The Repton narrator offers an alternative script for our present (possible) experience with a future (possible) experience. "Surely" we will have more delight thinking about the road becoming part of the approach rather than simply bordering the estate. The Red Books, Rogger concludes, "provided a vessel in which constituents from a broad range of topical discourses could be individually blended" (102). That blending narratively "forms new combinations in the mind" of the reader.

The winding and combining of the approach is frequently repeated in its narrative description, as we saw in chapter 1. Tewin Water (seat of Henry Cowper, Esq.) has a second approach from Hertford (the first, discussed in chapter 1 and below, was from Welwyn): "by approaching the house in two ways each road has its separate advantages and its separate beauties" (*Tewin Water* 47). This second approach also describes a narrative winding with a dual consciousness:

> From the new high road the approach will enter the park in a plantation that extends along the proposed head of the lake. This road will be the most natural as well as the most interesting, because it is the nearest and because it passes within view of the water, which from its colour and shape will be far more attractive than the high ground of the park, and from various parts of this road the house will appear to advantage. (*Tewin Water* 69)

The approach (metonymic for visitor) enters, extends along, and passes within view; the house appears at the end of the sentence as at the end of the experience. The experience is projected: the approach "will be" the most natural and interesting; the water "will be" more attractive; the house "will appear" to more advantage; Repton as narrator positions the route to the house and the house itself in front of Henry Cowper the Customer and his future guests and visitors, inserting his aesthetic judgments as their own.

In describing the approach to Blaise Castle, Repton confesses: "I can shew the effect of a new house instead of an old one, but I cannot describe those numberless beauties which may be brought before the eye in succession by the windings of a road, or the contrast of ascending and descending thro' a deep ravine of rich hanging woods." The landscape surrounding the castle is a "grand and sublime combination of rocks and trees"; the general inaccessibility of the sublime makes it "peculiarly desirable to have an easy road of approach thro' a part of the ground not interfering with these walks, that connect the house with the castle." Closer to the house are "more common objects of pleasure" than the picturesque; "the approach for a certain distance will serve as the line of communication betwixt the house and some objects highly interesting": a cottage, and a view from inside the mouth of a cavern that features "a winding valley of wood and rock terminated by a smooth hill," "enlivened by frequent groups of carriages and company who visit the spot, and produce an astonishing contrast to the solemn dignity of this awful scene."[119] Once again, the approach is designed to multiply perspectives and generate different views upon each turn; here, it is defined as a "line of communication" between the outer interesting objects and the house.[120] The approach *connects* the house with cottages and caverns, carriages and company; it provides access to "objects highly interesting" that might otherwise be overlooked; it is a passage to the visible. Under a different ("highly interesting") sense of "communication," the *OED* gives an example from James Beattie's *Elements of Moral Science* (1793): "Communication [. . .] takes place when a speaker or writer assumes his hearer or reader as a partner in his sentiments and discourse, saying we, instead of I or ye."[121] Thus Repton's descriptions of his approaches, his projects, are themselves lines of communication that assume in some cases a dual voice, and in all cases a dual (or more) perspective. The approach connects the periphery and the interstices of the estate to its center through a winding set of turns; the description of the approach is a line of communication *between* the narrator and his client/reader, and a passage *into* the mind of his client/reader.

Blakey Vermuele's description of Jane Austen's use of free indirect discourse itself rather beautifully follows the Reptonian patterns of approach, beginning with an overview, entering the grounds, highlighting the "mental turns" prompted by thoughts of Pemberley, and then breaking into the open:

> Jane Austen begins to use free indirect discourse in an orderly way during a crucial scene in *Pride and Prejudice*. Elizabeth travels with her uncle and aunt, Mr. and Mrs. Gardiner, into Derbyshire. Her aunt suggests they visit Pemberley, Mr. Darcy's stately home. When they enter the grounds, Elizabeth, who has already turned down a marriage proposal from Mr. Darcy, begins to have

> second thoughts. As she doubts herself, thoughts crowd into her head. Austen depicts her thinking as—well—thinking: "Elizabeth's mind was too full for conversation." Her mental turn triggers free indirect discourse, just as the mental turn itself was triggered by the weight of Pemberley on her psyche (later Elizabeth jokingly remarks to her sister Jane that she fell in love with Mr. Darcy when she saw his house). Here is the scene where it breaks out into the open: (77)

And that is frequently how Austen's paragraphs of free indirect discourse actually function, narratively speaking. Their syntactic topography is an approach of winding, perspectival change, circling from a bird's-eye view overhead, swooping down through a mind, and popping out into direct discourse. Narrative parallax, we might say, is achieved when one sentence winds into the next for a different perspective. Consider this paragraph from the beginning of *Mansfield Park* (1814), after Mrs. Price has written to her sisters for help, and family relations are reestablished:

> Mrs. Norris was often observing to the others, that she could not get her poor sister and her family out of her head, and that much as they had all done for her, she seemed to be wanting to do more : and at length she could not but own it to be her wish, that poor Mrs. Price should be relieved from the charge and expense of one child entirely out of her great number. " What if they were among them to undertake the care of her eldest daughter, a girl now nine years old, of an age to require more attention than her poor mother could possibly give ? The trouble and expense of it to them, would be nothing compared with the benevolence of the action." Lady Bertram agreed with her instantly. " I think we cannot do better," said she, " let us send for the child."[122]

Like Vermuele's paragraph, but even more to the point, like Repton's narrative of the approach to Tewin Water discussed in chapter 1, which skirts and sweeps and passes, finally bursting upon the house with the reward of a view (p. 31), Austen's paragraph also skirts along, sweeps round, and bursts upon; it begins circling high overhead in the general space of a year, with a timelessly repetitive Mrs. Norris freely and indirectly observing; then she is indirectly quoted, in the third person; and then, with no textual space in between, Lady Bertram bursts with unusual force into direct discourse—in a narrative arc of approach.

Julie Park has recently made a similar connection between Repton's landscapes and Austen's technique, arguing that landscape gardening is more than just a well-recognized theme in *Mansfield Park*, it is also "spatial, cognitive, and technical" (170). Highlighting Repton's emphasis on views seen through windows (another form of David Marshall's "frame of art"), she notes that "Repton designed his landscapes with an understanding that domestic landscapes were, to a large extent, shaped by interiority—by the experience of being situated in an interior space" and that his "visual sophistication [. . .] characterizes in particular the narrative technologies of perspective and free indirect discourse that Austen uses for presenting her dark narrative of domestic ideology, *Mansfield Park*" (171). Park connects the Reptonian landscape with the Austenian character and concludes that "what makes Austen's mastery of omniscient narration so accomplished in this particular novel" lies in the fact that "the character is the medium" (177).

I completely agree. Well, almost. I would simply expand that argument into the syntactical and typographical: the sentence, the paragraph, the page, are also the medium. (And I tend to pursue the patterns away from dark ideologies, across different psychological terrains.[123]) I will paraphrase Blakey Vermuele and suggest that free indirect discourse is the psycholiterary equivalent of the approach.[124] Watch, for example, the elaborate syntactic and psychological turns in this paragraph from *Emma* (1816), after Emma has spent her first evening with young Harriet Smith:

> Emma was as much pleased with her manners as her person, and quite determined to continue the acquaintance.
>
> She was not struck by any thing remarkably clever in Miss Smith's conversation, but she found her altogether very engaging—not inconveniently shy, not unwilling to talk—and yet so far from pushing, shewing so proper and becoming a deference, seeming so pleasantly grateful for being admitted to Hartfield, and so artlessly impressed by the appearance of every thing in so superior a style to what she had been used to, that she must have good sense and deserve encouragement. Encouragement should be given. Those soft blue eyes and all those natural graces should not be wasted on the inferior society of Highbury and its connections. The acquaintance she had already formed were unworthy of her. The friends from whom she had just parted, though very good sort of people, must be doing her harm. They were a family of the name of Martin, whom Emma well knew by character, as renting a large farm of Mr. Knightley, and residing in the parish of Donwell—very creditably she believed—she knew Mr. Knightley thought highly of them—but they must be coarse and unpolished, and very unfit to be the intimates of a girl who wanted only a little more knowledge and elegance to be quite perfect. *She* would notice her ; she would improve her ; she would detach her from her bad acquaintance, and introduce her into good society ; she would form her opinions and her manners. It would be an interesting, and certainly a very kind undertaking ; highly becoming her own situation in life, her leisure, and powers.[125]

The first sentence of the full paragraph moves from what is arguably simple narration ("She was not struck by any thing remarkably clever") almost straight into Emma's head, with the accumulating emphatics ("so far from pushing," "so proper," "so pleasantly," "so artlessly," "so superior") landing into a conclusion of their own making: "she must have good sense" (a conclusion rather pointedly undermined by its own first clause). The middle sentence, acknowledging what she knew to the Martins' credit (including Mr. Knightley's approbation), turns away firmly on a disjunction, in order to turn toward the "presumed certainty" of "must"—an irregular rock deliberately put in the way. The penultimate sentence piles up modal auxiliaries of intentions translating instantly and easily into results ("would notice her," "would improve her"), revealing the artfully winding approach of self-delusion that finally bursts into the self-certainty of her own "powers." Repton had recognized that "[t]here is as much absurdity in carrying an approach round, to include those objects which do not naturally fall within its reach, as there was formerly in cutting through a hill to obtain a straight line, pointing to the hall door."[126] Emma, clever as she is, is absurd. Self-deception is a convoluted, exaggerated, parody of picturesque. As Vermuele says, free indirect discourse "is not benign. Writers use it to slice the heads off their characters" (72).

We have already spent time on the *Pride and Prejudice* approach to Pemberley in chapter 1, with Darcy himself the Noun of House bursting out at its end (p. 48). But here we could revisit Elizabeth's reading and rereading Darcy's letter of explanation in volume II, chapter XIII in terms of the narrative approach of free indirect discourse. She begins the letter "[w]ith a strong prejudice against every thing he might say."[127] But then comes the "circuit" of sentence and paragraph "in which the meaning is suspended, until the whole is finished" (Robertson 90): "She read, with an eagerness which hardly left her power of comprehension, and from impatience of knowing what the next sentence might bring, was incapable of attending to the sense of the one before her eyes" (*PP* 204). She is the visitor so eagerly looking ahead toward the house that she misses (like Catherine Morland) the lodges, the views, the openings, the details on the way. (We have read his letter already ourselves, in the previous chapter; if we are rereaders, we already know the ground well. And we already know how rich the *re*-rereading is. No well-designed approach is self-exhausting.) The first paragraph ends in a dark center: "It was all pride and insolence."

The next paragraph turns on a "but." Elizabeth reads more slowly Darcy's account of Wickham and pauses at the natural obstacle in her way, which forces the turn that "must overthrow every cherished opinion of his worth."

The paragraph is punctuated with desperate direct discourse: "She wished to discredit it entirely, repeatedly exclaiming, ' This must be false ! This cannot be ! This must be the grossest falsehood ! ' "

The third paragraph finds her rereading again, and "command[ing] herself so far as to examine the meaning of every sentence" (205). Sentence by sentence she follows the arc of narrative, seeing things differently, forming new combinations, on every turn:

> Again she read on. But every line proved more clearly that the affair, which she had believed it impossible that any contrivance could so represent, as to render Mr. Darcy's conduct in it less than infamous, was capable of a turn which must make him entirely blameless throughout the whole. (205)

Every line offers a new turn. The previous example of Emma's thoughts showed the narrator slicing off her head; here, Elizabeth slices open her own: "for a few moments, she flattered herself that her wishes did not err. But when she read, and re-read with the closest attention, [. . .] again she was forced to hesitate." Each turn, each sentence, each detail reveals something different on second, third, and fourth looks; it is more the obverse of the architectural approach with its "charm of expectation" and the new delights of retravel. But it still gets you to the center.

Anthony Mandal has demonstrated that "Austen's presentation of dialogue presents a clear line of development, from her early reliance on the Johnsonian speech-patterns of the eighteenth century to a more sustained and naturalistic style of rendering conversation." He shows how, in *Sense and Sensibility* (1811), for example, Elinor's speech rhythms are aphoristic, "the balanced syntax and careful matching of verbs and nouns reflecting her own moral perceptions," while Marianne's are declamatory. In her later writings, Austen blends both into "modulated combinations of long and short sentences, which reflect the urgency or effusiveness of the speaker."[128] Or in other words, the later Austen has also perfected the combinations of the "peculiar kind of beauty" that Gilpin attached to the picturesque: foreground, middle distance, background; parts contributing to the whole; careful distribution of light and shade; varied textures and animated expressions; moods of place and time. Or: direct discourse, narration, free indirect discourse; synecdoche; irony; sentence lengths; verb tenses. Or: from Thomas Whately's approach to Caversham, the lodges at the entrance, the palisade between them, and the "whole breadth of a lovely valley" beyond; each part of the description matching each part of the approach, and those parts combining visually and narratively to the whole; the "gleams of light" and "shad-

Table 1. Correspondences

Gilpin's picturesque	Austen's narrative	Whately's (narrative) approach
foreground	direct discourse	lodges
middle distance	free indirect discourse	palisade
background	narration	the valley beyond
parts whole	synecdoche and metonymy	clauses matching topography
light and shade	irony	"gleams of light"; "shadows of various tints"
textures and expressions	sentence lengths and punctuation	sentence lengths and punctuation; slopes gentle and steep, groves thick or feathering
moods of time and place	grammatical moods; settings	"gloomy obscurity"; the "rich and extensive prospect"

ows of various tints"; slopes gentle and steep, groves thick or feathering; the "gloomy obscurity" and the "rich and extensive prospect."[129] (See table 1.)

Franco Moretti has argued that "not much happens as long as free indirect style remains confined to western Europe."[130] But not much *would* happen if the perception of Austenian free indirect discourse is of Austenian heroines who speak in "the composed, slightly resigned voice of the *well-socialized individual* [. . .]—these young women who speak of themselves *in the third person,* as if from the outside" (Moretti 82). But "these young women" do *not* speak of themselves in the third person; that is simply taking free indirect discourse at face value. The characters, if not always having their heads sliced off, are sliced open, cross-sectioned; the narrator puts the third person *in between* their thoughts and her narration. It is not so much a dual voice as a triple turn. Even something like this grammatical half-turn, where Mr. Elton (who happens to be a young *man*) begs Emma to let him take her portrait of Harriet to London to be framed, showcases the complexity built into the tiniest of syntactic movements:

> His gallantry was always on the alert. " Might he be trusted with the commission, what infinite pleasure should he have in executing it ! he could ride to London at any time. It was impossible too say how much he should be gratified by being employed on such an errand."
>
> " He was too good !—she could not endure the thought !—she would not

give him such a troublesome office for the world"—brought on the desired repetition of entreaties and assurances,—and a very few minutes settled the business. (*Emma* 49)

Both Mr. Elton and Emma shield themselves behind gallantry on the one hand and politeness on the other; the visible distance of the third person alerts the reader to the distance between speaker and spoken. It is too early in the novel for the reader to be certain about Mr. Elton's motives—although even the most mildly alert reader is presumeably ahead of Emma in her directly recorded thoughts: "' This man is almost too gallant to be in love,' thought Emma. [. . .] ['H]e does sigh and languish, and study for compliments. [. . .] I come in for a pretty good share as a second. But it is his gratitude on Harriet's account'" (49). Yet the quotation marks and the third person inserted within them ask us to look a second time at the utterance. We already know Emma's motives; *her* third-person protestations and dashes and exclamation points are *not* a surprise turn toward the settling of business. But they may make us return to the quoted discourse above with a different eye. *Pace* Moretti, I would say that much, much happens in Austenian free indirect style.

The traditional "historical" account of free indirect discourse—that it appears when third-person fiction enters the domain of first-person epistolary and confessional narrative at the end of the eighteenth century, or in Moretti's terms, "halfway between social *doxa* and the individual voice," and "a good indicator of their changing balance of forces" (82)—is more a description than an explanation. I see a narrative strategy and a psychological innovation literally grounded in a changed landscape most vividly described by the architectural approach that self-consciously replaced the avenue, its focal point the mansion, with a winding line that temporarily obscured its object in favor of its subject. The emphasis is on the perceptions of the viewer, the visitor, the one outside the frame just entering the picture; the interest is in the glimpse, the opening—in the prepositional, the *within* and *in-between*.

CODA

A Topographical Page

The printed page is, in C. F. Partington's words, "the ' form and texture' of one's thoughts."[1] *Grammars of Approach* has argued from a variety of perspectives that the eighteenth-century page wrought by author and printer has its own landscape that renders the form and texture of its culture. The 1960s spawned the perception-changing psychedelic, the buildings of Louis Kahn and I. M. Pei, the fonts Filmsense and Benguiat Zenedipity, and far-out prose. Similarly, the eighteenth-century *text* is not only an "[artifact] of the era's typographical culture"[2] but also formally, aesthetically, and ontologically linked to a literal landscape. Looking *at* the eighteenth-century page in the context of its material world gives us more interpretive purchase when looking *through* it.[3] The perception-changing "ROAD peculiar to a house in the country," designed to "form new combinations on every movement of the spectator," was part of a larger cultural shift in which all sorts of landscapes were changing.[4]

Landscape behaves rather like Caroline Levine's definition of "form"; it "indicates *an arrangement of elements—an ordering, patterning, or shaping*" and its patterns and shapes "differ," "overlap," "intersect," and "travel."[5] In the literal landscape (the most visual and obvious of its forms), from Capability Brown to the picturesque movement and everything in between, interest grew in the *in-between*. Brown's undulating grounds afforded views over, across, between; the famous clumps were meant to break the lines at nonsymmetrical moments. Repton favored a landscape in motion—running waters and pluming smoke. His slides hid and revealed. The picturesque was all about the unexpected, the irregular, the surprise.

"Landscape" also means "The depiction or description of something in words" (*OED* 4g). In one sense, to describe something is to give it a *dif-*

ferent shape. But I have been considering here the ways that words on a page *can* actually map its meaning. We have seen from several perspectives how Thomas Whately's description of the approach to Caversham narratively and typographically suggests description-as-cartography, as clauses and sentences arrange themselves around the patterns and shapes of their particular subject. The description follows the contours and opens the views of the approach.

Every great work, as Virginia Woolf says, is "based [. . .] on the sentence that was current at the time,"[6] and every sentence has an identity made up of typographic as well as syntactic gestures. The contours of letter, line, spacing, pointing; the grammatical shifts, paratactical accumulation, hypotactical organization—all provide the landscape of *narrative*, of meaning, their forms differing in and traveling over time. Defoe's layered clauses and Haywood's bristling pages are physically as well as linguistically different from Richardson's prepositions and Radcliffe's commas.

I agree with Levine in challenging the long-held idea (from Milton to Marxists) that "form is disturbing because it imposes powerful controls and containments" (4). Alexander Pope—heroic coupleteer, micromanager of his capitals, italics, punctuation, and spacing—embraced the constraint and taught us: "True Ease in Writing comes from Art, not Chance, / As those move easiest who have learn'd to dance."[7] The architectural "approach" was a "form" intended to liberate the visitor, the viewer, from the predeterminacy of the avenue, the domination of the House looming larger with every step. The approach wended, planning its views and its burstings-upon-the-house, but essentially giving the experience over to that visitor, to the movement of the spectator. The approach would differ on every experience; as with any good novel, there is simply too much to be taken in at first reading. And that eighteenth-century nominalized verb ("A means or way of approach; an access, passage, avenue" [*OED* 5a]) opened the term to its wider figurative use today: "A way of considering or handling something, esp. a problem" (*OED* 5b).[8] The first and oldest definition—"The act of coming nearer (relatively), or of drawing near (absolutely), in space" (*OED* 1)—acts more like an avenue: linear, straight, predetermined. The eighteenth-century cultivation of an approach in which we are encouraged to look not simply ahead but to this side and that, underneath and in between, vastly widens the territory. It is, in a sense, an early exercise in close reading. Elizabeth Bennett rereads Darcy's explanatory letter in an epistemological approach. She begins the letter with "a strong prejudice against every thing he might say,"[9] but then comes the "circuit" of sentence and paragraph "in which the meaning is suspended, until the whole is finished,"[10] as she finally lifts up the Reptonian slide and, obversely, sees not what she wants to see but *what is*.

The page is three-dimensional, then, in the sense that it has a readerly topography, with a modeled surface and a historical underground; it shares its textures with the textures of its world. It is worth visiting as an approach, watching the turn of lines, experiencing "the charm of expectation" in a series of clauses,[11] reaching the point where meaning bursts open, where we understand how the author, with Capability Brown, sees her landscape and says, "Now *there*," (pointing a finger), "I make a comma, and there" (pointing to another spot where a more decided turn is proper), "I make a colon: at another part (where an interruption is desirable to break the view) a parenthesis—now a full stop, and then I begin another subject."[12]

I would like to close by considering two forms of the topographical page, as art and exercise. The first is exemplified by the recent work of Chicago web designer Nicholas Rougeux, *Between the Words: Exploring the Punctuation in Literary Classics* (2016). Rougeux explores the "visual rhythm of punctuation" by stripping out all the words, numbers, and spaces from famous literary works and leaving *only* the punctuation marks, which he then spins into one continuous spiraling line, with an illustration at the center. (For a virtual "figure 24," see https://www.c82.net/work/?id=347 for his punctuation-only text of *Pride and Prejudice*.)His work gives us a stylized, contoured insight into punctuational patterns, which can suggest interesting comparisons and which certainly push us into looking *at* the page rather than *through* it. But this image *only* really allows us to look *at* it; there is no "through" to meaning. (Very postmodern.)

The second is the kind of exercise I have been practicing in my own reading and teaching, to open up more ways to look at the page while looking through it, to see meaning simultaneously on multiple levels. In a way, this is what close reading has always done, whether New Critical or Deconstructivist, though typically ahistorically. (It is also the work of the compositor, the corrector, the copy editor, and the proofreader.) The topographical page invites us to cross-section the layers of punctuation and syntax, landscape and root systems, the literal and the figurative, the historical and the hermeneutic. Plate IX is a multiply highlighted transcription of the scene in *Northanger Abbey* examined in chapter 3 (pp. 134–35) for the performances of its dash-hybrids and revisited here to capture the textual layers of a remarkable metaphorical approach. The green marks the approach itself: Catherine Morland takes an "extraordinary [. . .] road from the break-fast-parlour to [her] apartment" that culminates in "the end of the gallery," "her own room," and the end of the "visions of romance."[13] The lavender illuminates the punctuation and formatting, particularly those dash-hybrids that are so ineffective for Catherine changing the subject, and so effective for Henry bringing it back. Rose looks at grammar and syntax in the cumulative weight of Henry's catechism, leavened by his repetition of "your own" and the last new intensifier, tenderly if almost invisibly introduced: "Dearest Miss Morland" (186). And goldenrod highlights the free indirect discourse of Catherine's mind, suffering and ashamed, but not, from the perspective of Growing Up, undeservedly so: her youth sails her to another emotionally imaginative extreme, where her folly "now seemed even criminal" and Henry "must despise her forever" (187). Except we know that Henry is generally a level-headed lad, and there is always that "Dearest" as the impress of the invisible.

What I hope from this example, and from this book, is that more of us literary readers look *at* the page as we read it; that we look sideways into small changes; that our "close reading" includes form as well as content, page as well as plot; that the pleasures of rereading highlight the previously unseen underbrush of the first reading; that the printed book brings us closer to the "real world" in unexpectedly material ways; and that any text becomes freshly three-dimensional as a hand-held landscape of the book.[14]

Notes

A Note on My Text

1 John Smith, *The Printer's Grammar* (London: Printed for the Editor, and sold by W. Owen, 1755), 101. "Even the comma," he says, "is not under a necessity to clinge to the Matter so close as it always does, in England[.]"

Introduction

1 Humphry Repton, *Observations on the Theory and Practice of Landscape Gardening* (London: Printed by T. Bensley for J. Taylor, 1803), 34. *Observations* was reprinted in 1805 with different typesettings but not advertised as a second edition. My citations throughout will be to the 1803 text, but they correspond to the 1805, which is digitally available through Hathi Trust.

2 J. C. Loudon, *A Treatise on Forming, Improving, and Managing Country Residences*, 2 vols. (London: Printed for Longman, Hurst, Rees, and Orme, 1806), 2:590.

3 Uvedale Price, *Essays on the Picturesque*, 3 vols. (London: Printed for J. Mawman, 1810), 1:31.

4 Thomas Whately, "Approach to Caversham," in Whatley, *Observations on Modern Gardening, Illustrated by Descriptions* (London: Printed for T. Payne, 1770), 140.

5 Tessa Murdoch, ed., *Noble Households: Eighteenth-Century Inventories of Great English Houses: A Tribute to John Cornforth* (Cambridge: John Adamson, 2006).

6 Tim Mowl and Brian Earnshaw, *Trumpet at a Distant Gate: The Lodge as Prelude to the Country House* (London: Waterstones, 1985), vi.

7 Benjamin Franklin to Noah Webster (Philadelphia, 26 December 1789), in Franklin, *Writings*, ed. J. A. Leo Lemay (Library of America, 1987), 1176–77.

8 Bertrand Harris Bronson, "Printing as an Index of Taste," in Bronson, *Facets of the Enlightenment: Studies in English Literature and Its Contexts* (Berkeley and Los Angeles: University of California Press, 1968), 348.

9 Richard Wendorf, "Abandoning the Capital in Eighteenth-Century London," in *Reading, Society, and Politics in Early Modern England*, ed. Kevin Sharpe and Steven N. Zwicker (Cambridge: Cambridge University Press, 2003), 72–98.

10 Peter de Bolla, *The Education of the Eye: Painting, Landscape, and Architecture in Eighteenth-Century Britain* (Stanford: Stanford University Press, 2003), 2.

11 William Mason, *The English Garden* (1786), qtd. in Humphry Repton, *Humphry Repton: The Red Books for Brandsbury and Glemham Hall* (1789, 1791), intro. Stephen Daniels (Washington, DC: Dumbarton Oaks Research Library and Collection, 1994), n.p.

12 Joseph Robertson, *An Essay on Punctuation*, 2nd ed. (London: J. Walter, 1786), 90.

13 In January 2013 Monika Fludernik organized a conference in Turku, Finland, in which she wanted to bring together the too-often-separate approaches of narratologists and literary critics, historicizing narratology and theorizing critical history. It was a wonderful conference, and I thank Professor Fludernik for her linguistic and narratological help along the way in this project.

14 Franco Moretti, *Graphs, Maps, Trees: Abstract Models for Literary History* (London: Verso Books; Scranton, PA: W. W. Norton, 2007), 76.

15 Dror Wahrman and Jonathan Sheehan, *Invisible Hands: Self-Organization and the Eighteenth Century* (Chicago: University of Chicago Press, 2015).

16 Robert Boyle, *An Essay of the Great Effects of Even Languid and Unheeded Motion* (London: M. Flesher for Richard Davis, 1685), 4–5.

17 Jayne Elizabeth Lewis, private correspondence. Best. Phrase. Ever.

18 Samuel Richardson, *Clarissa; or, The History of a Young Lady*, 7 vols. (London: Printed for S. Richardson, 1747–48), 4:206.

19 Caroline Levine, *Forms: Whole, Rhythm, Hierarchy, Network* (Princeton: Princeton University Press, 2015), 17.

20 This point might seem to glide glibly by "the dark side of the landscape," and in fact I am considering primarily the middle and upper classes throughout this book. However, as we will see (particularly in chapters 2 and 5), the tenants and the interiors of huts and cottages emerge as part of the new ways of looking.

21 Hugh Kenner, "In Memoriam, Etaoin Shrdlu," in Kenner, *The Mechanic Muse* (Oxford: Oxford University Press, 1987), 14.

22 Richard Johnson, *Grammatical Commentaries* (London: S. Keble et al., 1706), 3; A[nne] Fisher, *A Practical New Grammar*, 6th ed. (Newcastle upon Tyne: Printed for Thomas Slack, 1759), 1; James Buchanan, *The British Grammar* (London: Printed for A. Millar, 1762), 3 (my emphasis). Linguistic historian Tom Lundskær-Nielsen elaborates on these arguments in *Prepositions in English Grammars until 1801—With a Survey of the Western European Background* (Odense: University Press of Southern Denmark, 2011). He himself is on Buchanan's side.

23 Clifford Siskin and William Warner, "This Is Enlightenment: An Invitation in the Form of an Argument," in *This Is Enlightenment*, ed. Siskin and Warner (Chicago: University of Chicago Press, 2010), 5.

24 This approach, too, is not new, just newly reconfigured; as Richard Lanham says of close reading in general, "Analysis [. . .] makes us look *at* words and not *through* them." Richard A. Lanham, *Analyzing Prose* (New York: Charles Scribner's Sons, 1983), 2.

25 Hannah More, *Memoirs of the Life and Correspondence of Mrs. Hannah More: By William Roberts, Esq.*, 3rd ed., 4 vols. (London: R. B. Seeley and W. Burnside, 1835), 1:267.

26 "Was there a moment in history when Congreve and Tonson, two intelligent, sensitive and original men, decided to make their pages speak, to edit and design their plays in a way which gave typography a voice in the hand-held theatre of the book?" D. F. McKenzie, "Typography and Meaning: The Case of William Congreve," in *The Book and the Book Trade in Eighteenth-Century Europe*, ed. Giles Barber and Bernhard Fabian (Hamburg: Dr. Ernst Hauswedell and Co., 1977), 83.

27 John Smith, *The Printer's Grammar* (London: Printed for the Editor and sold by W. Owen, 1755), 88.

28 Anna Lætitia Barbauld, "The Life of Samuel Richardson," in *The Correspondence of Samuel Richardson*, 6 vols. (London: Printed for Richard Phillips, 1804), 1:lxxxiii.

29 Henry Peacham, *The Garden of Eloquence* (London: H. Jackson, 1577), Oiiii$_v$.

30 Frances Burney, *Camilla; or, A Picture of Youth*, 5 vols. (London: Printed for T. Payne, T. Cadell Jun., and W. Davies, 1796), vol. 1, bk. 2, ch. 13.

31 "The pleasure arising from beholding, as it were, the 'form and texture' of one's thoughts, is a sensation much easier felt than described." C. F. Partington, *The Printer's Complete Guide* (London: Printed for Sherwood, Gilbert, and Piper, 1825), 246.

Chapter One

1 J. C. Loudon, *A Treatise on Forming, Improving, and Managing Country Residences*, 2 vols. (London: Printed for Longman, Hurst, Rees, and Orme, 1806), 2:590.

2 Humphry Repton, *Observations on the Theory and Practice of Landscape Gardening* (London: Printed by T. Bensley for J. Taylor, 1803), 34.

3 J. C. Loudon, *An Encyclopædia of Cottage, Farm, and Villa Architecture and Furniture* (London: Printed for Longman, Rees, Orme, Brown, Green, and Longman, 1833; rpt. Cambridge: Cambridge University Press, 2014), 769.

4 Mark Girouard, *Life in the English Country House: A Social and Architectural History* (New Haven: Yale University Press, 1978). See chapter 1, "The Power Houses."

5 Richard Payne Knight, *An Analytical Inquiry into the Principles of Taste*, 4th ed. (London: T. Payne, 1808), 154; Raymond Williams, *The Country and the City* (Oxford: Oxford University Press, 1973), 120; John Barrell, *The Idea of Landscape and the Sense of Place, 1730–1840* (Cambridge: Cambridge University Press, 1972), 59; Stephen Daniels, *Humphry Repton: Landscape Gardening and the Geography of Georgian England* (New Haven: Yale University Press, 1999), 2, 28, 47, 48; Peter de Bolla, *The Education of the Eye: Painting, Landscape, and Architecture in Eighteenth-Century Britain* (Stanford: Stanford University Press, 2003), 2; David Marshall, *The Frame of Art: Fictions of Aesthetic Experience, 1750–1815* (Baltimore: Johns Hopkins University Press, 2005), 9.

6 Peter Collins, *Changing Ideals in Modern Architecture, 1750–1950* (1965), 2nd ed. (Montreal and Kingston: McGill-Queen's University Press, 1998), 27. He

is quoting "the dictionary" here; dictionary not identified. The *Oxford English Dictionary* gives as its first definition: "Difference or change in the apparent position or direction of an object as seen from two different points" (http://www.oed.com/view/Entry/137461?redirectedFrom=parallax#eid) (accessed 24 January 2016).

7 Robert Cawdrey, *A Table Alphabeticall, conteyning and teaching the true writing, and vnderstanding of hard vsuall English wordes, borrowed from the Hebrew, Greeke, Latine, or French. &c.* (London: Printed by I. R. for Edmund Weauer, 1604), rpt. as *The First English Dictionary, 1604*, ed. and intro. John Simpson (Oxford: Bodleian Library, 2006). Rebecca Shapiro has just published a wonderful anthology of the front matter of English-language dictionaries from 1602 to 1828 ("prefaces, introductions, dedicatory epistles, advertisements, and addresses to the reader," as Jack Lynch says in his foreword). The first entry is William Clark's *A Dictionarie in English and Latine for Children, and Yong beginners* (1602). Rebecca Shapiro, ed., *Fixing Babel: An Historical Anthology of Applied Lexicography* (Lewisburg: Bucknell University Press, 2018).

8 Other instances where "approach" does not appear include Elisha Coles, *An English Dictionary* (1685 and 1717) and Edward Cocker, *Cocker's English Dictionary* (1704).

9 "To APPROA'CH [of *approcher*, F.] to draw nigh to, or come near," N[athan] Bailey, *Dictionarium Britannicum* (London: Printed for T. Cox, 1730); "APPROA'CH (*v. int. from the* French approacher *to come Near*)," John Ash, *The New and Complete Dictionary of the English Language*, 2 vols. (London: Printed for Edward and Charles Dilly, 1775). The definitions remain the same in the 1795 edition.

10 Ephraim Chambers, *Cyclopædia; or, An Universal Dictionary of Arts and Sciences*, 7th ed., 2 vols. (London: Printed for W. Innys et al., 1751), 1:119. The first edition (1728) gives only the military definition.

11 Samuel Johnson, *A Dictionary of the English Language*, 2 vols. (London: Printed by W. Strahan for J. and P. Knapton et al., 1755). The first brackets—"[from the verb]"—are Johnson's.

12 Webster's: "4. A way, passage, or avenue by which a place or buildings can be approached; an access."

13 See also Kersey's *Dictionarium Anglo-Britannicum* (1715, 1721) and Egbert Buys, *A New and Complete Dictionary of Terms of Art* (Amsterdam: K. de Veer, 1768–69): "*Lines of* APPROACH', (in *Fortification*) Trenches cut in the Ground, the Earth of which is thrown up in the Form of a Parapet, on the Side towards the Enemy, in order to approach the covert Way, without being exposed to the Cannon of the Besieged."

14 James Elmes, *A General and Bibliographical Dictionary of the Fine Arts* (London: Printed for Thomas Tegg; Dublin: R. M. Tims; Glasgow: R. Griffin and Co., 1826).

15 Elmes was, however, vice president of the Royal Architectural Society from 1806 to 1848, so presumably *au courant*. Worth noting in the ongoing relationships between the architectural and literary arts, he also edited the *Annals of the Fine Arts* from 1816 to 1820, in which he published poems by Keats and Wordsworth. See the entry for Elmes by C. J. Robinson in *The Dictionary of National Biography*, ed. Leslie Stephen (London: Smith, Elder, and Co., 1889), 17:308–9.

16 John Dixon Hunt and Peter Willis, introduction to *The Genius of the Place: The English Landscape Garden, 1620–1820*, ed. Hunt and Willis (New York: Harper and Row, 1975), 1.

17 When Brown died in 1783, Walpole reported with typical whimsied dolefulness to a friend: "Your dryads must go into black gloves, Madam: their father-in-law, Lady Nature's second husband, is dead! Mr Brown dropped down at his own door yesterday. The death of the second monarch of landscape is a considerable event to me, the historian of that kingdom." Horace Walpole, *The Yale Edition of Horace Walpole's Correspondence*, ed. W. S. Lewis et al., 48 vols. (New Haven: Yale University Press, 1937–83), 33:385 (to Lady Ossory, Saturday, 8 February 1783).

18 Anna Pavord describes "two sides of the landscape coin," where agricultural reformers accomplished their own reshapings: "Arthur Young's *Annals of Agriculture* coincided with Gilpin's *Observations* on the Lake District." Pavord, *Landskipping: Painters, Ploughmen and Places* (London: Bloomsbury, 2016), 94.

19 Stephen Daniels, *Humphry Repton: Landscape Gardening and the Geography of Georgian England* (New Haven: Yale University Press, 1999), 2. Repton employs the "field of vision" to correct a(nother) "mistake of the admirers of painters' landscape," which is that even "the finest pictures of Claude [. . .] seldom consist of more than one-fifth of that field of vision which the eye can with ease behold, *without any motion of the head, viz.* about 20 degrees out of 90; and we may farther add, *without moving the body*, our field of vision is extended to 180 degrees" (*Observations* 117).

20 I do not intend to ignore the political and social implications of all this reshaping and reappropriating of the land—Barrell's "dark side of the landscape." Repton himself, particularly later in his career, was well aware of the political and social ramifications of architectural design. As we will see in chapter 2, he paid close attention to the park gate lodge as a place where someone would actually have to live; his plans for the removal of villages were reformist (however flawed that might be); he argued for approaches and drives that would accommodate the elderly and infirm and wheelchair-bound; and he was deeply interested in the idea of "appropriation" not so much as a move for power but as a psychologically aesthetic advantage open to anyone. See also my essay "The Impress of the Invisible: Lodges and Cottages," *ELH* 79:4 (Winter 2012): 989–1012.

21 See Dorothy Stroud, *Capability Brown* (1950; London: Faber and Faber, 2000); Laura Mayer, *Capability Brown and the English Landscape Garden* (Oxford: Shire Publications, 2011); Roger Turner, *Capability Brown and the Eighteenth-Century English Landscape* (London: Weidenfeld and Nicolson, 1985).

22 Lancelot Brown, "Copy of Letter sent to the Revd. Mr. Dyer, June 2, 1775, to go into Frame with a Plan," qtd. in Stroud, *Capability Brown*, 157.

23 Humphry Repton, *An Enquiry into the Changes of Taste in Landscape Gardening* (London: Printed for J. Taylor, 1806), 6.

24 Brown could achieve such radical transformations of boring or overstimulated land extraordinarily quickly. Since most of his clients were extremely wealthy and presumably used to having their own way, they often didn't want to wait for young trees to grow into graceful maturity, so Brown figured out a way to

move even ancient oak trees from one part of an estate to a more acceptable other.

25 John Barrell, "Geometry and the Garden," program notes to the 1994 Theatre Royal Haymarket production of Sir Tom Stoppard's *Arcadia*, directed by Trevor Nunn, n.p.

26 David Streatfield positions Pope in the theoretical landscape as someone who transformed classical norms with a "personal aesthetic vision" based on "contrasts, which included variety; the management of surprises; and the concealment of the boundaries"; Burlington's garden at Chiswick House, though originating in Italian Renaissance design, was innovative for its displacement of centrality: "The *allées* of the *patte d'oie* focus upon a series of garden buildings with irregular paths in the woods between them." Streatfield, "Art and Nature in the English Landscape Garden: Design Theory and Practice, 1700–1818," in *Landscape in the Gardens and the Literature of Eighteenth-Century England*, ed. Donald M. Roberts (Los Angeles: William Andrews Clark Memorial Library, UCLA, 1981), 24, 22–23.

27 William Shenstone, "Unconnected Thoughts on Gardening," in *The Works in Verse and Prose, of William Shenstone, Esq.*, 2 vols. (London: Printed for R. and J. Dodsley, 1764), 2:130.

28 Horace Walpole, *The History of the Modern Taste in Gardening* (1770, 1782), intro. John Dixon Hunt (New York: Ursus Press, 1995), 28. Hunt's editorial note explains: "This edition is based on the 1782 edition of the text, which was published by the Strawberry Hill Press under the title 'The History of the Modern Taste in Gardening' in the last volume of *Anecdotes of Painting in England*. The original spelling and punctuation have been preserved" (16).

29 As Christopher Hussey noted long ago, "Price was also the first defender of avenues since Capability Brown. Burke had said something in their favour, as tending to suggest infinity and thence the sublime. Price felt their analogy to the twilight of Gothic aisles. He tells us of one that he attempted, in vain, to preserve, and of how he was approaching by moonlight 'a venerable castle-like mansion, built in the beginning of the fifteenth century.'" Hussey, *The Picturesque: Studies in a Point of View* (London: G. P. Putnam's Sons, 1927), 176. For Repton, too, sometimes an avenue can be "most pleasing," as at Langley Park, where it "climbs up a hill and, passing over the summit, leaves the fancy to conceive its termination." Humphry Repton, *Sketches*, in *The Art of Landscape Gardening by Humphry Repton*, ed. John Nolen (London: Archibald Constable; New York: Houghton Mifflin, 1907), 25.

30 He adds: "'Romanticism' is an idea that needed a Classical mind to have it." Program notes to the 1994 Theatre Royal Haymarket production of Sir Tom Stoppard's *Arcadia*, directed by Trevor Nunn, n. p. N.B.: *Daily Mail*, 13 June 2015: "Playwright Sir Tom Stoppard has admitted making up a quote in the programme of one of his most famous plays, and then making up a professor to say it." (J. F. Shade is presumably an allusion to John Francis Shade, the poet in Nabokov's *Pale Fire*.)

31 Laura Mayer, *Capability Brown and the English Landscape Garden*, 25.

32 David Streatfield, for example, points out in "Art and Nature in the English Landscape Garden" that "Kent's famous athletic feat was not the first" and

argues that "Walpole's obstinate chauvinism has obscured the role of the French garden" in English history (33).

33 William Gilpin, *An Essay upon Prints*, 2nd ed. (London: Printed by G. Scott for J. Robson, 1768), x.

34 Uvedale Price, *Essays on the Picturesque,* 3 vols. (London: Printed for J. Mawman, 1810), 1:31.

35 William Gilpin, *Observations on the River Wye* (London: Printed for R. Blamire, 1782), 33.

36 Sir Walter Scott, when planning his gardens at Abbotsford, studied Price's works; William Wordsworth visited him twice; Sir Joshua Reynolds painted his wife, and Sir Thomas Lawrence painted Price himself. Price was made a baronet in 1828, and when eighty years old was still, according to Knight, "all life and spirits, and as active in ranging about his woods as a setter-dog." William Knight, *The Life of William Wordsworth,* 3 vols. (Edinburgh: W. Patterson, 1889), 3:130.

37 Ian McLean, "The Expanded Field of the Picturesque: Contested Identities and Empire in *Sydney-Cove 1794*," *Art and the British Empire*, ed. Tim Barringer, Geoff Quilley, and Douglas Fordham (Manchester: Manchester University Press, 2007), 27.

38 Richard Payne Knight, *The Landscape, A Didactic Poem. In Three Books. Addressed to Uvedale Price, Esq.* (London: Printed by W. Bulmer for G. Nicol, 1794), bk. 1, ll. 287–88; bk. 2, ll. 73–76.

39 John Byng, *The Torrington Diaries*, ed. C. Bruyn Andrews, 4 vols. (London: Eyre and Spottiswood, 1934), 1:375–76.

40 Ronald Paulson, "The Pictorial Circuit and Related Structures in Eighteenth-Century England," in *The Varied Pattern: Studies in the Eighteenth Century*, ed. Peter Hughes and David Williams (Toronto: A. M. Hakkert, 1971), 166.

41 John Dixon Hunt, "Ut Pictura Poesis, Ut Pictura Hortus, and the Picturesque," *Word and Image* 1 (1985): 87.

42 Hannah More, *Memoirs of the Life and Correspondence of Mrs. Hannah More: By William Roberts, Esq.*, 3rd ed., 4 vols. (London: R. B. Seeley and W. Burnside, 1835), 1:267.

43 J. C. Loudon, "Biographical Notice," in Loudon, *The Landscape Gardening and Landscape Architecture of the Late Humphry Repton,* 11.

44 Humphry Repton, *Sketches and Hints on Landscape Gardening*, in ibid., 30.

45 Dorothy Stroud, *Humphry Repton* (London: Country Life Limited, 1962), 12.

46 See Streatfield, "Art and Nature in the English Landscape Garden," 67–69. Knight connected the Grecian and Gothic styles of architecture with Poussin and Claude; Price argued that buildings exhibit similar qualities to scenery; Repton believed the late-century Gothic styles were easiest to assimilate to landscapes; and both Repton and Knight believed that the building should declare the character of its own age.

47 Brown, Repton argues, "frequently mistook the character of running water; he was too apt to check its progress, by converting a lively river into a stagnant pool"; "The *rippling motion* of water is a circumstance to which Improvers have seldom paid sufficient attention" (*Observations* 40, 41).

48 Thus he generally kept the area around the house slightly more formal, reintroducing flower beds and gravel walks, preserving avenues and terraces, approv-

ing neatly mown lawns; the park around the immediate house grounds would be more natural, with deer and sheep animating the landscape from a safely ha-ha'd distance; the agricultural business of the house would be firmly separate from the rest. He advocated architectural consistency or "appropriation," in which the house and grounds not only balanced each other but extended an influence into the surrounding country.

49 John Lucas, "Places and Dwellings: Wordsworth, Clare and the Anti-Picturesque," in *The Iconography of Landscape: Essays on the Symbolic Representation, Design and Use of Past Environments,* ed. Denis Cosgrove and Stephen Daniels (Cambridge: Cambridge University Press, 1988), 83. Lucas is quoting Christopher Salveson, *The Landscape of Memory: A Study of Wordsworth's Poetry* (Lincoln: University of Nebraska Press, 1965), 66.

50 Humphry Repton, *Humphry Repton: The Red Books for Brandsbury and Glemham Hall* (1789, 1791), intro. Stephen Daniels (Washington, DC: Dumbarton Oaks Research Library and Collection, 1994). Repton notes: "**Brandsbury was begun in 1789—& all planted in 1790.*"

51 Humphry Repton, *Fragments on the Theory and Practice of Landscape Gardening* (London: Printed by T. Bensley and Son for J. Taylor, 1816), Fragment XIV, 62.

52 Those other "improvers" included but were not limited to those undergardeners of Brown's, and the gardeners on the estates who took over from or displaced Repton in carrying out his designs.

53 Humphry Repton, *Humphry Repton's Red Books for Panshanger and Tewin Water, Hertfordshire, 1799–1800*, intro. Twigs Way (Hertfordshire: Hertfordshire Record Society, 2011), 67.

54 The mansion was built between 1731 and 1743 by Joseph Thompson and later bought by Samuel Farmer in 1799.

55 Thomas Whately, *Observations on Modern Gardening, Illustrated by Descriptions* (London: Printed for T. Payne, 1770), A3v.

56 George Mason, in his *Essay on Design in Gardening* (1768), offhandedly mentions the concept: "Beeches in particular should never be cleared of underwood, till their size is considerable; they only look like the approach to a *witch-house**, whose inhabitants had encouraged a nursery of broom-sticks." Mason, *An Essay on Design in Gardening. First Published in MDCCLXVIII. Now Greatly Augmented* (London: Printed by C. Roworth for Benjamin and John White, 1795), 73.

57 *The Papers of Thomas Jefferson Digital Edition*, ed. Barbara B. Oberg and J. Jefferson Looney (Charlottesville: University of Virginia Press, Rotunda, 2008), 369. Online ed.: http://rotunda.upress.virginia.edu/founders/TSJN.html (accessed 14 August 2012).

58 John Macky, *A Journey through England. In Familiar Letters from a Gentleman Here, to His Friend Abroad*, 2 vols. (London: Printed for J. Pemberton, 1722), 2:6.

59 Daniel Defoe, *A Tour Thro' the Whole Island of Great Britain*, 3 vols. (London: Printed and sold by G. Strahan et al., 1724–26). The letters are separately paginated within the volumes; further references will be to volume, letter, page: 2.3:9.

60 Daniel Defoe, *A Tour Thro' the Whole Island of Great Britain.* [. . .] *The Fifth Edition. With very great Additions, Improvements, and Corrections; which bring it down to the Year 1753,* 4 vols. (London: Printed for S. Birt et al., 1753), 1:109.

Richardson "periodically edited and brought up to date Defoe's *Tour.* [. . .] Four editions of this work were revised by Richardson, beginning with the third edition in 1742 and continuing with the fourth, fifth, and sixth in 1748, 1753, and 1761–62." William M. Sale Jr., *Samuel Richardson: Master Printer* (Ithaca: Cornell University Press, 1950), 80.

61 George Bickham, *The Beauties of Stow* (1750), intro. George B. Clarke, William Andrews Clark Memorial Library Publication, nos. 185–86 (Los Angeles: University of California Press, 1977), 1–2.

62 Richard Pococke, "Travels through England" (1750–57), British Library ms., qtd. in Hunt and Willis, *The Genius of the Place*, 264, 266.

63 Caroline Lybbe Powys, *Passages from the Diaries of Mrs. Philip Lybbe Powys of Hardwick House, Oxon. A.D. 1756 to 1808,* ed. Emily J. Climenson (London: Longmans, Green, 1899), 9, 27.

64 Charlotte Smith, *The Old Manor House* (1793), ed. Anne Henry Ehrenpreis (London: Oxford University Press, 1969), 3, 14.

65 Ann Radcliffe, *The Italian; or, The Confessional of the Black Penitents, a Romance,* 3 vols. (London: Printed for T. Cadell Jr. and W. Davies, 1797), 3:4–5.

66 Samuel Richardson, *The History of Sir Charles Grandison, In a Series of Letters published from the Originals by the Editor of Pamela and Clarissa* (1753), 6 vols. (Oxford: Basil Blackwell, 1931), 6:26 (LETTER V. *Lady* GRANDISON, *To Mrs.* SHIRLEY. *Grandison-hall, Saturday* 12 *o'clock, Dec.* 9).

67 Stephanie Fysh points out that there is "no particular organization to the description" of the gardens of Grandison Hall: "It begins with an indication of layout, a sense of space and of the possibility of movement within that space. [. . .] Lucy's description then follows various avenues through the park, beginning with the winding trout stream, noble cascade, and rudely disposed rock-work to the north of the park. Like Richardson's novels, which could be read for their stories or for their sentiments (using tables of contents, indices, or collections of quotations), so too can the gardens of Grandison-hall be seen from varying perspectives." Fysh, *The Work(s) of Samuel Richardson* (Newark: University of Delaware Press, 1997), 114.

68 Anna Lætitia Barbauld, "The Life of Samuel Richardson," in *The Correspondence of Samuel Richardson*, 6 vols. (London: Printed for Richard Phillips, 1804), 1:lxxxiii–lxxxiv.

69 See, for example, John Lucas, "Wordsworth and the Anti-Picturesque," in Lucas, *Romantic to Modern Literature: Essays and Ideas of Culture, 1750–1900* (Sussex: Harvester Press, 1982), 50–67.

70 In his *Sketches*, Repton recognizes that the aesthetics of ancient and modern, avenue and approach, are a tangled root system in themselves: "It seems to have been as much the fashion of the present century to condemn avenues as it was in the last to plant them; and yet the subject is so little understood that most people think they sufficiently justify their opinion, in either case, by merely saying, 'I like an avenue,' or, 'I hate an avenue': it is my business to analyse this approbation or disgust." He balances a "love of order, of unity, antiquity, greatness of parts, and continuity" on one side of the scale and the resistance to "eye-trap[ping]" compulsion, "tedious sameness," and the unfortunate tendency of avenues to act as "wind-spouts to direct cold blasts" on the other (*Art of Landscape Gardening* 25). See note 29 for Price as late defender of the avenue.

71 James Boswell, *Boswell's Life of Johnson*, ed. George Birkbeck Hill, rev. L. F. Powell, 6 vols. (Oxford: Clarendon Press, 1934–50), 2:175.

72 Henry Fielding, letter to Samuel Richardson, 15 October 1748.

73 Quoted in Dorothy Van Ghent, "On Clarissa Harlowe," in Van Ghent, *The English Novel: Form and Function* (New York: Rinehart, 1953), 63.

74 Samuel Richardson, *Clarissa; or, The History of a Young Lady*, 7 vols. (London: Printed for S. Richardson, 1747–48), 1:60, letter X.

75 See Deborah D. Rogers, introduction to *The Critical Response to Ann Radcliffe*, ed. Rogers (Westport, CT: Greenwood Press, 1994), xxx.

76 Ann Radcliffe, *The Mysteries of Udolpho, A Romance; Interspersed with Some Pieces of Poetry*, 4 vols. (London: Printed for G. G. and J. Robinson, 1794), 2:164–68.

77 Sir Walter Scott, *Lives of the Novelists*, 2 vols. (Paris: A. and W. Galignani, 1825), 1:254–55.

78 Jane Austen, *Pride and Prejudice* (1813), vol. 2 of *The Novels of Jane Austen*, ed. R. W. Chapman, 3rd ed. (Oxford: Oxford University Press, 1932), 245.

Chapter Two

1 Jane Austen, *Pride and Prejudice* (1813), vol. 2 of *The Novels of Jane Austen*, ed. R. W. Chapman, 3rd ed. (Oxford: Oxford University Press, 1932), 245.

2 Maurice Howard illustrates how a number of the Tudor hunting lodges were enlarged and transformed from temporary accommodations into principal dwellings; hence "many large English houses are called 'lodges' to this day." Howard, "The Hunting Lodge in England, 1500–1650," in *Maison des champs dans l'Europe de la Renaissance*, ed. Monique Chatenet (Paris: Éditions A et J Picard, [2006]), 291.

3 Johannes Kip and Leonard Knyff, *Britannia Illustrata; or, Views of Several of the Queens Palaces, as Also of the Principal seats of the Nobility and Gentry of Great Britain, Curiously Engraven on 80 Copper Plates* (London: D. Mortier, 1707). See also Sir Robert Atkyns, *The Ancient and Present State of Glostershire* (London: W. Bowyer for Robert Gosling, 1712).

4 Tim Mowl and Brian Earnshaw, *Trumpet at a Distant Gate: The Lodge as Prelude to the Country House* (London: Waterstones, 1985), vi.

5 Thomas Dyche, *A New General English Dictionary*, 3rd ed. (London: Printed by Richard Ware, 1740).

6 James Harris, *Hermes; or, A Philosophical Inquiry Concerning Language and Universal Grammar* (London: Printed by H. Woodfall for J. Nourse and P. Vaillant, 1751), 268.

7 Mark Girouard, *Life in the English Country House: A Social and Architectural History* (New Haven: Yale University Press, 1978), 212.

8 Roger Griffiths, *A Description of the River Thames* (London: Printed for T. Longman, 1758), 40, my emphasis.

9 J. C. Loudon, *A Treatise on Forming, Improving, and Managing Country Residences*, 2 vols. (London: Longman, Hurst, Rees, and Orme, 1806), 2:592. A number of the facts, images, and quotations, and the occasional full sentence, in this section first appeared in "The Impress of the Invisible: Lodges and Cot-

tages," *ELH* 79:4 (Winter 2012): 989–1012, but the rest of the material has been redigested, reorganized, and rewritten.

10 Humphry Repton, *Fragments on the Theory and Practice of Landscape Gardening* (London: Printed by T. Bensley and Son for J. Taylor, 1816), Fragment XXX, 184–85.

11 John B. Papworth, *Rural Residences* (London: J. Diggens for R. Ackermann, 1818), 77.

12 P. F. Robinson, *Designs for Gate Cottages, Lodges, and Park Entrances, in Various Styles, from the Humblest to the Castellated*, 3rd ed. (London: Henry G. Bohn, 1837), ii.

13 T. D. W. Dearn, *Designs for Lodges and Entrances* (London: J. Taylor, 1811), 6.

14 Humphry Repton, *Observations on the Theory and Practice of Landscape Gardening* (London: T. Bensley for J. Taylor, 1803), 143.

15 See also Stephen Daniels, *Humphry Repton: Landscape Gardening and the Geography of Georgian England* (New Haven: Yale University Press, 1999), 230.

16 Jane Austen, *Northanger Abbey* (1818), vol. 5 of *The Novels of Jane Austen*, ed. R. W. Chapman, 3rd ed. (Oxford: Oxford University Press, 1933), 85; hereafter cited *NA* in the text.

17 Ann Radcliffe, *The Mysteries of Udolpho, A Romance; Interspersed with Some Pieces of Poetry*, 4 vols. (London: Printed for G. G. and J. Robinson, 1794), 2:164.

18 Humphry Repton, *Red Book for Blaise Castle* (1796), "The Approach" (Bristol: Friends of Blaise, n.d.), n.p., my emphasis. Repton built Coombe Hill Lodge, the entrance to Blaise Castle, in 1801. *Northanger Abbey*, though written c. 1794 and thereby predating the lodge, was revised in 1802 and sold to Crosby and Co. in 1803.

19 Tessa Murdoch, ed., *Noble Households: Eighteenth-Century Inventories of Great English Houses: A Tribute to John Cornforth* (Cambridge: John Adamson, 2006), 68.

20 Ruth Perry, "Home Economics: Representations of Poverty in Eighteenth-Century Fiction," in *A Companion to the Eighteenth-Century English Novel and Culture*, ed. Paula R. Backscheider and Catherine Ingrassia (Oxford: Blackwell, 205), 442.

21 John Martin Robinson, introduction to Humphry Repton, *Observations on the Theory and Practice of Landscape Gardening* (Oxford: Phaidon Press, 1980), n.p.

22 See, for example, the essays in Ann Bermingham, ed., *Sensibility & Sensation: Viewing Gainsborough's "Cottage Door"* (New Haven: Yale University Press, 2005), especially her introduction; and John Styles, "Picturing Domesticity: The Cottage Genre in Late Eighteenth-Century Britain," in *Imagined Interiors: Representing the Domestic Interior since the Renaissance*, ed. Jeremy Aynsley and Charlotte Grant, with Harriet McKay (London: V&A Publications, 2006), 154–55. See also chapter 4 in this book.

23 Michael McMordie, "Picturesque Pattern Books and Pre-Victorian Designers," *Architectural History* 18 (1975), 43.

24 Stephen Daniels, introduction to *Humphry Repton: The Red Books for Brandsbury and Glemham Hall* (1789, 1791; Washington, DC: Dumbarton Oaks Research Library and Collection, 1994), ix.

25 As Sir Edward Coke declared in 1628, in *The Institutes of the Laws of England*: "For a man's house is his castle, *et domus sua cuique est tutissimum refugium* [and each man's home is his safest refuge]."

26 T. F. Hunt, "Address," in Hunt, *Half a Dozen Hints on Picturesque Domestic Architecture* (London: Longman et al., 1825), n.p.

27 Ian Michael, *English Grammatical Categories and the Tradition to 1800* (Cambridge: Cambridge University Press, 1970), 454.

28 But not so much in travel writing. It is, of course, the business of travel writers to notice all of their surroundings and comment on them. They are more than tourists—they are professional (or amateur) observers. So John Byng is a noticer of lodges. When he visits Sheffield Place (now Sheffield Park), purchased by John Baker Holroyd (later the 1st Earl of Sheffield) in 1769, he rides through the grounds designed by Capability Brown, with house and lodges designed by James Wyatt: "I came under Ld Sheffields park pales, when I rode through his grounds, and around the house, which is placed pleasantly, and surrounded greenly, and by some good trees, and with lakish ponds in front. / Returning by the lodge, of good Gothic taste." John Byng, *The Torrington Diaries*, ed. C. Bruyn Andrews, 4 vols. (London: Eyre & Spottiswoode, 1934), 1:373. Later that same afternoon (24 August 1788) he comments on the "two most solid stone lodges" of Brambletye (1:374).

29 John Bunyan, *The Pilgrim's Progress* (1678), ed. Cynthia Wall (New York: W. W. Norton, 2008), 38.

30 Marilyn Butler glosses the "triangular modern folly" of Blaise Castle in her Penguin edition (2003); John Davies's Oxford World's Classic edition of 1971 and 1988 does not gloss the scene at all; Claudia Johnson, in her 2003 re-edition of Davies, locates the historical folly on the map as well; Susan Fraiman's 2004 Norton Critical Edition refers to Claire Grogan's account of John Thorpe's ignorance and blatant lies about the matter; Barbara M. Benedict and Deirdre Le Faye mention the gothic folly in their 2006 Cambridge edition. Susan Wolfson's Annotated Edition (Cambridge, MA: Belknap Press of Harvard University Press, 2014) spells out Thorpe's bluff and bluster and gives the accurate historical details (154n7). No edition has anything to say about the "lodges of a modern appearance" at Northanger Abbey, although Wolfson defines "porter's lodge" and quotes the approach to Udolpho (238n20).

31 There is not a single mention of an architectural approach in all five volumes of *Camilla*, although about a dozen times in each novel someone is affected by the approach of someone else.

32 Frances Burney, *Camilla; or, A Picture of Youth*, 5 vols. (London: Printed for T. Payne, T. Cadell Jun., and W. Davies, 1796), 5:395–96.

33 Frances Burney, *Journals and Letters*, ed. Peter Sabor and Lars Troide (London: Penguin, 2001), 131.

34 Jane Austen, *Mansfield Park* (1814), vol. 3 of *The Novels of Jane Austen*, ed. R. W. Chapman, 3rd ed. (Oxford: Oxford University Press, 1934), 376–77.

35 "Old Portsmouth: Landport Gate," *Memorials and Monuments in Portsmouth*, http://www.memorials.inportsmouth.co.uk/old-portsmouthlandport_gate.html (accessed 4 May 2012).

36 Richard Gough, *Anecdotes of British Topography* (London: Printed by W. Richardson and S. Clark for T. Payne and W. Brown, 1768), iii.

37 Tim Clayton, *The English Print, 1688–1802* (New Haven: Yale University Press, 1997), 180.

38 See Tim Clayton, "Publishing Houses: Prints of Country Seats," in *The Georgian Country House: Architecture, Landscape and Society*, ed. Dana Arnold (Stroud, Gloucestershire: Alan Sutton, 1998), 43; see also Ronald Russell, *Guide to British Topographical Prints* (Newton Abbot, London, and North Pomfret, VT: David and Charles, 1979), 57–58; Ann Payne, *Views of the Past: Topographical Drawings in the British Library* (London: British Library, 1987), 6, 11–23; and Michael Raeburn, "Catherine the Great and the Image of Britain," in *The Green Frog Service*, ed. Michael Raeburn, Ludmila Voronikhina, and Andrew Nurnberg (London: Cacklegoose Press, 1995), 52.

39 To [Henry] Zouch, Friday, 12 January 1759. Walpole does qualify that it is not "the study itself" but its generally "wretched execution"—as Clayton shows, it will be another decade or so before the execution becomes artistically worthy. Horace Walpole, *The Yale Edition of Horace Walpole's Correspondence*, ed. W. S. Lewis et al., 48 vols. (New Haven: Yale University Press, 1937–83), 16:25.

40 Clayton cites in particular here the otherwise "exemplary" Eileen Harris, *British Architectural Books and Writers, 1556–1785* (Cambridge: Cambridge University Press, 1990).

41 For more on the changing status of description in the eighteenth century, see Wall, *The Prose of Things*, chapter 1.

42 Samuel Johnson, *Rasselas; Prince of Abissinia. A tale.* [. . .] *A New Edition*, 2 vols. (London: Printed for T. Johnstone, W. Taylor, and J. Davies, 1790), 1:72–73.

43 See Wall, *The Prose of Things*, chapter 7.

44 See, for example, Ian McLean, "The Expanded Field of the Picturesque: Contested Identities and Empire in *Sydney-Cove 1794*," in *Art and the British Empire*, ed. Tim Barringer, Geoff Quilley, and Douglas Fordham (Manchester: Manchester University Press, 2007), 23–37; and Elizabeth K. Helsinger, "Land and National Representation in Britain," *Prospects for the Nation: Recent Essays in British Landscape, 1750–1880*, ed. Michael Rosenthal, Christiana Payne, and Scott Wilcox (New Haven: Yale University Press, 1997), 13–35.

45 Ludmila Voronikhina, "The Green Frog Service and Its History in Russia," Michael Raeburn, Ludmila Voronikhina, and Andrew Nurnberg, eds., *The Green Frog Service* (London: Cacklegoose Press, 1995), 10. In case you're wondering, "the commission specified that each piece of the Service should incorporate in the design the image of a green frog" (9).

46 Qtd. in Voronikhina, "The Green Frog Service," 11n16: "Cited by Williamson, op. cit., p. 61" (George Williamson, *The Imperial Russian Dinner Service*, 1909).

47 *The Polite Repository, or Pocket Companion. Containing an almanack,* [. . .] *and various other articles of useful information. Ornamented with Elegant Engravings* (London: Printed [by T. Rickaby] for W. Peacock, 1800), British Library Ephemerides C.58.aa.12.

48 Much of this information is digested from Nigel Temple, "Humphry Repton, Illustrator, and William Peacock's 'Polite Repository,' 1790–1811," *Garden History* 16:2 (Autumn 1988): 161–73.

49 Temple tracks the full range of contributors to the *Repository*, noting that "the issues for the years prior to 1793 and after 1795 do not necessarily show on places where Repton's recommendations had been adopted. [. . .] Repton's

illustrations would have appeared in every issue from 1790 to 1809 inclusive, but not thereafter" (163–64). Although the print run was seven thousand copies annually, very few copies survive. Repton's designs were handed down in his family, and the Lewis Walpole Library has *An Album of engraved views from Peacock's Polite Repository, ca. 1790–1831* (75 R 299 788).

50 Susan Stewart, *On Longing: Narratives of the Miniature, the Gigantic, the Souvenir, the Collection* (Baltimore: Johns Hopkins University Press, 1984), 45.

51 Many thanks to Deidre Lynch, my fellow *Repository* reader in the British Library (July 2016), for drawing my attention to this in "her" copy. She is making use of the same information for her own exquisite purposes, I expect. The owner also transcribes Priestley on Marie Antoinette on the first blank pages, registers the French Constitution as "happily concluded" in September ("*Ca ira! Ca ira! Ca ira!*"), scribbles "ecclaircissement" [*sic*] in October, and quotes various bits of poetry. He or she also "need[s] a Letter" in February and is "at" and "return'd from" Charsfield Hall in March. British Library C.129.a.9.

52 Susan Owens, *The Art of Drawing: British Masters and Methods since 1600* (London: V&A Publishing, 2013), 77.

53 Ralph Hyde, *A Prospect of Britain: The Town Panoramas of Samuel and Nathaniel Buck* (London: Pavilion Books, 1994), 7.

54 Clayton points to William Oram's mid-1740s proposals for views of "the most extraordinary Natural Prospects" in Derbyshire, Staffordshire, and Yorkshire, in which he would take great pains "in the Choice of Prospects as well as in the Points of View, in order to render them the most Picturesque that have hitherto appeared" (qtd. in *The English Print* 158).

55 The "Album of landscape drawings by [William] Mason, [William] Gilpin, and [John] Holland [England, not after 1797?]" in the Lewis Walpole Library (Fol. 75 G 42 797) features seventy-six drawings, aquatints, and watercolors, all of which pointedly ignore or exclude anything like a proper, well-kept house or much in the way of people, unless it's a gentleman or two exploring a cave or a ruined tower.

56 André Rogger, *Landscapes of Taste: The Art of Humphry Repton's Red Books* (London: Routledge, 2007), 90.

57 William Angus, *The Seats of the Nobility and Gentry, in Great Britain and Wales. In a Collection of Select Views, Engraved by W. Angus. From Pictures and Drawings by the most Eminent Artists. With Descriptions of each View* (London: W. Angus, 1787), description of plate I. Note, in relation to the next chapter, how Angus uses the capitalized common nouns and italicized place names throughout—decades after the typographical shift to uniformity.

58 William Gilpin, *An Essay upon Prints,* 2nd ed. (London: Printed by G. Scott for J. Robson, 1768), 6.

59 Hans-Ulrich Beck, "Pieter Molyn and His Duplicate Drawings," *Master Drawings* 35:4 (Winter 1997): 341.

60 Maurice Rickards and Michael Twyman, *The Encyclopedia of Ephemera: A Guide to the Fragmentary Documents of Everyday Life for the Collector, Curator, and Historian* (London: British Library, 2000), 310. The entry notes that W. H. Pyne set things going with his collection of sketches *Microcosm: or, A Picturesque Delineation of the Arts, Agriculture, Manufactures, &c. of Great Britain* (1803–6), which offered more than six hundred groups of small figures—mostly tradesmen and laborers—to add to your landscape.

61 See Alison E. Martin, "The Traveller as Landschaftsmaler: Industrial Labour and Landscape Aesthetics in Johanna Schopenhauer's Travel Writing," *Modern Language Review* 99:4 (October 2004): 968–82, esp. 972.

62 Bruce MacEvoy, "The Topographical Tradition," ©2007, http://www.handprint.com/HP/WCL/artist02.thml (accessed 4 July 2015).

63 F[rancis] O[rpen] Morris, ed., *A Series of Picturesque Views of Seats of the Noblemen and Gentlemen of Great Britain and Ireland with Descriptive and Historical Letterpress,* 6 vols. (London: William MacKenzie, [c. 1880]), 1:n.p. (preface).

64 Benjamin Bennett, *Beyond Theory: Eighteenth-Century German Literature and the Poetics of Irony* (Ithaca: Cornell University Press, 1993), 29.

65 For more happy dogs in Angus's *Seats of the Nobility and Gentry,* see also Saltram, Brough Hall, Hare Hall, Panton House, Bradwell Lodge, Lumley Castle, Cirencester House, Lee, Bradbourn, and Gunnersbury House (though these might be sheep).

66 From "a private collection, England" (Rogger 249n34).

67 Much of the information and the prose for this section, though almost none of the argument, has been lifted from my essay "The Business of Houses: The Problem of Old London Bridge," in *Essays in Honor of John Richetti,* ed. Albert J. Rivero and George Justice, *Eighteenth-Century Novel* 6–7 (2009): 261–305.

68 Putney Bridge, between London Bridge and Kingston, was built in 1729, but that was the Outskirts then.

69 The bridge also acquired two other proverbial prepositions from the dangerous water rapids channeled through its narrow starlings: "*London* Bridge was made for wise men to pass over, and for fools to pass under." John Ray, *A Collection of English Proverbs* (Cambridge: Printed by John Hayes for W. Morden, 1670), 16.

70 From James Howell's (c. 1594–1666) translation of lines by the Italian poet Jacobus Sannazarius (1456–1530). The Ponte Vecchio in Florence (1345) had three arches and buildings of three stories; the Ponte di Rialto in Venice (1588) had one arch, one story; the Pont au Change in Paris (1639) had five arches, six stories; in England, the Old Tyne Bridge in Newcastle (thirteenth century) had a prison, a gatehouse, and a few shops and houses perched on it. With its twenty arches, 905-foot-length, six-story houses, and 622 years of habitation, London Bridge had earned Sannazarius's prize as the "Bridge of Wonders."

71 Jacob Rathgeb, *A True and Faithful Narrative of the bathing cxcursion* [. . .] *to the far-famed Kingdom of England,* ed. William Brenchley Rye (London: John Russell Smith, 1865), 9.

72 Paul Hentzner, *A Journey into England. By Paul Hentzner, In the Year M.D.XC. VIII,* trans. Horace Walpole ([Twickenham, London]: Printed at Strawberry-Hill, 1757), 4–5.

73 British Library Maps 3540.(19): "Photo-engraved by the courtesy of Sir Sidney Lee from an impression, unique in this state, engraved in the year 1597."

74 John Stow, *A Svrvay of London: Containing, the Originall, Antiquitie, Encrease, and more Moderne Estate of the sayd Famous Citie.* [. . .] *Written in the yeare 1598. By Iohn Stow, Citizen of London* (London: Imprinted by John Wolfe, 1598), 21.

75 *The Curiosities of London and Westminster Described in Four Volumes* (London: Printed for E. Newbery, 1786), 71–72.

76 Nehemiah Wallington, *Historical Notices of Events Occurring Chiefly in the Reign*

of Charles I. By Nehemiah Wallington, of St. Leonard's, Eastcheap, London. Edited from the Original Mss. with Notes and Illustrations, ed. R. Webb, 2 vols. (London: Richard Bentley, 1869), 1:19–20.

77 Gordon Home, *Old London Bridge* (London: John Lane, Bodley Head, 1931), 223–26; Ambrose Heal, *Old London Bridge Tradesmen's Cards and Tokens* (Oxford: John Lane, Bodley Head, 1931), 318–22.

78 Ephraim Hardcastle [William Henry Pyne], *Wine and Walnuts; or, After Dinner Chit-Chat*, 2 vols. (London: Printed for Longman, Hurst, Rees, Orme, and Brown, 1823), 2:112.

79 *A New and Compleat Survey of London, in Ten Parts*, 2 vols. (London: S. Lyne, 1742), 1:142.

80 John Stow, *A Survey of the Cities of London and Westminster* [. . .] *Corrected, Improved, and very much Enlarged* [. . .] by John Strype, 4 vols. (London: Printed for A. Churchill et al., 1720), 1:57.

81 *English Architecture; or, The Publick Buildings of London and Westminster* (London: Printed for T. Osborne, 1756), 63.

82 *Companion to Every Place of Curiosity and Entertainment* (London: Printed for J. Lawrence et al., 1767), 32–33.

83 Walter Harrison, *A New and Universal History, Description and Survey* [. . .] *of London* (London: J. Cooke, 1776), 25.

84 Thomas Pennant, *The Antiquities of London: Comprising Views and Historical Descriptions of its Principal Buildings* (London: J. Coxhead et al., 1814), 13.

85 As in G. Herbert Rodwell's rather magnificently melodramatic and Dickensian novel, *Old London Bridge: A Romance of the Sixteenth Century* (1845), 2 vols. (London: George Routledge and Sons, [1887]).

86 J. C. Loudon, *An Encyclopædia of Cottage, Farm, and Villa Architecture and Furniture* (London: Printed for Longman, Rees, Orme, Brown, Green, and Longman, 1833; rpt. Cambridge: Cambridge University Press, 2014), 769.

87 "Avenue," in N[athan] Bailey, *Dictionarium Britannicum* (London: Printed for T. Cox, 1730).

88 S. Palmer, *The General History of Printing* (London: S. Palmer, 1729), 93–95.

Chapter Three

1 Joseph Moxon, in *Mechanick Exercises on the Whole Art of Printing* (1683–84), notes that "[i]f the *Compositor* is not firmly resolv'd to keep himself strictly to the Rules of good Workmanship, he is now tempted to make *Botches*" (ed. Herbert Davis and Harry Carter [London: Oxford University Press, 1958], 210). The Edinburgh printer James Watson recounts how one person, the widowed Mrs. Anderson, "gave such a Chock to our promising Hopes [of revival], and so clogg'd our Art, and damp'd all ingenious Attempts of advancing It" for forty years: from 1671 to 1711 her husband and then she kept a stranglehold on the "Gift of being the King's Printer" and were far more interested in "gaining of Money by printing Bibles at any Rate," which were "the most illegible and uncorrect [. . .] that ever were printed in any one Place in the World" (*The History of the Art of Printing* [. . .] *and A Preface by the Publisher to The Printers in Scotland* [Edinburgh: Printed by James Watson, 1713], 11, 13). John Smith, in his 1755 *Printer's Grammar*, makes constant distinctions between neat and good

workmanship and the various temptations of sloth. And "The greatest disgrace that can attach to a compositor, is that of being considered a foul or slovenly workman" (C. S. Van Winkle, *The Printer's Guide* [New York: Printed by C. S. Van Winkle, 1818], 92–93).

2 Geofroy Tory, *Champ Fleury. Wherein is contained the Art & Science of the proper & true Proportions of Attic Letters, otherwise called Antique Letters, and in common speech Roman Letters, proportioned according to the human Body and Face* (Paris, 1526), trans. George B. Ives (New York: Grolier Club, 1927), 49–51. In his 1689 *Histoire de l'imprimerie*, Jean de la Caille writes: "Puisque nous venon de parler de la beauté des caracteres, que [Conrad] BADIUS avoit commencé à perfectionner, il est bon d'ajouster qui'ils furent mis dans leur derniere perfections par GEOFROY TORY Libraire, qui pour ce suject composa un Traité de la proportion de toutes sortes de caracters, intitulé *le Champ fleury, &c.*" (75–76). Garamond, Granjon, and others continue the succession of French perfections.

3 Thomas Sheridan, *A Discourse Delivered in The Theatre at Oxford, in The Senate-House at Cambridge, and At Spring-Garden in London.* [. . .] *Being Introductory to His Course of Lectures on Elocution and the English Language* . [. . .] (London: Printed for A. Millar et al., 1759), 21.

4 James Boswell, *Boswell's Life of Johnson*, ed. George Birkbeck Hill, rev. L. F. Powell, 6 vols. (Oxford: Clarendon Press, 1934–50), 4:315.

5 Margaret Anne Doody, *The Daring Muse: Augustan Poetry Reconsidered* (Cambridge: Cambridge University Press, 1985), 223.

6 I rather relish this poorly written, spelled, and formatted entry from Wikipedia: "Poetic Contractions are archaic and obsolete contractions of words not commonly used today in modern english [*sic*], but are still found used extensively in early modern English poetry, particular that of William Shakespeare. The extent to which the usage of poetic contractions really helps with matching poetic meters is neglectable [*sic*], and modern readers prefer to substitute the contractions with the actual words they imply for clarity, rather than adhere to obsolete words for the purpose of archaic nostalgia." "Poetic Contraction," https://en.wikipedia.org/wiki/Poetic_contraction (accessed 1 April 2016).

7 The year of Percy Simpson's *Shakespearean Punctuation*; in 1927 another landmark essay by Laura Riding Jackson and Robert Graves argued for a return to the original punctuation and spelling of Renaissance works in modern editions: "William Shakespeare and E. E. Cummings: A Study in Original Punctuation and Spelling," in Jackson and Graves, *A Survey of Modernist Poetry* (London: William Heinemann, 1927). See also Stephen Booth, ed., *Shakespeare's Sonnets* (New Haven: Yale University Press, 1977), who argues for the primacy of the original reading experience rather than the original text (inconsistent spelling and pointing is more distracting for modern audiences). Thomas M. Greene, who is somewhere in between, emphasizes the distance from the text experienced by the original typography and orthography. Greene, "Anti-hermeneutics: The Case of Shakespeare's Sonnet 129," in *Poetic Traditions of the English Renaissance*, ed. Maynard Mack and George deForest Lord (New Haven: Yale University Press, 1982), 143–61.

8 J. C. Loudon, *A Treatise on Forming, Improving, and Managing Country Residences*, 2 vols. (London: Printed for Longman, Hurst, Rees, and Orme, 1806), 2:590, 591.

9 Gérard Genette, *Paratexts: Thresholds of Interpretation*, ed. Thomas Macksey, trans. Jane E. Lewin (1987; Cambridge: Cambridge University Press, 1997).

10 Uvedale Price, *Essays on the Picturesque*, 3 vols. (London: Printed for J. Mawman, 1810), 1:31.

11 In thinking about this book in relation to my previous book, *The Prose of Things* (2006), I would say that the transformation of the eighteenth-century page was also the obverse of the transformation of eighteenth-century description: while the spare visual worlds of Defoe, Haywood, Behn, and Fielding were increasingly upholstered by the descriptions of Richardson, Radcliffe, Dickens, and Brontë, we might say the well-brocaded and -embroidered early text was replaced with clean linen.

12 D. F. McKenzie, "Typography and Meaning: The Case of William Congreve," in *Buch und Buchhandel in Europa im achtzehnten Jahrhundert: The Book and the Book Trade in Eighteenth-Century Europe*, ed. G. Barber and B. Fabian (Hamburg: Dr. Ernst Hauswedell and Co., 1981), 83.

13 R. B. McKerrow had stated that there is "very little evidence that many authors exercised any care about [punctuation] whatever. [. . .] Such punctuation as is to be found in ordinary MSS. of the sixteenth and seventeenth centuries is indeed most erratic [. . .] [S]uch rules as there were existed chiefly among the printers." McKerrow, *An Introduction to Bibliography for Literary Students* (1927), 2nd impression, corr. (1928; Oxford: Clarendon Press, 1951), 250. This view persisted as a signboard for modern bibliographers—at least in the minds of some literary scholars. But G. Thomas Tanselle trenchantly critiques those scholarly attacks on analytical bibliography in the 1990s. Stephen Orgel's opening essay for the 1996 special forum "Editing Early Modern Texts" (*Shakespeare Studies* 24:19–78), for example, "contains a single paragraph (the third one) that is perhaps the densest concentration of misstatements about analytical bibliography that I have ever seen. He claims one of the 'traditional assumptions of modern bibliography' to be the 'idea that spelling and punctuation have no rules in the period, and are a function of the whim of the compositor' (an opinion that no analytical bibliographer has ever uttered) and that 'there are elements of a text that are inessential or merely conventional,' which don't affect the meaning and we can therefore safely change them' (an interpretation of Greg's 'accidentals' that not only is incorrect but has nothing whatever to do with bibliography)." Tanselle, *Textual Criticism since Greg: A Chronicle, 1950–2000* (Charlottesville: Bibliographical Society of the University of Virginia, 2005), 325.

14 And earlier. Ben Jonson's editors, C. H. Herford and Percy Simpson, have suggested that he "took great care to check punctuation *in proof*," and Alexander Top's poem, *The Oliue Leafe* (1603), bewails,

> Diuine Conceite, *I wish thy selfe hadst drawen*
> *This* Grammatique *before it past to presse:*
> *It came to me as t'were by interception:*
> *And (as I thinke) not two lynes puncted right* [. . .]

Qtd. in Vivian Salmon, "Early Seventeenth-Century Punctuation as a Guide to Sentence Structure," *Review of English Studies*, n.s., 13 (1962): 348, 349.

15 John Smith, *The Printer's Grammar* (London: Printed for the Editor and sold

by W. Owen, 1755), 88. There is no sturdy biographical information on "John Smith"—that may not even be his name. But "internal evidence from the book suggests that he may have spent some time in northern Germany, and he also shows familiarity with aspects of French printing, so it is possible that he may have been a compositor or a printer's reader" (front matter, the Cambridge Library Collection facsimile reprint of *The Printer's Grammar* [Cambridge: Cambridge University Press, 2014]).

16 Quoted in Keith Maslen, "Samuel Richardson and Smith's *Printer's Grammar*," *Book Collector* 18:4 (Winter 1969): 518.

17 John Baskerville, preface to *The Works of Mr. William Congreve. In Three Volumes. Consisting of His Plays and Poems* (Birmingham: Printed by John Baskerville for J. and R. Tonson, London, 1761). He is referring to Pierre Bayle's *Dictionnaire Historique et Critique*, published in two volumes in 1697, three volumes in 1702, and in English in 1709.

18 C. F. Partington, *The Printer's Complete Guide: Containing a Sketch of the History and Progress of Printing, to its Present State of Improvement; Details of its Several Departments; Numerous Schemes of Imposition; Modern Improvements in Stereotype, Presses, and Machinery, &c. &c.* (London: Printed for Sherwood, Gilbert, and Piper, 1825), 243, 246.

19 This chapter thus positions itself against the various sheep-and-goat arguments about "substantives" (those matters of text "that affect the author's meaning or the essence of his expression") versus "accidentals" ("spelling, punctuation, word-division, and the like, affecting mainly its formal presentation") as drawn by W. W. Greg in 1950 ("The Rationale of Copy-Text," *Studies in Bibliography* 3 [1950]: 21). As Doody says, the Augustans knew what they were doing: they "were as self-conscious in spelling as in style and were careful that the word as spelled should reflect its sound; they are exact as to numbers of syllables. 'Enjoy'd' for instance is quite obviously only two syllables, while 'crabbed' is a full two syllables, the 'ed' counting as one. The Augustans write 'Heav'n' when they mean the sound 'Heav'n' and not 'Heav-en'; they write 'simp'ring,' 'thro',' 'powder'd with di'monds'" (Doody 223).

20 Peter J. De Voogd, "Tristram Shandy as Aesthetic Object," *Word and Image Conference Proceedings* 4:1 (1988); Alastair Johnson, "The Author as Typographer," *Ampersand*, Summer 1991, 3.

21 Richardson scholars tend to agree with Joe Bray that "though he may not have stood over his compositors while they were working, it does seem likely that, in Greg's words, Richardson 'took responsibility . . . in respect of accidentals no less than substantive readings' for all the revised editions of his works published in his lifetime." "'Attending to the *minute*': Richardson's Revisions of Italics in *Pamela*," in *Ma(r)king the Text: The Presentation of Meaning on the Page*, ed. Joe Bray, Miriam Handley, and Anne C. Henry (Aldershot: Ashgate, 2000), 107. Thomas Keymer, for example, has demonstrated how "*Clarissa* pioneered a range of techniques for the expressive use of typography, which, whether intended or not to foster the mimetic illusion, tended in practice to accentuate the literariness of the work. These include the printed fold-out of music that accompanies Clarissa's 'Ode to Wisdom'; printers' indices (☞) used to mark Lovelace's annotations to a letter by Anna; the skewed and rotated type of the verse fragments drawn up by Clarissa after the rape [. . .]; the unusual scriptorial typeface used for two of Clarissa's signatures in the first edition (a 'coun-

terfeit signing' in which, the *Gentleman's Magazine* protested, 'there appears to be some degree of affectation'); and the thematically loaded 'Rape of Europa' ornament, which Richardson appears to have had cut expressly for the volume containing the rape." Keymer, *Sterne, the Moderns, and the Novel* (Oxford: Oxford University Press, 2002), 67.

22 For the French version, see Geofroy Tory, *Champ Fleury ou l'Art et science de la proportion des lettres,* reproduction phototypique de l'édition princeps de Paris, 1529, ed. Gustave Cohen (Paris: Charles Bosse, 1921), E.j.–E.j.v.

23 Tanselle traces the various debates in "Historicism and Critical Editing: 1979–1985," in *Textual Criticism since Greg* (121–35). Fredson Bowers, influenced by Greg, had developed an editorial approach that emphasized authorial intention (127); McKenzie in the 1970s moved toward a "sociology of the text," in which authorship is more collaborative (intentionally or otherwise), embedded in the cultural networks of publishers and technologies (122); Jerome J. McGann takes this view even further in *A Critique of Modern Textual Criticism* (Chicago: University of Chicago Press, 1983) and argues for an editorial theory that privileged the social over the authorial: "'words do not by themselves constitute a system of communication' and [. . .] 'literary works are not produced without arrangements of some sort.' Thus, for [McGann], the very existence of works (and not merely their publication) depends on collaborative effort: 'the authority for the value of literary productions does not rest in the author's hands alone' (pp. 47–48)" (Tanselle, *Textual Criticism* 128). Tanselle points out, quite sanely, that "editors in the Bowers tradition [. . .] have habitually made judgments to distinguish which revisions made or suggested by others (whether publishers or acquaintances) were fully accepted by the author in the spirit of active and welcome collaboration, and they have rejected only those revisions that the author appears to have accepted grudgingly or been forced into accepting. These editors have normally recognized the social side of authorship by acknowledging that an author's intention can sometimes include the results of collaboration" (132). I'm with him.

24 Janine Barchas, *Graphic Design, Print Culture, and the Eighteenth-Century Novel* (Cambridge: Cambridge University Press, 2003), 1–5.

25 Alice D. Schreyer (Roger and Julie Baskes Vice President for Collections and Library Services at the Newberry Library) has told me that Madame Dacier translated *The Iliad* in 1711 into French as a novel for two reasons: "she thought it was impossible to translate Homer into French in verse and she wanted to provide morally uplifting material to the female readers devouring contemporary French fiction. John Ozell translated Dacier's text into English as blank verse but [Bernard] Lintot printed it as prose (1712) to save space" (private email, 31 May 2016). See David Wray, "Quarreling over Homer in France and England, 1711–1715," in *Homer in Print: A Catalogue of the Bibliotheca Homerica Langiana at the University of Chicago Library*, ed. Glenn W. Most and Alice Schreyer (Chicago: University of Chicago Press, 2013).

For a particularly elegant treatment of poetry on the page, see J. Paul Hunter, "Poetry on the Page: Visual Signalling and the Mind's Ear," in *The Work of Form: Poetics and Materiality in Early Modern Culture*, ed. Ben Burton and Elizabeth Scott-Baumann (Oxford: Oxford University Press, 2014), 179–96. See also his "Form as Meaning: Pope and the Ideology of the Couplet," *Eighteenth Century: Theory and Interpretation* 37:3 (Fall 1996): 257–70.

26 For the past few years I have been sending my first-year students to Special Collections to read any work on the syllabus in its original or early form, and to write a page on how the reading experience changed. It's become a favorite exercise. They find, for example, that the three-volume editions of *Frankenstein* or *Pride and Prejudice* are both more impressive and more friendly; they're agreeably surprised by the tactility of reading the thick, nice-smelling, well-spaced, short-lined pages. "It reads *faster*!"

27 John Grice, *Punctuation: A Printer's Study* (Stroud: Evergreen Press, 2001), preface. My thanks to Paul Gehl of The Newberry Library for bringing this to my attention (Wing oversize ZPP 2045 .E 94).

28 And "paper" could be a section as well, but I will save that for another time.

29 Mark Bland, "The Appearance of the Text in Early Modern England," *Text* 11 (1998): 126.

30 Samuel Palmer, *The General History of Printing* (London: S. Palmer and J. Roberts, 1729), 93–95.

31 Charles Butler, *The English Grammar; or, The Institution of Letters, Syllables, and Words, in the English tongue. Whereunto is annexed An Index of Words Like and Unlike* (Oxford: Printed by William Turner for the author, 1633), 51–52.

32 "A / Contemplation / UPON / The Mystery of MAN'S REGENERATION, / In Allusion to the MYSTERY of / PRINTING." The body of *The Art of Printing* is John Spottiswoode's translation of Jean de la Caille's *Histoire de l'imprimerie et de la librairie, où l'on voit son origine & son progrés, jusqu'en 1689*, 2 vols. (Paris: Jean de la Caille, 1689). The original French version does *not* conclude with a poem on printing as an allegory for life.

33 As part of my homework for this chapter, I spent a number of hours in the printing room of the University of Virginia Rare Book School, playing Compositor (with endless thanks to Amanda Nelsen, who taught and then guided me, and to David Whitesell, for answering endless questions during and after his RBS course), and proudly produced some reasonable facsimiles of pages from Radcliffe and Sterne in 18-point Baskerville. It's one thing to know the theory, and another to experience, as a novice, the difficulties and dangers of trying to fit a vulnerable kerned *f* next to an *i*, and *then realizing the reasons for and beauties of the ligature fi*. Humbling, but somehow thrilling.

34 Sarah Hyndman, *Why Fonts Matter* (London: Virgin Books, 2016), 9. She opens the book with "Font Fortunes": choose one of five unnamed sample typefaces, and then see what that says about you. A Baskervillean has "traditional values and can be a bit of a perfectionist at times"; Helvetica is "practical and versatile"; Didot "poised and thoughtful"; Gill Sans discovers a "traditionalist who likes to think of yourself as modern"; and Clarendon bespeaks "quiet, assured confidence" (142).

35 Stanley Morison, *On Type Designs Past and Present* (1926), new ed. (London: Ernest Benn, 1962), 28.

36 Perla Pequeno, https://www.behance.net/gallery/9622393/Type-Poster-Layout-Jenson (accessed 6 April 2016).

37 Stanley Morison and Holbrook Jackson, *A Brief Survey of Printing History and Practice* (New York: Alfred A. Knopf, 1923), 47. Some say Aldus invented italics to save space and make it possible to produce his octavo classics.

38 Samuel Richardson, letter to Stinstra, 26 November 1755, in *The Richardson-Stinstra Correspondence*, ed. William C. Slattery (Carbondale and Edwards-

ville: Southern Illinois University Press; London and Amsterdam: Feffer and Simons, 1969), 98–99.

39 John Baskerville, preface to *Paradise Lost. A Poem in Twelve Books. The Author John Milton. From the Text of Thomas Newton D. D.* (Birmingham: Printed by John Baskerville for J. and R. Tonson, London, 1758), A3.

40 A[nne] Fisher, *A Practical New Grammar*, 6th ed. (Newcastle upon Tyne: Thomas Slack, 1759), 1; *OED* 6a.

41 John Nichols, *Literary Anecdotes of the Eighteenth Century*, 6 vols. (London: Nichols, Son, and Bentley, 1812), 3:459.

42 Bertrand Harris Bronson, "Printing as an Index of Taste," in Bronson, *Facets of the Enlightenment: Studies in English Literature and Its Contexts* (Berkeley and Los Angeles: University of California Press, 1968), 348. Note the font.

43 John Baskerville, preface to *The Works of Mr. William Congreve. In Three Volumes. Consisting of His Plays and Poems* (Birmingham: Printed by John Baskerville for J. and R. Tonson, London, 1761), n.p.

44 John Baskerville, *Letters of the Famous 18th Century Printer John Baskerville of Birmingham*, ed. Leonard Jay (Birmingham: Birmingham School of Printing, 1932), 26.

45 Benjamin Franklin, *Writings*, ed. J. A. Leo Lemay (Library of America, 1987), 781.

46 Pierre Simon Fournier, le jeune, *Manuel typographique, utile aux gens de lettres*, 2 vols. (Paris: Barbou, 1764–66), 2:xxxix.

47 Alexander Lawson, "Baskerville," in *Anatomy of a Typeface* (Boston: David R. Godine, 1990), 190.

48 "Are Some Fonts More Believable than Others?" 21 March 2015, http://www.fastcodesign.com/1670556/are-some-fonts-more-believable-than-others. See also Hyndman 58–59. She qualifies the conclusion a bit: "I think it is important to take context into consideration before crowning *Baskerville* as the king of believability. Trust is created when the typeface matches the content and this suggests to me that the readers who read the article set in *Baskerville* found it to be the most authentic and credible for the *New York Times*. There will be other situations in which it would not score so highly" (59). (The *NYT* actually uses the Imperial typeface, and has done since 1967, she notes.)

49 Jonathan Swift, *On Poetry: A Rapsody* ("Printed at Dublin, and re-printed at London: and sold by J. Huggonson [. . .]," 1733), ll. 91–100.

50 Though not corrected in the 1734 edition printed in Edinburgh.

51 Samuel Johnson, preface to *A Dictionary of the English Language*, 2 vols. (London: Printed by W. Strahan for for J. and P. Knapton et al., 1755), fol. C.

52 See David Foxon, *Pope and the Early Eighteenth-Century Book Trade*, rev. and ed. James McLaverty (Oxford: Clarendon Press, 1991), 180.

53 John Jones, *Practical Phonography; or, The New Art of Rightly Speling* [*sic*] *and Writing Words By the Sound thereof* (1701), ed. Eilert Ekwall (Halle: Max Niemeyer, 1907), 140–41. See Foxon, *Pope and the Early Eighteenth-Century Book Trade*, 180–82.

54 Thomas Dyche, *A Guide to the English Tongue*, 23rd ed. (London: Printed for Richard Ware, 1736), 103.

55 Benjamin Franklin, "To Noah Webster, Philad[a], Dec[r] 26, 1789," in *Writings*, 1176.

56 Jonathan Swift, *Gulliver's Travels* (1726), ed. Paul Turner (Oxford: Oxford University Press, 1994), 177.

57 Joseph F. Loewenstein, "*Idem:* Italics and the Genetics of Authorship," *Journal of Medieval and Renaissance Studies* 20:2 (Fall 1990), 221.

58 *The History of Printing* (London: Printed for the Society for Promoting Christian Knowledge, 1855), 40.

59 Daniel Defoe, *A Journal of the Plague Year* (1722), ed. Cynthia Wall (London: Penguin Classics, 2003), 79. (I'm afraid as editor I didn't follow the eighteenth-century spacing of punctuation *exactly*. I wish I had read this book.)

60 In my "Poems on the Stage" in the *Oxford Handbook of British Poetry, 1660–1800*, ed. Jack Lynch (2016), I argue that in the otherwise impressive *Broadview Anthology of Restoration and Early Eighteenth-Century Drama* edited by J. Douglas Canfield and Maja-Lisa Von Sneidern (2001), the modernization (in the name of "readability") of spelling, punctuation, and typography has actually endangered the interpretation of the text by distorting its appearance, reorganizing its lines and "regularizing" its previously ambiguous italics. The case study is George Lillo's *The London Merchant* (1731) (*British Poetry* 31).

61 Ephraim Chambers, *Cyclopædia; or, An Universal Dictionary of Arts and Sciences*, 2 vols. (London: Printed for James and John Knapton et al., 1728), 1:154. However, by the sixth edition of 1750, the capitals-and-italics act was cleaned up:

> The English printers have carried *Capitals* to a pitch of extravagance ; making it a rule, to begin almost every substantive with a *Capital* ; which is a manifest perversion of the design of *Capitals*, as well as an offence against beauty and distinctness. Some of them begin now to retrench their superfluous *Capitals,* and to fall into the measures of the printers of other nations. See LETTER.

62 William Stow, preface to *Remarks on London* (London: Printed for T. Norris et al., 1722), A5. As this passage comes from a preface, the province of italics, all the proper names are in roman; I've reversed things here to highlight the usual in-text patterns.

63 See Foxon, *Pope and the Early Eighteenth-Century Book Trade.*

64 Robert Dodsley, ed., *A Select Collection of Old Plays*, 12 vols. (London: R. Dodsley, 1744), 1:xxxv.

65 Joseph Robertson, *An Essay on Punctuation*, 2nd ed. (London: Printed for J. Walter, 1786), 137.

66 *The Printer's Grammar: Containing a Concise History of the Origin of Printing;* [. . .] *Chiefly collected from* SMITH*'s Edition* [. . .] (London: Printed by L. Wayland, 1787), 149.

67 R. B. McKerrow, *An Introduction to Bibliography for Literary Students* (1927), 2nd impression, corr. (Oxford: Clarendon Press, 1928), 82; Philip Gaskell, *A New Introduction to Bibliography* (Oxford: Oxford University Press, 1972), 53.

68 *Notes and Queries*, 6th ser., 5 (January–June 1882): 466; 6 (July–December 1882): 93, respectively.

69 Theodore Low De Vinne, *The Practice of Typography* (New York: Century, 1901), 142–43.

70 Roy Stokes, *A Bibliographical Companion* (1989; Lanham, MD; Toronto; Plymouth, UK: Scarecrow Press, 2011), 50.

71 Manuel Portela, "Typographic Translation: The Portuguese Edition of *Tristram Shandy* (1997–98)," in *Ma(r)king the Text: The Presentation of Meaning on*

the Literary Page, ed. Joe Bray, Miriam Handley, and Anne C. Henry (Aldershot: Ashgate, 2000), 303.

72 Email conversation, 26 June 2017. I am very grateful to Mr. Kristensen for his time and counsel, and to Amanda Nelsen, director of programs and education at the Rare Book School, University of Virginia, for virtually introducing us.

73 Specifically: 8 are names or titles ("Sir," "Mrs"), 46 are meaningful verbs, adjectives, and nouns, and the rest (105, or two-thirds) are pronouns, exclamations, intensifiers, auxiliary verbs, headers ("LET-" for the next letter), and others of the lesser sort. Significant words dear to Pamela's heart, such as "Master," do not appear—except once, on p. 155, and then *fractured*: "Ma-" on the last line, "-ster" as catchword; thus "Master" is neatly castrated, as it were, on the way to page 156. "Master" is a typically sized catchword: no *need* to slice.

74 Rivington and Osborn also published Burney's *Camilla*; a continuation of this study would look at catchwords there, to see if the same compositors are at work with the same proclivities.

75 Ann Radcliffe, *The Italian; or, The Confessional of the Black Penitents, a Romance*, 3 vols. (London: Printed for T. Cadell Jun. and W. Davies, 1797), 1:155.

76 Gaskell relates Charles Manby Smith's story "of a man who spent all day checking every word of a newspaper for the printer, but who still called for the same paper in the evening to read it for the sake of its contents" (113). Anyone who proofreads knows this experience of *looking at* the words rather than reading them. But it is possible to do both simultaneously, although it takes effort and practice. That is what I am trying to do with this book.

77 He cautions here as well: "(You shouldn't, however, place too much importance on that evidence; hand composition of justified lines in ordinary early books was often quite crude, at least compared to the great evenness of machine-set lines.)" (Kristensen email, 26 June 2017.)

78 For example, there appear to be eight compositors for the first edition of *Udolpho*, as they identified their sections of work by a number (1–8, though not in any order) in the direction line. After looking at volume 1 in detail, I could argue that compositors 2, 4, and 7 included the longest words (seven or more letters) as catchwords; compositors 3 and 4 were more inclined to hyphenate (2, 5, and 7 not so much). Most interesting are the examples where the compositor could have hyphenated a long catchword and decided not to: *exhibiting, hereafter, pleasure, softened, parlour, pressing, resumed, depended, affliction, comfortable, declared, mentioned, opposite, a stranger, chamber, following, terrific, condition, chateau, sufficiently, continued, violence, favourite, Gascony, vindicate,* and *struggled* are only a few examples from the first volume.

79 Anne J. Krush, "The Historical and Archaeological Significance of Medieval Bench End Carvings in Some Parish Churches in Suffolk, England," *Transactions of the Nebraska Academy of Sciences* 12 (1984): 104. The carvings "without any symbolic meaning" include a woman walking her dog, a woman spanking her child, a harp-playing pig, various "rabbits, horses, mules, camels, elephants, squirrels" (106).

80 See, for example, the wonderful and busy little cats in the medieval manuscripts reprinted in Katherine Walker-Miekle, *Medieval Cats* (London: British Library Publishing, 2011).

81 Paul F. Gehl, "Texts and Textures: Dirty Pictures and Other Things in Medieval Manuscripts," *Corona* (1983): 68.

82 See Salmon, "Early Seventeenth-Century Punctuation."

83 Milton, *Paradise Lost*, Baskerville ed., A3, A3v, A3v–A4.

84 See J. Paul Hunter, "Seven Reasons for Rhyme," in *Ritual, Routine, and Regime: Repetition in Early Modern British and European Cultures*, ed. Lorna Clymer (Toronto: University of Toronto Press in assoc. with the UCLA Center for Seventeenth- and Eighteenth-Century Studies and the William Andrews Clark Memorial Library, 2006), 172–98; see esp. 196n13.

85 John Harris, *Punctuation Personified; or, Pointing Made Easy. By Mr. Stops.* (London: J. Harris and Son, 1824), 2.

86 See Ellen Lupton, "Telegrammar: From Writing to Speech," in *Period Styles: A History of Punctuation*, exh. cat. (New York: Herb Lubalin Study Center of Design and Typography, Cooper Union for the Advancement of Science and Art, 1988), 7. See also Walter Ong, "Historical Backgrounds of Elizabethan and Jacobean Punctuation," *PMLA* 59 (1944): 349–60. Vivian Salmon traces the binary argument to C. C. Fries, "Shakespearean Punctuation," *University of Michigan Studies in Shakespeare, Milton and Donne* (New York, 1925), 67–86. She argues that its "possible function is much more complex than a simple contrast between marking pause for 'rhetorical' reasons or structure for 'grammatical' reasons, and different marks have different types of function. Fundamentally, all punctuation is a method (albeit a very crude one) of conveying meaning which is not expressed lexically"—grammatical, emotional, or logical ("Early Seventeenth-Century Punctuation" 347–48).

87 In "English Punctuation Theory, 1500–1800," *Anglia: Zeitschrift für Englische Philologie* 106:3–4 (1988): 285–314, Vivian Salmon tracks the evolution of punctuation theory through three centuries (and among translators, schoolmasters, lawyers, and grammarians).

88 *Some Rules for Speaking and Action; To be observed At the Bar, in the Pulpit, and the Senate, and by every one that Speaks in Public*, 3rd ed. (London: Printed for W. Mears, 1716), 25. See also Isaac Watts, *The Art of Reading and Writing English; or, The Chief Principles and Rules of Pronouncing Our Mother-Tongue, Both in Prose and Verse*, 2nd. ed. (London: Printed for John Clark et al., 1722), 39–46.

89 For a lovely new study of communal reading, see Abigail Williams, *The Social Life of Books: Reading Together in the Eighteenth-Century Home* (New Haven: Yale University Press, 2017). See also the rich new study by Paula McDowell, *The Invention of the Oral: Print Commerce and Fugitive Voices in Eighteenth-Century Britain* (Chicago: University of Chicago Press, 2017), especially chapter 5, "How to Speak Well in Public: The Elocution Movement Begins in Earnest."

90 Elizabeth Hamilton, *Memoirs of the Late Mrs Elizabeth Hamilton*, ed. E Benger, 2 vols. (London, 1819), qtd. in Williams, *Social Life of Books*, 4.

91 John Brightland and Charles Gildon, *A Grammar of the English Tongue* (London: Printed for John Brightland, 1711), 149. This grammar was very popular and so presumably influential; it was in its eighth edition by 1759.

92 William Cockin, *The Art of Delivering Written Language; or, An Essay of Reading: In Which the Subject is Treated Philosophically as Well as with a View to Practice* (London: Printed by H. Hughs for J. Dodsley, 1775), 101n.

93 James Buchanan, *A Regular English Syntax* (London: Printed for J. Wren, 1767), 180.

94 Jane Austen, *Northanger Abbey* (1818), in *Northanger Abbey and Persuasion*, vol. 5 of *The Novels of Jane Austen*, ed. R. W. Chapman, 3rd ed. (Oxford: Oxford University Press, 1933), 27.

95 Park Honan, "Eighteenth- and Nineteenth-Century Punctuation Theory," *English Studies* 41 (1960), 97.

96 William Chauncey Fowler, *English Grammar*, rev. and enl. (New York: Harper and Brothers, 1877), 743.

97 M. B. Parkes, *Pause and Effect: An Introduction to the History of Punctuation in the West* (Aldershot, Hants.: Scolar Press, 1992), 92.

98 Nicholson Baker, "The History of Punctuation," in *The Size of Thoughts* (New York: Vintage Books, 1997), 82: "(so I name them, because naming makes analysis possible)."

99 Elisha Coles, *An English Dictionary* (London: Printed for Peter Parker, 1685). This was first published in 1676. Even in the seventeenth century, however, the grammars would pay more attention to the comma, as in Christopher Cooper's *The English Teacher; or, The Discovery of the Art of Teaching and Learning the English Tongue* (London: Printed by John Richardson, 1687); rpt. as *Christopher Cooper's English Teacher*, ed. Bertil Sundby (Lund: C. W. K. Gleerup; Copenhagen, Ejnar Munksgaard, 1953):

> 5. The *Comma* is set after other depending Clauses; either shorter sentences, or compounded propositions; whether they are conditional, causal, or relative, or copulative, disjunctive, or discretive; which are join'd to the principal Verb, and are neither whole members, nor half members. *To fear where, there is no fear, or to be bold, where there is no reason; argues a foolish, or fool hardy temper.* Or after words which supply the place of a sentence; whether they be Nouns, Verbs, or Adverbs; As, *The Sun, Earth, Sea, Air, and all Creatures are designed for the Glory of God, and the service of Man. Sooner, later, all must dye.* I would here also farther suggest, that a *Comma* should be placed before *or* the disjunctive, but not when it serves only to explain the foregoing word, or sentence. It is set also instead of
>
> 6. A *Semicomma*. (114)

100 Edward Phillips, *The New World of English Words* (London: Printed by E. Tyler for Nath. Brooke, 1658).

101 A pleasurable performative potted history:

> THE SYSTEM OF ARISTOPHANES IS THE BASIS FOR THE MODERN COMMA·COLON. AND PERIOD˙ WHOSE FORMS WERE ESTABLISHED BY THE SEVENTEENTH CENTURY˙ IN THE LATE MIDDLE AGES THE VIRGULE/A THIN/ DIAGONAL SLASH STILL USED AS A FRACTION BAR AND AN EITHER/OR SIGN/ WAS OFTEN USED TO INDICATE SHORT PAUSES/AND IT EVENTUALLY SANK AND DEVELOPED A CURVE, LIKE THE MODERN COMMA, WHILE A VERTICAL PAIR OF DOTS CAME TO MARK THE COLON: THE PERIOD BECAME A POINT RESTING ON THE LINE.

Ellen Lupton and J. Abbott Miller, "Period Styles: A Punctuated History," in *Period Styles: A History of Punctuation*, exh. cat. (New York: Herb Lubalin

Study Center of Design and Typography, Cooper Union for the Advancement of Science and Art, 1988), 2.

102 The relationship between punctuation and musical notation dates back to medieval texts. Quintilian's *Institutio Oratoria*, a common school text from the sixteenth through the eighteenth centuries, "makes a general association between music and grammar which may well have influenced his English readers. He argues: 'Tum neque citra musicen grammatice potest esse perfecta, cum ei de metris rhythmisque dicendum sit' ('Nor can [the study of language] be regarded as complete, if it stop short of music, for [the teacher] has to speak of metre and rhythm'; I.iv.4)." Salmon, "English Punctuation," 302.

103 Respectively, Edward Cocker, *Cocker's English Dictionary* (London: Printed for A. Back and A. Bettesworth, 1704); John Kersey, *Dictionarium Anglo-Britannicum*, 2nd ed., corr. (London: Printed by J. Wilde, 1715); Edward Phillips, *The New World of Words*, 7th ed. (London: Printed for J. Phillips et al., 1720); N[athan] Bailey, *Dictionarium Britannicum* (London: Printed for T. Cox, 1730).

104 Dyche, *Guide to the English Tongue* (1736), 105; Thomas Dyche, *A New General English Dictionary*, 3rd ed. (London: Printed by Richard Ware, 1740).

105 William F. Brooks, a music scholar at the University of York and a fellow Newberry Library Fellow in 2016, saw parallels to the architectural and linguistic approach in the late eighteenth-century music world with the developments in the sonata in the Classical and Romantic periods, and the corresponding changes in musical notation. An approach to approach one day.

106 "The Comma, marked thus (,) is the shortest Pause, and distinguishes the smallest Members of Sentences ; as, The Lord God is merciful, long-suffering, slow to Wrath, abounding in Goodness and Truth. It is used after every distinct Noun and Verb ; as, the Enemy advanced with Drums, Trumpets, Clarions, Fifes, &c. and fought with Guns, Swords, Spears, &c. but here the Verb is understood to every Noun after the first : This Man laughs, sings, whistles, dances, &c. and then cries, swears, prays, &c. Here again a Noun is understood to every Verb after the first. The Case is, that if there be several distinct Nouns belonging to one Verb, or several distinct Verbs belonging to one Noun, the Nouns and Verbs must be construed equal in Number : For every Verb must have its Noun expressed or understood, and every Noun its Verb expressed or understood ; and every distinct Verb or Noun, expressed or understood, must have a Comma to distinguish it.

"The Comma distinguishes Adverbs of a contrary Meaning ; as, Man is mortal, and *sooner*, or *later*, all must die. It lies scattered *here, there,* and every where" (Buchanan 180–81).

107 C. S. Van Winkle, who recapitulates Stower's *The Printer's Grammar* (1808, an extension of Smith's) for an American readership, lists twenty-two rules for the comma (15–22).

108 Ann Radcliffe, *The Mysteries of Udolpho, A Romance; Interspersed with Some Pieces of Poetry*, 4 vols. (London: Printed for G. G. and J. Robinson, 1794), 1–2.

109 Kathryn Sutherland, "Speaking Commas \ Reading Commas: Punctuating *Mansfield Park*," in *Ma(r)king the Text: The Presentation of Meaning on the Page*, ed. Joe Bray, Miriam Handley, and Anne C. Henry (Aldershot: Ashgate, 2000), 226.

110 Jane Austen, manuscript alternate ending to *Persuasion*, ed. John Davie

(Oxford: Oxford University Press, 1990), appendix 238. The chapter (10) is dated July 1816; the novel was posthumously published in 1817, dated 1818.

111 And if we want to follow the comma into the nineteenth century, we can call on Counsellor Comma, from John Harris's *Punctuation Personified* (1824):

> Here counsellor Comma the reader may view,
> Who knows neither guile nor repentance ;
> A straight forward path he resolves to pursue
> By dividing short parts of a sentence ;
> As "Charles can sing, whistle, leap, tumble, & run,"—
> Yet so BRIEF is each pause, that he merely counts ONE. (3)

112 Most—but not all—nineteenth- and twentieth-century editions of Defoe's works apologized for and modernized the spelling, capitalization, italicization, and punctuation. The editor of the Shilling Entertaining Library edition of *A Journal of the Plague Year*, for example (retitled *The History of the Great Plague* and published in 1863), was out to produce "readable" works for children and the working class: "Children freed from irksome tasks, and working men wearied with a hard day's toil, cannot possibly be induced to read until they find out what a wealth of entertainment is concealed under the hard, ungraceful forms of typography. [. . .] Grammatical constructions which are too involved and difficult will be simplified; modern words and idioms will be substituted for such as have become obsolete or nearly obsolete; and in all cases passages which are unsuitable to the young will be expunged." Defoe, *The History of the Great Plague*, ed. J. S. Laurie, Shilling Entertaining Library (London: Longman, Green, Longman, Roberts, and Green, 1863), introduction (n.p.).

113 Daniel Defoe, *Robinson Crusoe* (1719), ed. Thomas Keymer (Oxford: Oxford University Press, 2007), 130. There were seven editions published in Defoe's lifetime, collated by J. Donald Crowley for the Oxford edition on which this edition is based; as Keymer notes in the introduction, "spelling, italicization, and punctuation remain unaltered from the first edition, which offers, for all its evident flaws, the closest available approach to the original style and rhythm of Defoe's prose" (xl–xli).

114 Janine Barchas has written in *Graphic Design* on the "enthusiasm" with which "Richardson seizes [. . .] upon the interpretive function of punctuation marks—particularly the use of the dash," as well as the way he "awakens the ability of the [printer's] ornaments to punctuate, organize, and mark emphasis" to gain "greater control over [. . .] fiction's temporal dimensions" (152). See also the various works by Thomas Keymer: *"Pamela" in the Marketplace: Literary Controversy and Print Culture in Eighteenth-Century Britain and Ireland*, with Peter Sabor (Cambridge: Cambridge University Press, 2005); *Richardson's "Clarissa" and the Eighteenth-Century Reader* (Cambridge: Cambridge University Press, 1992); *Sterne, the Moderns, and the Novel* (Oxford: Oxford University Press, 2002). See also Christopher Flint, *The Appearance of Print in Eighteenth-Century Fiction* (Cambridge: Cambridge University Press, 2011). Julie Choi writes on emotive punctuation and free indirect discourse in "Feminine Authority? Common Sense and the Question of Voice in the Novel," *New Literary History* 27:4 (Autumn 1996): 641–62. Jennifer DeVere Brody writes on the performative aspects of punctuation more generally in *Punctuation: Art,*

Politics and Play (Durham: Duke University Press, 2008). And of course there is Terry Castle's brilliant first book, *Clarissa's Ciphers: Meaning and Disruption in Richardson's "Clarissa"* (Stanford: Stanford University Press, 1982), which is a thorough study of "the hermeneutic violence readers wage against authorial intentions" and of "Clarissa's own act[s] of textual interference" (131).

115 J. M. D. Meiklejohn, *The English Language: Its Grammar, History, and Literature* (Edinburgh and London: William Blackwood and Sons, 1886), 171.

116 Samuel Richardson, *Clarissa; or, The History of a Young Lady* [. . .], 7 vols. (London: Printed for S. Richardson, 1747–48), 1:145. See also figure 18 for an analysis of the use of dashes in this passage, p. 000, and chapter 4, p. 000, for its prepositional displays.

117 It is still a common cataloguing convention, at least with colons:

> London : Printed for S. Richardson; [etc., etc.], MDCCXLVIII [1748] (Newberry Library 2nd ed., Case Y 1585 .R388)

> Clarissa : a critical analysis of Samuel Richardson's novel in letters. Zanforlin, Nicolette Whitteridge. (University of Virginia Virgo entry)

118 In another notable colon-scene, Clarissa lays out for Lady Betty Lawrance all the reasons she cannot marry Lovelace; they are articulated in paragraphs separated by colons. See *Clarissa* 1748, 6:29–30 (LETTER XIII. *Miss* CLARISSA HARLOWE, *To Lady* BETTY LAWRANCE, *Monday, July* 3). See also the treatment of prepositions in this scene in chapter 4.

119 Robertson is actually quoting Hugh Blair's lecture XI, "Structure of Sentences":

> I proceed to a third rule, for preserving the unity of sentences; which is, to keep clear of all parenthesis in the middle of them. On some occasions, these may have a spirited appearance; as prompted by a certain vivacity of thought, which can glance happily aside, as it is going along. But, for the most part, their effect is extremely bad; being a sort of wheels within wheels; sentences in the midst of sentences; the perplexed method of disposing of some thought, which a writer wants art to introduce in its proper place.

Hugh Blair, *Lectures on Rhetoric and Belles Lettres,* 2 vols. (London: Printed for W. Strahan and T. Cadell; Edinburgh: Printed for W. Creech, 1783), 1:222.

120 "Too much in a hurry for good manners [Another parenthesis, Jack ! Good manners are so little natural, that we ought to be *compos'd* to observe them : Politeness will not live in a storm], I cannot stay to answer questions, cries the wench—tho' desirous to answer [A third parenthesis—Like the people crying proclamations, running away from the customers they want to sell to]. This hurry puts the lady in a hurry to ask [A fourth, by way of embellishing the third !] as the other does the people in a hurry to buy. And I have in my eye now a whole street raised, and running after a proclamation or express crier, as if the first was a thief, the other his pursuers" (*Clarissa* 4:206–7).

121 Maurya Simon and Cheryl Jacobsen, *A Brief History of Punctuation: Poems by Maurya Simon : : Calligraphy by Cheryl Jacobsen* (Winona, MN: Sutton Hoo Press, 2002), "VI. "Parentheses: A Bestiary," l. 2. My thanks again to Paul Gehl

of The Newberry Library for introducing me to this book, Wing folio ZPP 2083 .S882.

122 Henry Beadnell, *Spelling and Punctuation, a Manual for Authors, Students, and Printers* (London: Wyman and Sons, 1880), qtd. in H. W. Fowler and F. G. Fowler, *The King's English*, 3rd ed. (Oxford: Clarendon Press, 1930), 274.

123 The proscription is in place at least by 1901. In *The Practice of Typography*, De Vinne says that the "doubling of points should be avoided. [. . .] There is seldom any need of the comma, semicolon, or colon before the dash, as ,– ;– :– . The dash is the boldest and most striking of the minor points, and the greater should carry the less. The dash after minor points can be safely used only in the sentence that is overstudded with commas, and where it is selected as the equivalent of the parenthesis, for which it is an improper substitute" (291).

124 "What comet or glacier made them die out? This may be the great literary question of our time. I timidly tried to use a semi-colash in an essay for *The Atlantic Monthly* in 1983: the associate editor made a strange whirring sound in her throat, denoting inconceivability, and I immediately backed down" (Baker 86).

125 Laura All, "To '*Write upon Nothing*': Swift and the Literary Lacuna," chapter 1 of PhD dissertation in progress at the University of Virginia, 61.

126 Neal Curtis astutely notes that "punctuation is exempt from the coded 'character' [Lovelace] uses with Belford." After Clarissa has escaped, he "continues to attempt to imagine her interiority: 'But how she must abhor me to run all these risks' (Richardson 740 [Penguin]). Em dashes puncture the rest of the paragraph, indicating the trouble he is having penetrating Clarissa's subjectivity. [. . .] [I]n his very inarticulacy, the event of inscription and our encounter of his printed words finally collapse, or merge: here we may finally see a true 'equivalence' between inner state and outward representation." Curtis, unpublished course paper, "Dangers of Counterfeit: Lovelace's Flickering Boundaries in Richardson's *Clarissa*," 6 December 2016.

127 Samuel Richardson, *The History of Clarissa Harlowe*, vols. 1–8 of *The British Novelists: With An Essay; and Prefaces, Biographical and Critical, by Mrs. Barbauld*, ed. Anna Lætitia Barbauld (London: Printed for F. C. and J. Rivington et al., 1810), 1:157–58.

128 Anna Lætitia Barbauld, "The Life of Samuel Richardson," in *The Correspondence of Samuel Richardson*, 6 vols. (London: Printed for Richard Phillips, 1804), 1: lxxxiii–lxxxiv.

129 This compositor of this passage was an exception to the rule of separating punctuation marks other than the comma and period "from the matter" (Smith, *PG* 101), particularly at the ends of his sentences.

130 Jane Austen, *Northanger Abbey* (1818), vol. 5 of *The Novels of Jane Austen*, ed. R. W. Chapman, 3rd ed. (Oxford: Clarendon Press, 1933), 195. Of course, there is the Kathryn Sutherland/Geoff Nunberg debate about Austen's punctuation: Sutherland's examination of over a thousand manuscript pages that differ markedly (so to speak) from the early printed works leads her to suggest that William Gifford may have edited—"corrected" or "modernized"—her works, rather as Henry Fielding did for (to) his sister Sarah's. But as Janine Barchas has argued for the rhetorical power of Sarah Fielding's dashes (and Sutherland acknowledges the older speaking-style of Austen's punctuation), so Nunberg argues that Austen's prose stands in its syntactical power even without editorial intervention.

131 R. W. Chapman, "Punctuation," in *Emma*, vol. 4 of *The Novels of Jane Austen*, 3rd ed. (Oxford: Oxford University Press, 1933), 516.

132 Blair, *Lectures* (1783), lecture XIII, "Harmony of Sentences," 1:249; lecture XII, "Structure of Sentences," 1:237.

Chapter Four

1 James Buchanan, *The British Grammar* (London: Printed for A. Millar, 1762), 3 (my emphasis).

2 Tom Lundskær-Nielsen, *Prepositions in English Grammars until 1801* (Odense: University Press of Southern Denmark, 2011), 196.

3 James Buchanan's correction of Johnson's definition is in a footnote on his own definition in *The British Grammar* (that "Grammar is the Art of expressing the Relations of Words in Construction"): "The abovementioned Definition of Grammar is certainly the best and most comprehensive that has yet been given; and is only an Improvement on the judicious Mr. Johnson's, who says, Grammar is the Art of expressing the Relations of Things in Construction, with due Accent in Speaking, &c. but he should have said of Words, not Things, as Grammar treats of Words and not of Things" (3n).

4 James Harris, *Hermes; or, A Philosophical Inquiry Concerning Language and Universal Grammar* (London: Printed by H. Woodfall for J. Nourse and P. Vaillant, 1751), 263–64.

5 Jonathan Swift, *Gulliver's Travels* (1726), ed. Paul Turner (Oxford: Oxford University Press, 1994), 177–78. They therefore decided to "carry about them, such Things as were necessary to express the particular Business they are to discourse on [. . .] which hath only this Inconvenience attending it; that if a Man's Business be very great, and of various Kinds, he must be obliged in Proportion to carry a greater Bundle of Things upon his Back, unless he can afford one or two strong Servants to attend him."

6 H. C., "Preface to the Reader," in H. C., *Aristotle's Rhetoric; or, The True Grounds and Principles of Oratory* (London: Printed by T. B. for Randal Taylor, 1686), $A4_v$.

7 J. M. D. Meiklejohn, *The English Language: Its Grammar, History, and Literature* (Edinburgh and London: William Blackwood and Sons, 1886), 58.

8 Sir Joshua Reynolds, Discourse XIII (11 December 1786), in *Discourses on Art*, ed. Robert R. Wark (New Haven: Yale University Press, 1975), 242.

9 Joseph Robertson, *An Essay on Punctuation*, 2nd ed. (London: J. Walter, 1786), 90. Hugh Blair, *Lectures on Rhetoric and Belles Lettres*, 2 vols. (London: Printed for W. Strahan and T. Cadell; Edinburgh: Printed for W. Creech, 1783), lecture XIII, "Harmony of Sentences," 1:249; lecture XII, "Structure of Sentences," 1:237.

10 The first English grammar (about English and written in English) appeared in 1586; "grammar in England before 1586 simply *was* Latin grammar" (Lundskær-Nielsen 94), based on William Lily's *Syntax* (1513, 1533, etc.) and *A Short Introduction of Grammar* (1748/49), by Lily and Colet, known as Lily's Grammar.

11 Ian Michael, *English Grammatical Categories and the Tradition to 1800* (Cambridge: Cambridge University Press, 1970), 588. Michael analyzes the "rise of the English grammar" from the sixteenth through the eighteenth centu-

ries, counting 32 in the seventeenth century and 231 in the eighteenth. Ingrid Tieken-Boon van Ostade argues that the increase in grammar production in the early eighteenth century "seems due to the fact that it finally became clear, after the death of Queen Anne in 1714, that England would never have an Academy, despite recurrent pleas for one by men of letters such as Dryden in the early 1660s, Defoe in 1697, Addison in 1711 and Swift in 1712. One of the functions of such an academy would have been to publish an authoritative grammar of English, alongside a dictionary, as had been done previously by the Italian and French academies and would be done similarly by the Spanish Academy which would be founded in 1713. When various individuals decided that they themselves could attempt to deal with what was commonly acknowledged to be an important desideratum, calls for the need of an academy finally dwindled." Tieken-Boon van Ostade, "Grammars, Grammarians and Grammar Writing: An Introduction," in *Grammars, Grammarians and Grammar-Writing in Eighteenth-Century England*, ed. Ingrid Tieken-Boon van Ostade (Berlin: Mouton de Gruyter, 2008), 4.

12 Carol Percy, "Mid-century Grammars and Their Reception in the *Monthly Review* and the *Critical Review*," in Tieken-Boon van Ostade, *Grammars, Grammarians and Grammar-Writing in Eighteenth-Century England,* 128.

13 Laurel J. Brinton and Leslie K. Arnovick, *The English Language: A Linguistic History* (Oxford: Oxford University Press, 2006), 357.

14 Andrew Elfenbein, "Romantic Poetry and the Standardization of English," in *The Cambridge Companion to British Romantic Poetry*, ed. James Chandler and Maureen N. McLane (Cambridge: Cambridge University Press, 2008), 80.

15 The success of Murray's *Grammar*, Lundskær-Nielsen argues, "was probably due to the fact that it was *not* innovative but represented a practice of grammar writing that gradually crystallised into an accepted system towards the end of the eighteenth century and which was respectful of traditional views and yet prepared to analyse the English language on its own terms" (261).

16 Otto Jespersen, *The System of Grammar* (London: Allen and Unwin; Copenhagen: Munksgaard, 1933), 46.

17 Indeed, Elfenbein notes that these grammarians tended to be not English but Scots, Irish, or American, and that, "while their introductions often claim to reflect general usage, the writers' specific decisions usually arise from their own sense of what they like" (78).

18 Robert Lowth, *A Short Introduction to English Grammar:* [1762]. *A New Edition, Corrected* (London: J. Dodsley, T. Cadell, 1775), 127. Elizabeth Closs Traugott notes that although "Lowth and other eighteenth-century grammarians favored the co-occurrence of relative and preposition, [. . .] most of them saw that the language favored splitting the two, as in *The man whom I voted for*. It is not until the nineteenth century that prescriptivists insisted that the split was wrong; there is little evidence this this [*sic*] dictum had any substantive effect on the spoken language." Traugott, *The History of English Syntax: A Transformational Approach to the History of English Sentence Structure* (New York: Holt, Rinehart, and Winston, 1972), 184.

19 Ben Jonson, *English Grammar*, in *Workes* (1640), written before 1623 (qtd. in Lundskær-Nielsen 114).

20 Edward Phillips, *The New World of English Words* (London: Printed by E. Tyler for Nath. Brooke, 1658).

21 Elisha Coles, *An English Dictionary* (London: Printed for Peter Parker, 1685).

22 Edward Cocker, *Cocker's English Dictionary* (London: Printed for A. Back and A. Bettesworth, 1704).

23 Edward Phillips, *The New World of Words,* 7th ed. (London: Printed for J. Phillips et al., 1720).

24 Ephraim Chambers, *Cyclopædia; or, An Universal Dictionary of Arts and Sciences*, 2 vols. (London: Printed for James and John Knapton et al., 1728), 1:177.

25 Richard Johnson, *Grammatical Commentaries* (London: Printed for the Author and sold by S. Keble et al., 1706), 3; A[nne] Fisher, *A Practical New Grammar, with Exercises of Bad English*, 6th ed. (Newcastle upon Tyne: Printed for Thomas Slack, 1759), 1, and all the later editions through 1795.

26 William Cobbett, *A Grammar of the English Language*, 2nd ed. (London: Printed for the Author and sold by Thomas Dolby, 1819), 8.

27 Thomas Dyche, *A New General English Dictionary,* 3rd ed. (London: Printed by Richard Ware, 1740). The definition is the same in the second edition of 1737.

28 "So not only is grammar a *science,* it is the foundation of all the others, although it has to be said that the notion of 'science' in those days differed somewhat from ours. Even so, few people would probably express themselves so boldly nowadays" (Lundskær-Nielsen 197). He quotes from *A New Grammar* of 1745, of which no copy survives; the second edition was published in 1750, and in 1762 the editions' title changes to *A Practical New Grammar,* which is the seventh edition "Enlarged and much Improved" (although identical to the 1754 fourth edition); thirty-five editions appeared before 1800 (195, 199).

29 Samuel Johnson, *A Dictionary of the English Language*, 2 vols. (London: Printed by W. Strahan for J. and P. Knapton et al., 1755). Later editions, such as the eighth (London: Printed for J. Johnson, 1799), add another example: "To be accurate in the *grammar* and idioms of the tongues, and then as a rhetorician to make all their graces serve his eloquence. *Fell.*"

30 Thomas Dilworth, *A New Guide to the English Tongue* (1740), 13th ed. (London: Printed by T. Henry Kent, 1751), 85. The first edition appeared in 1740, but the earliest surviving copy is the fifth (1744). Scolar Press used the thirteenth edition (1751) for its facsimile (see Lundskaer-Nielsen 185).

31 John Ash, *The New and Complete Dictionary of the English Language*, 2 vols. (London: Printed for Edward and Charles Dilly, 1775).

32 William Perry, *The Royal Standard English Dictionary* (Boston: Thomas and Andrews et al., [1777?].

33 *The Female Miscellany* (Salop [Shropshire]: Printed by Stafford Pryse, 1770), 1.

34 Duncan Mackintosh and His Two Daughters, *A Plain, Rational Essay on English Grammar* (Boston: Printed by Manning and Loring, 1797), 17. (And no, I haven't figured out what those superscript numbers mean. But every single sentence throughout the tome is painstakingly superscripted in that way.)

35 N[athan] Bailey, *Dictionarium Britannicum* (London: Printed for T. Cox, 1730).

36 Carol Percy, "The English Language," in *Samuel Richardson in Context,* ed. Peter Sabor and Betty A. Schellenberg (Cambridge: Cambridge University Press, 2018), 179.

37 George Dalgarno, *Ars Signorum* (*The Art of Signs*, London, 1661), ed. and trans. David Cram and Jaap Maat in their *George Dalgarno on Universal Language* (Oxford: Oxford University Press, 2001), 131.

38 William Ward, *An Essay on Grammar* (London: Robert Horsfield, 1765), 439.

39 It-narratives themselves, as a rising popular genre, are interested in the little things, the things out of the normal field of vision, the things in between.

40 Jonathan Swift, *Gulliver's Travels* (1726), ed. Paul Turner (Oxford: Oxford University Press, 1994), 177.

41 Richard Wendorf, "Abandoning the Capital in Eighteenth-Century London," in *Reading, Society, and Politics in Early Modern England*, ed. Kevin Sharpe and Steven N. Zwicker (Cambridge: Cambridge University Press, 2003), 86.

42 Ray S. Jackendoff, "The Base Rules for Prepositional Phrases," in *A Festschrift for Morris Halle*, ed. Stephen R. Anderson and Paul Kiparski (New York: Holt, Rinehart, and Winston, 1973), 345.

43 Charles Coote, *Elements of the Grammar of the English Language* (London: Printed for the Author and sold by C. Dilly, 1788), 6.

44 Margaret Anne Doody, *The Daring Muse: Augustan Poetry Reconsidered* (Cambridge: Cambridge University Press, 1985), 226.

45 Clifford Siskin and William Warner, "This Is Enlightenment: An Invitation in the Form of an Argument," in *This Is Enlightenment*, ed. Siskin and Warner (Chicago: University of Chicago Press, 2010), 5.

46 William Clare, *A Compleat System of Grammar, English and Latin* (London: Printed for H. Walwyn, 1690), 97.

47 Charles Butler, *The English Grammar* (Oxford: Printed by William Turner for the Author, 1633), 51.

48 Jeremiah Wharton, *The English Grammar* (1654; Menston: Scolar Press, 1970), 58.

49 John Kersey, *Dictionarium Anglo-Britannicum; or, A General English Dictionary*, 2nd ed., corr. (London: Printed by J. Wilde, 1715); the definitions are the same in the 1721 (3rd) edition.

50 Bailey, *Dictionarium Britannicum* (1730).

51 John Brightland and Charles Gildon, *A Grammar of the English Tongue* (London: Printed for John Brightland, 1711); John Collyer, *The General Principles of Grammar* (Nottingham: Printed by Tho. Collyer, 1735). A few more examples of the spare approach:

> 1755: In the Preface to the *Dictionary*, Samuel Johnson "leaps straight into the word classes without any introduction" and "there are no headings for adverbs, prepositions, conjunctions or interjections as separate classes, or as members of a more general class" (Lundskær-Nielsen 203).
>
> 1765: "PREPOSI'TION, (S.) In Grammar, a Particle so called from it's [*sic*] being placed before the noun, *&c. L.*" *A Pocket Dictionary; or, Complete English Expositor: Shewing Readily the Part of Speech to which Each Word Belongs* (1753), 3rd ed. (London: Printed for J. Newbery, 1765).
>
> 1785: "A Preposition is a Word put before others to explain some particular Circumstance; as, He went out *from* me—He came *into* Town ; or, it is joined to another Word, as, he *out*-went him, he *over*-came his Enemy." John Corbet, *A Concise System of English Grammar* (Madeley: Printed by J. Edmunds, 1785), 24.

52 *A Compleat Guide to the English Tongue* (London: Printed for Richard Wild, c. 1708), 77.

53 Ephraim Chambers, *Cyclopædia; or, An Universal Dictionary of Arts and Sciences*, 2nd ed., 2 vols. (London: Printed for D. Midwinter et al., 1738).

54 Cobbett, *A Grammar of the English Language*, 73. Cobbett actually picks out portmanteau prepositions—those "which are joined to verbs or other words" (such as "outlive," "undervalue," to be "overdone")—for this particularly dismissive treatment, but it fits in with his advice to his son James (to whom the work is addressed, in the form of letters) as well as the soldiers, sailors, and apprentices "who will have to earn what you eat and what you drink and what you wear": it is important "to avoid every thing that tends not to real utility."

55 John Marchant, *A New and Complete English Dictionary* (London: Printed for J. Fuller, 1760). See also William Perry, *The Royal Standard English Dictionary* (Boston: Thomas and Andrews et al., [1777?]: "Prep-o-si-tion, *s.* a particle governing a case."

56 John Baskerville, *A Vocabulary, or Pocket Dictionary. To Which is Prefixed, A Compendious Grammar of the English Language* (Birmingham: Printed by John Baskerville for Dod, Rivington et al., 1765), b2.

57 John Wilkins, *An Essay Towards a Real Character, and a Philosophical Language* (London: Printed for Samuel Gellibrand and John Martyn, 1668), 309. Lundskær-Nielsen argues that Wilkins's schema foreshadows some modern analyses (139).

58 John Locke, *An Essay Concerning Humane Understanding* (London: Printed for Tho. Basset and sold by Edward Mory, 1690), 228.

59 James Greenwood, *An Essay Towards a Practical English Grammar* (London: Printed by R. Tookey, 1711), 69.

60 Philip Dormer Stanhope, 4th Earl of Chesterfield, *Lord Chesterfield's Letters*, ed. David Roberts (Oxford: Oxford University Press, 2008), 245 (letter 71, to his son, 19 December, O.S. 1751).

61 James Elphinston, *The Principles of the English Language Digested; or, English Grammar Reduced to Analogy*, 2 vols. (London: Printed by James Bettenham for P. Vaillan et al., 1765), 2:139, 129.

62 William Scott, *A Short System of English Grammar; with Examples of Improper and Inelegant Construction, and Scotticisms* [. . .] (Edinburgh: Printed for Peter Hill, 1793), 18n.

63 Hugh Blair, *Lectures on Rhetoric and Belles Lettres* (1783), 8th American ed. (New York: Jas. and John Harper, 1819), 84.

64 William C. Fowler, *English Grammar: The English Language in its Elements and Forms* (New York: Harper and Brothers, 1850), 323–25.

65 Jo Rubba, "Grammaticization as Semantic Change: A Case Study of Preposition Development," in *Perspectives on Grammaticalization*, ed. William Pagliuca (Amsterdam and Philadelphia: John Benjamins, 1994), 98–99.

66 Eve Kosofsky Sedgwick, "Around the Performative: Periperformative Vicinities in Nineteenth-Century Narrative," in *Touching Feeling: Affect, Pedagogy, Performativity* (Durham: Duke University Press, 2003), 75. Her periperformative sentences are themselves highly prepositional creatures in relation to their Austinian performative utterances, which makes her vocabulary so useful for me here: "Periperformative utterances aren't just about performative utter-

ances in a referential sense: they cluster around them, they are near them or next to them or crowding against them; they are in the neighborhood of the performative" (68).

67 Anna Lætitia Barbauld, "The Life of Samuel Richardson," in *The Correspondence of Samuel Richardson*, 6 vols. (London: Printed for Richard Phillips, 1804), 1:lxxxiii.

68 It goes without saying that in the hands of *every* great writer throughout time, the preposition and every other part of language, large and small, central and peripheral, are used in a new way. As Margaret Doody argues for Augustan poetry in *The Daring Muse*: "The Augustans want us to see connected and connectedness in a new way. The oxymorons (in *aromatic pain*, in *Majesty* of *Mud*) strike out new connections which are related to ourselves, to our customary ways of seeing and describing, and to our sense-reactions, by the quiet use of normal prepositions, introducing the modifying phrase and connecting it with the strange noun and verb, themselves likewise oddly linked" (226). The point is to try to capture the differences of the new.

69 Samuel Richardson to Johann Stinstra, 2 June 1753, in *The Richardson-Stinstra Correspondence and Stinstra's Prefaces to Clarissa*, ed. William C. Slattery (Carbondale and Edwardsville: Southern Illinois University Press; London and Amsterdam: Feffer and Simons, 1969), 24.

70 Keith Maslen, "Samuel Richardson: Printer-Novelist," in *Approaches to Teaching the Novels of Samuel Richardson*, ed. Lisa Zunshine and Jocelyn Harris (New York: Modern Language Association of America, 2006), 39.

71 Stephanie Fysh, *The Work(s) of Samuel Richardson* (Newark: University of Delaware Press, 1997), 7. The short list of important scholars of Richardson as master printer includes Alan Dugald McKillop and William Sale Jr. in the 1930s, Eaves and Kimpel in the 1970s, and M. B. Parkes, Margaret Anne Doody, Florian Stuber, Peter Sabor, Jocelyn Harris, Thomas Keymer, Albert Rivero, O M Brack, John Dussinger, and Janine Barchas, more recently.

72 John Nichols, "Samuel Richardson," in *Literary Anecdotes of the Eighteenth Century*, 6 vols. (London: Nichols, Son, and Bentley, 1812), 4:578.

73 Qtd. in Keith Maslen, "Samuel Richardson and Smith's *Printer's Grammar*," note 322, *Book Collector* 18:4 (Winter 1969), 518.

74 "The Case of Samuel Richardson, of London, Printer, on the Invasion of his Property in the History of Sir Charles Grandison, before publication, by certain Booksellers in Dublin," 14 September 1753 (Nichols 4:586–88).

75 Joe Bray, "'Attending to the *minute*': Richardson's Revisions of Italics in *Pamela*," in *Ma(r)king the Text: The Presentation of Meaning on the Page*, ed. Joe Bray, Miriam Handley, and Anne C. Henry (Aldershot: Ashgate, 2000), 107.

76 T. C. Duncan Eaves and Ben D. Kimpel, *Samuel Richardson: A Biography* (Oxford: Clarendon Press, 1971), 91.

77 John Mullan, *Sentiment and Sociability: The Language of Feeling in the Eighteenth Century* (Oxford: Clarendon Press, 1988), 93.

78 Christopher Flint, "The Material Book," in Sabor and Schellenberg, *Samuel Richardson in Context*, 124.

79 Peter Sabor, "Teaching *Pamela* and *Clarissa* through Richardson's Correspondence," in *Approaches to Teaching the Novels of Samuel Richardson*, ed. Lisa Zunshine and Jocelyn Harris (New York: Modern Language Association of America, 2006), 32.

80 Maurya Simon and Cheryl Jacobsen, *A Brief History of Punctuation: Poems by Maurya Simon : : Calligraphy by Cheryl Jacobsen* (Winona, MN: Sutton Hoo Press, 2002), "VI. "Parentheses: A Bestiary," l. 2.

81 The fourth edition of 1759 is identical to the third (*Clarissa* 1759, 4:275–76).

82 Unless otherwise noted, all further references to *Clarissa* will be to the first edition.

83 Gaston Bachelard, *The Poetics of Space* (1958), trans. Maria Jolas (Boston: Beacon Press, 1964), 146.

84 Margaret Anne Doody, introduction to *Pamela*, ed. Peter Sabor (Harmondsworth: Penguin, 1980), 11.

85 Albrecht von Haller, "A Critical Account of *Clarissa*," *Gentleman's Magazine* 19 (1749): 346. I am indebted to Keymer's citation in *Richardson's "Clarissa"* (181), and to his headnote to "Albrecht von Haller's review of *Clarissa* with Richardson's Annotations" in *Samuel Richardson's Published Commentary on "Clarissa,"* ed. Florian Stuber and Margaret Anne Doody, 3 vols. (London: Pickering and Chatto, 1998), 1:140–46.

86 See William Harmon, *A Handbook to Literature*, 10th ed. (Upper Saddle River, NJ: Pearson/Prentice Hall, 2006), 386.

87 Thomas Keymer and Peter Sabor, *"Pamela" in the Marketplace: Literary Controversy and Print Culture in Eighteenth-Century Britain and Ireland* (Cambridge: Cambridge University Press, 2005), 14.

88 Mark Bibbins, "In the Corner of a Room Where You Would Never Look," *New Yorker*, 10 February 2014, 71.

89 See Wall, *The Prose of Things*, chapter 5.

90 Thomas Keymer, *Richardson's "Clarissa" and the Eighteenth-Century Reader* (Cambridge: Cambridge University Press, 1992), 179.

91 Sharon Olds, "The Prepositions," *New Yorker*, 2 April 1990, 48. "I'd / walk, day and night, into the / Eden of the list, *hortus conclusus*, where / everything had a place. I was *in / relation to, upon, with* [. . .] / [. . .] the breaking of childhood, beginning of memory."

92 *Critical Remarks on Sir Charles Grandison, Clarissa, and Pamela. Enquiring, Whether they have a Tendency to corrupt or improve the Public Taste and Morals. In a Letter to the Author. By a Lover of Virtue* (London: Printed for J. Dowse, 1754), 4–5. Full text:

> Our language, though capable of great improvements, has, I imagine, been for some time on the decline, and your works have a manifest tendency to hasten that on, and corrupt it still farther. Generally speaking, an odd affected expression is observable throughout the whole, particularly in the epistles of Bob Lovelace. His many new-coin'd words and phrases, Grandison's *meditatingly*, Uncle Selby's *scrupulosities*, and a vast variety of others, all of the same Stamp, may possibly become current in common Conversation, be imitated by other writers, or by the laborious industry of some future compiler, transferred into a Dictionary, and sanctioned by your great Authority. Your success has farther corrupted our taste, by giving birth to an infinite series of other compositors all of the same kind, and equally, if not more, trifling that your's. [. . .] I can foretel, that if ever a good taste universally prevails, your romances, as well as all others, will be as universally neglected, and that in any event their fate will not be much better ; for what

> recommends them to the notice of the present age is, their novelty, and their gratifying an idle and insatiable curiosity. In a few years that novelty will wear off, and that Curiosity will be equally gratified by other Compositions, it may be, as trifling, but who will then have the additional charm of novelty, to recommend them. Such, Sir, must be the fate of all works which owe their success to a present capricious humor, and have not real intrinsic worth to support them. (*Critical Remarks* 4–5)

Although intended as cutting irony, these predictions of course all came true—unlike his final one: "if ever a good taste universally prevails, your romances, as well as all others, will be as universally neglected" because they are based on a "capricious humour" rather than "intrinsic merit" (*Critical Remarks* 4).

He later gives his own sample of "the manner and stile *Richardsonian, that is my word,* [. . .] with which, no less than eighteen large volumes are stuffed from beginning to end":

> *Let me whisper you, Charlotte.—Ought not this writer of the amorous class (could his future genius for oose and lascivious description have been known) to have been strangled in his cradle?—I see the charming archness rising in your eyes, which makes one both love you and fear you.—Yet you look meditatingly—Tell me, thou dear flighty creature—Am I not right?—Very right, Sir.—Huzzah, Sam.—well said—that's a good girl, give me a buss for that, Hussy—Heyday* SIRR*—Who allows you these liberties,* SIRR*!—I take them, Charlotte.—Do not think you have wemmell'd me quite—so none of your scrupulosities with me Varletess—but oh! What an eye-beam was there,—she has soul-harrow'd me by her frowns,—yet her anger may slide off on it own ice.—Then hey for lady Goosecap,—O Jack, the charmingest bosom, ever mine eyes beheld.* * * * * * * * * * * * * * (*Critical Remarks* 47–48)

93 Samuel Richardson, *Pamela* (1740), ed. Thomas Keymer and Alice Wakely (Oxford: Oxford University Press, 2001), 34. Have you noticed by now the *absence* of eighteenth-century punctuation-spacing here?

94 Alan Dugald McKillop, *Samuel Richardson: Printer and Novelist* (Chapel Hill: University of North Carolina Press, 1936), 159–225.

95 See Cynthia Wall, "Teaching Space in *Sir Charles Grandison*," in *Approaches to Teaching the Novels of Samuel Richardson*, ed. Lisa Zunshine and Jocelyn Harris (New York: Modern Language Association of America, 2006), 162–68.

96 Samuel Richardson, *The History of Sir Charles Grandison*, 3rd ed., 7 vols. (London: Printed for S. Richardson, 1754), 7:18.

97 Alistair Duckworth, "Fiction and Some Uses of the Country House Setting from Richardson to Scott," in *Landscape in the Gardens and the Literature of Eighteenth-Century England*, ed. Donald M. Roberts (Los Angeles: William Andrews Clark Memorial Library, University of California, 1981), 96.

98 Samuel Richardson, *Sir Charles Grandison* (1753), ed. Jocelyn Harris (Oxford: Oxford University Press, 1972), 481n.

99 Sarah Berkowitz, email, 21 December 2016.

Chapter Five

1 *OED*: 5. To measure with a (surveyor's) chain. Also with out.
1610 W. Folkingham Feudigraphia ii. v. 55 Extende lines from each station . . . (chayning the stationall line onely).
1816 U. Brown in Maryland Hist. Mag. XI. 224 [But for the rain] I should Certainly have Caused this line on the river to have been Correctly run and Chain'd.
1845 J. F. Cooper Chainbearer II. x. 141 You're welcome to chain out just as much of this part of the patent as you see fit.

2 Ian A. Gordon, *The Movement of English Prose* (London: Longman, 1966), 12.

3 Richard A. Lanham, *Analyzing Prose* (New York: Charles Scribner's Sons, 1983), 61.

4 Caroline Levine, *Forms: Whole, Rhythm, Hierarchy, Network* (Princeton: Princeton University Press, 2015), 6.

5 This chapter originally had a section on Fielding, but for reasons of textual economy it was left behind.

6 Uvedale Price, *Essays on the Picturesque*, 3 vols. (London: J. Mawman, 1810), 1:25.

7 Benjamin Franklin, letter to Noah Webster (26 December 1789), in Franklin, *Writings*, ed. J. A. Leo Lamay (New York: Library of America, 1987), 1177.

8 George Saintsbury, *A History of English Prose Rhythm* (London: Macmillan, 1912), 294.

9 *Gentleman's Magazine*, n.s., 22 (July 1844): 15–16.

10 Virginia Woolf, *A Room of One's Own* (London: Hogarth Press, 1929), 114–15. She was referring specifically to the great male novelists of the nineteenth century—Thackeray, Dickens, Balzac—and pointing out that their hefty, periodic, Johnsonian-inspired sentences were not readily packaged for the nineteenth-century woman writer: "The sentence that was current at the beginning of the nineteenth century ran something like this perhaps: 'The grandeur of their works was an argument with them, not to stop short, but to proceed. They could have no higher excitement or satisfaction than in the exercise of their art and endless generations of truth and beauty. Success prompts to exertion; and habit facilitates success.' That is a man's sentence; behind it one can see Johnson, Gibbon and the rest. It was a sentence that was unsuited for a woman's use. Charlotte Brontë, with all her splendid gift for prose, stumbled and fell with that clumsy weapon in her hands. George Eliot committed atrocities with it that beggar description. Jane Austen looked at it and laughed at it and devised a perfectly natural, shapely sentence proper for her own use and never departed from it" (114–16).

11 Elizabeth Closs Traugott, *The History of English Syntax: A Transformational Approach to the History of English Sentence Structure* (New York: Holt, Rinehart, and Winston, 1972), 173.

12 Joseph Robertson, *An Essay on Punctuation*, 2nd ed. (London: J. Walter, 1786), 90.

13 William Minto, *A Manual of English Prose Literature*, 3rd ed. (Edinburgh and London: William Blackwood and Sons, 1886), 5.

14 Stanley Fish, *How to Write a Sentence and How to Read One* (New York: Harper, 2011), 2.

15 Robert Lowth, *A Short Introduction to English Grammar: With Critical Notes* [1762]. *A New Edition, Corrected* (London: J. Dodsley, T. Cadell, 1775), iii.

16 "'By greatness,' says Mr. Addison, in the Spectator, No. 412, 'I do not only mean the bulk of any single object, but the largeness of a whole view.' Here the place of the adverb *only*, renders it a limitation of the following word mean. 'I do not only mean.' The question may then be put, What does he more than mean ? Had he placed it after *bulk*, still it would have been wrong. 'I do not mean the bulk *only* of any single object.' For we might then ask, What does he mean more than the bulk ? Is it the colour ? Or any other property ? Its proper place, undoubtedly, is, after the word object" (103–4). Hugh Blair, *Lectures on Rhetoric and Belles Lettres* (1783), 8th American ed. (New York: Jas. and John Harper, 1819), 103–4.

17 Respectively, *Gentleman's Magazine* (1741), 488; Minto, *Manual of English Prose Literature*, 352, 356; John J. Richetti, *Popular Fiction before Richardson* (1969; rpt. with new introduction Oxford: Clarendon Press, 1992), 188, 262.

18 Carey McIntosh, *The Evolution of English Prose, 1700–1800: Style, Politeness, and Print Culture* (Cambridge: Cambridge University Press, 1998), 28.

19 Henry Peacham, *The Garden of Eloquence* (London: H. Jackson, 1577), Oiii$_{v}$.

20 Bits and bobs of this section echo moments in my essays "Bunyan and the Spaces of Religious Writing," in *The Blackwell Companion to British Literature*, ed. Robert DeMaria Jr., Heesok Chang, and Samantha Zacher (Oxford: Blackwell, 2014), 342–58; and "Bunyan and the Early Novel," in *The Oxford Handbook of John Bunyan*, ed. Michael Davies and W. R. Owens (Oxford: Oxford University Press, 2018), 521–36.

21 John Bunyan, *The Pilgrim's Progress* (1678), Norton Critical Edition, ed. Cynthia Wall (New York: W. W. Norton, 2009). All quotations from *The Pilgrim's Progress* will be from this edition unless otherwise noted; hereafter cited *TPP* in the text. Sadly, from my pre-punctuation-spacing-awareness days.

22 See Wall, *The Prose of Things*, chapter 2.

23 Qtd. in Roger Sharrock, ed., *Bunyan: The Pilgrim's Progress: A Casebook* (London: Macmillan, 1976), 49.

24 Samuel Taylor Coleridge, *Coleridge's Miscellaneous Criticism*, ed. Thomas Middleton Raysor (London: Constable, 1936), 31, 406.

25 William Cowper, *Tirocinium; or, A Review of Schools* (1784), ll. 37–38, qtd. in Sharrock, *Bunyan* [. . .] *Casebook*, 52.

26 C. H. Firth, ed., *The Pilgrim's Progress* (London: Methuen, 1898), xxv.

27 C. S. Lewis, "The Vision of John Bunyan," in *Selected Literary Essays*, ed. Walter Hooper (Cambridge: Cambridge University Press, 1969), 150.

28 Dorothy Van Ghent, *The English Novel: Form and Function* (New York: Rinehart, 1953), 31–32.

29 John Bunyan, *Grace Abounding to the Chief of Sinners*, 6th ed., corr. (London: Printed for Nathaniel Ponder, 1688), 15–16, §33. Roger Sharrock describes the first edition of 1666, published by the young and inexperienced George Larkin, as "poorly produced for the popular market," but sees "some improvement" in the later editions printed by Francis Smith and Nathaniel Ponder. Ponder took over with the fifth edition in 1680; the "sixth edition adds no new sections and differs from the fifth only in a few minor points" (introduction to his edition of *Grace Abounding* [Oxford: Clarendon Press, 1962], xxxvi, xxxvii). I am thus

using the 1688 edition as the last in Bunyan's lifetime; hereafter cited *GA* in the text. The section numbers can differ slightly.

30 Henri A. Talon, *John Bunyan: The Man and His Works* (1948), trans. Barbara A. Wall (London: Rockliff, 1951), 217.

31 See chapter 4; Richard Johnson, *Grammatical Commentaries* (1706) and A[nne] Fisher, *A Practical New Grammar* (1759 ff.).

32 Sharrock, introduction to Bunyan, *Grace Abounding* (1962), xxxviii.

33 James Blanton Wharey, introduction to John Bunyan, *The Pilgrim's Progress from this World to That which is to Come* (1678), ed. Wharey; 2nd ed. by Roger Sharrock (Oxford: Clarendon Press, 1960), xcv–xcvi. This introduction gives the full publishing and editing history of the thirteen lifetime editions (and more!), concluding that "the first three only are of substantive character" (xcii). Sharrock for the second edition bases his text on the first rather than Wharey's choice of a "diplomatic text of the third edition" ("Preface to the Second Edition" v).

34 "It was [. . .] the printer of the second and third editions who was responsible for trimming and polishing Bunyan's English" (Wharey xcv).

35 *Gentleman's Magazine*, n.s., 22 (July 1844): 15–16.

36 William Cobbett, *Rural Rides* (1830), 2 vols. (London: J. M. Dent, 1832), 1:255, 1:177.

37 Although Wharey acknowledges that it is impossible to determine whether Bunyan was responsible for all the marginal glosses (some "are so colourless that they might very easily have been added by another hand"), it "would be difficult to persuade oneself that any other hand than Bunyan's was responsible" for the "raciness" of some of the others (lxxxiii).

38 John Smith, *The Printer's Grammar* (London: Printed for the Editor and sold by W. Owen, 1755), 14.

39 Joseph F. Loewenstein, "*Idem:* Italics and the Genetics of Authorship," *Journal of Medieval and Renaissance Studies* 20:2 (Fall 1990), 224.

40 C. F. Partington, *The Printer's Complete Guide* (London: Printed for Sherwood, Gilbert, and Piper, 1825), 243, 246.

41 Samuel Taylor Coleridge, *The Literary Remains of Samuel Taylor Coleridge*, ed. Henry Nelson Coleridge, 4 vols. (London: William Pickering, 1836), 3:406–7.

42 Coleridge was commenting on some "exquisite paragraphs" in the *Farther Adventures*; qtd. in *Defoe: The Critical Heritage* , ed. Pat Rogers (Boston: Routledge and Kegan Paul, 1972), 84.

43 W. R. Owens and P. N. Furbank, "Defoe and the 'Improvisatory' Sentence," *English Studies* 67:2 (1986): 158.

44 Laura A. Curtis, for example, argues that "the problems some Defoe scholars have with his 'loose' sentence structure appear to be caused by their insistence on applying grammatical standards that were not developed until long after Defoe's death. As a result, the same scholars neglect documented, conventional qualities of seventeenth-century prose and of the oral/aural principles that gave that prose its shape." Curtis, "A Rhetorical Approach to the Prose of Daniel Defoe," *Rhetorica: A Journal of the History of Rhetoric* 11:3 (Summer 1993), 318n. She analyzes Defoe's rhetorical (vs. syntactical) styles (high, middle, and low) and concludes that "such sentences are no more 'unconsciously' typical of Defoe's style than the balanced sentence [. . .]. Quite the contrary: it is Defoe's

conscious rhetorical choices, shaped in part by his schooling in rhetoric, that controls his prose. It seems clear, therefore, that a rhetorical approach to Defoe's style can indeed be more fruitful than a grammatical one" (319).

45 Daniel Defoe, *The Life and Strange Surprizing Adventures of Robinson Crusoe, of York, Mariner* [. . .], 3rd ed. (London: Printed for W. Taylor, 1719), 68–69 (my emphasis).

46 Other Roxana phrases include "*I say,*" "*as I have said,*" "*by the way,*" "except as hereafter," "But to return to my Story," and "But of that in its Place," but these are far less frequent, and are more returns from digressions than compressions.

47 For a nonfictional contrast: *A Tour Thro' the Whole Island of Great Britain* (1724–26, 3 vols.) uses "in a word" 39 times (or 2.87% of a total of 1357 pages) and "in short" 9 (0.66%). The total page numbers of the first editions: *Roxana* 412; *Moll Flanders* 436; *Journal of the Plague Year* 291; *Robinson Crusoe* 371.

48 Try it. The results from my search on 2 October 2017 are different from the results on 22 September 2017, and there are the usual caveats about such data, but the overall trajectories are similar enough for the generalizations: https://books.google.com/ngrams/graph?content=in+a+word%2Cin+short%2Cin+fine&year_start=1700&year_end=2000&corpus=15&smoothing=3&share=&direct_url=t1%3B%2Cin%20a%20word%3B%2Cc0%3B.t1%3B%2Cin%20short%3B%2Cc0%3B.t1%3B%2Cin%20fine%3B%2Cc0.

49 Daniel Defoe, *Roxana, the Fortunate Mistress* (1724), ed. John Mullan (Oxford: Oxford University Press, 1996, reissued 2008), 17–18. "This edition is based on the British Museum copy of the first edition of 1724. The long 's' has been modernized, but the spelling, punctuation, italicization, and capitalization of the original have been preserved" (xxix). I will add with pleasure that Mullan keeps the original spacings between words and punctuation as well.

50 "Mrs. Heywood had written a number of stories resembling, in the licentiousness of their character and the flimsiness of their construction, the novels of Mrs. Behn." Bayard Tuckerman, *A History of English Prose Fiction* (New York: G. P. Putnams's Sons, Knickerbocker Press, 1886), 193.

51 John Richetti, *Popular Fiction before Richardson* (1969; rpt. with new introduction Oxford: Clarendon Press, 1992), 179. William H. McBurney was the first to make the connection: "In 1719 appeared the first parts of two novels which in terms of book sales share with *Gulliver's Travels* the distinction of being the most popular English fiction of the eighteenth century before *Pamela.* These were *Love in Excess; or, The Fatal Enquiry* and *The Life and Strange Surprizing Adventures of Robinson Crusoe.*" McBurney, "Mrs. Penelope Aubin and the Early Eighteenth-Century English Novel," *Huntington Library Quarterly* 20 (1957), 250. Patrick Spedding has since moderated this claim considerably: "*LiE* does not come anywhere near either work in popularity (measured in the number of editions) in the eighteenth century as a whole. *The English Short Title Catalogue* contains 193 entries for *Robinson Crusoe,* 65 for *Gulliver's Travels* and only seven for *LiE.*" Spedding, *A Bibliography of Eliza Haywood* (London: Pickering and Chatto, 2004), 89.

52 See, for example, the work of Kathryn King, Margaret Croskery and Anna Patchias, Alexander Pettit, Felicity Nussbaum, and David Oakleaf.

53 In his introduction to the reprinting of *Popular Fiction* some twenty years after writing it, Richetti grants more power—contemporary and lasting—to the

genre: "It now seems to me that formula fiction, in its very plenitude and variety, its inexhaustible supply of virtue/vice (male villains and female paragons), must have been in some way a challenge to an increasingly restricted and measured actuality" (xxviii).

54 David Fairer, "'Light Electric Touches': Sterne, Poetry, and Empirical Erotics," in *Eighteenth-Century Poetry and the Rise of the Novel Reconsidered*, ed. Kate Parker and Courtney Weiss Smith (Lewisburg, PA: Bucknell University Press, 2014), 148.

55 Eliza Haywood, *Lasselia; or, The Self-Abandon'd* (London: Printed for D. Browne Jun. and S. Chapman, 1724), 23. Fairer ends his quotation at "turn," but the last pair of clauses in the sentence continues and confirms his point.

56 Eliza Haywood, *Love in Excess; or, The Fatal Enquiry, a Novel* (London: Printed for W. Chetwood and R. Francklin and sold by J. Roberts, 1719), 1:28–29; hereafter cited as *LE* in the text.

57 "Phrases P1 with a preposition [. . .] in a word (also in one word, †with a word): in a simple or short (esp. comprehensive) statement or phrase; briefly, concisely, in short" (*OED* e [a]).

58 At this point I have run a word search on five early Haywood works, with these results: *Fantomina* (1); *Love in Excess* (6); *Idalia* (7); *The Surprize, or, Constancy Rewarded* (2); *The Fatal Secret* (3). Of these, "in short" appears once, in *Idalia*, and "in a word," not at all. None of Defoe's novels uses the phrase (though for Moll and Roxana there are many fine fabrics, fine jewels, fine plate, fine words, and fine boys), nor Fielding's, nor Sterne's; Smollett uses it once in *Roderick Random* and once in *Humphry Clinker*; Burney uses it six times in *Camilla* but none in *Evelina* or *Cecilia*; Radcliffe and Smith, not at all. In fine, it's Haywoodian.

59 "In conclusion, in sum; finally; (also) in short" (*OED* "fine," "Phrases b").

60 Eliza Haywood, *Fantomina: or, Love in a Maze. Being a Secret History of an Amour Between Two Persons of Condition* (London: D. Browne jun. and S. Chapman, 1725), 262–63.

61 Eliza Haywood, *The Fatal Secret; or, Constancy in Distress*, 3rd ed. (London: D. Browne Jun. and S. Chapman, 1725), 212.

62 David Oakleaf, "A Note on the Text," in Eliza Haywood, *Love in Excess; or, The Fatal Enquiry*, ed. David Oakleaf (Peterborough, Ont.: Broadview Press, 1994), 25–26.

63 "Editorial changes consider but do not invariably follow the 1722 edition ('The fourth edition corrected'), which shows no signs of authorial revision but corrects some obvious slips. [. . .] [E]ven the different volumes of *Love in Excess* follow distinct recipes. The third volume, for example, prefers *D'Elmont* to *D'elmont* and accents rhetorical contrasts by changing typefaces: 'her *real perfidy*,' Frankville says of Camilla, 'shall be repaid with *seeming inconstancy* . . .' (221 [Broadview edition])" (Oakleaf 26).

64 Spedding records that this misprint is on the general title page of volume III of the "Second Edition" (71): *Secret Histories, Novels, and Poems, Written by Mrs. Eliza Haywood.* 2nd ed. 4 vols. L O N D O N : Printed for DAN. BROWNE *jun.* at the *Black-Swan* without *Temple-Bar*, and S. CHAPMAN, at the in *Angel Pall-mall* [*sic*] M.DCC.XXV.

65 Spedding footnotes (89n87): "Elizabeth Woodfall records the fact that Haywood's 'Maid Servt came very often from the s^{d} Mrs Haywood wth the proof

Sheets' to Ab.65 *Dalinda* in the deposition taken at the time of Haywood's arrest for publishing Ab.66 *HG*."

66 Virginia Woolf, "On First Reading a Contemporary Woman Writer," in Woolf, *A Room of One's Own* (London: Hogarth Press, 1929), 120–21.

67 Thomas Keymer, "Obscenity and the Erotics of Fiction," in *The Cambridge History of the English Novel*, ed. Robert L. Caserio and Clement Hawes (Cambridge: Cambridge University Press, 2012), 141.

68 William Sale believed that *A Wife to be Lett* was "the only link between Richardson and Mrs. Haywood. She certainly would have earned his disapproval, if he had known that she was the author of *Anti-Pamela; or, Feign'd Innocence Detected*." William M. Sale Jr., *Samuel Richardson: Master Printer* (Ithaca: Cornell University Press, 1950), 173. But as Thomas Keymer and Peter Sabor note, "New research has shown that [Richardson] printed, in 1728, the first edition of Haywood's *The Agreeable Caledonian*; in 1732, the first and final volumes of the third edition of Haywood's four-volume collection, *Secret Histories, Novels, and Poems* (1724); and, in 1735, the third edition of her comedy *A Wife to be Lett* (1723). Richardson's debt, in all of his novels, to amatory fiction of the kind he had printed in *Secret Histories* is obvious, yet it was a source he always refused to acknowledge." Keymer and Sabor, *"Pamela" in the Marketplace: Literary Controversy and Print Culture in Eighteenth-Century Britiain and Ireland* (Cambridge: Cambridge University Press, 2005), 84. That "new research" is Keith Maslen, *Samuel Richardson of London, Printer* (Dunedin: University of Otago Press, 2001), 90; Spedding, *Bibliography of Haywood*, 78, 131; and Katherine Ruth Williams, "Samuel Richardson and Amatory Fiction" (PhD diss., Oxford University, 2004).

69 Although his overall point remains with "erzatz": the typography "co-operates with the automatic and mindless erotic suggestion to build up the sexual 'intensity' Mrs. Haywood is after." And I expect that if he reads this chapter one day he will smile but remain completely unconvinced.

70 Quoted in James Elmes, *General and Bibliographical Dictionary of the Fine Arts*, "Landscape Gardening" (EE2); from "Walks around London," in *The Literary Pocket-Book; or, Companion for the Lover of Nature and Art, 1822. To be continued annually* (London: Printed for C. and J. Ollier, 1822).

71 All are Haywood titles, of course: *Love in Excess; or, The Fatal Enquiry* (1719–20); *The Fatal Secret; or, Constancy in Distress* (1724); *The Masqueraders; or, Fatal Curiosity* (1724); *The Fatal Fondness; or, Love Its Own Oppose* (1725).

72 Richard A. Lanham, *Analyzing Prose* (New York: Charles Scribner's Sons, 1983), 54.

73 Anthony Burgess compares Defoe's style to the "Latinate prose of those Elizabethans who fixed one eye on the Court and the Inns of Court"; Defoe consistently chooses the "loose sentence" ("the culmination of decades of search for a perfect narrative manner") because it is more "easily capable of giving the impression of immediacy"; the Elizabethan periodic sentence makes "the events described in narrative [seem] shaped by the writer, the image only fully revealed when we come to the full stop." Qtd. in Daniel Defoe, *A Journal of the Plague Year*, ed. Cynthia Wall (London: Penguin, 2003), 273.

74 Joseph Robertson, *An Essay on Punctuation*, 2nd ed. (London: J. Walter, 1786), 90. He also defines *any* complete or independent English sentence as a period, broadening the Greek and Latin sense of "verborum Ambitus," or circuit of

words, because, while the ancients "were at liberty to throw the first word in construction to the end of the sentence," English and other modern languages "do not so readily admit of such a circuitous arrangement" (90–91).

In 1850 William Fowler repeats that definition: "A PERIOD SENTENCE, or a Period, is a Sentence so framed that the Grammatical structure will not admit of a close before the end of it; or it is one in which the meaning remains suspended until the whole is finished." Fowler, *English Grammar* (New York: Harper and Brothers, 1850), 636. And in 1886, in *Manual of English Prose Literature*, William Minto points out that "*[t]he effect of the periodic structure* is to keep the mind in a state of uniform or increasing tension until the *dénouement*" (5).

75 Humphry Repton, *Humphry Repton's Red Books for Panshanger and Tewin Water, Hertfordshire, 1799–1800*, intro. Twigs Way (Hertfordshire: Hertfordshire Record Society, 2011), 67.

76 As with any other argument about a period (periodic argument? or argument, period?), not everything fits in. Much of Hugh Blair's analysis of sentence and paragraph style smacks of the anti-approach; e.g., "during the course of the sentence, the scene should be changed as little as possible"; the egregious example:

> The following sentence, from a translation of Plutarch, is still worse: 'Their march,' says the author, speaking of the Greeks under Alexander, 'their march, was through an uncultivated country, whose savage inhabitants fared hardly, having no other riches than a breed of lean sheep, whose flesh was rank and unsavory, by reason of their continually feeding upon sea-fish.' Here the scene is changed again and again. 'The march of the Greeks, the description of the inhabitants through whose country they travelled, the account of their sheep being ill-tasted food, form a jumble of objects, slightly related to each other, which the reader cannot, without much difficulty, comprehend under one view. (Hugh Blair, *Lectures on Rhetoric and Belles Lettres* [1783], 8th American ed. [New York: Jas. and John Harper, 1819], 107.)

77 [Samuel Taylor Coleridge?], review of *The Mysteries of Udolpho* in *Critical Review* 11, August 1794 (London: A. Hamilton, 1794), 361–62. The attribution, I believe widely accepted, is noted in Deborah D. Rogers, ed., *The Critical Response to Ann Radcliffe* (Westport, CT: Greenwood Press, 1994), 17.

78 Humphry Repton, *Sketches and Hints on Landscape Gardening*, in *The Landscape Gardening and Landscape Architecture of the Late Humphry Repton, Esq.*, ed. J. C. Loudon (London: Longman; Edinburgh: A. and C. Black, 1840), 91.

79 [William Enfield], review in *Monthly Review*, n.s., 15 (November 1794): 278–83.

80 Richard Payne Knight, *The Landscape, A Didactic Poem* (London: W. Bulmer for G. Nicol, 1794), ll. 177, 192–96.

81 See also the Marquis de Sade, in writing on *The Monk* and Radcliffe: "[In this kind of writing] one must choose one of two things: either one must bring forth the magic spell, after which interest is lost, or one must never raise the curtain at all, and then one enters the realms of the most frightful *truthlessness*" ("Idee sur les romans" in *Les Crimes de l'Amour* [Paris, 1800]).

82 Enduring thanks to Matthew Dowiatt, from my graduate seminar on the eighteenth-century novel (ENEC 8600, Fall 2012), who got intrigued and first

performed this search, and to Evan Cheney, who continued the word searches for all the word phrases analyzed in chapter 5 in Spring 2017.

83 This is according to my own hunt-and-peck research of literary texts in ECCO, as confirmed by Google Books Ngram Viewer, accessed 22 September 2017 and 2 October 2017: https://books.google.com/ngrams/graph?content=at+length&year_start=1600&year_end=2000&corpus=15&smoothing=3&share=&direct_url=t1%3B%2Cat%20length%3B%2Cc0.

84 "At length" appears in *Robinson Crusoe* 22 times, or 5.9% in 371 pages—about the same as the combined "in short" and "in a word" (0.8% and 6.1% respectively); 16 times in *Moll Flanders* (3.66%, compared to 5% for "in short" and 6.65% for "in a word" in 436pp.); 10 times in *A Journal of the Plague Year* (3.43%, with "in a word" at 4.1% and "in short" at 1.7%, 291pp.); and 6 times in *Roxana* (1.45%), compared to 45 times for "in short" (10.9%) and 32 times for "in a word" (7.76%), 412 pp. Fielding uses "at length a total of 30 times in the two volumes of *Joseph Andrews*, and 67 times over the four volumes of *Tom Jones* (not at all in *Amelia*).

85 The phrase shows up in earlier works: the *OED* offers several sixteenth- and seventeenth-century usages, including Spenser: "At length it brought them to a hollowe cave" (1590), the King James bible, and Milton ("Of thy birth at length, Announc't by Gabriel" [1671]). Various online definitions offer: "after some time; eventually" or "for a considerable time; fully"; "for a long time" or "at last, finally"; "in full, extensively" or "after a long time."

86 Deborah Rogers, ed., *The Critical Response to Ann Radcliffe* (Westport, CT: Greenwood Press, 1994), xxx.

87 Ann Radcliffe, *The Mysteries of Udolpho, A Romance; Interspersed with Some Pieces of Poetry,* 2nd ed., 4 vols. (London: Printed for G. G. and J. Robinson, 1794), 2:164. The citations in the following reading will be volume and page numbers only.

88 Bertrand Bronson, "Printing as an Index of Taste," in Bronson, *Facets of the Enlightenment: Studies in English Literature and Its Contexts* (Berkeley and Los Angeles: University of California Press, 1968), 348.

89 Ann Radcliffe, *The Italian; or, The Confessional of the Black Penitents, a Romance,* 3 vols. (London: Printed for T. Cadell Jun. and W. Davies, 1797), 1:51.

90 Peter Collins, *Changing Ideals in Modern Architecture 1750–1950* (1965), 2nd ed. (Montreal: McGill University Press, 1998), 27.

91 See Wall, *The Prose of Things*, 213.

92 In *Evelina* (1778), the phrase is used thirty times over three volumes; in *Cecilia* (1782), just over fifty times (five volumes); in *Camilla* (1796), forty times (five volumes).

93 Some of this section is adapted from my essay "Approaching the Interior of the Eighteenth-Century English Country House," Special Edition, "Narrative Perspectives and Interior Spaces in Literature Before 1850," ed. Monika Fludernik and Suzanne Keen, *Style* 48:4 (Winter 2014): 543–62.

94 Humphry Repton, *An Enquiry into the Changes of Taste in Landscape Gardening* (London: Printed for J. Taylor, 1806), 103–4.

95 William Gilpin, *An Essay upon Prints*, 2nd ed. (London: Printed by G. Scott for J. Robson, 1768), 6–7.

96 See, for example, Bruce Robbins, *The Servant's Hand: English Fiction from Below* (New York: Columbia University Press, 1986); John Richetti, "Repre-

senting an Under Class: Servants and Proletarians in Fielding and Smollett," in *The New Eighteenth Century: Theory, Politics, English Literature*, ed. Felicity Nussbaum and Laura Brown (New York: Methuen, 1987); Ruth Perry, "Home Economics: Representations of Poverty in Eighteenth-Century Fiction," in *A Companion to the Eighteenth-Century English Novel and Culture*, ed. Paula R. Backscheider and Catherine Ingrassia (Oxford: Blackwell, 2005); see also work by John Barrell, Tim Hitchcock, Donna Landry, and Kristina Straub.

97 J. C. Loudon, *Treatise on Forming, Improving, and Managing Country Residences*, 2 vols. (London: Longman, Hurst, Rees, and Orme, 1806), 1:124–25.

98 John B. Papworth, *Rural Residences* (London: Printed by J. Diggens for R. Ackermann, 1818), 10. His arguments for a comfortable and graceful cottage and its good effects for labor contrast with "the broken casement, the patched wall, the sunken roof, the hatch unhinged, the withered shrub," which are "corresponding testimonies of the husbandman's relaxed energies and broken spirit" (10). Dearn's *Designs for Lodges and Entrances* (1811) and Hunt's *Half a Dozen Hints on Picturesque Domestic Architecture* (1825) are discussed in chapter 2.

99 For a more extended analysis of country house guides, see Wall, *The Prose of Things*, chapter 7.

100 George Bickham, *The Beauties of Stow* (1750), intro. George B. Clarke, William Andrews Clark Memorial Library Publication, nos. 185–86 (Los Angeles: University of California Press, 1977), 1–2. The second-person address of the tour guide goes back to the rhetorical arts of the London topographies of the late seventeenth and early eighteenth centuries; see Wall, *The Literary and Cultural Spaces of Restoration London* (Cambridge: Cambridge University Press, 1998).

101 George Bickham and P. Norbury, *A Short Account of the Principal Seats and Gardens in and about Richmond and Kew* (Brentford: Printed and sold by P. Norbury and George Bickham, 1763), 3.

102 The Twickenham Museum notes that Ragman's Castle was "built on a long strip of land running up Orleans Road, adjacent to the Orleans House Estate. Might have been the great new house in the lane of Richard Ell as listed in the 1661 parish survey. Site of an ale house known as The Dog and Partridge." It was bought by William and Hannah Pritchard in 1755; he died in 1763, and the house was sold. It was demolished in 1850.

103 Humphry Repton, "View from the House continued," in *Glemham Hall in Suffolk A Seat of Dudley Long North Esqr.*" (1791), in *The Red Books for Brandsbury and Glemham Hall*, intro. Stephen Daniels (Washington, DC: Dumbarton Oaks, 1994), n.p.

104 David Marshall, *The Frame of Art: Fictions of Aesthetic Experience, 1750–1815* (Baltimore: Johns Hopkins University Press, 2005), 17.

105 Batty Langley, *The Builder's Chest-Book* (London: J. Wilcox, 1727).

106 Elizabeth Burton, *The Georgians at Home* (1967; London: Arrow, 1973), 110–11.

107 Caroline Lybbe Powys, *Passages from the Diaries of Mrs. Philip Lybbe Powys of Hardwick House, Oxon. A.D. 1756 to 1808*, ed. Emily J. Climenson (London: Longmans, Green, 1899), 6.

108 J. C. Loudon, *An Encyclopædia of Cottage, Farm, and Villa Architecture and Furniture* (London: Printed for Longman, Rees, Orme, Brown, Green, and Longman, 1833; rpt. Cambridge: Cambridge University Press, 2014), 272, 274.

109 Alison E. Martin, "The Traveller as Landschaftsmaler: Industrial Labour and

Landscape Aesthetics in Johanna Schopenhauer's Travel Writing," *Modern Language Review* 99:4 (October 2004): 972.

110 Frances Burney, *Camilla; or, A Picture of Youth* (London: Printed for T. Payne, T. Cadell Jun., and W. Davies, 1796), 1:299.

111 Henry Austen, "Biographical Notice of the Author" (1817), in *Northanger Abbey and Persuasion*, vol. 5 of *The Novels of Jane Austen*, ed. R. W. Chapman, 3rd ed. (Oxford: Oxford University Press, 1933), 7.

112 Sir Walter Scott, unsigned review of *Emma, Quarterly Review* 14 (dated October 1815, issued March 1816): 188–201, in *Jane Austen: The Critical Heritage*, ed. B. C. Southam (London: Routledge and Kegan Paul; New York: Barnes and Noble, 1968), 68.

113 Alistair M. Duckworth, "Landscape," in *Jane Austen in Context*, ed. Janet Todd (Cambridge: Cambridge University Press, 2005), 285.

114 Blakey Vermuele gives an excellent summary and analysis of free indirect discourse from Geoffrey Chaucer through Madame de Lafayette, Horace Walpole, and William Godwin, to Austen, George Eliot, Flaubert, and James, in *Why Do We Care about Literary Characters?* (Baltimore: Johns Hopkins University Press, 2010), 72.

115 Julie Park, "What the Eye Cannot See: Interior Landscapes in *Mansfield Park*," *Eighteenth Century: Theory and Interpretation* 54:2 (Summer 2013): 70.

116 Dorrit Cohn, *Transparent Minds: Narrative Modes for Presenting Consciousness in Fiction* (Princeton: Princeton University Press, 1978), 103.

117 See, for example, Cohn, *Transparent Minds*, 105; Roy Pascal, *The Dual Voice: Free Indirect Speech and Its Functioning in the Nineteenth-Century European Novel* (Manchester: Manchester University Press, 1977); and Suzanne Keen, *Narrative Form* (Hampshire: Palgrave Macmillan, 2003), 61.

118 André Rogger, *Landscapes of Taste: The Art of Humphry Repton's Red Books* (London: Routledge, 2007), 91.

119 Humphry Repton, "The Approach," *Humphry Repton's Red Book for Blaise Castle* (1795), (Bristol: Friends of Blaise, n.d.), n.p.

120 "Access or means of access between two or more persons or places; the fact of being connected by a physical link, or by a practicable route; connection, passage (between two places, vessels, spaces, etc.)" (*OED* 9a).

121 "†8. Rhetoric. The device of appearing to consult one's audience or opponent, as by introducing questions into a speech; = anacoenosis n. Also: (rare) the use of we in order to include the hearer or reader in the speaker or writer's sentiments. Obs." [1793 J. BEATTIE *Elem. Moral Sci.* II.iv.i.465]

122 Jane Austen, *Mansfield Park* (1814), vol. 3 of *The Novels of Jane Austen*, ed. R. W. Chapman, 3rd ed. (Oxford: Oxford University Press, 1934), 5.

123 "Dark ideologies" include, among others, Nina Auerbach's in *Romantic Imprisonment* (New York: Columbia University Press, 1985), 22–37; Tony Tanner, introduction to *Mansfield Park* (Harmondsworth: Penguin, 1966); Lionel Trilling, *The Opposing Self* (New York: Viking Press, 1955); and William Galperin, "The Missed Opportunities of *Mansfield Park*," in *Companion to Jane Austen*, ed. Claudia Johnson and Clara Tuite (Chichester: Blackwell, 2009), 123–32.

124 She argues that "[f]ree indirect discourse is the psycholiterary equivalent of economics" in chapter 4 (78), expanded in chapter 8.

125 Jane Austen, *Emma* (1816), vol. 4 of *The Novels of Jane Austen*, ed. R. W. Chapman, 3rd ed. (Oxford: Oxford University Press, 1933), 23–24.

126 Humphry Repton, *An Enquiry into the Changes of Taste in Landscape Gardening* (London: Printed for J. Taylor, 1806), 107.

127 Jane Austen, *Pride and Prejudice* (1813), vol. 2 of *The Novels of Jane Austen*, ed. R. W. Chapman, 3rd ed. (Oxford: Oxford University Press, 1932), 204.

128 Anthony Mandal, "Language," in *Jane Austen in Context*, ed. Janet Todd (Cambridge: Cambridge University Press, 2005), 28.

129 Thomas Whately, "The Approach to Caversham," in Whately, *Observations on Modern Gardening, Illustrated by Descriptions* (London: Printed for T. Payne, 1770), 140–44.

130 Franco Moretti, *Graphs, Maps, Trees: Abstract Models for Literary History* (London: Verso Books; Scranton, PA: W. W. Norton, 2007), 82.

Coda

1 C. F. Partington, *The Printer's Complete Guide* (London: Printed for Sherwood, Gilbert, and Piper, 1825), 246.

2 Deidre Shauna Lynch, *The Economy of Character: Novels, Market Culture, and the Business of Inner Meaning* (Chicago: University of Chicago Press, 1998), 28.

3 Richard A. Lanham, *Analyzing Prose* (New York: Charles Scribner's Sons, 1983), 61.

4 J. C. Loudon, *A Treatise on Forming, Improving, and Managing Country Residences,* 2 vols. (London: Printed for Longman, Hurst, Rees, and Orme, 1806), 2:590–91.

5 Caroline Levine, *Forms: Whole, Rhythm, Hierarchy, Network* (Princeton: Princeton University Press, 2015), 3.

6 Virginia Woolf, *A Room of One's Own* (London: Hogarth Press, 1929), 115.

7 Alexander Pope, *An Essay on Criticism* (1711), ll. 362–63.

8 The illustrative quotations for the figurative meaning of "approach" begin with the twentieth century: "1905 R. B. Perry *Approach to Philos.* 1 (heading) Approach to the problem of philosophy"; also, "1969 *Mod. Lang. Rev.* LXIV. 876 The typological approach . . . does not preclude other methods of interpreting Milton's symbolism," and "1986 *N.Y. Times* 7 May a10/4 We reaffirm the continued importance of the case-by-case approach to international debt problems."

9 Jane Austen, *Pride and Prejudice* (1813), vol. 2 of *The Novels of Jane Austen*, ed. R. W. Chapman, 3rd ed. (Oxford: Oxford University Press, 1932), 204.

10 Joseph Robertson, *An Essay on Punctuation,* 2nd ed. (London: J. Walter, 1786), 90.

11 Uvedale Price, *Essays on the Picturesque,* 3 vols. (London: J. Mawman, 1810), 1:250.

12 Adapted from Hannah More, *Memoirs of the Life and Correspondence of Mrs. Hannah More: By William Roberts, Esq.,* 3rd ed., 4 vols. (London: R. B. Seeley and W. Burnside, 1835), 1:267.

13 Jane Austen, *Northanger Abbey*, in *Northanger Abbey and Persuasion,* 4 vols. (London: John Murray, 1818), 2:178, 186, 187.

14 Paraphrasing one last time McKenzie's "hand-held theatre of the book." D. F. McKenzie, "Typography and Meaning: The Case of William Congreve," *Buch und Buchhandel in Europa im achtzehnten Jahrhundert: The Book and the Book Trade in Eighteenth-Century Europe,* ed. G. Barber and B. Fabian (Hamburg: Dr. Ernst Hauswedell and Co., 1981), 83.

Bibliography

Primary Sources

Adams, Thomas F. *Typographia; or, The Printer's Instructor* (1837). Rpt. with an introduction by John Bidwell. New York: Garland, 1981.

Addison, Joseph. *Remarks on Several Parts of Italy*. London: J. and R. Tonson, 1767.

———. *Spectator* 135, Saturday, August 4, 1711.

Allardyce, Paul [i.e., George Paul Macdonell]. *"Stops"; or, How to Punctuate*. London: T. F. Unwin, 1884.

Angus, William. *The Seats of the Nobility and Gentry, in Great Britain and Wales. In a Collection of Select Views, Engraved by W. Angus. From Pictures and Drawings by the most Eminent Artists. With Descriptions of each View*. London: W. Angus, 1787.

Armstrong, Mostyn John. *An Actual Survey of the Great Post-Roads between London and Edinburgh*. London: Printed for the Author, 1776.

Arnold, Matthew. *Poetry and Criticism of Matthew Arnold*. Ed. A. Dwight Culler. Boston: Houghton Mifflin, 1961.

Ash, John. *The New and Complete Dictionary of the English Language*. 2 vols. London: Edward and Charles Dilly, 1775.

———. *The New and Complete Dictionary of the English Language*. 2nd ed. 2 vols. London: Edward and Charles Dilly, 1795.

Atkyns, Sir Robert. *The Ancient and Present State of Glostershire*. London: W. Bowyer for Robert Gosling, 1712.

Austen, Jane. *Emma: A Novel*. 3 vols. London: John Murray, 1816.

———. *Emma* (1816). Vol. 4 of *The Novels of Jane Austen*. Ed. R. W. Chapman. 3rd ed. Oxford: Oxford University Press, 1933.

———. *Mansfield Park: A Novel*. 3 vols. London: T. Egerton, 1814.

———. *Mansfield Park* (1814). Vol. 3 of *The Novels of Jane Austen*. Ed. R. W. Chapman. 3rd ed. Oxford: Oxford University Press, 1934.

———. *Mansfield Park* (1814). Ed. Tony Tanner. Harmondsworth: Penguin, 1966.

———. *Mansfield Park* (1814). Ed. James Kinsley. Intro. Jane Stabler. Oxford: Oxford University Press, 2003.

———. *Northanger Abbey and Persuasion.* 4 vols. London: John Murray, 1818.

———. *Northanger Abbey* (1818). Vol. 5 of *The Novels of Jane Austen.* Ed. R. W. Chapman. 3rd ed. Oxford: Clarendon Press, 1933.

———. *Northanger Abbey* (1818). Ed. James Kinsley and John Davie. Intro. Claudia L. Johnson. Oxford: Oxford University Press, 2003.

———. *Northanger Abbey: An Annotated Edition.* Ed. Susan Wolfson. Cambridge, MA: Belknap Press of Harvard University Press, 2014.

———. *Persuasion.* In *Northanger Abbey and Persuasion.* 4 vols. London: John Murray, 1818.

———. *Persuasion* (1818). Vol. 5 of *The Novels of Jane Austen.* Ed. R. W. Chapman. 3rd ed. Oxford: Clarendon Press, 1933.

———. *Persuasion* (1818). Ed. John Davie. Oxford: Oxford University Press, 1990.

———. *Pride and Prejudice* (1813). Vol. 2 of *The Novels of Jane Austen.* Ed. R. W. Chapman. 3rd ed. Oxford: Oxford University Press, 1932.

———. *Pride and Prejudice* (1813). Ed. James Kinsley. Intro. and notes by Fiona Stafford. Oxford: Oxford University Press, 2004.

B., N. *The Antiquities of London and Westminster.* London: H. Tracy, 1722.

Bailey, N[athan]. *Dictionarium Britannicum; or, A More Compleat Universal Etymological English Dictionary.* London: T. Cox, 1730.

———. *Dictionarium Britannicum* [. . .] 2nd ed. London: T. Cox, 1736.

———. *The Universal Etymological English Dictionary: In Two Parts.* London: T. Cox, 1727.

———. *An Universal Etymological English Dictionary.* 4th ed. London: J. Darby et al., 1728.

———. *An Universal Etymological Dictionary Comprehending the Derivations of the Generality of Words in the English Tongue.* 21st ed. London: T. Osborne et al., 1766.

Barbauld, Anna Lætitia. "Life of Samuel Richardson, with Remarks on his Writings." *The Correspondence of Samuel Richardson, Author of Pamela, Clarissa, and Sir Charles Grandison.* Ed. Anna Lætitia Barbauld. 6 vols. London: Richard Phillips, 1804.

Baskerville, John. *Letters of the Famous 18th Century Printer John Baskerville of Birmingham, Together with a Bibliography of Works Printed by Him at Birmingham.* Ed. Leonard Jay. Birmingham: Birmingham School of Printing, 1932.

———. Preface to *Paradise Lost. A Poem in Twelve Books. The Author John Milton. From the Text of Thomas Newton D. D.* Birmingham: John Baskerville for J. and R. Tonson, 1758.

———. Preface to *The Works of Mr. William Congreve. In Three Volumes. Consisting of His Plays and Poems.* Birmingham: John Baskerville for J. and R. Tonson, London, 1761.

———. *Some Correspondence concerning the Making of Printing Type by John Baskerville of Birmingham.* Foreword, typography, composition, and presswork by Charles Whitehouse. Zurich: Hand Press, 1991.

———. *A Vocabulary, or Pocket Dictionary. To Which is Prefixed, A Compendious Grammar of the English Language.* Birmingham: John Baskerville for Dod, Rivington et al., 1765.

Bickham, George. *The Beauties of Stow* (1750). Intro. George B. Clarke. William Andrews Clark Memorial Library Publication nos. 185–86 (Los Angeles: University of California Press, 1977).

Bickham, George, and P. Norbury. *A Short Account of the Principal Seats and Gardens in and about Richmond and Kew*. Brentford: P. Norbury and George Bickham, 1763.

Bickham, George, Junior. *A Curious Antique Collection of Birds-Eye-Views of the Several Counties in England & Wales; Exhibiting a Pleasing Landscape of Each County; with a Variety of Rustic Figures, Ruins, &c. &c. And the Names of the Principal Towns and Villages, interspersed according to their apparent Situation*. London: Robert Laurie and James Whittle, 1796.

Blair, Hugh. *Lectures on Rhetoric and Belles Lettres*. 2 vols. London: W. Strahan and T. Cadell; Edinburgh: W. Creech, 1783.

———. *Lectures on Rhetoric and Belles Lettres*. 8th American ed. New York: Jas. and John Harper, 1819.

Boswell, James. *Boswell's Life of Johnson*. Ed. George Birkbeck Hill. Rev. L. F. Powell. 6 vols. Oxford: Clarendon Press, 1934–50.

———. *Life of Johnson*. Ed. R. W. Chapman. Oxford: Oxford University Press, 1980.

Boyle, Robert. *An Essay of the Great Effects of Even Languid and Unheeded Motion*. London: M. Flesher for Richard Davis, 1685.

Brightland, John, and Charles Gildon. *A Grammar of the English Tongue*. London: John Brightland, 1711.

Brown, John. *Bunyan's Home*. London: E. Nister, 1890.

Browne, Moses. *Percy-Lodge, A Seat of the Duke and Duchess of Somerset, A Poem; Written by Command of their late Graces, (In the Year 1749)*. London: W. Owen et al., 1755.

Brydall, John. *Camera Regis; or, A Short View of London*. London: William Crooke, 1676.

Buchanan, James. *The British Grammar; or, An Essay, in Four Parts, Towards Speaking and Writing the English Language Grammatically, and Inditing Elegantly. For the Use of the Schools of Great Britain and Ireland, and of Private Young Gentlemen and Ladies*. London: A. Millar, 1762.

———. *A Regular English Syntax. Wherein is exhibited, The whole Variety of English Construction, properly exemplified. To which is added, The elegant Manner of arranging Words, and Members of Sentences. The whole Reduced to Practice, for the Use of private young Gentlemen and Ladies, as well as of our most eminent Schools*. London: J. Wren, 1767.

Bunyan, John. *A Discourse on the Building, Nature, Excellency, and Government of the House of God*. London: George Larkin, 1688.

———. *Grace Abounding to the Chief of Sinners; or, A Brief and Faithful Relation of the exceeding Mercy of God in Christ, to His poor Servant John Bunyan*. 6th ed., corr. London: Nathaniel Ponder, 1688.

———. *Grace Abounding to the Chief of Sinners* (1666). Ed. Roger Sharrock. Oxford: Clarendon Press, 1962.

———. *The Pilgrim's Progress from this World, to That which is to come: Delivered under the Similitude of a Dream Wherein is Discovered, The manner of his setting out, His Dangerous Journey; And safe Arrival at the Desired Countrey*. London: Nathaniel Ponder, 1678.

———. *The Pilgrim's Progress* (1678). Ed. C. H. Firth. London: Methuen, 1898.

———. *The Pilgrim's Progress from this World to That which is to Come* (1678). Ed. James Blanton Wharey. 2nd ed. by Roger Sharrock. Oxford: Clarendon Press, 1960.

———. *The Pilgrim's Progress* (1678). Ed. Cynthia Wall. New York: W. W. Norton, 2009.

———. *The Pilgrim's Progress From This World to That Which Is to Come* (1678). Chicago: Bible Institute Corporate Association, 1904.

Burney, Frances. *Camilla: or, A Picture of Youth.* 5 vols. London: T. Payne, T. Cadell Jun., and W. Davies, 1796.

———. *Camilla* (1796). Ed. Edward A. Bloom and Lillian D. Bloom. Oxford: Oxford University Press, 1989.

———. *Journals and Letters.* Ed. Peter Sabor and Lars Troide. London: Penguin, 2001.

Butler, Charles. *The English Grammar; or, The Institution of Letters, Syllables, and Words, in the English tongue. Whereunto is annexed An Index of Words Like and Unlike.* Oxford: William Turner for the Author, 1633.

Buys, Egbert. *A New and Complete Dictionary of Terms of Art. Containing a sufficient explication, of all words derived from the Hebrew, Arabic, Greek, Latin, Spanish, French, English, German, Dutch and other languages; made use of to express any art, science, custom, sickness, medicine, plant, flower, fruit, tool, machine, &c.* [. . .] 2 vols. Amsterdam: K. De Veer, 1768–69.

Byng, John, Viscount Torrington. *The Torrington Diaries* [. . .] *1781–1794.* Ed. C. Bruyn Andrews. 4 vols. London: Eyre and Spottiswoode, 1934.

Caille, Jean de la. *Histoire de l'Imprimerie et de la librairie, où l'on voit son origine & son progrés, jusqu'en 1689.* 2 vols. Paris: Jean de la Caille, 1689.

Cawdrey, Robert. *A Table Alphabeticall, conteyning and teaching the true writing, and vnderstanding of hard vsuall English wordes, borrowed from the Hebrew, Greeke, Latine, or French. &c.* London: I. R. for Edmund Weaver, 1604.

Chamberlayne, John. *Magnæ Britanniæ Notitia; or, The Present State of Great Britain; With diverse Remarks upon The Ancient State thereof.* London: S. Birt, A. Millar et al., 1755.

Chambers, Ephraim. *Cyclopædia; or, An Universal Dictionary of Arts and Sciences.* 2 vols. London: James and John Knapton et al., 1728.

———. *Cyclopædia; or, An Universal Dictionary of Arts and Sciences.* 2nd ed. 2 vols. London: D. Midwinter et al., 1738.

———. *Cyclopædia; or, An Universal Dictionary of Arts and Sciences.* 4th ed. 2 vols. London: W. Innys et al., 1741.

———. *Cyclopædia; or, An Universal Dictionary of Arts and Sciences.* 6th ed. 2 vols. London: W. Innys, et al., 1750.

———. *Cyclopædia; or, An Universal Dictionary of Arts and Sciences. With the Supplement and Modern Improvements, Incorporated in one Alphabet. By Abraham Rees.* 4 vols. London: J. F. and C. Rivington et al., 1786.

Clare, John. *Cottage Tales.* Ed. Eric Robinson, David Powell, and P. M. S. Dawson. Manchester: Carcanet Press, 1993.

———. *The Lodge House. A Gossips Tale.* In *The Early Poems of John Clare, 1804–1822.* 2 vols. Ed. Eric Robertson and David Powell. Oxford: Clarendon Press, 1989.

Clare, William. *A Compleat System of Grammar, English and Latin.* London: H. Walwyn, 1690.

Cobbett, William. *A Grammar of the English Language, In a Series of Letters. Intended for the Use of Schools and of Young Persons in general; but, more especially for the Use of Soldiers, Sailors, Apprentices, and Plough-boys.* 2nd ed. London: Thomas Dolby, 1819.

———. *Rural Rides* (1830). 2 vols. London: J. M. Dent and Sons, 1832.

Cocker, Edward. *Cocker's English Dictionary: Interpreting the Most Refined and Difficult Words.* London: A. Back and A. Bettesworth, 1704.

Cockin, William. *The Art of Delivering Written Language; or, An Essay of Reading: In Which the Subject is Treated Philosophically as Well as with a View to Practice.* London: H. Hughs for J. Dodsley, 1775.

Coleridge, Samuel Taylor. *Coleridge's Miscellaneous Criticism.* Ed. Thomas Middleton Raysor. London: Constable and Co., 1936.

———. *The Literary Remains of Samuel Taylor Coleridge.* Ed. Henry Nelson Coleridge. 4 vols. London: William Pickering, 1836).

Coles, Elisha. *An English Dictionary, Explaining the difficult Term That are used in Divinity, Husbandry, Physick, Phylosophy, Law, Navigation, Mathematicks, and other Arts and Sciences. Containing Many thousands of hard Words (and proper names of Places) more than are in any other English Dictionary or Expositor.* London: Peter Parker, 1685.

———. *An English Dictionary.* [. . .] London: S. Collins for R. Bonwick, 1717.

A Collection of the Names of the Merchants Living in and about the City of London. London: Samuel Lee, 1677.

Collyer, John. *The General Principles of Grammar: Especially Adapted to the English Tongue. With a Method of Parsing and Examination. For the Use of Schools.* Nottingham: Tho. Collyer, 1735.

A Companion To every Place of Curiosity and Entertainment In and about London and Westminster. London: J. Lawrence et al., 1767.

A Compleat Guide to the English Tongue. London: Printed for Richard Wild, [cataloguer's pencil: (c. 1708)].

Coote, Charles. *Elements of the Grammar of the English Language.* London: C. Dilly, 1788.

Corbet, John. *A Concise System of English Grammar.* Madely: J. Edmunds, 1785.

Critical Remarks on Sir Charles Grandison, Clarissa, and Pamela. Enquiring, Whether they have a Tendency to corrupt or improve the Public Taste and Morals. In a Letter to the Author. By a Lover of Virtue. London: J. Dowse, 1754.

Croker, the Rev. Temple Henry, Thomas Williams, and Samuel Clark. *The Complete Dictionary of Arts and Sciences.* 3 vols. London: J. Wilson and J. Fell et al., 1764.

Crouch, John. *A Mixt Poem, Partly Historicall, partly Panegyricall, upon the Happy Return of His Sacred Majesty Charls* [*sic*] *the Second, and his Illustrious Brothers, the Dukes of York and Glocester,* With Honourable Reflections upon some State-martyrs, and the Renowned Generall. Not forgetting the Rump *and its Appurtenances.* London: Thomas Bettertun [*sic*], 1660.

The Curiosities of London and Westminster Described in Four Volumes. London: E. Newbery, 1786.

Dalton, William Hugh. *The New and Complete English Traveller; or, A New Historical Survey and Modern Description of England and Wales. A Work calculated equally to please the Polite—entertain the Curious—instruct the Uninformed—and direct the Traveller.* London: Alex. Hogg, [1794].

Dalgarno, George. *The Art of Signs* (1661). Ed. and trans. David Cram and Jaap Maat. In Cram and Maat, *George Dalgarno on Universal Language.* Oxford: Oxford University Press, 2001.

Dallaway, James. "Supplementary Anecdotes of Gardening in England." In *Anecdotes of Painting in England; With Some Account of the Principal Artists; and Incidental*

Notes on other Arts. Also, A Catalogue of Engravers, who have been born or resided in England. Collected by the late George Vertue; Digested and Published from his Original Mss. by Horace Walpole; with additions by the Rev. James Dallaway. A New edition, revised, with additional notes. By Ralph N. Wornum. 3 vols. London: Henry G. Bohn, 1849.

Dearn, T. D. W. *Designs for Lodges and Entrances.* London: J. Taylor, 1811.

Decorations for Parks and Gardens, Designs for Gates, Garden Seats, Alcoves, Temples, Baths, Entrance Gates, Lodges, Facades, Prospect Towers, Cattle Sheds, Ruins, Bridges, Greenhouses. [. . .] London: J. Taylor, [1800].

Defoe, Daniel. *An Essay upon Projects.* London: R. R. for Tho. Cockerill, 1697.

———. *Essays upon Several Projects: Or, Effectual Ways for advancing the Interest of the Nation.* London: The Booksellers of London and Westminster, 1702.

———. *Every-Body's Business, is No-Body's Business; or, Private Abuses, Publick Grievances.* By Andrew Moreton, Esq. London: T. Warner, A. Dodd, and E. Nutt, 1725.

———. "Fleeing For Refuge To The hope Sett before us." In *The Meditations of Daniel Defoe.* Ed. George Harris Healey. Cummington, MA: The Cummington Press, 1946.

———. *The Fortunes and Misfortunes of the Famous Moll Flanders* (1722). Ed. G. A. Starr. Oxford: Oxford University Press, 1971.

———. *A Journal of the Plague Year* (1722). Retitled *The History of the Great Plague.* Ed. J. S. Laurie. Shilling Entertaining Library. London: Longman, Green, Longman, Roberts, and Green, 1863.

———. *A Journal of the Plague Year* (1722). Ed. Cynthia Wall. London: Penguin Classics, 2003.

———. *The Life and Strange Surprizing Adventures of Robinson Crusoe, of York, Mariner* [. . .] *Written by Himself.* 3rd ed. London: W. Taylor, 1719.

———. *Robinson Crusoe.* (1719). Ed. Thomas Keymer. Oxford: Oxford University Press, 2007.

———. *Roxana, the Fortunate Mistress* (1724). Ed. John Mullan. Oxford: Oxford University Press, 1996, reissued 2008.

———. *A Tour Thro' the Whole Island of Great Britain, Divided into Circuits or Journeys.* [. . .] 3 vols. London: Printed and sold by G. Strahan et al., 1724–26.

———. *A Tour Thro' the Whole Island of Great Britain. Divided into Circuits or Journeys.* [. . .] *The Fifth Edition. With very great Additions, Improvements, and Corrections; which bring it down to the Year 1753.* 4 vols. London: S. Birt et al., 1753.

———. *A Tour Through the Whole Island of Great Britain* (1724–26). Ed. P. N. Furbank, W. R. Owens, and A. J. Coulson. New Haven: Yale University Press, 1991.

Delany, Mary. *The Autobiography and Correspondence of Mary Granville, Mrs. Delany.* Ed. Lady Llanover. 1st–2nd ser. London: R. Bentley, 1861–62. Rpt. New York: AMS Press, 1974.

Dictionarium Rusticum, Urbanicum and Botanicum: or, A Dictionary of Husbandry, Gardening, Trade, Commerce, And all Sorts of Country-Affairs. 2nd ed. London: J. Nicholson, W. Taylor, and W. Churchill, 1717.

Dibdin, Thomas Frognall. *Typographical Antiquities; or, The History of Printing in England, Scotland, and Ireland.* 4 vols. London: William Miller, 1810.

Dilworth, Thomas. *A New Guide to the English Tongue* (1740). 13th ed. London: Henry Kent, 1751.

———. *A New Guide to the English Tongue, In Five Parts.* [. . .] *A New Edition.* 1st ed. 1740. Boston: T. and J. Fleet, 1789.

Dodsley, Robert. *The Correspondence of Robert Dodsley, 1733–1764*. Ed. J. E. Tierney. Cambridge: Cambridge University Press, 1988.

———. *A Select Collection of Old Plays*. 12 vols. London: R. Dodsley, 1744.

Dutens, M. L. *Journal of Travels made through the Principal Cities of Europe*. Trans. John Highmore. London: J. Wallis, 1782.

Dyche, Thomas. *Guide to the English Tongue*. London: Samuel Butler, 1707.

———. *A Guide to the English Tongue*. 23rd ed. London: Richard Ware, 1736.

———. *A New General English Dictionary; Peculiarly calculated for the Use and Improvement of such as are unacquainted with the Learned Languages.* [. . .] *now finish'd by William Pardon, Gent.* 3rd ed. London: Richard Ware, 1740.

Edgeworth, Maria. *Love and Law. A Drama in Three Acts*. In *Tales and Novels: The Longford Edition (1893)*. Vol. 8. Hildesheim: Georg Olms Verlagsbuchhandlung, 1969.

Elmes, James. *A General and Bibliographical Dictionary of the Fine Arts. Containing Explanations of the Principal Terms Used in the Arts of Painting, Sculpture, Architecture, and Engraving, in All Their Various Branches.* London: Printed for Thomas Tegg; Dublin: R. M. Tims; Glasgow: R. Griffin and Co., 1826.

Elphinston, James. *The Principles of the English Language Digested; or, English Grammar Reduced to Analogy*. 2 vols. London: James Bettenham for P. Vaillan et al., 1765.

[Enfield, William.] Review of *The Mysteries of Udolpho. Monthly Review*, n.s., 15 (November 1794): 278–83.

England Illustrated; or, A Compendium of the Natural History, Geography, Topography, and Antiquities Ecclesiastical and Civil, of England and Wales. 2 vols. London: R. and J. Dodsley, 1764.

English Architecture; or, The Publick Buildings of London and Westminster. London: T. Osborne, 1756.

Ernesti, J. H. G. *Die Wol-eingerichtete Büchdrückerey*. 2nd ed. Nuremberg: J. A. Endter, 1733.

Evelyn, John. *The Diaries of John Evelyn*. Ed. E. S. De Beer. 6 vols. Oxford: Clarendon Press, 1955.

Farington, Joseph. *The Diary of Joseph Farington*. Ed. Kenneth Garlick and Angus Macintyre. 17 vols. New Haven: Yale University Press, 1978–1998.

The Female Miscellany: In Two Parts. Part I. Containing a Sketch of English Grammar; an Abridgment of the Holy History; a small Collection of Fables, &c. Part II. Consisting of a Series of Letter addressed to a young Lady who has made some Progress in Reading. For the Use of a Boarding School. Salop [Shropshire]: Stafford Pryse, 1770.

Fertel, Martin Dominique. *La Science pratique*. Saint Omer: Marchand Libraire, 1723.

Fielding, Henry. *The History of Tom Jones, a Foundling* (1749). Wesleyan Edition. Ed. Fredson Bowers. Intro. Martin C. Battestin. Wesleyan, OH: Wesleyan University Press, 1975.

———. *Joseph Andrews* (1742). Ed. Martin C. Battestin. Oxford: Clarendon Press, 1967.

Fiennes, Celia. *The Illustrated Journeys of Celia Fiennes, 1685–c. 1712*. Ed. Christopher Morris. London: Macdonald, 1982. New ed., Stroud: Alan Sutton, 1995.

Fisher, A[nne]. *A New Grammar, with Exercises of Bad English; or, An Easy Guide to Speaking and Writing the English Language Properly and Correctly*. 3rd ed. London: Printed for the Author, 1753.

———. *A Practical New Grammar, with Exercises of Bad English; or, An Easy Guide to Speaking and Writing the English Language Properly and Correctly.* 6th ed. Newcastle upon Tyne: Thomas Slack, 1759.

———. *A Practical New Grammar.* [. . .]. 7th ed. Newcastle: Thomas Slack, 1762.

———. *A Practical New Grammar.* [. . .] 15th ed. London: G. Robinson., 1795.

Fosbroke, T. D. *A Picturesque and Topographical Account of Cheltenham, and Its Vicinity.* Cheltenham: S. C. Harper; London: Nichols and Son, and O. B. Whittaker, 1826.

Fournier, Pierre Simon, le jeune. *Manuel typographique, utile aux gens de lettres.* 2 vols. Paris: Barbou, 1764–66.

Fowler, William Chauncey. *English Grammar. The English Language in its Elements and Forms. With a History of Its Origin and Development Designed for Use in Colleges and Schools.* New York: Harper and Brothers, 1850.

———. *English Grammar: The English Language in its Elements and Forms.* [. . .] Rev. and enl. New York: Harper and Brothers, 1877.

Franklin, Benjamin. *Writings.* Ed. J. A. Leo Lamay. New York: Library of America, 1987.

Free, John. *An Essay Towards an History of the English Tongue.* 4th ed. London: W. Brown, W. Ash, 1788.

A Full and True Account of a most Horrid and Barbarous Design, intended to be Executed upon the Body of Mr. J. Frampton, a Wire-worker, Living upon London-Bridge: Who by Providence hath escaped the Wicked Conspiracy of Mary Roberts; the Effects of which was to have ended in his Death, and utter Ruine of his whole Family. London: E. Baldwin, 1698.

Gastineau, Henry. *North Wales Illustrated.* London: Jones, 1830. Rpt. Wakefield, West Yorkshire: EP Publishing, 1977.

Gessner, Christian Friedrich. *Die so nöthig als nützliche Buchdruckerkunst und Schriftgiesserey.* Leipzig: Christian Friedrich Gessner, 1740.

Gilpin, William. *An Essay upon Prints: Containing Remarks upon the Principles of Picturesque Beauty; the Different Kinds of Prints; and the Characters of the Most Noted Masters: Illustrated by Criticisms upon Particular Pieces: To which are added, Some Cautions that may be useful in collecting Prints.* 2nd ed. London: G. Scott for J. Robson, 1768.

———. *Observations on the River Wye, and Several Parts of South Wales, &c. Relative Chiefly to Picturesque Beauty; Made in the Summer of the Year 1770.* London: R. Blamire, 1782.

Gough, James, and John Gough. *A Practical Grammar of the English Tongue.* [. . .] *For the Use of Schools.* 2nd ed. Dublin: Isaac Jackson, 1760.

Gough, Richard. *Anecdotes of British Topography.* London: W. Richardson and S. Clark for T. Payne and W. Brown, 1768.

Greenwood, James. *An Essay Towards a Practical English Grammar.* London: R. Tookey, 1711.

Griffiths, Roger. *A Description of the River Thames &c. with the City of London's jurisdiction and conservancy thereof proved, Both in Point of Right and Usage.* London: T. Longman, 1758.

Grose, Francis. *A Classical Dictionary of the Vulgar Tongue.* London: S. Hooper, 1785.

———. *A Classical Dictionary of the Vulgar Tongue.* 3rd ed. London: Hooper and Wigstead, 1796.

Grunden, John. *Convenient and Ornamental Architecture, Consisting of Original*

Designs, for Plans, Elevations, and Sections: Beginning with the Farm House, and regularly ascending to the most grand and magnificent Villa. London: Henry Wesley, 1767.

Gyfford, E. *Designs for Elegant Cottages and Small Villas, Calculated for the Comfort and Convenience of Persons of Moderate and of Ample Fortune.* London: J. Taylor, J. Harding, J. Carpenter, 1806.

Halfpenny, William. *Useful Architecture in Twenty-one New Designs for Erecting Parsonage-Houses, Farm-Houses, and Inns.* London: Robert Sayer, 1752.

Halfpenny, William, and John Halfpenny. *The Country Gentleman's Pocket Companion and Builder's Assistant, for Rural Decorative Architecture. Containing, Thirty-two New Designs, Plans and Elevations of Alcoves, Floats, Temples, Summer-Houses, Lodges, Huts, Grotto's, andc. In the Augustine, Gothick and Chinese Taste, With proper Directions annexed.* London: Robert Sayer, 1753.

Haller, Albrecht von. "A Critical Account of *Clarissa.*" *Gentleman's Magazine* 19 (1749): 345–49.

Hamilton, Elizabeth. *Memoirs of the Late Mrs. Elizabeth Hamilton: With a Selection from her Correspondence, and Other Unpublished Writings.* Ed. E. Benger. 2 vols. London: Longman, Hurst, Rees, Orme, and Brown, 1818.

Hansard, Thomas C. *Typographia.* London: Baldwin, Cradock, and Joy, 1825.

Hardcastle, Ephraim [William Henry Pyne]. *Wine and Walnuts; or, After Dinner Chit-Chat.* 2 vols. London: Longman, Hurst, Rees, Orme, and Brown, 1823.

Harley, George. *A Guide to Landscape Drawing in Pencil and Chalk.* London: George Rowney and Co., 1848.

Harris, James. *Hermes; or, A Philosophical Inquiry Concerning Language and Universal Grammar.* London: H. Woodfall for J. Nourse and P. Vaillant, 1751.

Harris, John. *Punctuation Personified; or, Pointing Made Easy. By Mr. Stops.* London: J. Harris and Son, 1824.

Harrison, Walter. *A New and Universal History, Description and Survey* [. . .] *of London.* London: J. Cooke, 1776.

Hawksmoor, Nicholas. *A Short Historical Account of London-Bridge; with A Proposition for a new Stone-Bridge at Westminster.* London: J. Wilcox, 1736.

Haywood, Eliza. *Fantomina: or, Love in a Maze. Being a Secret History of an Amour Between Two Persons of Condition.* London: D. Browne jun. and S. Chapman, 1725.

———. *The Fatal Secret; or, Constancy in Distress.* 3rd ed. London: D. Browne jun. and S. Chapman, 1725.

———. *Lasselia; or, The Self-Abandon'd. A Novel.* London: D. Browne jun. and S. Chapman, 1724.

———. *Love in Excess; or, The Fatal Enquiry, a Novel.* London: W. Chetwood and R. Francklin and sold by J. Roberts, 1719.

———. *Love in Excess; or, The Fatal Inquiry* (1719). Ed. David Oakleaf. Peterborough, Ont.: Broadview Press, 1994, 1996.

———. *Secret Histories, Novels, and Poems, Written by Mrs. Eliza Haywood.* 2nd ed. 4 vols. London: D. Browne jun. and S. Chapman, 1725.

Hazlitt, William. *Lectures on the English Comic Writers.* London: Taylor and Hessey, 1819.

H. C. *Aristotle's Rhetoric; or, The True Grounds and Principles of Oratory; Shewing, the Right Art of Pleading and Speaking in full Assemblies and Courts of Judicature.* London: T. B. for Randal Taylor, 1686.

Heely, Joseph. *Letters on the Beauties of Hagley, Envil, and the Leasowes*. 2 vols. London: R. Baldwin, 1777.

Hentzner, Paul. *A Journey into England. By Paul Hentzner, In the Year M.D.XC.VIII.* Trans. Horace Walpole. [Twickenham, London]: Strawberry-Hill, 1757.

The History of Printing. London: Society for Promoting Christian Knowledge, 1855.

Howell, James. *Londinopolis; An Historicall Discourse or Perlustration Of the City of London*. London: J. Streater for Henry Twiford et al., 1657.

Howlett, Bartholomew. *A Selection of Views in the County of Lincoln* (1805). Sleaford, Lincolnshire: Heritage Lincolnshire, 2001.

Hunt, T. F. *Half a Dozen Hints on Picturesque Domestic Architecture, in A Series of Designs for Gate Lodges, Gamekeepers' Cottages, and Other Rural Residence*. London: Longman et al., 1825.

Hurlstone, Thomas. *Crotchet-Lodge: A Farce in Two Acts. As Performed at the Theatre-Royal, Covent-Garden*. London: T. N. Longman, 1796.

Jefferson, Thomas. *The Papers of Thomas Jefferson Digital Edition*. Ed. Barbara B. Oberg and J. Jefferson Looney. Charlottesville: University of Virginia Press, Rotunda, 2008. http://rotunda.upress.virginia.edu/founders/TSJN.html.

Johnson, John. *Typographia; or, The Printers' Instructor*. 2 vols. London: Longman et al., 1824.

Johnson, Richard. *Grammatical Commentaries; being an Apparatus To a New National Grammar, by way of Animadversion upon the Falsities, Obscurities, Redundancies, and Defects of Lilly's System Now in Use*. London: S. Keble et al., 1706.

Johnson, Samuel. *A Dictionary of the English Language; In which the Words are Deduced from their Originals, and Illustrated in their Different Significations by Examples from the Best Writers. To which are Prefixed a History of the Language, and all English Grammar*. 2 vols. London: W. Strahan for J. and P. Knapton et al., 1755.

———. *Rasselas; Prince of Abissinia. A tale.* [. . .] *A New Edition*. 2 vols. London: T. Johnstone, W. Taylor, and J. Davies, 1790.

Jones, Harriet. *Belmont Lodge. A Novel*. 2 vols. London: Minerva Press, 1799.

Jones, John. *Practical Phonography; or, The New Art of Rightly Speling* [*sic*] *and Writing Words By the Sound thereof* (1701). Ed. Eilert Ekwall. Halle: Max Niemeyer, 1907.

Kersey, John. *Dictionarium Anglo-Britannicum; or, A General English Dictionary*. London: J. Wilde, 1708.

———. *Dictionarium Anglo-Britannicum*. [. . .] 2nd ed., corr. London: Printed by J. Wilde, 1715.

———. *Dictionarium Anglo-Britannicum*. [. . .] 3rd ed., corr. and enl.. London: J. Phillips, 1721.

King, Richard. *The Complete Modern London Spy, For the present Year, 1781*. [. . .] London: Alex. Hogg et al., [1781].

Kip, Johannes, and Leonard Knyff. *Britannia Illustrata; or, Views of Several of the Queens Palaces, as Also of the Principal seats of the Nobility and Gentry of Great Britain, Curiously Engraven on 80 Copper Plates*. London: D. Mortier, 1707.

Knight, Richard Payne. *An Analytical Inquiry into the Principles of Taste*. 4th ed. London: T. Payne, 1808.

———. *The Landscape, A Didactic Poem. In Three Books. Addressed to Uvedale Price, Esq*. London: W. Bulmer for G. Nicol, 1794.

Knight, William. *The Life of William Wordsworth*. 3 vols. Edinburgh: W. Patterson, 1889.

Laing, D. *Hints for Dwellings: Consisting of Original designs for Cottages, Farm-Houses, Villas, andc. Plain and Ornamental; With Plans to Each: in which strict attention is paid to unite convenience and elegance with economy. Including some Designs for Town Houses.* [. . .] *A new edition.* London: S. Gosnell for J. Taylor, 1818.

Langley, Batty. *The Builder's Chest-Book; or, A Complete Key to the Five Orders of Columns in Architecture.* London: J. Wilcox, 1727.

La Roche, Sophie von. *Sophie in London 1786, being the Diary of Sophie v. la Roche.* Trans. Clare Williams. Foreword by G. M. Trevelyan. London: Jonathan Cape, 1933.

Lemon, George William. *English Etymology.* London: G. Robinson, 1783.

A Letter Written from Dover, to the Commissioners for the Customs, London, May 26. Relating certain Passages of His Majesties Arrival and Reception There. London: Thomas Johnson, 1660.

Lichtenberg, Georg Christoph. "Über den deutschen roman" (1775). In *Lichtenberg: Aphorismen, Essays, Briefe.* Ed. K. Batt. Leipzig: Dieterich, 1970.

Lightoler, Timothy. *The Gentleman and Farmer's Architect.* London: Robert Sayer, 1762.

The Literary Pocket-Book; or, Companion for the Lover of Nature and Art, 1822. To be continued annually. London: C. and J. Ollier, 1822.

Locke, John. *An Essay Concerning Humane Understanding.* London: Tho. Basset, 1690.

London Bridge. Assignments of Leases in the "middle east" part of London Bridge, 1666–86. Guildhall Library.

London Bridge, Householders. Guildhall Ms. 2785.

Loudon, J. C. *An Encyclopædia of Cottage, Farm, and Villa Architecture and Furniture.* London: Longman, Rees, Orme, Brown, Green, and Longman, 1833. Rpt. Cambridge: Cambridge University Press, 2014.

———. *An Encyclopædia of Cottage, Farm, and Villa Architecture and Furniture.* [. . .] *A New Edition, With Numerous Corrections, and with Many of the Plates Re-engraved.* London: Longman, Rees, Orme, Brown, Green, and Longman, 1836.

———. *A Treatise on Forming, Improving, and Managing Country Residences; and on the Choice of Situations Appropriate to Every Class of Purchasers.* 2 vols. London: Longman, Hurst, Rees, and Orme, 1806.

Lowth, Robert. *A Short Introduction to English Grammar: With Critical Notes* [1762]. *A New Edition, Corrected.* London: J. Dodsley, T. Cadell, 1775.

Luckombe, Philip. *The Beauties of England: or, a Comprehensive View of the Antiquities of this Kingdom; the Seats of the Nobility and Gentry;* [. . .] *Intended as a Travelling Pocket Companion.* London: L. Davis and C. Reymers, 1764.

———. *A Concise History of the Origin and Progress of Printing; with Practical Instructions to the Trade in General. Compiled from those who have wrote on this curious art.* London: W. Adlard and J. Browne, 1770.

———. *The History and Art of Printing, in Two Parts.* London: W. Adlard and J. Browne for J. Johnson, 1771.

Macaulay, Thomas Babington. "*The Pilgrim's Progress, with a Life of John Bunyan,* by Robert Southey, Esq., LL.D., Poet-Laureate. Illustrated with Engravings. 8vo. London. 1830" (1832). In *Reviews and Essays from "The Edinburgh."* London: Ward, Lock, and Tyler, [1874–78]. Pp. 239–49.

Mackintosh, Duncan, and His Two Daughters. *A Plain, Rational Essay on English*

Grammar: The Main Object of Which is to Point Out a Plain, Rational and Permanent Standard of Pronunciation. To which is given, A Gamut or Key, Still more simple, plain and easy than that given to Music. [. . .] Boston: Manning and Loring, 1797.

Macky, John. *A Journey through England. In Familiar Letters from a Gentleman Here, to His Friend Abroad.* 2 vols. London: J. Pemberton, 1722.

Maitland, William. *The History and Survey of London from its Foundation to the Present Time. In Two Volumes.* London: T. Osborne, 1760.

———. *The History and Survey of London from its Foundation to the Present Time. In Two Volumes.* London: T. Osborne and J. Shipton et al., 1761.

———. *The History of London, from its Foundations by the Romans, to the Present Time.* [. . .] London: Samuel Richardson, 1739.

Marchant, John. *A New and Complete English Dictionary* [. . .]*: wherein difficult words and technical terms, in all faculties and professions* [. . .] *are fully explained.* [. . .] London: J. Fuller, 1760.

Marshall, William. *Planting and Ornamental Gardening; A Practical Treatise.* London: J. Dodsley, 1785.

Mason, George. *An Essay on Design in Gardening. First Published in MDCCLXVIII. Now Greatly Augmented.* London: Printed by C. Roworth for Benjamin and John White, 1795.

Mason, William. *The English Garden: A Poem. Book the First.* London: R. Horsfield et al., 1772.

Mavor, William. *New Description of Blenheim, The Seat of His Grace the Duke of Marlborough.* London: T. Cabell et al., 1793.

Meiklejohn, J. M. D. *The English Language: Its Grammar, History, and Literature.* Edinburgh and London: William Blackwood and Sons, 1886.

Minto, William. *A Manual of English Prose Literature, Biographical and Critical, Designed Mainly to Show Characteristics of Style* (1872). 3rd ed. Edinburgh and London: William Blackwood and Sons, 1886.

Miège, Guy. *English Grammar.* London: Richard Wild, 1688.

Miller, J. *The Country Gentleman's Architect, in a Great Variety of New Designs; for Cottages, Farm-Houses, Country-Houses, Villas, Lodges for Park or Garden Entrances, and Ornamental Wooden Gates.* [. . .] London: J. and J. Taylor, 1787.

More, Hannah. *Memoirs of the Life and Correspondence of Mrs. Hannah More: By William Roberts, Esq.* 3rd ed. 4 vols. London: R. B. Seeley and W. Burnside, 1835.

Morgan, William. *Ogilby's and Morgan's Pocket-Book of the Roads, with their Computed and Measured Distances, and the Distinction of Market and Post-Towns.* [. . .] 10th ed., corr. London: J. Brotherton et al., 1745.

Moritz, Karl Philipp von. *Travels, Chiefly on Foot, through Several Parts of England, in 1782. Described in Letters to a Friend. Translated from the German, by a Lady.* London: G. G. and J. Robinson, 1795.

Morris, F. O., ed. *A Series of Picturesque Views of Seats of the Noblemen and Gentlemen of Great Britain and Ireland with Descriptive and Historical Letterpress.* 6 vols. London: William MacKenzie, [ca.1880].

Moxon, Joseph. *Mechanick Exercises on the Whole Art of Printing* (1683–84). Ed. Herbert Davis and Harry Carter. London: Oxford University Press, 1958.

Murray, Lindley. *English Grammar* (1795). Menston: Scholar Press, 1968.

———. *An English Grammar: Comprehending The Principles and Rules of the Lan-*

guage. [. . .] 2nd ed. 2 vols. York: Thomas Wilson and Son for Longman, Hurst et al., 1809.

A New and Compleat Survey of London, in Ten Parts. 2 vols. London: S. Lyne, 1742.

A New English Dictionary, Containing a Brief and Concise Explication of Most Words in the English Language. Glasgow: C. Hutcheson, 1759.

Newbery, John. *A Pocket Dictionary, or, Complete English Expositor* [. . .] 3rd ed., greatly improved. London: J. Newbery, 1765.

———. *A Spelling-Dictionary of the English Language, to which is Prefixed a Compendious English Grammar.* London: J. Newbery, 1757.

Nichols, John. *Literary Anecdotes of the Eighteenth Century.* 6 vols. London: Nichols, Son, and Bentley, 1812.

[Nichols, John Gough.] *London Pageants. I. Accounts of Fifty-Five Royal Processions and Entertainments in the City of London; Chiefly Extracted from Contemporary Writers. II. A Bibliographical List of Lord Mayors' Pageants.* London: J. B. Nichols and Son, 1831.

Norden, John. *Civitas Londini. This Description of the Moste Famous Citty London was pperformed in* [. . .] *1600* [. . .] *By the Industry of John Norden.* London: London Topographical Society, 1961.

Ogilby, John. *The Entertainment of His Most Excellent Majestie Charles II, in His Passage through the City of London to his Coronation: Containing an exact Accompt of the whole Solemnity; the Triumphal Arches, and Cavalcade, delineated in Sculpture; the Speeches and Impresses illustrated from Antiquity.* [. . .] London: Richard Mariot and Thomas Dring, 1662.

Palmer, Samuel. *The General History of Printing, From Its first Invention in the City of Mentz, to Its first Progress and Propagation thro' the most celebrated Cities in Europe.* [. . .] London: S. Palmer and J. Roberts, 1732.

Papworth, John B. *Rural Residences, Consisting of A Series of Designs for Cottages, Decorated Cottages, Small Villas, and other Ornamental Buildings.* [. . .] London: J. Diggens for R. Ackermann, 1818.

Partington, C. F. *The Printer's Complete Guide: Containing a Sketch of the History and Progress of Printing, to its Present State of Improvement; Details of its Several Departments; Numerous Schemes of Imposition; Modern Improvements in Stereotype, Presses, and Machinery &c. &c.* London: Sherwood, Gilbert, and Piper, 1825.

Peacham, Henry. *The Garden of Eloquence, Conteyning the Figures of Grammer and Rhetorick.* [. . .] London: H. Jackson, 1577.

Peacock, William. *The Polite Repository, or Pocket Companion. Containing an Almanack,* [. . .] *and various other articles of useful information. Ornamented with Elegant Engravings.* [. . .] London: T. Rickaby for W. Peacock, 1787 [same for 1791, 1796, 1797, 1799, 1800, 1831 eds.].

Pennant, Thomas. *The Antiquities of London: Comprising Views and Historical Descriptions of its Principal Buildings; Also Anecdotes of Eminent Persons Connected Therewith.* London: J. Coxhead, et al., 1814.

———. *The Journey from Chester to London.* London: B. White, 1782.

———. *A Journey from London to the Isle of Wight.* 4 vols. London: E. Hardinge, 1801.

Pepys, Samuel. *The Diary of Samuel Pepys.* Ed. Robert Latham and William Matthews. 11 vols. London: Bell and Hyman, 1970–83.

Perry, William. *The Royal Standard English Dictionary: in which the words are not only rationally divided into syllables, accurately accented, and their part of speech prop-*

erly distinguished; but likewise by a key to this work. Boston: Thomas and Andrews et al., [1777?].

Phillips, Edward. *The New World of English Words; or, A General Dictionary: Containing the Interpretations of Such Hard Words as Are Derived From Other Languages.* [. . .] London: E. Tyler for Nath. Brooke, 1658.

———. *The New World of Words; or, Universal English Dictionary.* [. . .] *The Sixth Edition, revised, corrected, and improved; with the addition of near twenty thousand words* [. . .] *by J. Kersey.* London: J. Phillips et al., 1706.

———. *The New World of Words; or, Universal English Dictionary.* 7th ed. London: J. Phillips et al., 1720.

Picturesque Views of the Principal Seats of the Nobility and Gentry in England and Wales. By the most eminent British artists. With a description of each seat. London: Harrison, 1786–88.

Piozzi, Hester Lynch. *British Synonymy; or, An Attempt at Regulating the Choice of Words in Familiar Conversation.* 2 vols. London: G. G. and J. Robinson, 1794.

A Pocket Dictionary; or, Complete English Expositor: Shewing Readily the Part of Speech to which Each Word Belongs. London: J. Newbery, 1753.

———. 3rd ed., greatly improved. London: J. Newbery, 1765.

A Pocket-Guide to the English Traveller: Being a Compleat Survey and Admeasurement Of all the Principal Roads and most Considerable Cross-Roads in England and Wales. In One Hundred Copper-Plates. London: J. Tonson, J. Watts, 1719.

Pococke, Richard. "Travels through England." In *The Genius of the Place: The English Landscape Garden, 1620–1820.* Ed. John Dixon Hunt and Peter Willis. New York: Harper and Row, 1975. Pp. 264–67.

Powys, Caroline Lybbe. *Passages from the Diaries of Mrs. Philip Lybbe Powys of Hardwick House, Oxon. A.D. 1756 to 1808.* Ed. Emily J. Climenson. London: Longmans, Green, 1899.

Price, O. *English orthographie.* Oxford: Francis Titon, 1668.

———. *English Orthography* (1668). Menston: Scolar Press, 1972.

Price, Uvedale. *Essays on the Picturesque, as Compared with the Sublime and the Beautiful; and, on the Use of Studying Pictures, for the Purpose of Improving Real Landscape.* 3 vols. London: J. Mawman, 1810.

A Professional Survey of the Old and New London Bridges, and their Approaches, including Historical Memorials of Both Structures; with Remarks on the Probable Effects of the Changes in Progress on the Navigation of the Thames. With a Portrait of the Late John Rennie, Esq. And Thirteen other Illustrative Plates. 2nd ed. London: M. Salmon, 1831.

Radcliffe, Ann. *The Italian; or, The Confessional of the Black Penitents, a Romance.* 3vols. London: T. Cadell Jun. and W. Davies, 1797.

———. *The Italian* (1797). Ed. Frederick Garber. Oxford: Oxford University Press, 1968, 1981.

———. *The Mysteries of Udolpho, A Romance; Interspersed with Some Pieces of Poetry.* 2nd ed. 4 vols. London: G. G. and J. Robinson, 1794.

———. *The Mysteries of Udolpho* (1794). Ed. Bonamy Dobrée. Intro. Terry Castle. Oxford: Oxford University Press, 1998.

———. *The Romance of the Forest: Interspersed with Some Pieces of Poetry.* 2nd ed. 3 vols. London: T. Hookham and J. Carpenter, 1792.

Rathgeb, Jacob. *A True and Faithful Narrative of the bathing excursion, which His Serene Highness Frederick, duke of Wirtemberg, count Mümppelgart, knight of the*

Garter, made a few years ago to the far-famed kingdom of England; as it was noted down daily in the most concise manner possible at his Highness's gracious command by his private secretary (Jacob Rathgeb), who accompanied him. [. . .] *In England as seen by foreigners in the days of Elizabeth and James the First.* Ed. William Brenchley Rye. London: John Russell Smith, 1865.

Ray, John. *A Collection of English Proverbs, Digested into a convenient Method for the speedy finding any one upon occasion; with Short Annotations. Whereunto are added Local Proverbs with their Explications, Old Proverbial Rhythmes, Less known or Exotick Proverbial Sentences, and Scottish Proverbs. By J. R., M.A. and Fellow of the Royal Society.* Cambridge: John Hayes for W. Morden, 1670.

Reed, Joseph. *Saint Peter's Lodge: A Serio-comi-legendary Tale. In Hudibrastic Verse. By the Author of the* Register-Office. London: L. Davis, J. and T. Egerton, J. Bew, 1786.

Repton, Humphry. An album of engraved views from *Peacock's Polite Repository.* England, ca. 1790–1831. [graphic] Lewis Walpole Library 75 R299 788.

———. *The Art of Landscape Gardening by Humphry Repton Esq. Including his Sketches and Hints on Landscape Gardening and Theory and Practice of Landscape Gardening.* Ed. John Nolen. London: Archibald Constable; New York: Houghton Mifflin, 1907.

———. *An Enquiry into the Changes of Taste in Landscape Gardening. To Which are Added, Some Observations on its Theory and Practice, Including a Defence of the Art.* London: J. Taylor, 1806.

———. *Fragments on the Theory and Practice of Landscape Gardening, Including some remarks on Grecian and Gothic Architecture* [. . .] *By H. Repton, assisted by his son J. Adey Repton, F.A.S.* London: T. Bensley and Son for J. Taylor, 1816.

———. *Humphry Repton: The Red Books for Brandsbury and Glemham Hall* (1789, 1791). Intro. Stephen Daniels. Washington, DC: Dumbarton Oaks Research Library and Collection, 1994.

———. *Humphry Repton's Red Book for Blaise Castle* (1795). Bristol: Friends of Blaise, n.d.

———. *Humphry Repton's Red Books for Panshanger and Tewin Water, Hertfordshire, 1799–1800.* Intro. Twigs Way. Hertfordshire: Hertfordshire Record Society, 2011.

———. *Memoirs.* Ed. Ann Gore and George Carter. Wilby, Norwich: Michael Russell, 2005.

———. *Observations on the Theory and Practice of Landscape Gardening.* London: T. Bensley for J. Taylor, 1803.

———. *Observations on the Theory and Practice of Landscape Gardening.* Ed. John Martin Robinson. Oxford: Phaidon Press Ltd, 1980.

———. *Sketches and Hints on Landscape Gardening, collected from designs and observations now in the possession of the different noblemen and gentlemen for whose use they were originally made: the whole tending to establish fixed principles in the art of laying out ground* (1795). In *The Landscape Gardening and Landscape Architecture of the Late Humphry Repton, Esq.* Ed. J. C. Loudon. London: Longman; Edinburgh: A. and C. Black, 1840.

———. *Variety: A Collection of Essays. Written in the Year 1787.* London: T. Cadell, 1788.

Reynolds, Sir Joshua. *Discourses on Art.* Ed. Robert R. Wark. New Haven: Yale University Press, 1975.

Richardson, Samuel. *Clarissa; or, The History of a Young Lady: Comprehending The most Important Concerns of Private Life; And particularly shewing, The Distresses that may attend the Misconduct Both of Parents and Children, In Relation to Marriage*. 7 vols. London: S. Richardson, 1747–48.

———. *Clarissa; or, The History of a Young Lady*. [. . .] 2nd ed. 8 vols. London: S. Richardson, 1749.

———. *Clarissa; or, The History of a Young Lady*. [. . .] *In Eight Volumes. To Each of which is added A Table of Contents. The Third Edition, in which Many Passages and some Letters are restored from the Original Manuscripts. And to which is added, An ample Collection of such of the moral and Instructive Sentiments interspersed throughout the Work, as may be presumed to be of general Use and Service*. 8 vols. London: S. Richardson, 1751.

———. *Clarissa; or, The History of a Young Lady*. [. . .] 4th ed. 8 vols. London: S. Richardson, 1759.

———. *Clarissa; or, The History of a Young Lady*. [. . .] 5th ed. 8 vols. London: J. Rivington et al., 1764.

———. *The History of Clarissa Harlowe*. Vols. 1–8 of *The British Novelists: With an Essay; and Prefaces, Biographical and Critical, by Mrs. Barbauld*. Ed. Anna Lætitia Barbauld. London: F. C. and J. Rivington et al., 1810.

———. *The Correspondence of Samuel Richardson, Author of Pamela, Clarissa, and Sir Charles Grandison. Selected from the Original Manuscripts, Bequeathed by Him to His Family, To which are prefixed, A Biographical Account of that Author, and Observations on His Writings. By Anna Lætitia Barbauld*. 6 vols. London: Richard Phillips, 1804.

———. *The History of Sir Charles Grandison, in a Series of Letters Published from the Originals, By the Editor of Pamela and Clarissa*. 3rd ed. 8 vols. London: S. Richardson, 1754.

———. *The History of Sir Charles Grandison, In a Series of Letters published from the Originals by the Editor of Pamela and Clarissa* (1753). 6 vols. Shakespeare Head Edition. Oxford: Basil Blackwell, 1931.

———. *Sir Charles Grandison* (1753). Ed. Jocelyn Harris. 4 vols. Oxford: Oxford University Press, 1972.

———. *Pamela; or, Virtue Rewarded. In a Series of Familiar Letters from a Beautiful Young Damsel, to her Parents*. [. . .] 2nd ed. 4 vols. London: C. Rivington and J. Osborn, 1741.

———. *Pamela* (1740). Ed. Peter Sabor. Intro. Margaret A. Doody. Harmondsworth: Penguin, 1980.

———. *Pamela* (1740). Ed. Thomas Keymer and Alice Wakely. Oxford: Oxford University Press, 2001.

———. *The Richardson-Stinstra Correspondence and Stinstra's Prefaces to Clarissa*. Ed. William C. Slattery. Carbondale and Edwardsville: Southern Illinois University Press; London and Amsterdam: Feffer and Simons, 1969.

———. *Samuel Richardson's Published Commentary on Clarissa*. Ed. Florian Stuber and Margaret Anne Doody. 3 vols. London: Pickering and Chatto, 1998.

Robertson, Joseph. *An Essay on Punctuation*. 2nd ed. London: J. Walter, 1786.

Robinson, P. F. *Designs for Gate Cottages, Lodges, and Park Entrances, in Various Styles, from the Humblest to the Castellated*. 3rd ed. London: Henry G. Bohn, 1837.

Rodwell, G. Herbert. *Old London Bridge: A Romance of the Sixteenth Century* (1845). 2 vols. London: George Routledge and Sons, [1887].

Savage, William. *A Dictionary of the Art of Printing*. London: Longman, Brown, Green, and Longmans, 1841.

———. *Practical Hints on Decorative Printing*. London: William Savage, 1818.

Scott, Walter. *Lives of the Novelists*. 2 vols. Paris: A. and W. Galignani, 1825.

———. Unsigned review of Jane Austen's *Emma*. *Quarterly Review* 14 (March 1816): 188–201.

Scott, William. *A Short System of English Grammar; with Examples of Improper and Inelegant Construction, and Scotticisms*. [. . .] Edinburgh: Peter Hill, 1793.

Shenstone, William. *The Works in Verse and Prose, of William Shenstone, Esq.* 2 vols. London: R. and J. Dodsley, 1764.

Sheridan, Thomas. *A Complete Dictionary of the English Language, both with Regard to Sound and Meaning* [. . .] *To which is prefixed a prosodial grammar*. 2nd ed. London: C. Dilly, 1789.

———. *A Complete Dictionary of the English Language*. [. . .]. 4th ed. London: C. Dilly, 1797.

———. *A Discourse Delivered in The Theatre at Oxford, in The Senate-House at Cambridge, and At Spring-Garden in London*. [. . .] *Being Introductory to His Course of Lectures on Elocution and the English Language*. [. . .] London: A. Millar et al., 1759.

A Short Historical Account of Bristol Bridge; [. . .] *Likewise, An Account of some Bridges of Note in England*. [. . .] Bristol: E. Ward, 1759.

Smith, Charlotte. *The Old Manor House* (1793). Ed. Anne Henry Ehrenpreis. London: Oxford University Press, 1969.

Smith, John. *The Printer's Grammar: Wherein are Exhibited, Examined, and Explained, The Superficies, Gradation, and Properties of The different Sorts and Sizes of Metal Types, cast by Letter Founders*. London: W. Owen, 1755.

———. *The Printer's Grammar: Containing A Concise History of the Origin of Printing;* [. . .] *Chiefly collected from Smith's Edition*. [. . .] London: Printed by L. Wayland, 1787.

Some Rules for Speaking and Action; To be observed At the Bar, in the Pulpit, and the Senate, and by every one that Speaks in Public. In a Letter to a Friend. [. . .] 3rd ed. London: W. Mears, 1716.

Spencer, Nathaniel. *The Complete English Traveller; or, A New Survey and Description of England and Wales*. [. . .] London: J. Cooke, 1771.

Stanhope, Philip Dormer, 4th Earl of Chesterfield. *Lord Chesterfield's Letters*. Ed. David Roberts. Oxford: Oxford University Press, 2008.

Steel, David, Jr. *Elements of Punctuation: Containing Remarks on an "Essay on Punctuation;" and Critical Observations on some Passages in Milton*. London: G. G. J. and J. Robinson et al., 1786.

Sterne, Laurence. *The Life and Opinions of Tristram Shandy, Gentleman* (1759–67). Ed. Ian Campbell Ross. Oxford: Oxford University Press, 1983.

Stops, Mr. *Punctuation Personified; or, Pointing Made Easy. By Mr. Stops*. London: J. Harris and Son, 1824.

Stow, John. *A Svrvay of London: Containing, the Originall, Antiquitie, Encrease, and more Moderne Estate of the sayd Famous Citie*. [. . .] *Written in the yeare 1598. By Iohn Stow, Citizen of London*. London: John Wolfe, 1598.

Stow, John. *A Survey of the Cities of London and Westminster* [. . .] *Corrected, Improved, and very much Enlarged* [. . .] *By John Strype. In Six Books*. [. . .] London: A. Churchill et al., 1720.

Stow, William. *Remarks on London; Being an Exact Survey of the Cities of London and Westminster* [. . .] London: T. Norris et al., 1722.

Stower, Caleb. *The Printer's Grammar.* London: B. Crosby, 1808.

———. *The Printer's Manual, An Abridgment of Stower's Grammar* (1817). Intro. John Bidwell. New York: Garland Publishing, 1981.

Stuart, Robert. *A Dictionary of Architecture; Historical, Descriptive, Topographical, Decorative, Theoretical, and Mechanical. Alphabetically Arranged, Familiarly Explained, and Adapted to the Comprehension of Workmen* [. . .] 3 vols. London: Jones and Co., [1830].

Sun Insurance Office. *Memorandum Book, c. 1710–1830*. Guildhall Library Ms. 15,057.

Swift, Jonathan. *A Proposal for Correcting, Improving and Ascertaining the English Tongue.* 2nd ed. London: Benj. Tooke, 1712.

———. *Gulliver's Travels* (1726). Ed. Paul Turner. Oxford: Oxford University Press, 1994.

———. *On Poetry: A Rapsody.* "Printed at Dublin, and re-printed at London: and sold by J. Huggonson [. . .]," 1733.

[Thomson, Richard.] *The Chronicles of London Bridge by an Antiquary.* London: Smith, Elder, and Col, 1827.

Timperley, Charles Henry. *The Printers' Manual.* London: H. Johnson, 1838.

Tory, Geofroy. *Champ Fleury ou l'Art et science de la proportion des lettres.* Reproduction phototypique de l'édition princeps de Paris, 1529. Ed. Gustave Cohen. Paris: Charles Bosse, 1921.

———. *Champ Fleury. Wherein is contained the Art & Science of the proper & true Proportions of Attic Letters, otherwise called Antique Letters, and in common speech Roman Letters, proportioned according to the human Body and Face* (1529). Trans. George B. Ives. New York: Grolier Club, 1927; New York: Dover, 1967.

A Treatise of Stops, Points, or Pauses (1680). Menston: Scolar Press, 1968.

Tuckerman, Bayard. *A History of English Prose Fiction.* New York: G. P. Putnams's Sons, Knickerbocker Press, 1886.

Upcott, William. *A Bibliographic Account of the Principal Works Relating to British Topography.* 3 vols. London: Richard and Arthur Taylor, 1818.

Van Winkle, C. S. *The Printer's Guide; or, An Introduction to the Art of Printing: including an Essay on Punctuation, and Remarks on Orthography.* New York: C. S. Van Winkle, 1818.

Walker, John. *A Dictionary of the English Language.* London: T. Becket, 1775. [also 1823 ed.]

Wallington, Nehemiah. *Historical Notices of Events Occurring Chiefly in the Reign of Charles I. By Nehemiah Walllington, of St. Leonard's, Eastcheap, London. Edited from the Original Mss. with Notes and Illustrations.* Ed. R. Webb. 2 vols. London: Richard Bentley, 1869.

Walpole, Horace. *The Castle of Otranto, A Story. Translated by William Marshal, Gent. From the Original Italian of Onuphrio Muralto, Canon of the Church of St. Nicholas at Otranto.* London: Tho. Lownds, [1764].

———. *A Description of the Villa of Mr. Horace Walpole at Strawberry-Hill near Twickenham, Middlesex. With an Inventory of the Furniture, Pictures, Curiosities, andc.* Strawberry-Hill: Thomas Kirgate, 1784.

———. *The History of the Modern Taste in Gardening* (1770, 1782). Intro. John Dixon Hunt. New York: Ursus Press, 1995.

———. *The Yale Edition of Horace Walpole's Correspondence.* Ed. W. S. Lewis. 48 vols. New Haven: Yale University Press, 1937–83.

Ward, John. *Four Essays upon the English Language; Namely, I. Observations on the Orthography. II. Rules for the Division of Syllables. III. The Use of the Articles. IV. The Formation of the Verbs, and their Analogy with the Latin.* London: J. Ward, 1758.

Ward, William. *An Essay on Grammar, as it may be applied to the English Language. In Two Treatises.* [. . .] London: Robert Horsfield, 1765.

Watson, James. *The History of the Art of Printing: Containing an Account of It's [sic] Invention and Progress in Europe: With The Names of the Famous Printers, The Places of Their Birth, And the Works printed by Them. And A Preface by the Publisher to The Printers in Scotland.* Edinburgh: James Watson, 1713.

Watts, Isaac. *The Art of Reading and Writing English; or, The Chief Principles and Rules of Pronouncing Our Mother-Tongue, Both in Prose and Verse.* 2nd ed. London: John Clark et al., 1722.

Watts, William. *The Seats of the Nobility and Gentry, in a Collection of the Most Interesting and Picturesque Views, engraved by W. Watts, from Drawings by the Most Eminent Artists. With Descriptions of Each View.* Chelsea: W. Watts, 1779 -1786.

Whately, Thomas. *Observations on Modern Gardening, Illustrated by Descriptions.* London: T. Payne, 1770.

Wilkins, John. *An Essay Towards a Real Character, and a Philosophical Language.* London: Samuel Gellibrand and John Martyn, 1668.

Woolgar, William. *Youth's Faithful Monitor; or, The Young Man's Best Companion. Containing A compendious English Grammar, proper for all Youth to be acquainted with.* [. . .] *The Fifth Edition, Improved, enlarged and corrected by John Wright, Gent.* [. . .] London: Hawes et al., 1769.

Wright, William. *Grotesque Architecture, or, Rural Amusement; Consisting of Plans, Elevations, and Sections, for Huts, Retreats, Summer and Winter Hermitages, Terminaries, Chinese, Gothic, and Natural Grottos, Cascades, Baths, Mosques, Moresque Pavilions, Grotesque and Rustic Seats, Green Houses, &c.* [. . .] London: Henry Webley, 1767.

Secondary Sources

Andrews, Malcolm. *The Search for the Picturesque: Landscape Aesthetics and Tourism in Britain, 1760–1800.* Aldershot: Scolar Press, 1987.

———, ed. *The Picturesque: Literary Sources and Documents.* 3 vols. Robertsbridge: Helm Information, 1994.

Arnold, Dana, ed. *The Georgian Country House: Architecture, Landscape and Society.* Stroud, Gloucestershire: Sutton Publishing, 1998, 2003.

Auerbach, Nina. *Romantic Imprisonment.* New York: Columbia University Press, 1985.

Bachelard, Gaston. *The Poetics of Space* (1958). Trans. Maria Jolas. Boston: Beacon Press, 1964.

Baker, Nicholson. *The Size of Thoughts: Essays and Other Lumber.* New York: Vintage Books, 1997.

Banfield, Ann. *Unspeakable Sentences: Narration and Representation in the Language of Fiction.* Boston: Routledge and Kegan Paul, 1982.

Barchas, Janine. *Graphic Design, Print Culture, and the Eighteenth-Century Novel.* Cambridge: Cambridge University Press, 2003.

Barker, Nicolas. "Typography and the Meaning of Words: The Revolution in the Layout of Books in the Eighteenth Century." In *Buch und Buchhandel in Europa im achtzehnten Jahrhundert: The Book and the Book Trade in Eighteenth-Century Europe*. Ed. G. Barber and B. Fabian. Hamburg: Dr. Ernst Hauswedell and Co., 1981. Pp. 126–65.

Barrell, John. *The Dark Side of the Landscape: The Rural Poor in English Painting, 1730–1840*. Cambridge: Cambridge University Press, 1980.

———. *The Idea of Landscape and the Sense of Place, 1730–1840: An Approach to the Poetry of John Clare*. Cambridge: Cambridge University Press, 1972.

Baudin, Fernand. "The Visual Editing of Texts." *Visible Language* 18 (1984): 81–86.

Baugh, Albert C., and Thomas Cable. "The Appeal to Authority, 1650–1800." *A History of the English Language*. 5th ed. Upper Saddle River, NJ: Prentice Hall, 2001.

Beck, Hans-Ulrich. "Pieter Molyn and His Duplicate Drawings." *Master Drawings* 35:4 (Winter 1997): 341–66.

Bennett, Benjamin. *Beyond Theory: Eighteenth-Century German Literature and the Poetics of Irony*. Ithaca: Cornell University Press, 1993.

Berkson, William. "Readability and Revival: The Case of Caslon." *Printing History* 10 (July 2011): 3–24.

Bermingham, Ann, ed. *Sensation & Sensibility: Viewing Gainsborough's "Cottage Door."* New Haven: Yale University Press, 2005.

Besant, G. B. *London Bridge*. London: Selwyn and Blount, 1927.

Bibbins, Mark. "In the Corner of a Room Where You Would Never Look." *New Yorker*, 10 February 2014, 71.

Bland, Mark. "The Appearance of the Text in Early Modern England." *Text* 11 (1998): 91–154.

Booth, Stephen, ed. *Shakespeare's Sonnets*. New Haven: Yale University Press, 1977.

Bornstein, Diane. *Readings in the Theory of Grammar from the 17th to the 20th Century*. Cambridge: Winthrop, 1976.

Börsch-Supan, Helmut. "Caspar David Friedrich's Landscapes with Self-Portraits." *Burlington Magazine* 114:834 (September 1972): 620–30.

Bowers, Fredson. *Principles of Bibliographic Description*. Princeton: Princeton University Press, 1949, 1986; Winchester: St Paul's Bibliographies no. 15, 1986.

Brandon, Peter. "The Diffusion of Designed Landscapes in South-East England." In *Change in the Countryside: Essays on Rural England, 1500–1900*. Ed. H. S. A. Fox and R. A. Burlin. London: Institute of British Geographers, 1979. Pp. 165–85.

Braunmuller, A. R. "Accounting for Absence: The Transcription of Space." In *New Ways of Looking at Old Texts: Papers of the Renaissance English Text Society, 1985–1991*. Ed. W. Speed Hill. Binghamton, NY: Renaissance English Text Society, 1993. Pp. 47–56.

Bray, Joe. "'Attending to the *minute*': Richardson's Revisions of Italics in *Pamela*." In *Ma(r)king the Text: The Presentation of Meaning on the Page*. Ed. Joe Bray, Miriam Handley, and Anne C. Henry. Aldershot: Ashgate, 2000. Pp. 105–19.

Bray, Joe, Miriam Handley, and Anne C. Henry, eds. *Ma(r)king the Text: The Presentation of Meaning on the Page*. Aldershot: Ashgate, 2000.

Brewer, John. *The Pleasures of the Imagination: Culture in Eighteenth-Century England*. London: HarperCollins, 1997.

Brimacombe, Peter. *Capability Brown, the Master Gardener*. Pitkin Biographical Series, 2001.

Brinton, Laurel J., and Leslie K. Arnovick. *The English Language: A Linguistic History*. Oxford: Oxford University Press, 2006.
Brodey, Inger Sigrun. *Ruined by Design: Shaping Novels and Gardens in the Culture of Sensibility*. New York: Routledge, 2008.
Brody, Jennifer DeVere. *Punctuation: Art, Politics and Play*. Durham: Duke University Press, 2008.
Bronson, Bertrand Harris. "Printing as an Index of Taste." In Bronson, *Facets of the Enlightenment: Studies in English Literature and Its Contexts*. Berkeley and Los Angeles: University of California Press, 1968. Pp. 326–65.
Brownell, Morris R. *Alexander Pope's Villa. Views of Pope's Villa, Grotto and Garden: A Microcosm of English Landscape*. Exhibition catalogue. London: Marble Hill House, 1980.
Bruning, Ted, and Keith Paulin, eds. *The David and Charles Book of Historic English Inns*. Newton Abbot, London, and North Pomfret VT: David and Charles, 1982.
Burke, John. *The English Inn*. New York: Holmes and Meier Publishers, 1981.
Burke, Thomas. *English Inns*. London: Collins, 1944.
Burrows, George Thomas. *Some Old English Inns*. London: T. Werner Laurie, [1907].
Burton, Elizabeth. *The Georgians at Home* (1967). London: Arrow, 1973.
Caffyn, Lucy. "Housing in an Industrial Landscape: A Study of Workers' Housing in West Yorkshire." *World Archaeology* 15:2 (1983): 173–83.
Campbell, Jeremy. *Grammatical Man: Information, Entropy, Language, and Life*. New York: Simon and Schuster, 1982.
Campbell, Jill. "Fielding's Style." *ELH* 72:2 (Summer 2005): 407–28.
Carr, Dan. "Beyond Fine Printing: Typographic Punchcutting and the Evolution of a Poet's Voice on the Page." *Book Club of California Quarterly News Letter* 63:1 (Winter 1997): 3–17.
Carter, George. "Humphry Repton at Hare Street, Essex." *Garden History* 12:2 (Autumn 1984): 120–31.
Carter, Ronald, and John McRae. *The Routledge History of Literature in English: Britain and Ireland*. London: Routledge, 1997.
Castle, Terry. *Clarissa's Ciphers: Meaning and Disruption in Richardson's "Clarissa."* Stanford: Stanford University Press, 1982.
Chartier, Roger. *The Author's Hand and the Printer's Mind*. Trans. Lydia G. Cochrane. Cambridge: Polity Press, 2014.
———. *Forms and Meanings: Texts, Performances, and Audiences from Codex to Computer*. Philadelphia: University of Pennsylvania Press, 1995.
Choi, Julie. "Feminine Authority? Common Sense and the Question of Voice in the Novel." *New Literary History* 27:4 (Autumn 1996): 641–62.
Christiansen, C. Paul. *Memorials of the Book Trade in Medieval London: The Archives of Old London Bridge*. Cambridge: D. S. Brewer, 1987.
Clarke, Michael. *The Tempting Prospect: A Social History of English Watercolours*. London: Colonnade Books, British Museum Publications, 1981.
Clayton, Tim. *The English Print, 1688–1802*. New Haven: Yale University Press, 1997.
———. "Publishing Houses: Prints of Country Seats." In *The Georgian Country House: Architecture, Landscape and Society*. Ed. Dana Arnold. Stroud, Gloucestershire: Alan Sutton, 1998. Pp. 43–60.
Cohen, Murray. *Sensible Words: Linguistic Practice in England, 1640–1785*. Baltimore: Johns Hopkins University Press, 1977.
Cohn, Dorrit. *Transparent Minds: Narrative Modes for Presenting Consciousness in Fiction*. Princeton: Princeton University Press, 1978.

Collins, Christopher. *Reading the Written Image: Interpretation, Verbal Play, and the Roots of Iconophobia*. University Park: Pennsylvania State University Press, 1991.

Collins, Peter. *Changing Ideals in Modern Architecture, 1750–1950* (1965). 2nd ed. Montreal and Kingston: McGill-Queen's University Press, 1998.

Coote, Stephen. *The Innholders: A History of the Worshipful Company of Innholders*. Cirencester, Gloucestershire: Collectors Books, 2002.

Cosgrove, Denis, and Stephen Daniels, eds. *The Iconography of Landscape: Essays on the Symbolic Representation, Design and Use of Past Environments*. Cambridge: Cambridge University Press, 1988.

Cox, Barrie. *English Inn and Tavern Names*. Nottingham: Center for English Name Studies, University of Nottingham, 1994.

Cox, H., and H. Brewer. *Old London Illustrated*. London: Builder, c. 1950.

Crawford, Rachel. "Verbal Representations." In *A Cultural History of Gardens in the Age of Enlightenment*. Ed. Stephen Bending. London: Bloomsbury, 2013. Pp. 141–66.

Crowley, John E. "'In Happier Mansions, Warm and Dry': The Invention of the Cottage as the Comfortable Anglo-American House." *Winterthur Portfolio* 32:2/3 (Summer/Autumn 1997): 169–88.

Curran, Louise, and Sören Hammerschmidt. "Mediation, Authorship, and Samuel Richardson: An Introduction." *Eighteenth-Century Fiction* 29:2 (Winter 2016–17): 121–29.

Curtis, Laura A. "A Rhetorical Approach to the Prose of Daniel Defoe." *Rhetorica: A Journal of the History of Rhetoric* 11:3 (Summer 1993): 293–319.

Daniels, Stephen. *Fields of Vision: Landscape Imagery and National Identity in England and the United States*. Princeton: Princeton University Press, 1993.

———. *Humphry Repton: Landscape Gardening and the Geography of Georgian England*. New Haven: Yale University Press, 1999.

———. "The Political Iconography of Woodland in Later Georgian England." In *The Iconography of Landscape: Essays on the Symbolic Representation, Design and Use of Past Environments*. Ed. Denis Cosgrove and Stephen Daniels. Cambridge: Cambridge University Press, 1988. Pp. 43–82.

Daniels, Stephen, and Denis Cosgrove. "Iconography and Landscape." In *The Iconography of Landscape: Essays on the Symbolic Representation, Design and Use of Past Environments*. Ed. Denis Cosgrove and Stephen Daniels. Cambridge: Cambridge University Press, 1988. Pp. 1–10.

Davidson, Jenny. *Reading Style: A Life in Sentences*. New York: Columbia University Press, 2014.

De Bolla, Peter. *The Education of the Eye: Painting, Landscape, and Architecture in Eighteenth-Century Britain*. Stanford: Stanford University Press, 2003.

Denison, David. *English Historical Syntax*. London: Longman, 1993.

De Vinne, Theodore Low. *The Practice of Typography: Correction Composition, a Treatise on Spelling Abbreviations, the Compounding and Division of Words, the Proper Use of Figures and Numerals, Italic and Capital Letters, Notes, Etc. With Observations on Punctuation and Proof-Reading*. New York: Century, 1901.

De Voogd, Peter J. "Tristram Shandy as Aesthetic Object." *Word and Image Conference Proceedings* 4:1 (1988): 383–92.

Doody, Margaret Anne. *The Daring Muse: Augustan Poetry Reconsidered*. Cambridge: Cambridge University Press, 1985.

Duckworth, Alistair. "Fiction and Some Uses of the Country House Setting from Richardson to Scott." In *Landscape in the Gardens and the Literature of Eighteenth-Century England*. Ed. Donald M. Roberts. Los Angeles: William Andrews Clark Memorial Library, University of California, 1981. Pp. 88–138.

———. *The Improvement of the Estate: A Study of Jane Austen's Novels* (1971). Baltimore: Johns Hopkins University Press, 1994.

———. "Landscape." In *Jane Austen in Context*. Ed. Janet Todd. Cambridge: Cambridge University Press, 2005. Pp. 278–88.

Eaves, T. C. Duncan, and Ben D. Kimpel. *Samuel Richardson: A Biography*. Oxford: Clarendon Press, 1971.

Elam, Kimberly. *Expressive Typography: The Word as Image*. New York: Van Nostrand Reinhold, 1990.

Elfenbein, Andrew. "Romantic Poetry and the Standardization of English." In *The Cambridge Companion to British Romantic Poetry*. Ed. James Chandler and Maureen M. McLane. Cambridge: Cambridge University Press, 2008. Pp. 76–97.

Eliot, Simon, and Jonathan Rose. *A Companion to the History of the Book*. Oxford: Blackwell Publishing, 2007.

Evans, Joan, ed. *The Flowering of the Middle Ages*. London: Thames and Hudson, 1966.

Fairer, David. "'Light Electric Touches': Sterne, Poetry, and Empirical Erotics." In *Eighteenth-Century Poetry and the Rise of the Novel Reconsidered*. Ed. Kate Parker and Courtney Weiss Smith. Lewisburg, PA: Bucknell University Press, 2014. Pp. 135–160.

Ferguson, Frances. "*Emma* and the Impact of Form." *Modern Language Quarterly* 61 (March 2000): 157–80.

———. *Solitude and the Sublime: Romanticism and the Aesthetics of Individuation*. New York: Routledge, 1992.

Finch, Jonathan, and Kate Giles. *Estate Landscapes: Design, Improvement and Power in the Post-Medieval Landscape*. London: Boydell and Brewer, 2007.

Fish, Stanley. *How to Write a Sentence and How to Read One*. New York: Harper, 2011.

Flint, Christopher. *The Appearance of Print in Eighteenth-Century Fiction*. Cambridge: Cambridge University Press, 2011.

———. "The Material Book." In *Samuel Richardson in Context*. Ed. Peter Sabor and Betty A. Schellenberg. Cambridge: Cambridge University Press, 2018. Pp. 119–27.

Fludernik, Monica. *The Fictions of Language and the Languages of Fiction: The Linguistic Representation of Speech and Consciousness*. New York: Routledge, 1993.

———. "Histories of Narrative Theory (II): From Structuralism to the Present." In *A Companion to Narrative Theory*. Ed. James Phelan and Peter J. Rabinowitz. Oxford: Blackwell, 2005, 2008. Pp. 36–59.

Flynn, Carol Houlihan. "Samuel Richardson." In *The Cambridge History of the English Novel*. Ed. Robert L. Caserio and Clement Hawes. Cambridge: Cambridge University Press, 2012. Pp. 97–112.

Fowler, H. W., and F. G. Fowler. *The King's English* (1906). 3rd ed. Oxford: Clarendon Press, 1930.

Foxon, David. "Poets and Compositors." Unpublished sixth Lyell Lecture.

———. *Pope and the Early Eighteenth-Century Book Trade*. Rev. and ed. James McLaverty. Oxford: Clarendon Press, 1991.

Fried, Michael. *Art and Objecthood*. Chicago: University of Chicago Press, 1998.

Fries, Charles C. "Shakespearean Punctuation." In *Studies in Shakespeare, Milton, and Donne*. New York: Haskell House, 1964. Pp. 67–86.

Fussell, Paul. *The Rhetorical World of Augustan Humanism: Ethics and Imagery from Swift to Burke*. Oxford: Clarendon Press, 1965.

Fysh, Stephanie. *The Work(s) of Samuel Richardson*. Newark: University of Delaware Press, 1997.

Gallagher, Catherine, and Stephen Greenblatt. *Practicing New Historicism*. Chicago: University of Chicago Press, 2000.

Galperin, William. "The Missed Opportunities of *Mansfield Park*." In *Companion to Jane Austen*. Ed. Claudia Johnson and Clara Tuite. Chichester: Blackwell, 2009. Pp. 123–32.

Gaskell, Philip. *A New Introduction to Bibliography*. New York and Oxford: Oxford University Press, 1972.

Gehl, Paul F. "Texts and Textures: Dirty Pictures and Other Things in Medieval Manuscripts." *Corona* (1983): 68–77.

Genette, Gérard. *Paratexts: Thresholds of Interpretation*. Ed. Thomas Macksey. Trans. Jane E. Lewin (1987). Cambridge: Cambridge University Press, 1997.

Gibney, Somerville. *The Maid of London Bridge. A Story of the Time of Kett's Rebellion* (1892). 3rd ed. London: Jarrold and Sons, 1895.

Girouard, Mark. *A Country House Companion*. New Haven: Yale University Press, 1987.

———. *Life in the English Country House: A Social and Architectural History*. New Haven: Yale University Press, 1978.

Gokak, V. K. *The Poetic Approach to Language, with Special Reference to the History of English*. Oxford: Oxford University Press, 1950.

Goldblatt, David. "The Dislocation of the Architectural Self." In *What is Architecture?* Ed. Andrew Ballantyne. London: Routledge, 2002. Pp. 153–72.

Goodman, Frederick. *Magick Symbols*. London: Brian Trodd, 1989.

Greene, Thomas M. "Anti-hermeneutics: The Case of Shakespeare's Sonnet 129." In *Poetic Traditions of the English Renaissance*. Ed. Maynard Mack and George deForest Lord. New Haven: Yale University Press, 1982. Pp. 143–61.

Greetham, G. Foreword to Jerome J. McGann, *Critique of Modern Textual Criticism*. Chicago: University of Chicago Press, 1983.

Greg, W. W. "The Rationale of Copy-Text." *Studies in Bibliography* 3 (1950): 19–36.

Grice, John. *Punctuation: A Printer's Study*. Stroud, Gloucestershire: Evergreen Press, 2001.

Gordon, Ian A. *The Movement of English Prose*. London: Longman, 1966.

Gregory, Derek. "The Fiction of Distance? Information Circulation and the Mails in Early Nineteenth-Century England." *Journal of Historical Geography* 13 (1987): 130–54.

Hagstrum, Jean. *The Sister Arts: The Tradition of Literary Pictorialism from Dryden to Gray*. Chicago: University of Chicago Press, 1958.

Hamilton, Frederick W. *A Brief History of Printing in England: A Short History of Printing in England from Caxton to the Present Time*. Published by the Committee on Education, United Typothetae of America, 1918.

Harmon, William. *A Handbook to Literature*. 10th ed. Upper Saddle River, NJ: Pearson/Prentice Hall, 2006.

Harris, John. *The Artist and the Country House: A History of Country House and Garden View Painting in Britain, 1540–1870*. London: Sotheby Parke Bernet, 1979.

———. "English Country House Guides, 1740–1840." In *Concerning Architecture: Essays on Architectural Writing Presented to Nikolaus Pevsner*. Ed. John Summerson. Baltimore: Penguin Books, 1968. Pp. 345–56.

Harrison, D. F. "Bridges and Economic Development, 1300–1800." *Economic History Review*, n.s., 45:2 (May 1992): 240–61.

Harrowen, Jean. *Riddles and Legends of London Bridge*. Norwich: Borrowdale Press, 1979.

Hartley, James, and Peter Burnhill, eds. "The Spatial Arrangement of Text." *Visible Language* 15:1 (1981): 1–120.

Harwood, Edward S. "Personal Identity and the Eighteenth-Century English Landscape Garden." *Journal of Garden History* 13:1–2 (Spring–Summer 1993): 36–48.

Heal, Ambrose. *Old London Bridge Tradesmen's Cards and Tokens*. Oxford: John Lane, Bodley Head, 1931.

Hearsey, John E. N. *Bridge, Church and Palace in Old London*. London: John Murray, 1961.

Helsinger, Elizabeth K. "Clare and the Place of the Peasant Poet." *Critical Inquiry* 13:3 (Spring 1987): 509–31.

———. "Land and National Representation in Britain." In *Prospects for the Nation: Recent Essays in British Landscape, 1750–1880*. Ed. Michael Rosenthal, Christiana Payne, and Scott Wilcox. New Haven: Yale University Press, 1997. Pp. 13–35.

———. *Rural Scenes and National Representation: Britain, 1815–1850*. Princeton: Princeton University Press, 1997.

Henry, Anne C. "The Re-markable Rise of '. . .': Reading Ellipsis Marks in Literary Texts." In *Ma(r)king the Text: The Presentation of Meaning on the Page*. Ed. Joe Bray, Miriam Handley, and Anne C. Henry. Aldershot: Ashgate, 2000. Pp. 120–142.

Hind, A. M. *The History of Engraving and Etching*. 3rd ed. (1923). Rpt. New York: Dover Publications, 1963.

Hindle, Steve. "Representing Rural Society: Labor, Leisure, and the Landscape in an Eighteenth-Century Conversation Piece." *Critical Inquiry* 41 (Spring 2015): 615–54.

Home, Gordon. *Old London Bridge*. London: John Lane, Bodley Head, 1931.

Honan, Park. "Eighteenth- and Nineteenth-Century Punctuation Theory." *English Studies* 41 (1960): 92–102.

Hoskins, W. G. *The Making of the English Landscape*. London: Hodder and Stoughton, 1955.

Houston, Keith. *Shady Characters: Ampersands, Interrobangs and Other Typographical Curiosities*. London: Penguin Group, Particular Books, 2013.

Howard, Maurice. "The Hunting Lodge in England, 1500–1650." In *Maison des champs dans l'Europe de la Renaissance*. Ed. Monique Chatenet. Paris: Éditions A et J Picard, [2006]. Pp. 291–98.

Hunt, John Dixon. *The Figure in the Landscape: Poetry, Painting and Gardening during the Eighteenth Century*. Baltimore: Johns Hopkins University Press, 1976.

———. *Gardens and the Picturesque: Studies in the History of Landscape Architecture*. Cambridge, MA: MIT Press, 1992.

———. "Ut Pictura Poesis, Ut Pictura Hortus, and the Picturesque," *Word and Image* 1 (1985): 87–107.

Hunt, John Dixon, and Peter Willis, eds. *The Genius of the Place: The English Landscape Garden, 1620–1820*. New York: Harper and Row, 1975.

Hunter, J. Paul. *Before Novels: The Cultural Contexts of English Fiction*. New York: W. W. Norton, 1990.

———. "Couplets." In *The Oxford Handbook of British Poetry, 1660–1800*. Ed. Jack Lynch. Oxford: Oxford University Press, 2016. Pp. 373–85.

———. *Occasional Form: Henry Fielding and the Chains of Circumstance*. Baltimore: Johns Hopkins University Press, 1975.

———. "Poetry on the Page: Visual Signalling and the Mind's Ear." In *The Work of Form: Poetics and Materiality in Early Modern Culture*. Ed. Ben Burton and Elizabeth Scott-Baumann. Oxford: Oxford University Press, 2014. Pp. 179–96.

———. *The Reluctant Pilgrim: Defoe's Emblematic Method and Quest for Form in "Robinson Crusoe."* Baltimore: Johns Hopkins University Press, 1966.

———. "Serious Reflections on Farther Adventures: Resistances to Closure in Eighteenth-Century English Novels." In *Augustan Subjects: Essays in Honor of Martin Battestin*. Ed. Albert J. Rivero. Newark: University of Delaware Press and Associated University Presses, 1997. Pp. 276–94.

———. "Seven Reasons for Rhyme." In *Ritual, Routine, and Regime: Repetition in Early Modern British and European Cultures*. Ed. Lorna Clymer. Toronto: University of Toronto Press, in assoc. with the UCLA Center for Seventeenth- and Eighteenth-Century Studies and the William Andrews Clark Memorial Library, 2006. Pp. 172–98.

Hussey, Christopher. *The Picturesque: Studies in a Point of View*. London: G. P. Putnam's Sons, 1927.

Hyde, Ralph. *A Prospect of Britain: The Town Panoramas of Samuel and Nathaniel Buck*. London: Pavilion Books, 1994.

Hyndman, Sarah. *Why Fonts Matter*. London: Virgin Books, 2016.

Jackendoff, Ray. "The Base Rules for Prepositional Phrases." In *A Festschrift for Morris Halle*. Ed. Stephen R. Anderson and Paul Kiparski. New York: Holt, Rinehart, and Winston, 1973.

Jackson, Laura Riding, and Robert Graves. "William Shakespeare and E. E. Cummings: A Study in Original Punctuation and Spelling." In Jackson and Graves, *A Survey of Modernist Poetry*. London: William Heinemann, 1927. Pp. 59–82.

Jackson, Peter. *London Bridge*. London: Cassell, 1971.

Jespersen, Otto. *The System of Grammar*. London: Allen and Unwin; Copenhagen: Munksgaard, 1933.

Johns, Adrian. *The Nature of the Book: Print and Knowledge in the Making*. Chicago: University of Chicago Press, 1998.

Johnson, Alastair. "The Author as Typographer." *Ampersand* (Summer 1991): 2–5.

Johnson, Claudia, and Clara Tuite. *Companion to Jane Austen*. Chichester: Blackwell, 2009.

Jones, David. *In Parenthesis; seinnyessit e gledyf ym penn mameu*. London: Faber and Faber, 1937.

Jones, T. D. "Ackermann's *Repository* 1809–1823." *British Art Journal* 11:1 (2010): 69–74.

Keen, Suzanne. *Narrative Form*. Hampshire: Palgrave Macmillan, 2003.

Keesey, W. M., illus. *Tales of Old Inns: The History, Legend and Romance of Some of Our Older Hostelries*. 2nd ed. London: Trust Houses, 1929.

Kellert, Jan. *Old London Bridge*. Malvern: De Walden Press, 2002.

Kelsall, Malcolm. *The Great Good Place: The Country House and English Literature*. New York: Columbia University Press, 1993.

Kenner, Hugh. *The Mechanic Muse*. Oxford: Oxford University Press, 1987.

Keymer, Thomas. "Obscenity and the Erotics of Fiction." In *The Cambridge History of the English Novel*. Ed. Robert L. Caserio and Clement Hawes. Cambridge: Cambridge University Press, 2012. Pp. 131–46.

———. *Richardson's "Clarissa" and the Eighteenth-Century Reader*. Cambridge: Cambridge University Press, 1992.

———. *Sterne, the Moderns, and the Novel*. Oxford: Oxford University Press, 2002.

Keymer, Thomas, and Peter Sabor. *"Pamela" in the Marketplace: Literary Controversy and Print Culture in Eighteenth-Century Britain and Ireland*. Cambridge: Cambridge University Press, 2005.

King, Kathryn R. *A Political Biography of Eliza Haywood*. London: Pickering and Chatto, 2012; London: Routledge, 2016.

Klein, Manfred, Yvonne Schwemer-Scheddin, and Erik Spiekermann, eds. *T and T: Type and Typographers*. London: Architecture Design and Technology Press, 1991.

Kowsky, Francis R. "H. H. Richardson's Ames Gate Lodge and the Romantic Landscape Tradition." *Journal of the Society of Architectural Historians* 50:2 (June 1991): 181–88.

Kramnick, Jonathan. *Making the English Canon: Print-Capitalism and the Cultural Past, 1700–1770*. Cambridge: Cambridge University Press, 1998.

Krush, Anne J. "The Historical and Archaeological Significance of Medieval Bench End Carvings in Some Parish Churches in Suffolk, England." *Transactions of the Nebraska Academy of Sciences* 12 (1984): 103–8.

Kvande, Marta. "Printed in a Book: Negotiating Print and Manuscript Cultures in *Fantomina* and *Clarissa*." *Eighteenth-Century Studies* 46:2 (Winter 2013): 239–57.

Lanham, Richard A. *Analyzing Prose*. New York: Charles Scribner's Sons, 1983.

Latour, Bruno. *Reassembling the Social: An Introduction to Actor-Network Theory*. Oxford: Oxford University Press, 2005.

Lawson, Alexander. *Anatomy of a Typeface*. Boston: David R. Godine, 1990.

Lennard, John. "InVisible Punctuation." *Visible Language* 45:1/2 (2011): 121–38.

Leonard, Sterling A. *The Doctrine of Correctness in English Usage 1700–1800*. Madison: University of Wisconsin Press, 1929.

Levenston, Edward A. *The Stuff of Literature: Physical Aspects of Texts and Their Relation to Literary Meaning*. Albany: State University of New York Press, 1992.

Levine, Caroline. *Forms: Whole, Rhythm, Hierarchy, Network*. Princeton: Princeton University Press, 2015.

Lewis, C. S. "The Vision of John Bunyan." In *Selected Literary Essays*. Ed. Walter Hooper Cambridge: Cambridge University Press, 1969. Pp. 146–53.

Lewis, Jayne Elizabeth. *Air's Appearance: Literary Atmosphere in British Fiction, 1660–1794*. Chicago: University of Chicago Press, 2012.

Lieberman, J. Ben. *Type and Typefaces* (1967). 2nd ed. New Rochelle, NY: Myriade Press, 1978.

Lipking, Lawrence. *The Ordering of the Arts in Eighteenth-Century England*. Princeton: Princeton University Press, 1970.

Liu, Alan. *Wordsworth: The Sense of History*. Stanford: Stanford University Press, 1989.

Loewenstein, Joseph. "*Idem*: Italics and the Genetics of Authorship." *Journal of Medieval and Renaissance Studies* 20:2 (Fall 1990): 205–24.

London Buildings and Sites: A Guide for Researches in Guildhall Library. London: Guildhall Library Publications, 2006.

Long, George. *English Inns and Road-Houses*. London: T. Werner Laurie, 1937.

Lounsbury, T. R. *History of the English Language*. Rev. ed. New York: Henry Holt; London: G. Bell and Sons, 1924.

Lucas, John. "Places and Dwellings: Wordsworth, Clare and the Anti-Picturesque." In *The Iconography of Landscape: Essays on the Symbolic Representation, Design and Use of Past Environments*. Ed. Denis Cosgrove and Stephen Daniels. Cambridge: Cambridge University Press, 1988. Pp. 83–97.

———. "Wordsworth and the Anti-Picturesque." In Lucas, *Romantic to Modern Literature: Essays and Ideas of Culture, 1750–1900*. Sussex: Harvester Press, 1982. Pp. 50–67.

Luna, Paul. "Marks, Spaces and Boundaries: Punctuation (and Other Effects) in the Typography of Dictionaries." *Visible Language* 45:1/2 (2011): 139–60.

Lundskær-Nielsen, Tom. *Prepositions in English Grammars until 1801—With a Survey of the Western European Background*. Odense: University Press of Southern Denmark, 2011.

Lupton, Ellen. "Telegrammar: From Writing to Speech." In *Period Styles: A History of Punctuation*, exh. cat. New York: Herb Lubalin Study Center of Design and Typography, Cooper Union for the Advancement of Science and Art, 1988. Pp. 6–8.

Lupton, Ellen, and J. Abbott Miller. "Period Styles: A Punctuated History." In *Period Styles: A History of Punctuation*, exh. cat. New York: Herb Lubalin Study Center of Design and Typography, Cooper Union for the Advancement of Science and Art, 1988. Pp. 1–5.

Lupton, Julia. "SHAKESPEARE AND e. e. CUMMINGS: Elizabethan Punctuation and Modernist Poetics." In *Period Styles: A History of Punctuation*, exh. cat. New York: Herb Lubalin Study Center of Design and Typography, Cooper Union for the Advancement of Science and Art, 1988. Pp. 9–11.

Lynch, Deidre Shauna. *The Economy of Character: Novels, Market Culture, and the Business of Inner Meaning*. Chicago: University of Chicago Press, 1998.

———. "Novels in the World of Moving Goods." In *Concise Companion to the Restoration and Eighteenth Century*. Ed. Cynthia Wall. Oxford: Blackwell, 2005. Pp. 121–43.

Macartney, Mervyn. *English Houses and Gardens in the 17th and 18th Centuries: A Series of Bird's-eye Views Reproduced from Contemporary Engravings by Kip, Badeslade, Harris and Others*. London: B. T. Batsford, 1908.

MacEvoy, Bruce. "Watercolour Artists." ©2007. http://www.handprint.com/HP/WCL/artist02.html.

Mak, Bonnie. *How the Page Matters*. Toronto: University of Toronto Press, 2011.

Mandal, Anthony. "Language." In *Jane Austen in Context*. Ed. Janet Todd. Cambridge: Cambridge University Press, 2005. Pp. 23–32.

Manley, Lawrence. *Literature and Culture in Early Modern London*. Cambridge: Cambridge University Press, 1995.

Manzalaoui, M. A. "Typographical Justification and Grammatical Change in the Eighteenth Century." *Papers of the Bibliographical Society of America* 56 (1962): 248–51.

Marshall, David. *The Frame of Art: Fictions of Aesthetic Experience, 1750–1815*. Baltimore: Johns Hopkins University Press, 2005.

———. "The Problem of the Picturesque." *Eighteenth-Century Studies* 35:3 (Spring 2002): 413–437.

Marsten, Jeffrey, Peter Stallybrass, and Nancy J. Vickers. *Language Machines: Technologies of Literary and Cultural Production*. New York: Routledge, 1997.

Martin, Alison E. "The Traveller as Landschaftsmaler: Industrial Labour and Landscape Aesthetics in Johanna Schopenhauer's Travel Writing." *Modern Language Review* 99:4 (October 2004): 968–82.

Maslen, Keith. "Samuel Richardson and Smith's *Printer's Grammar*." *Book Collector* 18:4 (Winter 1969): 518–19.

———. *Samuel Richardson of London, Printer: A Study of His Printing Based on Ornament Use and Business Accounts*. Dunedin: University of Otago Press, 2001.

———. "Samuel Richardson: Printer-Novelist." In *Approaches to Teaching the Novels of Samuel Richardson*. Ed. Lisa Zunshine and Jocelyn Harris. New York: Modern Language Association of America, 2006. Pp. 39–47.

Matz, B. W. *Dickensian Inns and Taverns*. London: Cecil Palmer, 1922.

Mayer, Laura. *Capability Brown and the English Landscape Garden*. Oxford: Shire Publications, 2011.

McBurney, William H. "Mrs. Penelope Aubin and the Early Eighteenth-Century English Novel." *Huntington Library Quarterly* 20 (1957): 245–67.

McCaskill, A. *English Sentence Patterns*. Glasgow: Kelvin Press, [1962].

McDowell, Paula. *The Invention of the Oral: Print Commerce and Fugitive Voices in Eighteenth-Century Britain*. Chicago: University of Chicago Press, 2017.

McGann, Jerome J. *A Critique of Modern Textual Criticism*. Chicago: University of Chicago Press, 1983.

———. "The Socialization of Texts." In McGann, *The Textual Condition*. Princeton: Princeton University Press, 1991. Pp. 69–98.

McIntosh, Carey. *The Evolution of English Prose, 1700–1800: Style, Politeness, and Print Culture*. Cambridge: Cambridge University Press, 1998.

McKenzie, D. F. *Making Meaning: "Printers of the Mind" and Other Essays*. Ed. Peter D. McDonald and Michael F. Suarez. Amherst: University of Massachusetts Press, 2002.

———. "Typography and Meaning: The Case of William Congreve." In *Buch und Buchhandel in Europa im achtzehnten Jahrhundert: The Book and the Book Trade in Eighteenth-Century Europe*. Ed. G. Barber and B. Fabian. Hamburg: Dr. Ernst Hauswedell and Co., 1981. Pp. 81–125.

McKeon, Michael. *The Origins of the English Novel 1600–1740*. Baltimore: Johns Hopkins University Press, 1987.

———. *The Secret History of Domesticity: Public, Private, and the Division of Knowledge*. Baltimore: Johns Hopkins University Press, 2005.

McKerrow, Ronald B. *An Introduction to Bibliography for Literary Students* (1927). 2nd impression, corr. Oxford: Clarendon Press, 1928; rpt. 1951.

McKillop, Alan Dugald. *Samuel Richardson: Printer and Novelist*. Chapel Hill: University of North Carolina Press, 1936.

McLean, Ian. "The Expanded Field of the Picturesque: Contested Identities and Empire in *Sydney-Cove 1794*." In *Art and the British Empire*. Ed. Tim Barringer, Geoff Quilley, and Douglas Fordham. Manchester: Manchester University Press, 2007. Pp. 23–37.

McLaverty, James. *Pope, Print and Meaning*. Oxford: Oxford University Press, 2001.

McMorran, Will. *The Inn and the Traveller: Digressive Topographies in the Early Modern European Novel*. Oxford: European Humanities Research Centre, 2002.

McMordie, Michael. "Picturesque Pattern Books and Pre-Victorian Designers." *Architectural History* 18 (1975): 43–59, 109–12.

McMurtrie, Douglas C. "The Origin and Development of the Marks of Quotation." *Library*, 4th ser., 2 (1921): 133–34.

———. *Concerning Quotation Marks*. New York: Private printing, 1934.

Michael, Ian. *English Grammatical Categories and the Tradition to 1800*. Cambridge: Cambridge University Press, 1970.

Mitchell, W. J. T. *Landscape and Power*. 2nd ed. Chicago: University of Chicago Press, 1994, 2002.

Morison, Stanley. *On Type Designs Past and Present* (1926). New ed. London: Ernest Benn, 1962.

———. *Politics and Script: Aspects of Authority and Freedom in the Development of Graeco-Latin Script from the Sixth Century B.C. to the Twentieth Century A.D.* Ed. Nicolas Barker. Oxford: Clarendon Press, 1972.

———. *Selected Essays on the History of Letter-Forms in Manuscript and Print*. Ed. David McKitterick. 2 vols. Cambridge: Cambridge University Press, 1981.

———. *A Tally of Types*. Ed. Brooke Crutchley. Cambridge: Cambridge University Press, 1973.

———. *The Typographic Book, 1450–1935*. Chicago: University of Chicago Press, 1963.

Morison, Stanley, and Holbrook Jackson. *A Brief Survey of Printing History and Practice*. New York: Alfred A. Knopf, 1923.

Morley, Henry, ed. *The Earlier Life and the Chief Earlier Works of Daniel Defoe*. London: George Routledge and Sons, 1889.

Moretti, Franco. *Graphs, Maps, Trees: Abstract Models for Literary History*. London: Verso Books; Scranton, PA: W. W. Norton, 2007.

Morris, David. *Thomas Hearne and His Landscape*. London: Reaktion Books, 1989.

Mowl, Timothy. "The Evolution of the Park Gate Lodge as a Building Type." *Architectural History* 27 (1984): 467–80.

Mowl, Tim, and Brian Earnshaw. *Trumpet at a Distant Gate: The Lodge as Prelude to the Country House*. London: Waterstones, 1985.

Mosley, J. "S and f: The Origin and Use of the 'Long s.'" In *James Mosley: A Checklist of the Published Writings, 1958–1995*. Comp. S. Tuhoy. Over, Cambridgeshire: Rampant Lions Press, 1995. Pp. 20–22.

Mullan, John. *Sentiment and Sociability: The Language of Feeling in the Eighteenth Century*. Oxford: Clarendon Press, 1988.

Murdoch, Tessa, ed. *Noble Households: Eighteenth-Century Inventories of Great English Houses: A Tribute to John Cornforth*. Cambridge: John Adamson, 2006.

Ohmann, Richard M. "Prolegomena to the Analysis of Prose Style." In *Style in Prose Fiction: English Institute Essays, 1958*. Ed. Harold C. Martin. New York: Columbia University Press, 1959. Pp. 1–24.

Old London Bridge: An Historical Account of the Origins of London Bridge. Whitstable, Kent: Pryor Publications, 1982.

Olds, Sharon. "The Prepositions." *New Yorker*, 2 April 1990.

Ong, Walter. "Historical Backgrounds of Elizabethan and Jacobean Punctuation." *PMLA* 59 (1944): 349–60.

Owens, Susan. *The Art of Drawing: British Masters and Methods since 1600*. London: V&A Publishing, 2013.

Owens, W. R., and P. N. Furbank. "Defoe and the 'Improvisatory' Sentence." *English Studies* 67:2 (1986): 157–66.

———. "Stylometry and the Defoe Canon: A Reply to Irving Rothman." *Papers of the Bibliographical Society of America* 96:3 (September 2002): 463–65.

Park, Julie. "Pains and Pleasures of the Automaton: Frances Burney's Mechanics of Coming Out." *Eighteenth-Century Studies* 40:1 (Fall 2006): 23–49.

———. "What the Eye Cannot See: Interior Landscapes in *Mansfield Park*." *Eighteenth Century: Theory and Interpretation* 54:2 (Summer 2013): 169–81.

Parkes, M. B. *Pause and Effect: An Introduction to the History of Punctuation in the West.* Aldershot, Hants: Scolar Press, 1992.

Parry, Graham. *Hollar's England: A Mid-Seventeenth-Century View.* Wilton, England: Michael Russell, 1980.

Pascal, Roy. *The Dual Voice: Free Indirect Speech and Its Functioning in the Nineteenth-Century European Novel.* Manchester: Manchester University Press, 1977.

Paulson, Ronald. "The Pictorial Circuit and Related Structures in Eighteenth-Century England." In *The Varied Pattern: Studies in the Eighteenth Century.* Ed. Peter Hughes and David Williams. Toronto: A. M. Hakkert, 1971. Pp. 165–97.

Pavitt, W. T. and K. *The Book of Talismans.* London: William Rider and Sons, 1922.

Pavord, Anna. *Landskipping: Painters, Ploughmen and Places.* London: Bloomsbury, 2016.

Payne, Ann. *Views of the Past: Topographical Drawings in the British Library.* London: British Library, 1987.

Percy, Carol. "English Language." In *Samuel Richardson in Context.* Ed. Peter Sabor and Betty A. Schellenberg. Cambridge: Cambridge University Press, 2018. Pp. 178–85.

———. "Mid-century Grammars and Their Reception in the *Monthly Review* and the *Critical Review*." In *Grammars, Grammarians and Grammar-Writing in Eighteenth-Century England.* Ed. Ingrid Tieken-Boon van Ostade. Berlin: Mouton de Gruyter, 2008. Pp. 125–47.

Pérez-Gómez, Albert, and Louise Pelletier. *Architectural Representation and the Perspective Hinge.* Cambridge, MA: MIT Press, 1997.

Period Styles: A History of Punctuation. Exh. cat. Ellen Lupton, curator. New York: Herb Lubalin Study Center of Design and Typography, Cooper Union for the Advancement of Science and Art, 1988.

Perry, Ruth. "Home Economics: Representations of Poverty in Eighteenth-Century Fiction." In *A Companion to the Eighteenth-Century English Novel and Culture.* Ed. Paula R. Backscheider and Catherine Ingrassia. Oxford: Blackwell, 2005. Pp. 874–906.

Phibbs, John. "A Reconsideration of Repton's Contribution to the Improvements at Felbrigg, Norfolk, 1778–84." *Garden History* 13:1 (Spring 1985): 33–44.

Pierce, Patricia. *Old London Bridge.* London: Headline, 2001.

Portela, Manuel. "Typographic Translation: The Portuguese Edition of *Tristram Shandy* (1997–98)." In *Ma(r)king the Text: The Presentation of Meaning on the Literary Page.* Ed. Joe Bray, Miriam Handley, and Anne C. Henry. Aldershot: Ashgate, 2000. Pp. 291–308.

Pratchett, Terry. *Guards! Guards!* 1989. New York: HarperCollins, 2001.

Price, Martin. "The Picturesque Moment." In *From Sensibility to Romanticism.* Ed. F. W. Hilles and Harold Bloom. Oxford: Oxford University Press, 1965. Pp. 259–92.

Prince, Hugh. "Art and Agrarian Change, 1710–1815." In *The Iconography of Landscape: Essays on the Symbolic Representation, Design and Use of Past Environments.*

Ed. Denis Cosgrove and Stephen Daniels. Cambridge: Cambridge University Press, 1988. Pp. 98–118.

Raeburn, Michael. "Catherine the Great and the Image of Britain." In *The Green Frog Service*. Ed. Michael Raeburn, Ludmila Voronikhina, and Andrew Nurnberg. London: Cacklegoose Press, 1995. Pp. 42–56.

Raeburn, Michael, Ludmila Voronikhina, and Andrew Nurnberg, eds. *The Green Frog Service*. London: Cacklegoose Press, 1995.

Ramazani, Vaheed K. *The Free Indirect Mode: Flaubert and the Poetics of Irony*. Charlottesville: University Press of Virginia, 1988.

Ramsey, Stanley C. *Small Houses of the Late Georgian Period*. London: Technical Journals, 1919.

Reed, Alonzo, and Brainerd Kellog. "Higher Lessons in English" (1906). In *Readings in the Theory of Grammar from the 17th to the 20th Century*. Ed. Diane Bornstein. Cambridge: Winthrop, 1976. Pp. 49–51.

Richardson, A. E. *The Old Inns of England*. Foreword by Sir Edwin Lutyens, R. A. New York: Charles Scribner's Sons; London: B. T. Batsford, 1935.

Richetti, John J. "The Novel before 'the Novel.'" In *The Cambridge History of the English Novel*. Ed. Robert L. Caserio and Clement Hawes. Cambridge: Cambridge University Press, 2012. Pp. 14–29.

———. *Popular Fiction before Richardson* (1969). Rpt. with new introduction. Oxford: Clarendon Press, 1992.

Rickards, Maurice, and Michael Twyman. *The Encyclopedia of Ephemera: A Guide to the Fragmentary Documents of Everyday Life for the Collector, Curator, and Historian*. London: British Library, 2000.

Robinson, John Martin. "Model Farm Buildings of the Age of Improvement." *Architectural History* 19 (1976): 17–31.

———. Introduction to Humphry Repton, *Observations on the Theory and Practice of Landscape Gardening*. Oxford: Phaidon Press, 1980.

Rogers, Deborah D., ed. *The Critical Response to Ann Radcliffe*. Westport, CT: Greenwood Press, 1994.

Rogers, Kenneth. *Signs and Taverns round about Old London Bridge: Including Gracechurch Street, Fenchurch Street and Leadenhall Street*. London: Homeland Association, 1937.

Rogers, Pat, ed. *Defoe: The Critical Heritage*. Boston: Routledge and Kegan Paul, 1972.

Rogger, André. *Landscapes of Taste: The Art of Humphry Repton's Red Books*. London: Routledge, 2007.

Rothman, Irving. "Coleridge on the Semi-Colon in 'Robinson Crusoe': Problems in Editing Defoe." *Studies in the Novel* 27:3 (Fall 1995): 320–40.

Rougeux, Nicholas. *Between the Words: Exploring the Punctuation in Literary Classics*. Website. 2016. https://www.c82.net/work/?id=347.

Rubba, Jo. "Grammaticization as Semantic Change: A Case Study of Preposition Development." In *Perspectives on Grammaticalization*. Ed. William Pagliuca. Amsterdam and Philadelphia: John Benjamins, 1994. Pp. 81–102.

Russell, Ronald. *Guide to British Topographical Prints*. Newton Abbot, London, and North Pomfret, VT: David and Charles, 1979.

Sabor, Peter. Introduction to *Samuel Richardson's Published Commentary*. 3 vols. London: Pickering and Chatto, 1998. Pp. 2:vii–xxxviii.

———. "Teaching *Pamela* and *Clarissa* through Richardson's Correspondence." In

Approaches to Teaching the Novels of Samuel Richardson. Ed. Lisa Zunshine and Jocelyn Harris. New York: Modern Language Association of America, 2006. Pp. 32–38.

Sabor, Peter, and Betty A. Schellenberg, eds. *Samuel Richardson in Context*. Cambridge: Cambridge University Press, 2018.

Saintsbury, George. *A History of English Prose Rhythm*. London: Macmillan, 1912.

Sale, William M., Jr. *Samuel Richardson: A Bibliographical Record of His Literary Career with Historical Notes*. New Haven: Yale University Press, 1936.

———. *Samuel Richardson: Master Printer*. Ithaca: Cornell University Press, 1950.

Salmon, Vivian. "Early Seventeenth-Century Punctuation as a Guide to Sentence Structure." *Review of English Studies* 13:52 (1962): 347–60.

———. "English Punctuation Theory, 1500–1800." *Anglia: Zeitschrift für Englische Philologie*. 106:3–4 (1988): 285–314.

Schama, Simon. *Landscape and Memory*. New York: Vintage Books, 1995.

Scholz, Bernhard F. "Is Typography Textual? From Illustrated Epigram to Emblem: The Canonization of a Typographical Arrangement." In *New Ways of Looking at Old Texts: Papers of the Renaissance English Text Society, 1985–1991*. Ed. W. Speed Hill. Binghamton, NY: Renaissance English Text Society, 1993. Pp. 149–57.

Schulz, Max F. "The Circuit Walk of the Eighteenth-Century Landscape Garden and the Pilgrim's Circuitous Progress." *Eighteenth-Century Studies* 15 (Autumn 1981): 1–25.

Sedgwick, Eve Kosofsky. "Around the Performative: Periperformative Vicinities in Nineteenth-Century Narrative." In Sedgwick, *Touching Feeling: Affect, Pedagogy, Performativity*. Durham: Duke University Press, 2003. Pp. 67–91.

Shapiro, Rebecca. *Fixing Babel: An Historical Anthology of Applied English Lexicography*. Foreword by Jack Lynch. Lewisburg: Bucknell University Press, 2018.

Sharrock, Roger, ed. *Bunyan: The Pilgrim's Progress: A Casebook*. London: Macmillan, 1976.

Sharvit, Yael. "The Puzzle of Free Indirect Discourse." *Linguistics and Philosophy* 31:3 (2008): 353–95.

Shepherd, C. W. *A Thousand Years of London Bridge*. London: John Baker; New York: Hastings House, 1971.

Simon, Maurya, and Cheryl Jacobsen. *A Brief History of Punctuation: Poems by Maurya Simon : : Calligraphy by Cheryl Jacobsen*. Winona, MN: Sutton Hoo Press, 2002.

Simpson, Percy. *Proof-Reading in the Sixteenth, Seventeenth, and Eighteenth Centuries*. Oxford: Oxford University Press, 1935.

Simpson, John. Introduction to *The First English Dictionary, 1604*. Oxford: Bodleian Library, 2006.

Siskin, Clifford, and William Warner. "This Is Enlightenment: An Invitation in the Form of an Argument." In *This Is Enlightenment*. Ed. Siskin and Warner. Chicago: University of Chicago Press, 2010. Pp. 1–33.

Smith, Courtney Weiss. *Empiricist Devotions: Science, Religion, and Poetry in Early Eighteenth-Century England*. Charlottesville: University of Virginia Press, 2016.

Soltow, Lee. "The Distribution of Property Values in England and Wales in 1798." *Economic History Review*, n.s., 34:1 (February 1981): 60–70.

Spedding, Patrick. *A Bibliography of Eliza Haywood*. London: Pickering and Chatto, 2004.

Starr, G. A. "Defoe's Prose Style: 1. The Language of Interpretation." *Modern Philology* 71:3 (February 1974): 277–294.

Stein, Dieter, and Ingrid Tieken-Boon van Ostade, eds. *Towards a Standard English, 1600–1800*. Berlin: Mouton de Gruyter, 1994.

Stewart, Susan. *On Longing: Narratives of the Miniature, the Gigantic, the Souvenir, the Collection*. Baltimore: Johns Hopkins University Press, 1984.

Stokes, Roy. *A Bibliographical Companion* (1989). Lanham, MD: Toronto; Plymouth, UK: Scarecrow Press, 2011.

Streatfield, David C. "Art and Nature in the English Landscape Garden: Design Theory and Practice, 1700–1818." In *Landscape in the Gardens and the Literature of Eighteenth-Century England*. Ed. Donald M. Roberts. Los Angeles: William Andrews Clark Memorial Library, UCLA, 1981. Pp. 1–87.

Stroud, Dorothy. *Capability Brown* (1950). London: Faber and Faber, 1984.

———. *Humphry Repton*. London: Country Life Limited, 1962.

Stuart, Donald. *London's Historic Inns and Taverns*. Derby, England: Breedon Books, 2004.

Styles, John. "Picturing Domesticity: The Cottage Genre in Late Eighteenth-Century Britain." In *Imagined Interiors: Representing the Domestic Interior since the Renaissance*. Ed. Jeremy Aynsley and Charlotte Grant, with Harriet McKay. London: V&A Publications, 2006. Pp. 154-55.

Sutherland, Kathryn. "Speaking Commas \ Reading Commas: Punctuating *Mansfield Park*." In *Ma(r)king the Text: The Presentation of Meaning on the Page*. Ed. Joe Bray, Miriam Handley, and Anne C. Henry. Aldershot: Ashgate, 2000. Pp. 217–34.

Talon, Henri A. *John Bunyan: The Man and His Works* (1948). Trans. Barbara A. Wall. London: Rockliff, 1951.

Tames, Richard. *City of London Past*. London: Historical Publications, 1995.

Tanselle, G. Thomas. "Greg's Theory of Copy-Text and the Editing of American Literature." *Studies in Bibliography* 28 (1975): 167–225.

———. *A Rationale of Textual Criticism*. Philadelphia: University of Pennsylvania Press, 1989.

———. *Textual Criticism and Scholarly Editing*. Charlottesville: Bibliographical Society of the University of Virginia, 1990.

———. *Textual Criticism since Greg: A Chronicle, 1950–1985*. Charlottesville: Bibliographical Society of the University of Virginia, 1987.

Tattersfield, Nigel. *Thomas Bewick: Graphic Worlds*. London: British Museum, 2014.

Teller, Alex. "Finger-Pointing." Chicago: Newberry Library, 2016. https://www.newberry.org/finger-pointing (accessed 28 January 2016).

Temple, Nigel. "Humphry Repton, Illustrator, and William Peacock's 'Polite Repository,' 1790–1811." *Garden History* 16:2 (Autumn 1988): 161–73.

Thornbury, Walter. *Old and New London: A Narrative of Its History, Its People, and Its Places*. 6 vols. London, Paris, and New York: Cassell, Petter and Galpin, 1879–85.

Tieken-Boon van Ostade, Ingrid. *The Bishop's Grammar: Robert Lowth and the Rise of Prescriptivism in English*. Oxford: Oxford University Press, 2011.

———. *Grammars, Grammarians and Grammar-Writing in Eighteenth-Century England*. Berlin: Mouton de Gruyter, 2008.

Tillotson, Geoffrey. "Eighteenth-Century Capitalization." *Library*, 5th ser., 10 (1955): 49–54.

Toller, T. N. *Outlines of the History of the English Language*. Cambridge Series for Schools and Training Colleges. London: C. J. Clay and Sons, 1900.

Toner, Anne. "Seeing Punctuation." *Visible Language* 45:1/2 (August 2011): 6–19.
Traugott, Elizabeth Closs. *The History of English Syntax: A Transformational Approach to the History of English Sentence Structure*. New York: Holt, Rinehart and Winston, 1972.
Treip, Mindele. *Milton's Punctuation and Changing English Usage, 1582–1676*. London: Methuen, 1970.
Trilling, Lionel. *The Opposing Self*. New York: Viking Press, 1955.
Turner, Henry S. "Lessons from Literature for the Historian of Science (and Vice Versa): Reflections on 'Form.'" *Isis* 101 (2010): 578–89.
Turner, Roger. *Capability Brown and the Eighteenth-Century English Landscape*. London: Weidenfeld and Nicolson, 1985.
Twyman, Michael. *Printing, 1770–1970: An Illustrated History of Its Development and Uses in England* (1970). London: British Library, 1998.
Updike, Daniel Berkeley. *Printing Types: Their History, Forms and Use*. Cambridge, MA: Harvard University Press, 1922.
Van Ghent, Dorothy. *The English Novel: Form and Function*. New York: Rinehart, 1953.
Veeser, H. Aram, ed. *The New Historicism*. New York: Routledge, 1989.
Vermeule, Blakey. *Why Do We Care about Literary Characters?* Baltimore: Johns Hopkins University Press, 2010.
Viney, Brigit. *The History of the English Language*. Oxford: Oxford University Press, 2008.
Visser, F. Th. *An Historical Syntax of the English Language*. 4 vols. Leiden: E. J. Brill, 1984.
Voronikhina, Ludmila. "The Green Frog Service and Its History in Russia." In *The Green Frog Service*. Ed. Michael Raeburn, Ludmila Voronikhina, and Andrew Nurnberg. London: Cacklegoose Press, 1995. Pp. 9–16.
Wahrman, Dror, and Jonathan Sheehan. *Invisible Hands: Self-Organization and the Eighteenth Century*. Chicago: University of Chicago Press, 2015.
Walker-Miekle, Katherine. *Medieval Cats*. London: British Library Publishing, 2011.
Wall, Cynthia. "Approaching the Interior of the Eighteenth-Century English Country House." Special Edition, "Interior Spaces and Narrative Perspectives before 1900." Ed. Monika Fludernik and Suzanne Keen. *Style* 48:4 (Winter 2014): 543–562.
———. "The Business of Houses: The Problem of Old London Bridge." In *Essays in Honor of John Richetti*, ed. Albert J. Rivero and George Justice. *Eighteenth-Century Novel* 6–7 (August 2009): 261–305.
———. "The Impress of the Invisible: Lodges and Cottages." *ELH* 79:4 (Winter 2012): 989–1012.
———. *The Literary and Cultural Spaces of Restoration London*. Cambridge: Cambridge University Press, 1998.
———. "'The little words': The Close Reading of *Really* Small Things." Special Edition in Honor of Robert Langbaum. Ed. Marilyn Gaull and Michael Pickard. *Wordsworth Circle* (Spring 2016): 114–18.
———. *The Prose of Things: Transformations of Description in the Eighteenth Century*. Chicago: University of Chicago Press, 2006.
———. "Teaching Space in *Sir Charles Grandison*." In *Approaches to Teaching the Novels of Samuel Richardson*. Ed. Lisa Zunshine and Jocelyn Harris. New York: Modern Language Association of America, 2006. Pp. 162–68.

Webster's New International Dictionary of the English Language. 2nd ed. Unabridged. Utilizing all the experience and resources of more than one hundred years of Merriam-Webster Dictionaries. Springfield, MA: G. and C. Merriam, 1958.

Welch, Charles. *History of the Tower Bridge and of Other Bridges over Thames Built by the Corporation of London.* London: Smith and Elder, 1894.

Wendorf, Richard. "Abandoning the Capital in Eighteenth-Century London." In *Reading, Society, and Politics in Early Modern England.* Ed. Kevin Sharpe and Steven N. Zwicker. Cambridge: Cambridge University Press, 2003. Pp. 72–98.

———, ed. *Articulate Images: The Sister Arts from Hogarth to Tennyson.* Minneapolis: University of Minnesota Press, 1983.

———. *The Elements of Life: Biography and Portrait-Painting in Stuart and Georgian England.* Oxford: Clarendon Press, 1990.

———. "Robert Dodsley as Editor." *Studies in Bibliography* 31 (1978): 235–48.

———. *William Collins and Eighteenth-Century English Poetry.* Minneapolis: University of Minnesota Press, 1981.

Weymyss, General Sir Colville. *English Inns Illustrated.* London: Odhams Press, [1951].

White, J. G. *A Short History of Old London Bridge.* London: Printed for Private Circulation, 1900.

Williams, Abigail. *The Social Life of Books: Reading Together in the Eighteenth-Century Home.* New Haven: Yale University Press, 2017.

Williams, Raymond. *The Country and the City.* Oxford: Oxford University Press, 1973.

Willis, Peter. "Capability Brown in Northumberland." *Garden History* 9:2 (Autumn 1981): 157–83.

Wilson, Richard, and Alan Mackley. *Creating Paradise: The Building of the English Country House, 1660–1880.* London: Hambledon and London, 2000.

Woolf, Virginia. "Rambling Round Evelyn" (1925). In *The Common Reader, First Series.* Ed. Andrew McNeillie. London: Hogarth Press, 1984. Pp. 80–88.

———. *A Room of One's Own.* London: Hogarth Press, 1929.

Wray, David. "Quarreling over Homer in France and England, 1711–1715." In *Homer in Print: A Catalogue of the Bibliotheca Homerica Langiana at the University of Chicago Library.* Ed. Glenn W. Most and Alice Schreyer. Chicago: University of Chicago Press, 2013. Pp. 300–331.

Yañez-Bouza, Nuria. "Preposition Stranding in the Eighteenth Century: Something to talk about." In *Grammars, Grammarians and Grammar-Writing in Eighteenth-Century England.* Ed. Ingrid Tieken-Boon van Ostade. Berlin: Mouton de Gruyter, 2008. Pp. 251–77.

Index

Page numbers in italics refer to figures; color illustrations will be noted with plate numbers. 313